SECOND IMPRESSION

Percy H. Muir
1894-1979

SECOND IMPRESSION

RURAL LIFE WITH A RARE BOOKMAN

Barbara Kaye

(MRS. PERCY MUIR)

OAK KNOLL PRESS
& WERNER SHAW

Published in 1995 by OAK KNOLL PRESS,
414 Delaware Street, New Castle, DE 19720, USA

Published in the UK by WERNER SHAW, Suite 34,
26 Charing Cross Road, London WC2H 0DH, UK

ISBN 1-884718-04-3 (Oak Knoll Press)
ISBN 0-907961-08-8 (Werner Shaw)

Edited by Jill Mason
Designed at Oak Knoll Press
Printed in the United States of America

*Library of Congress
Cataloging-in-Publication Data*
Kaye, Barbara, 1908-
Second impression : rural life with a rare bookman / by
Barbara Kaye (Mrs. Percy Muir).
p.   cm.
Includes index.
ISBN 1-884718-04-3
1. Kaye, Barbara, 1908- . 2. Antiquarain booksellers' spouses—
Great Britain—Biography.   I. Title.
Z325.K33A3   1994
381'.45002'092—dc20
[B]   94-12220
CIP

For Howard
With love and gratitude

Also by Barbara Kaye

Fiction

CALL IT KINDNESS

HOME FIRES BURNING

FOLLY'S FABRIC

NO LEISURE TO REPRINT

PLEASANT BURDEN

THE GENTLEYS

BLACK MARKET GREEN

IN WHOSE CUSTODY?

FESTIVAL AT FROKE

CHAMPION'S MEAD

REBELLION ON THE GREEN

NEIGHBOURLY RELATIONS

LONDON-LYCHFORD RETURN

MINUS TWO

Non-Fiction

LIVE AND LEARN

THE COMPANY WE KEPT

Juvenile

THE WHITE MOUSE

Illustrations

Preface

My husband was still alive when I began writing a lighthearted account of the ups and downs of our life in an Essex village during the war. In his autobiographical book, *Minding My Own Business* (reprinted by Oak Knoll Books in 1991), Percy Muir had told the story of the firm of Elkin Mathews, publishers and antiquarian booksellers, from its establishment in London in 1887 up to its move to our home in Takeley in 1939. Percy had joined the company in 1930, and at the outbreak of the war he was the sole active director, the two other partners, Ian Fleming and Greville Worthington, both being on active service.

My idea was to carry on the story from my own point of view for a further six years up to the end of the war. Although I suspect my husband had some misgivings about such a project, he made no attempt to discourage me. While we did not discuss the content of the book, he would, from time to time, drop some correspondence onto my desk, remarking that I might find it useful "for whatever you are writing." He knew that I would seek his opinion when the first draft was finished, but by then, alas, he was no longer alive.

My book was published by Werner Shaw in 1986 under the title *The Company We Kept*. Although it sold well and was soon out of print, I had no plans to write a sequel. It was not until I began to read through a quantity of hitherto overlooked papers concerning the early days of the International League of Antiquarian Booksellers, together with personal correspondence of my husband's, unpublished writings, and an archive on the activities of book auction rings that I began to consider continuing the story for a further decade.

As a novelist, I have been a compulsive scribbler all my life; I had my diaries to refer to, the journals I had written during every one of our joint trips abroad, letters from my husband written to me when he had attended meetings or gone on buying trips without me, and my own letters from abroad written to my family, kept by my mother.

Some, at least, of the material we had both preserved seemed worth recording. It had all happened more than forty years ago — crowded years they had been for us. As I sorted, read, and gazed at old photographs, memories of people, places, and events began to surface and were soon demanding to be put down on paper. In the end the temptation was irresistible.

If a few inaccuracies have crept into this book, I alone must plead guilty and hope that those who spot them will be tolerant of an octogenarian's lapses of memory. In the final chapter, which I have called "A Postscript," all the material I have used — papers, correspondence, and press clippings — was compiled by Percy Muir at the time of the events described; nothing of significance has since been added.

In conclusion, I would like to thank friends and colleagues here and abroad who have helped with relevant information; in particular, I am grateful to Mr. Raymond Kilgarriff of Howes Bookshop, who allowed me access to ILAB archives. Nor shall I ever forget the unfailing help and patience of David Butcher of Langham Post Office, who guided my hesitant fingers into the mysteries of using a word processor and never failed to respond to my frantic SOS calls when things went wrong.

Finally, my warm thanks to Paul Wakeman and Robert Fleck for their kindness and encouragement while I have struggled to put into narrative form events in the lives of the Muirs going back nearly half a century.

Barbara Kaye

Chapter 1

"Back to normal," I recorded in my diary on May 10th, 1945. "Children back at school. . . ." The two-day V-E spree was over. Only the ashes of burnt-out bonfires on town bomb sites and village greens remained with a litter of spent fireworks, empty celebratory bottles, beer cans, and other such detritus to testify to the people's celebrations of the end of the war in Europe.

"Normal" did not mean an end to food and clothes rationing, electricity supply cuts, and all the other shortages and lack of services we had resignedly accepted throughout the war years, together with endless queuing and the black market. Anyone naive enough to suppose that better times were just around the corner was to be speedily disillusioned.

Hardly had the cheering crowds dispersed from outside the gates of Buckingham Palace, than the newspapers and radio were telling us the country was broke and the war in the Pacific might drag on for another year or more.

An incurable optimist, I was not to be cast down by gloomy prophecies. In 1940 I had refused to believe the pessimists who told us we hadn't a chance against the strength of German military might. With Europe freed from Nazi domination, I could persuade myself that our five-year-old son, David, and eight-year-old daughter, Helen, would grow up in a better, safer world. The iron curtain had yet to descend between East and West.

It was springtime; the tulips stood bright and bold in the garden, the apple trees were in a pink and white froth of blossom, and at dusk the nightingales sang their love songs in the tall elms bordering Hatfield Forest, just across the road from where we lived. Once again our black half-Siamese cat was in the family way.

For a business occupying elegant premises in Mayfair to transfer to a couple of converted hen houses in an Essex village might be said to have been a bit of a come-down, but in August 1939 we had been only too

1

thankful that we already had a home thirty miles from London where both we and the business could find sanctuary. Against the odds, the firm of Elkin Mathews, established in London in 1887, had not only survived during six years of rustication, it had even prospered in a modest way. In 1945 our make-do premises, with swags of purple clematis climbing around the doorway, had a certain rustic charm. To go to work Percy had only to stroll down the bricked garden path from house to office — and back again for lunch. He always had disliked commuting.

Elkin Mathews' Catalogue Number 100 had just been sent out. To mark the occasion appropriately, it offered "One Hundred Unusual Books, Manuscripts, Letters and Drawings." This had meant months of work on Percy's part, searching for literary rarities (some not then seriously collected) and then researching them. Not that he grudged the time spent; it was the part of bookselling that gave him as much satisfaction as selling the items he had catalogued. And if they didn't sell? Well, he had backed his judgement when he bought, and sooner or later a perspicacious customer was going to prove him right, as one almost invariably did.

After the V-E celebrations it was considered meet and proper that everyone should foregather in the local church and give thanks to the Almighty. "Took part in Church service and Victory Parade," I wrote in my diary, "wore my ARP [Air Raid Precautions] uniform for the last time."

I hadn't driven an ambulance since 1942, but I was still on standby and felt in honor bound to parade with the rest. Percy, who was CO of the Dunmow cadet corps, was involved in his company's parade elsewhere.

It was really the Home Guard's show, at least that was what their CO thought. No doubt he could have done without the ladies from the First Aid Post, the Land Girls, and the ARP, unsoldierly lot that we were. The church service over, we were marched somewhat raggedly along the main road up the hill to the forecourt of the village hall. There, lined up self-consciously in our respective groups, we waited for a visiting dignitary to inspect us. Villagers who had straggled along in our wake stood about at a respectful distance, watching to see how we comported ourselves. Naughty boys pulled faces at us behind their elders' backs.

The Land Girls, in their cord breeches and green pullovers, looked youthful and healthy; the first aid ladies, middle-aged and sensible; the air raid wardens in their thick navy blue uniforms, uncomfortably warm — as I was in mine. Puffed up with self-importance, belly straining against the confines of his khaki battle dress, the CO gave his men a final once-over. I stole a sideways glance at them. There they stood, eyes front, stiff as pokers, mostly middle-aged men, over-age for the call-up or else in reserved occupations — farmers and farm workers, a few veterans of World War I, one or two in office jobs. They were Dad's Army and proud of it. In five years of drills and exercises they had never been called upon to arrest fifth columnists or round up German parachutists, let alone fire a machine gun in earnest. All the same, back in 1940, volunteers to a man, they had been ready to defend the village and repel the Nazi invaders — with pikes if necessary.

The inspection began; the VIP (a retired general, I seem to remember) went conscientiously through the motions, walking along the ranks, beaming on us encouragingly, finishing the inspection with the appropriate "few words." He was proud of us, he said. For that matter, we were all quite pleased with ourselves. Then the onlookers began to drift away home, the men more likely to their delayed Sunday morning session at the pub. The Home Guard was dismissed; it would be some months before they were finally "stood down," when they would celebrate the event with a party not to be forgotten for years. According to the sergeant instructor in Percy's cadet unit, it wasn't the gin or even the port that caused him to land in a ditch on the way home from that party, but, he confessed afterwards, the parsnip wine, a war-time brew saved for such an occasion. "Real cunning ol' stuff, that wor," he told Percy with a rueful shake of a sore head.

The rest of us on the Home Front had had our pat on the back and were now redundant, or so I thought. Meantime, I mounted my ancient push-bike and sped home to feed my family, coasting down the hill where open farmland fell away gently on either side of the main road until, at the dip at the bottom, The Street began. Here on the north side were the remains of domestic architecture going back to Tudor times. Old timber-framed plaster-fronted houses, steep-gabled, red-tiled or thatched; a couple of pubs; our village shop. On the south side was a line of low-cost bungalows, the Johnny-come-latelys, built between the wars, with back gardens running down to our single-track railway line, soon to be closed. In one lived my mother-in-law, just a little too near for my taste.

Our house, called "Taylors," was at the farthest end of the street, next to a big, timbered barn no longer used for livestock and which had latterly become a doss-house for tramps. Picturesque Tudor cottages are seldom the most comfortable of dwellings. Friends over six feet tall had to bow their heads if they came into our kitchen and duck through every doorway. The upstairs floors sloped, the staircases were crooked. We grumbled, or cursed when heads met beams, but we still went on loving the house as one might love an eccentric but endearing relative.

The week after the victory parade I recorded in my diary: "To Cambridge with Percy. Bought my first hat for five years."

Hats had gone out of fashion during the war, except for the most formal of occasions. Before 1939 we had all gone to work wearing hat or cap. The tilt of a man's hat or the trimmings on a woman's gave a clue to the wearer's character. Bourne & Hollingsworth, a popular middle-income store in London's Oxford Street, was a millinery mecca for the suburban housewife. Many a happy morning could be spent sitting at a table before a three-sided mirror, trying on their latest collection from 7s. 6d. up to £5 or so for wedding finery.

The war had put an end to such frivolity; the all-purpose headscarf was classless, practical, and cheap. You could wear it turban-wise, if you wanted to cut a dash, or you could follow the example of the royal princesses at Balmoral and tie the ends under your chin or gypsy-wise under your hair at the back. My preferred solution for controlling my fine, unruly hair was a wide velvet band, which was what I was wearing that day in Cambridge. Percy had business to do at Gray's, our bookbinders in Green Street, and I was enjoying some dilatory window shopping, when an unexpected display of millinery caught my eye, filling me with an irresistible longing to be prettily hatted once again.

I succumbed to temptation and went in. I knew exactly what I wanted, the sort of hat a woman wears for a luncheon *à deux* in a smart restaurant. I had seen just the thing in the window. It was a saucy little bit of nonsense made of ersatz straw and velvet ribbon. "Yes, I'll take it. I'll wear it now," I said to the salesgirl. I put it on and smiled at myself in the mirror, feeling young and frivolous. I was thirty-six and felt no older than I had in 1939.

It was time to meet Percy at Gray's where, in March, he had staged an exhibition of fine bindings, many of them from the library of Paul Hirsch. The manager of the bindery was a genial character called Band, known to his friends as Dicky. Shortish, inclined to be tubby (a tendency not helped by the proximity of the Blue Boar hostelry), Dicky came into his own twice a year as producer for the Rodney Amateur Dramatic Society at the Cambridge Arts theater. An actor *manqué*, he always made sure of a bit part for himself whatever the play.

Our March exhibition had been an experiment. Paul Hirsch, who had let us have many fine bindings to sell on commission, had quit Germany in the mid-thirties with his family, bringing with him his extensive library and valuable music collection (now in the British Library in London) and settling in a large, comfortable house in Adams Road, Cambridge, not far from the university library, where it was arranged that his music collection should be on loan while he continued to work on it. Throughout the war years he had filtered books and manuscripts from his personal library onto the antiquarian market to augment his income, often by way of Elkin Mathews' catalogues. This arrangement had suited Percy admirably, allowing him to offer many highly collectible items without capital outlay. An additional bonus was the warm friendship that developed between the two men and their families.

With the war over, what we needed was a more appropriate showroom to display expensive or showy stock than a couple of converted chicken houses. True, there were a few customers who had no objection to "stopping off" at Bishop's Stortford railway station on their way to Cambridge and being ferried three and a half miles out to Takeley for an hour or two to see our stock, but undoubtedly there were many more who couldn't or wouldn't spare the time.

A solution would have been to take the business back to London, as some colleagues who, like us, had evacuated in 1939, had already done. London, they declared, was where the action was. To Percy it was where you worked doubly hard to keep up with overheads and had to spend hours in over-crowded trains in order to do so. Six years of working from premises in his own garden had convinced him that that was the way he wanted to live his life. To go all out for the big money was not for him. Nevertheless, he had no intention of marking time.

Dicky had liked the prestige and publicity created for Gray's by our March exhibition, but he was not at all sure about a permanent showroom for Elkin Mathews on the premises. He was not a man who went out of his way to look for extra work. Cautious and suspicious of what might be expected of him, he needed persuasion. Percy dangled the advantages: commission on sales, rent for the room, the possibility of new customers for the bindery. Dicky was weakening but still hemming and ha-ing when I made my entrance.

"You've bought a hat!" Percy said, looking at me with approval. "It suits you."

"Well, I was sick of that old band—" I began without thinking.

Percy chuckled. "'That old Band'," he echoed. "What d'you think, Dicky? Has she made her point?"

For a moment Dicky looked po-faced, then he grinned sheepishly.

"All right, old boy, I give in. I'll give it a try. Don't really see why it shouldn't work out so long as you'll be coming over fairly often to keep an eye on things. Suppose we all repair to the Blue Boar and drink to it?"

The new association between Gray's and Elkin Mathews was celebrated suitably next door, along with my first post-war hat. The room that we were to use at Gray's was upstairs, oak panelled with a fine Adams fireplace and a splendid octagonal library table for displaying quarto volumes. Before long we would find another rather different sales outlet nearer to home.

Chapter 2

When Parliament was dissolved at the end of June 1945, neither Percy nor I had any intention of taking part in political campaigning. It would be the first general election for nine years. As far as we knew, there would not be a Liberal candidate contesting the Saffron Walden division in which we lived, even though it had once been a safe Liberal seat. The sitting member was R. A. Butler, a war-time cabinet minister highly regarded in the constituency, even if some of his supporters, off the record, called him "a cold fish." No one thought he had much to fear from his Labour opponent, a Mr. Weech, who was hardly known. All the same, rumors were circulating that the tide had begun to turn in Labour's favor, especially in the armed forces, due, some Conservatives hinted gloomily, to subversive influences at work among those soon to be demobbed.

Not long after the date of the general election was announced we heard that it would, after all, be a three-horse race in our constituency. What was even more interesting was that the candidate so bravely joining the fight was someone we knew, although not well: an eccentric journalist and author who was putting up as an Independent Liberal.

From the first, George Edinger assumed that he could rely on our support. He needed someone to chair his meetings. Percy would do very well. Taking the chair was something Percy rather enjoyed, so he didn't refuse. I volunteered for the lowly task of addressing envelopes. We would probably have given him more support (for I rather enjoyed teasing my Conservative friends by being a Liberal activist) had it not been a time when Percy was hard pressed in the office.

Left with only a secretary, a one-day-a-week bookkeeper, a gardener-packer, and some sporadic help from me when I could squeeze time from writing and domestic chores, Elkin Mathews was seriously understaffed. With some difficulty Percy did manage to recruit an office girl locally (none we employed ever showed any ambition to learn more than basic office skills), but to find a good cataloguer of rare books in rural Essex was like trying to grow orange trees in the garden. An intelligent learner seemed the best answer: a young man who actually liked the idea of a job working with books and had no yearning for city lights. Pie in the sky, I thought, but I was to be proved wrong.

Meantime, I did what I could to help out, not that I was ever initiated into the mysteries of researching and cataloguing rare books. Although I had, some years before, been given one share in Elkin Mathews to make me a director of the firm, Percy was not going to waste his time teaching a "temp" who was more concerned with writing books herself than selling those of the firm's. Nor was I even allowed to do the filing ("If I let you loose on the files, I'll never be able to find anything I need"). Instead, I was given the job of selling, rather trying to sell, the run-of-the-mill stock that all bookdealers accumulate, by reporting items to other dealers through the *Clique*. This was the journal of the antiquarian and secondhand book trade, a drab, privately owned weekly publication in which dealers advertised for books they required. It had no competitors to speak of, so most of the trade subscribed to it, despite its uninspired editorial policy.

When the *Clique* arrived, Percy would run his eye down the columns of "Books Wanted," ticking those we had in stock (his memory was such that he could do this without ever having to check shelves or card index) and was willing to let me offer at trade discount. This was done at high speed, his eyes taking in a page almost at a glance; I would then be left to take the books from the shelves, quote the details on the catalogue cards, and offer them at a discount. Fairly boring routine work, but it did teach me something of values and the titles of books and names of authors currently in demand.

At first, in my innocence, I looked for a prompt reply with an order and check. The fairly frequent lack of any response to the quotes I posted soon taught me that this was no sure-fire way of selling secondhand books. In any case, I was puzzled as to why, if there was some demand for a certain book, we were prepared to part with it at a discount. If a competitor could buy it from us and then sell it at a higher price, why, I wanted to know, couldn't *we* find a customer to buy it and pay the full price?

Logic, I soon learned, does not operate in the rare and secondhand book trade — or in any other trade dealing in collector's items, for that matter. As Percy patiently explained to me, the fact that a fellow dealer has a customer for a book on your shelves is no guarantee that another customer will soon be along eager to buy it from you at your price. Rather, it could well stay disregarded in your shop for months if not years. More sensible, then, to make a more modest profit by passing it on to a colleague who does have a customer for it and use the money from the sale more advantageously — if you know how.

From Percy I learned to look out for the first published work of authors who were beginning to be esteemed, often after years of obscurity — that slim volume of poetry, perhaps privately printed in the author's youth, which unexpectedly becomes upwardly mobile, moving from a box of junk in an auction room to a provincial bookshop and then on again into an elegant glazed cabinet in a West End dealer's showroom, perhaps ending up as a prized possession in an important collector's library, making everyone who handled it some money on the way.

Good advice to store away for future book-buying forays in the UK and abroad. But potential high flyers were not the books I was required to quote. Percy, always percipient in the matter of trends, would back his judgement, putting aside (sometimes into his own collection) the early writings of authors he believed under valued. Siegfried Sassoon was one of these. Oliver Onions (who, alas, is still under valued) was another. My job was the mundane one of trying to sell the boring laggards that had lingered too long on our shelves.

I used to think that posting my batch of "quotes" off to the *Clique* was rather like fishing. One baited the hook, cast the bait on to the water, and waited for a catch. But others were fishing in the same pool, and the week's catch was often a disappointment.

As Percy's wife, I could hardly dodge the columns of the village money-raisers, especially when it came to the organization of the summer fête. The holding of that event, the most time-consuming of all village functions, was based on the assumption that the chosen day would be warm and sunny. Usually it was the reverse. Traditionally, in our village the fête was combined with the primary-school sports. This insured a good gate, bringing as it always did mums, grannies, and grand-dads to the field (fathers were apt to make the excuse that they were working; others were away in the forces) at the same time siphoning back into the funds, via the various sideshows, the sixpences and shillings pressed into the hot little hands of the winners of the various events.

Each year the same stalls and sideshows were run by the people who had been running them for years; country dancing by the schoolchildren, a few middle-aged men lining up sheepishly for the knobbly knees competition, and, as a finale, the men's tug of war, leaving a legacy of aching joints for the week to come.

9

"Can't we do something a bit different?" I unwisely asked at one of the preliminary meetings after the program outlined had sounded depressingly familiar.

"All right, then, what?" Predictably the question was bounced back at me.

"Well," I began, "how would it be if . . . ?"

"I'm going to do a production of *Midsummer Night's Dream* at the fête," I told Percy some while later.

"Good heavens, not the complete play?" he asked in alarm.

I reassured him. "No, just the one scene when Titania falls in love with Bottom. I shall stage it on the vicarage lawn, and I'm having a juvenile cast — at least it will be less boring than schoolchildren dancing around the maypole," I added defensively. I had already recruited my cast, two pretty young girls from a family down the road, a plump, pudding-faced high school girl with acting ambitions for Bottom, and my own daughter for one of the four fairies. I didn't dare mention that failing to cast a suitable Oberon, I had half a mind to take the part myself.

"Well, as long as you don't involve me," Percy said.

I promised I wouldn't. He had much else on his mind just then.

Chapter 3

Some while before the general election Percy had been tipped off that Bishop's Stortford's one and only bookshop might soon be up for sale. Without committing himself, he went along to have a look at it. It was a small but attractive little shop just off the main shopping area with a pleasing Georgian frontage. Next door was an old-established bespoke tailor, one of the oldest businesses in the town, where, according to a snobbish friend, "the county families buy their clothes." So, would they sometimes, as they went by to be measured up for their tweed suits, drop into the bookshop to buy a book or two? At least it could be said that the business was in the best part of the town. The ginger-haired rather taciturn Scot who had run the shop for some years was looking for someone to take over the lease by the end of the summer. He employed two part-time women assistants who were willing to stay on; there was a fair amount of saleable stock, and the place looked in good order. He said it had been bringing him around £500 a year. After the years of war-time restrictions on book publication, Percy could forecast that the market for new books would increase rapidly as paper rationing was phased out, enabling publishers to supply what he believed would be a surge of released demand. The shop clearly had potential. What was more, he expected it to prove a useful outlet for secondhand stock not worth the time and expense of cataloguing.

"I think it might well be a good investment," he said after he had been back for another look. He was clearly tempted, but he was not a man to plunge. Many years before, he had set up his first shop in Davies Street, just off Oxford Street, on borrowed capital. He had long since repaid the debt, but for years it had been a millstone round his neck. Now he was hesitant over whether he could risk funding the project, for we had little capital available, and, although our bank would undoubtedly have obliged, his aversion to raising even a modest loan was strong. This was an attitude that David Sachs, our neighbor, a financial whiz-kid later to become a director of the merchant bankers Guinness Mahon, found quite inexplicable. But no amount of argument from a man who understood how to use borrowed money to make more money (and would become a rich man) had any effect on Percy's built-in determination never to be in the red.

For my part, I was all for taking over the bookshop. I had once sold children's books at Harrods when they took on temporary staff for the run-up from November to Christmas, and I had enjoyed the experience. I was eager to help and, with an eye to the main chance, could picture a nice little display of my latest novel in the window along with the new edition, published that year, of Percy's successful *Book-Collecting for Everyman*.

"I think I'll get Ben McPeake to come and take a look at the shop," Percy said after his second visit. "He's interested in finding outlets for his publications, and he might consider taking a share in the business. I'll suggest that he come up one day soon to look it over."

Ben McPeake was in charge of the National Magazine Company's UK publishing interests. One of these was Gramol Publications, which had published Percy's book-collecting paperback. Percy was currently editing their *Collector's Book* Series. McPeake was an astute Irishman who combined charm and guile. At that time he and Percy were seeing a good deal of each other, but I had not yet met him.

For three weeks I rehearsed my youthful cast in our garden after school. The front lawn was our stage, lilac and laburnum trees the backdrop. June sunlight, beaming down on my blonde, nubile Titania recumbent on a pile of cushions, was my stage lighting. The four fairies ran around barefoot on the grass, clutching bunches of flowers, attendant on a well-developed, snub-nosed Bottom, while Puck observed the scene from behind the floribunda roses. It was not always quite so idyllic. The sun was sometimes disobliging, the wind chilly, the grass damp, and the cat made entrances and exits at will. Sometimes there would be an uninvited audience gathered outside the gate, gawping.

Since I had so rashly committed myself to giving the village a taste of Shakespeare, my priorities had become hopelessly mixed. When I ought to have been sitting at my typewriter finishing a chapter, or getting a meal ready, I would be pondering my scribbled stage directions or declaiming my part in front of the mirror in the bedroom. With some misgivings, I had taken on the part of Oberon.

Three days before the fête, Percy came over to the house to break the good news. Ben McPeake had risen to the bait and had rung up to say he would come and have a look at the bookshop the following Saturday.

"*Saturday?*" I echoed aghast. "But you know that's the day of the fête?"

"Oh, is it? I'd quite forgotten." For Percy it had been an easily forgettable date." I said we'd give him lunch. . . ." My expression told him he was adding insult to injury.

"No, I suppose not. Well, it's a pity, but I can't put him off now. I'll have to take him out to lunch in Stortford after we've looked at the shop. We might come along to the fête afterwards in time for your show if he isn't in a hurry to get back to London."

I had taken it for granted that Percy would be there to see my production. While by no means over confident, I had been secretly hoping for a pat on the back and an admission that he had underestimated my talents as an impresario. Probably just as well if he was not in the audience, I told myself, my confidence suddenly dipping. In any case, I definitely did not want a smart London publisher there.

"I wouldn't encourage him," I said hastily. "He'll only be bored to tears and probably turn sour on the shop as a result."

The day of the fête dawned with grey skies and drizzle. "Rain at seven, shine at eleven," I said to the children without much conviction, half hoping that the weather would be my let-out. The dress rehearsal hadn't gone too well; I was suffering from an attack of cold feet, telling myself that an embarrassing flop was what I deserved for having the temerity to edit a scene from Shakespeare for my purpose. A heavy shower or two and perhaps I could call the whole thing off. And disappoint my little troupe after they had faithfully learned their parts and given up so many evenings to rehearsals? No, the show would go on, somehow — even if the audience had to sit under umbrellas.

When I cycled up to the cricket field, the scene was typical morning of village fête. The trestle tables stood bare under dripping trees, the goods for sale had been stacked beneath them in cartons and baskets — jams and chutneys, homemade cakes, knitted baby clothes, aprons contrived from remnants, handmade lavender bags and oven gloves, many of which would be bought only to reappear at some future charity sale. As always there were the throw-outs from sheds and attics: the chipped cups and saucers, broken-spouted teapots, garish tin tea caddies, old flat-irons, and tasteless kitsch misguidedly bought on some long forgotten holiday or won at a fairground. Could anyone really want to buy such junk? After years of shortages, finding anything to put on the white elephant stall was scraping the bottom of the barrel, yet somehow the stall never failed to make money.

At least it had stopped raining. Having put up the trestle tables, the men had turned their attention to rigging up that common British fair game, the cocoanut shy; the women helpers stood around irresolutely, unwilling to risk covering the tables with old sheets brought for the purpose. The damp grass under their feet was already trampled dark green. Overhead, scudding grey clouds shredded by a blustery wind gave an occasional glimpse of pale blue, just enough to raise the hopes of the optimists.

"Well, that could come out fine later . . . it do look brighter than first thing . . . showers was what they said on the wireless. . . ."

A wicket gate led from the cricket field to the vicarage tennis court where my fairies would (I hoped) be dancing barefoot in a few hours' time. I went to inspect the pitch. At least the vicar had remembered to take the tennis net down, but the grass was not likely to dry out in time even with no further rain. If they caught cold, it was going to be my fault. Should I call the whole thing off? Why on earth had I ever volunteered to provide an entertainment? And the *Dream* of all things! I must have been mad. Despondently, I turned my back on the depressing scene and cycled home.

"Look, the sun's coming!" cried the children, rushing to meet me as I turned in through the gate. "There's enough blue in the sky to make a sailor a pair of trousers! It's going to be fine, after all!"

"Ladies and gentlemen. There will be a performance of a scene from *Midsummer Night's Dream* on the vicarage lawn, starting in five minutes time . . . ," boomed the loudspeaker from the cricket field. The fête had been officially opened in fitful sunshine and a cool breeze. The children's races had been run, the stalls and sideshows were in business. My little troupe, pink-cheeked with excitement, stood waiting by the open vicarage french windows. The four fairies, Pease-blossom, Cobweb, Moth, and Mustard-seed, in their dresses of dyed parachute-nylon, fidgeted and giggled. Bottom, in a boy's suit, had his head hidden in a contraption of cardboard and sacking, which was the best we could do to make an ass of him. Puck wore a green jerkin and a pixie hood; Titania, with her long blonde tresses falling around her shoulders, looked slim and pretty, if not exactly ethereal, in a dress of white butter muslin. My own costume was a rather doubtful combination of silk shirt and riding breeches. A portable wind-up gramophone standing just inside the door was to play Mendelssohn's "Midsummer Night's Dream" Overture. I peered out and scanned the audience coming onto the lawn to take their seats, an assortment of damp benches and deck chairs. Much to my relief, I couldn't spot Percy and McPeake among them.

14

"Ready?" I said to my little company. "Come on then, while the sun's still shining. Now!"

The vicar's wife started the gramophone, Titania and her fairies tripped out onto the grass, Oberon hitched up his breeches, counted ten, and followed.

"Ill met by moonlight, proud Titania!" Well, it was hardly moonlight, nor did the vicarage lawn much resemble a forest glade. It didn't matter. Caught up in the magic of the *Dream*, the poetry swept us along.

The adrenalin was still flowing when we returned to take our bows, to applause from an audience largely made up of the village mums, grannies, and aunties with a grandfather or two, few of whom had had much contact with any play of Shakespeare's since their schooldays.

"They done it nicely, didn't they . . . I like to see kiddies acting. . . ." As I gathered up our props while the audience filtered back to the cricket field, I caught a few comments: "Grass must've been a bit damp . . . well, it did turn out nice for them after all. Couldn't catch a lot of what they were sayin'. . . . Shakespeare, worn't it? Well, that makes a change . . ."

My players had quickly turned themselves back into mortals and run off to the cricket field to try their luck on the sideshows. There were marks of damp bare feet on the polished floor of the vicarage dining room and a scratch on the Mendelssohn record. Never mind, with the performance over, there were more important things to worry about, such as how Percy had been getting on showing Ben McPeake the bookshop.

Some while later I caught sight of the two men making their way across the field, looking, I thought, like visitors from another country coming to observe the natives at play. I was helping out looking after the "Guess the weight of the cake" competition when they spotted me and came up with broad smiles. They had clearly lunched well.

Ben was a good-looking man; he gripped my hand, and as he greeted me, I felt suffused in a blend of alcohol and Irish charm.

"I don't know why Percy's never let us meet before," he said, smiling warmly into my eyes. "I told him he'd just got to bring me along here this afternoon. Looks like everyone's having a good time." His Irish voice had a slight American overtone. "Percy was telling me you were putting on some Shakespeare. I wish we could have got to see it. I bet it was a big success." I said modestly that I thought we had got through without disaster. My venture into outdoor theater had become unimportant. I was dying to ask Percy how they had got on — apart from lunching well. I caught his eye, but it was McPeake who answered my unspoken question.

15

"Well, we went to see that bookshop Percy fancies. It seems like a nice little business. With Percy taking it in hand, it could be a good proposition, I'd say." He slapped Percy's shoulder encouragingly. "Anyway, that's what I've been telling him. We'll be talking about it some more."

Percy smiled and caught my eye but said nothing, and Ben turned his attention to the raffle prize cake, over-large and topped with half a week's sugar ration.

"That looks good. Are you going to sell me a slice?"

After I'd made them both pay their sixpences and guess the cake's weight they wandered off, their gambling instincts aroused, to try their skill at the bowling, the cocoanut shy, and the rest of the sideshows. Later, after he had taken Ben to catch his train Percy returned to the field in his role of honorary treasurer to collect the takings.

"Well, I should be able to take over the bookshop," he said as we drove home with our children. "Ben's definitely interested. If all goes well, we could be in business by the autumn." It had been a pretty satisfactory day, after all.

With the fête over, I could spare some time for George Edinger's election campaign, by then in its last two weeks. As one of his small band of supporters, mostly readers of the *Guardian* and the *News Chronicle*, trudging around pushing his election address through letter boxes, I would assure anyone willing to listen that the Liberals were about to make a great comeback until I almost came to believe it. George himself was remarkably calm, apparently unworried by the outcome. Kidding ourselves that it was all worthwhile, we rather enjoyed being a small band of believers.

Election day was July 25th. Winston Churchill, we learned from the radio, was returning from the Potsdam Conference that same afternoon in order to record his vote and would be in his own constituency of Wanstead & Woodford that evening. I drove around the village picking up a few declared Liberal voters and some undeclared ones whom I hoped might have a last minute change of heart, driving them to the polling station at the county primary school, where well-heeled Conservative tellers stood beside the gate looking complacent.

Percy and I did not attend the count, having no wish to witness George hopelessly outstripped by R. A. Butler, with Weech, for Labour, not far behind. But we did sit up into the early hours (no transistor to take up to bed with us in those days) listening to the results, as more and more Labour gains from Conservatives came through.

In the morning we learned that Butler was still our MP but with a considerably reduced majority. As for George, he had trailed third and lost his deposit, along with many other Liberal candidates. By no means cast down, he would live to fight another day.

There were those who talked of the country's ingratitude to Winston Churchill, without whose leadership we would surely have been defeated by the Nazis. But the election result had not been a rejection of Churchill, the war leader, still loved and admired by the vast majority of the British people, but of the Conservative Party, the party of privilege, in power too long. People had voted for change and, as they believed, for a fairer society.

Chapter 4

It is probably true to say that when the news came that atomic bombs had been dropped first on Hiroshima and then on Nagasaki, quickly followed by the announcement that Japan had surrendered, the initial reaction of most people in Britain was relief that the war was over. We were told that thousands of POW lives had been saved in the nick of time as well as those of the internees in the camps, that the alternative of a full-scale invasion of Japan by US land forces would inevitably have led to a heavy loss of life on both sides. Our realization of the implications for a world with a stockpile of nuclear weapons, together with revulsion at the horrific results of the bombing, would come later.

That it was the Americans who had carried out the bombing, not the British, helped to assuage the feelings of guilt of those who were aghast and ashamed at the hideous wholesale slaughter of non-combatants. It was convenient to overlook the fact that Attlee, our prime minister, and his government had been a party to the decision. Had an opinion poll been taken at that time on whether the use of atomic bombs was justified in order to bring the war to an end, it is likely that a majority in this country would have agreed with the decision.

Among our circle of friends there were endless arguments on the ethics of the bombing. Women, myself included, were mainly against the use of nuclear weapons in any circumstances. The men mostly fell back on the soldier's argument that the slaughter of innocents is one of the unhappy results of war and must be balanced against the larger number of lives saved by taking hard decisions.

In our village there were several families who had a father or a son in a Japanese POW camp. For them the Japanese surrender brought hope after as much as three and a half years of waiting and cruel uncertainty. A family living across the street was one of these; their son would be coming home at last. A little farther along the road a sad, childless young woman would wait in vain for her husband's return.

18

Again a two-day holiday was announced. Bonfires were lit; much alcohol was consumed. In our village, as in many others, the school-children were given a party. This time the jollifications were more low key. The wholesale killing might be over, but clearing up the mess was going to take a long, long time. On August 16th, 1945, I recorded in my diary: "V-J Day plus one. Still a holiday. Ate bad sausages and felt ill. Bonfire across the road. Percy went over with the children. Bed early and no celebrations."

A week before V-J Day a red-haired cockney evacuee came to see me and, to my astonishment, offered to come and work for us as a resident maid. Resident servants, especially English ones, being an almost extinct species at that time, I engaged her without hesitation. It was like an answer to a prayer. Even if she lasted only a matter of weeks, I was ready to take her on for the sake of a break from domestic chores and ties. All the same, I was curious to discover her motives for wanting the job.

She was an uncommunicative sort of girl, but the reason did emerge. Her family, a large one, had been bombed out during the flying bomb raids. They had fled from London's East End to Dunmow and for want of better accommodation had taken refuge in a disused church hall, where they had lived hugger-mugger ever since, with the minimum of amenities.

"We 'ung blankets across the middle of the 'all to make two rooms of it, like," she said. "There wasn't nowhere proper to wash. I just got sick of it."

All she wanted, I discovered, was a bedroom of her own and to be allowed to take a bath once a week. A modest enough wish that posed no problem. She could have our small single bedroom, I said, and unrationed baths any time our one and only bathroom was not being used by the family. Her weekly wage would be the £2 a week for which she asked.

With her fiery red hair, hazel eyes, and creamy skin, she was not a bad-looking girl in a sulky, unsmiling way. Smiling did not come easily to Esther, nor laughter. All the same, I expected to find a young man waiting at the doorstep on her days off. None ever appeared. She would walk to the bus stop wearing her one smart black dress, powdered, lipsticked, and alone. What she did or where she went when she was off duty I never learned. She turned out to be a good worker but as wary of overtures of friendship as a cat that has been ill-treated. My children accepted her rule just as they had accepted my previous domestic helps, the adult in charge in my absence, who looked at the clock and announced a mealtime or bedtime. She was matter-of-fact with them but not unkind.

19

As the eldest of a family of seven, she was used to looking after children and willing enough to take charge if necessary.

Throughout the war I had never felt able to leave my two overnight. When Percy had gone on book-buying trips, I had stayed at home. Now he saw no reason why I shouldn't go away with him for a few days.

At first I hesitated. The maternal shackles I had worn for six years were not easily cast off. Suppose one of the children was taken ill; was Esther to be trusted? Could she cope in a crisis? Well, but why should anything go wrong, I asked myself? We would only be away four nights and would be going no farther than Norfolk. The war was over, no bombs would fall. Still, the house could catch fire, I worried. Esther might entertain dubious boyfriends (even though she had shown no sign of having any), crooks, or drunks. My imagination painted sinister pictures . . .

"You really must make up your mind," said Percy. He had encountered my forebodings before and was not going to waste his breath telling me that they were quite irrational. "I'd like to have you with me, but I can't decide for you."

"Well, I would love to come with you, of course . . ."

It was harvest time as we drove through Constable country on our way to Ipswich. Sun-bleached stooks like little wigwams stood waiting to be carted. Horse-drawn reaper binders were at work in the barley fields cutting and throwing down the bound sheaves for the harvest hands. In other fields men were pitchforking the sheaves onto a tractor-drawn wagon, a back-aching task that I had done the summer before, helping our farmer neighbor. Few farmers then owned or could hire the combine-harvester that was going to halve labor costs.

For the first time since 1939 we had shed our role of parents and were away on our own. I was tasting freedom and liking it. A busman's holiday for Percy it might be; for me it felt like a second honeymoon. The fine old coaching inn where we were booked for the night, with its age-blackened timbers and open fireplaces, its country-hotel smell of furniture polish, wood fires, roast beef, and a hint of cooked cabbage, was just right for the occasion. So was our double bedroom with floral wallpaper and an old-fashioned king-sized double bed topped with a rose-patterned eiderdown.

We were in Ipswich to visit a secondhand bookshop run by an agreeable if somewhat eccentric dealer already known to Percy. Dumping our suitcases at the hotel, we made for Silent Street. Mr. Cook's shop was a rambling old building that promised bargains if only one knew where to search. Every shelf was crammed with volumes that looked as if they had been there, untouched, for years. Forewarned of our visit, he was there to welcome us.

"Glad to see you. I know you're interested in children's books, so I've put some aside for you to look over," he said. "I bought a collection of them not long ago. Haven't put them on the shelves yet."

Percy, who never wasted time in idle chat when book buying, was already casting his eye along the shelves. Noncommittal, as he always was in such circumstances, he said he would be glad to have a look at them. Cartons of old children's books were then dragged out from the back of the shop, and he settled down beside them. I knew he would go methodically through the lot, and it would take some time. Ipswich had been our nearest big town when I was a child and my parents were living near Orford as tenants of Sir Alfred Clark, Kenneth Clark's father, a man of wealth and substance. My father, one of Alfred Harmsworth's team of Fleetway House serial writers, had little substance to boast of, had he been a boasting man, which he was not. He was a good shot, so he would be invited to shoots now and then; otherwise, social contact between landlord and tenants was minimal. Rather oddly, once or twice a year my eldest sister, who was the same age as the future Lord Clark, would be asked to nursery tea at the Hall with young Kenneth, not an invitation a shy little girl much welcomed; perhaps he was not more enthusiastic. Either way, the friendship never really got off the ground.

My own childhood memories of Ipswich were mixed. A day's outing to the town was both an ordeal and a treat, for usually it meant our annual visit to the dentist. First we rode in the dogcart to Wickham Market, then took the slow train to Ipswich. Only rich, sporty people owned motorcars in those days. Making a virtue out of necessity, we thought them vulgar. After the dentist had made us squeak and spit, our spirits would rise with our appetites and we would sit down to a splendid blowout in an old-fashioned eating house, where, behind steamed-up plate-glass windows we would tuck into steak-and-kidney pudding and meringues and cream, for 1s. 9d. a head.

The eating house had disappeared, I couldn't even find the right street, but the I've-been-here-before feeling came and went as I wandered past old timbered houses that I had certainly passed as a small child. The Butter Market brought back memories, or was it just the name that had so pleased me once, conjuring visions of great slabs of the stuff patted into rounds on marble counters and smacked with a wooden pat that left the shape of a rose on top, as butter was sold in those days at Liptons' or the Home and Colonial stores.

When I returned to the bookshop, Percy was loading his purchases into the car, two or three cartons of them. Mr. Cook was happy to have got rid of stock that didn't interest him and had been bought cheaply. Percy was happy, too; he had found juvenile treasures galore, from early chapbooks to Beatrix Potter. Many would appear in future catalogues, some to end up in important collections of juvenilia, providing data to be stored for future bibliographical writings. By great good luck we had come to Ipswich at the right moment.

The town was quiet as we drove back to our hotel for a celebratory meal. It was not so long since it would have been full of off-duty Americans from one of the surrounding bases. Now the GIs had gone home and taken many of the girls with them.

The following day we crossed into Norfolk and went on to the town of Norwich. Neither of us had been there since before the war. We knew it was one of the cities that had suffered in the so-called Baedeker raids, but we were shocked by the extent of damage to the city center. The old city hall had gone and with it most of the surrounding buildings, many of them fine ones. The whole area looked flat and sad. "Found great devastation in Norwich," I wrote in my diary that night.

At least the bookshop we had planned to visit was still there, even more ramshackled than I remembered it, with little bare-floored rooms upstairs opening into each other. It was a shop I had visited on several occasions with my father, who was in the habit of ridding himself of books he was bored with for something of greater interest.

In this sort of shop, with a large and diverse stock, bargains could usually be found. Through my chore of reporting books to the *Clique* my perceptions of what might be worth buying had sharpened. On prewar book hunting trips with Percy I had been content to sit in a corner reading a novel that had taken my fancy while he worked his way along the shelves. On this trip I too began to scan the shelves for books we might be able to use. One day I meant to surprise and delight him with the bargain of the year, but it didn't happen that day in Norwich: "No, not in that condition . . . no, it's not the first edition . . . no, the price is too high . . . ," and back went my finds on to the shelf, while the books he had found piled up. Expertise was not picked up so easily.

We were staying overnight with a bachelor uncle of mine, and his widowed sister, my Aunt Kitty, by no means kittenish, who kept house for him. He was a big, gruff man, a civil engineer who had spent much of his life in China, where he had made a great deal of money. On his retirement he had bought a large country house near Norwich and settled

22

down to live the life of a country gentleman. He was the only one of my mother's family of eight who had never married.

We arrived in time for a stroll round the garden. The sweep of close-cut lawn, the borders abloom with late summer flowers, the latest acquisitions to the rose beds all testified to a good gardener's professional skill. Percy and Uncle John got on well together, and after I had duly admired all the beds and borders I left them together and was led by my aunt into the still-room to admire her contribution to good living. This consisted of row upon row of jars packed with fruit from the garden and even more rows of jams, chutneys, and pickles.

"I always like to have a nice stock of preserves," said my aunt, regarding the crowded shelves complacently. Where, I wondered, as I stared enviously at such plenty, had all the rationed sugar come from? It was better not to ask.

It was a pleasant, relaxing visit. The tempo of life for these elderly relatives seemed half the pace of ours; it was as if we had slipped back in time to the 1930s. There was afternoon tea with cucumber sandwiches and sherry or madeira at six-thirty, before we sat down to dinner promptly at eight o'clock, with Uncle John in his smoking jacket ("You don't need to change, dear, but we always do . . ."), followed by port and cigars and a game of billiards downstairs in the billiard room.

"What about the washing up, Aunt Kitty?" Somewhere in the background there must surely have been unseen domestic help.

"Don't worry, dear. It will be seen to in the morning." That Uncle John should take a tea cloth and dry up the glasses was unthinkable.

We went home the next day to find all was well. My forebodings of disaster had proved illusory. Good news awaited us. The owner of the bookshop had accepted Percy's offer for the stock and fittings, and the lease was ready for him to sign. We were now in the business of selling new books as well as old.

Chapter 5

Now that we had Esther to look after the children, Percy proposed that we should take up the Sadleirs' long-standing invitation to pay them a visit at Througham. He had stayed there before the war when Michael and Betty were in the habit of entertaining his bibliographical friends for bookish weekends. But that was before my time.

On the occasions when I had met Michael in London at literary functions he had appeared to me an Olympian figure, a distinguished author, the editor and publisher of the scholarly Bibliographia Series (to which Percy had contributed two volumes), and a well-known collector of Victorian fiction.

I had typed Percy's manuscript of *Points: Second Series*, soon after we were married and been thoroughly bemused by its content. Such terms as "variants," "cancels," and "first issues" meant nothing to me, and, secretly, I couldn't see what all the fuss was about.

It was not until I had read Michael's novel *Fanny by Gaslight* that I realized he wrote fiction. This brought him down a few steps from the Olympic Heights, from my point of view. His novel had been well timed when it appeared in 1940. People were reading more than ever, in air-raid shelters, on ARP duty, on disrupted train journeys. The novel's combination of high life and low life in Victorian times, with an old-fashioned love story, was a recipe for the bestseller it became. Sadleir had, in fact, already written four previous novels; his first, *Hyssop*, was published in 1915. But up to the publication of *Fanny* his reputation in literary circles rested on his bibliographical writings. These I had never attempted.

I had enjoyed the book, despite finding the unfortunate Fanny (she was inevitably "betrayed") a rather unconvincing character, probably because the author had written in the first person as a young girl, a method more likely to succeed with male readers than with women. But my main interest in meeting Michael again was that he was head of the publishing house of Constable. Like many an aspiring young novelist I had become disenchanted with my own publisher and was casting hopeful glances at other more up-market firms. The weekend at Througham would, I hoped, provide the opportunity for a chat with Michael on the novelist's craft in general and mine in particular.

To leave my children in the care of our red-head was still a worry, but my mother-in-law had promised to keep an eye on things, so Percy and I set off for the Cotswolds one damp autumn day. Ploughs were out on the fields slicing the stubble into wet chocolate-brown furrows, flocks of gulls swirling and crying in their wake. It was late afternoon when we drew up outside the Sadleirs' Cotswold home, built of the pale local stone, long and low, blending sympathetically into its surroundings.

Michael, a slim good-looking man in his late fifties, casually yet neatly dressed, appeared promptly to welcome us.

"Betty is busy with her dairy herd," he said. "So I'll take you up to your room. She'll be back soon to give us tea."

He led the way upstairs. There he paused. Along the wide landing, lined with shelves from floor to ceiling, was his much famed collection of yellow-backs, thus named because of the background of their lurid pictorial covers; cheap nineteenth-century editions of popular novels, designed to catch the eye of the lower classes looking for titillation or horrors. Astutely, Michael had been the first to work a neglected seam, and he had bought only the brightest, cleanest copies at giveaway prices.

The pause, before we proceeded to our bedroom, was to allow Michael to take down one or two of the rarest specimens for our closer inspection. Percy's interest was taken for granted, mine assumed. I was allowed to hold, briefly, Fergus Hume's *The Mystery of a Hansom Cab* ("a remarkably fine copy") while Percy was handed M. E. Braddon's *Lady Audley's Secret* to admire. The two titles were vaguely familiar to me as Victorian bestsellers, but why, I wondered silently, as I handed back my copy to Michael with a polite murmur of appreciation, were such crude little books desirable acquisitions?

As Michael led us on to our bedroom, we passed the open door of another room. I had time to glimpse an interior with rumpled bed whose recent occupant had obviously left in a hurry. Clicking his tongue in disapproval, Michael snapped the door shut. "Our daughter went back to London today. She seems to have left her room in a dreadful mess," he said with annoyance. It was the comment of an orderly man who expects his family to conform.

Home from attending to her dairy herd, Betty assumed her role of hostess and dispensed tea in their comfortable, tasteful drawing room. Her background was Church of England (her father had been a canon) and county. She looked pleasant and competent. Before long, Michael took Percy off to his study, Betty disappeared into the kitchen, and I settled down with a Constable novel until it was time to change. Later, as we sat over our drinks before dinner, Michael and Percy were still talking books, an inexhaustible subject for them both. While they capped each other's tales of remarkable bargains bought in unlikely places and looked back nostalgically to the pre-war days of the sixpenny box outside the shop door, Betty politely engaged me in small talk. Her reasonable assumption must have been that I couldn't possibly be interested in hearing of Michael's acquisition of yet another Trollope first edition.

So we talked of food, an inexhaustible subject for women in the 1940s, usually discussed with a degree of one-upmanship. Few could resist a boast of some clever trick of making boring food less boring, or of some friendly little corner shop where scarce delicacies were kept for best customers under the counter — quite as exciting to us, her tone suggested, as the sought-for first edition.

Cookery led the conversation to Betty's dairy herd, which must have been invaluable during the war. It was not a subject to grab Percy's attention, and the men did not join in. Whether or not Michael had played any part in this contribution to the war effort I have no idea, but their land girl did inspire him to verse. Her name was Thyrsa, and his poem in her praise contained a remarkable number of rhymes for her name. He must have been rather pleased with it, for he had it privately printed in a limited edition of seventeen copies and sent to his bibliophile friends for Christmas 1944.

At dinner Betty kept the conversation to general topics and news of mutual friends. I did discover that Michael was working on another novel, but as he showed no inclination to discuss it, I didn't make the hoped for progress along the road to Constable's fiction list. Still, I had *Fanny* up my sleeve, and there would be time to talk about her when the meal was over. Betty had fed us well, we had had plenty to drink, the atmosphere was convivial and relaxed.

"We'll leave the men to sit over their drinks a little longer, shall we?" Betty said, leading the way back to the drawing room. My offer to help wash up was waved aside; there was, she said, someone in the kitchen to cope and bring us coffee. Presently, the men appeared, chuckling over a shared joke. Percy was in an anecdotal mood, not unusual when he dined out in congenial company. He sat down beside Betty, but his stories were addressed to us all. Encouraged by an appreciative audience, he followed one with another. They were all pretty familiar to me. I could have told them myself, though not half so well.

"Ah, now that reminds me," Michael said when there was a pause. "There was something I forgot to show you before dinner. Now I've got you here, Percy, it's too good an opportunity to miss. You remember that Marryat I told you about? . . . You don't mind, do you, Barbara, if I take him away for a short while?"

Percy was sitting in an armchair looking very contented, but he rose obediently. There was no gainsaying an obsessional collector. Michael cast an apologetic smile at me and then at his wife, murmured that they wouldn't be long, and the two men were gone.

Betty smiled indulgently. "Men! You must forgive Michael. He does so enjoy having someone like Percy to talk to about his books."

We had already exhausted the subject of books. For a change we talked of my children. A good hostess, she asked all the right questions: their ages, their schools, their interests. Before the war we would have talked of nannies and our respective domestic staff. She asked if I had some help.

"At the moment, yes. If I didn't, I'd never get any work done," I said.

"Work? Oh yes, you write, don't you? Do tell me what sort of books. You must forgive me for not knowing them — I never seem to have enough time for reading. . . ." After that there didn't seem much point in developing the subject.

An hour later, when the men had still not returned and Betty was trying not to yawn, I gave up surreptitiously watching the door and bade my hostess good night, pleading weariness after the journey.

On the way up to bed I paused and rather guiltily borrowed one of Michael's yellow-backs to read in bed. Soon bored with it, I was half asleep when eventually Percy joined me.

"I'm sorry. I tried to get away before," he said apologetically. "Michael really has some remarkable books. . . ." But I didn't want to hear about them.

We left soon after breakfast the next morning. Michael was abstracted; it was one of his "writing days," Betty said. She was busy, too, having to go and see her cowman. We were going on to stay with Percy's oldest friend and colleague, Harold Edwards, and his wife, Olive, at Newbury. Like us, the Edwards had built a bookstore in their garden; and like us, they had no intention of taking their business back to London, where they had once had a shop in Cecil Court. It would be mostly book talk

27

again, but there would be the garden and the cats, breakfast in bed, endless cups of tea and gossip, and my ego would be restored by Olive, who actually read my novels.

Home again, refreshed by the break, we found that Esther had managed and all was well. Putting all thoughts of changing publishers out of my head (at least for the time being), I settled down at my typewriter to make up for lost time and was almost immediately interrupted.

"We are making a collection for the Help Holland Appeal," said the voice on the telephone. "Do you think you could cover your end of the village?"

In the approach to Christmas a spate of charitable organizations were telling us that even though rations were tight in the UK, we were incomparably better off than our neighbors across the channel, stripped bare by the Nazis. Before the war the Netherlands Countrywomen's Association had enjoyed close links with the British Women's Institutes. The Help Holland Appeal was intended as a collective effort on the part of various women's organizations in the UK in response to an appeal from Dutch housewives, who were, indeed, in need of help.

"All right," I said, suppressing a groan. I had done a good deal of knocking on doors during the war years, pestering my neighbors for scrap metal to make Spitfires (were those old prams and iron railings ever constructively used?) and rubber tires for recycling, not to mention books and old newspapers. It was true that no one had set the dog on me or even sworn at me, but it was a chore I had come to dislike heartily. All the same, my conscience would not allow me to refuse.

From the sharpish "Yes?" to the kindly "Hello, dear" the expression of the housewives who opened the door to me said the same: "She wants something!" All the same, no one refused me.

"Well, I don't know, dear. There's not much to spare, being most everything's pretty near worn out. 'Course we know there's folks worse off than we are. May be though there's something I could find for you. . . ."

Flannel trousers, odd jackets, cardigans, children's clothes; even a mothballed fur coat were handed over. At the collecting center we sorted the smelly and unacceptably scruffy from the just about wearable, packed the latter into cartons, and went back for more. Did Dutch husbands ever wear those long woollen pants with darned knees? Did their wives really pull on those voluminous grey bloomers as the temperature fell? But the blankets must have helped to keep someone warm in bed, along with the knitted bedsocks.

Our new bookshop in Bishop's Stortford was already proving a good investment. One of the middle-aged gentlewomen who had worked there previously was carrying on for the time being, and somehow the management of the business was fitted into the jigsaw of Percy's working week. Restocking was allowed to erode his weekend with Saturday morning journeys to the wholesaler, Simpkin Marshall, a long-established rival to W. H. Smith presently to become a victim of a Robert Maxwell raid. Simpkin's warehouse, stocked as it was with an enormous range of books, was invaluable to the small retail bookseller. Its closure would be much bemoaned by the trade.

Initially, my help was not required, but when Percy returned from one of his Saturday forays with a carload of bright, shiny new volumes, it was fun to look them over and discuss his choices. Pre-Christmas sales began early that year and were soon exceeding our expectations. Before long I was recruited as a temporary saleswoman to help cope with the rush.

The run-up to Christmas in 1945 was very different from previous years, at least in our shop. For an exhausting three weeks we found ourselves selling almost nonstop to a steady stream of customers who thought, very sensibly, that books were that winter's best buy, especially juveniles. Books were inexpensive, unrationed, and of a good deal better quality than much of the Christmas goods on display, including toys. Nor did they have to compete with television, still in its infancy.

To be selling books, rather than writing them, made a pleasant change. It was gratifying when on occasion I sold one of my own novels, and I was shameless in pushing Percy's *Book Collecting As a Hobby*. Customers, disciplined by years of war-time queuing awaited their turn patiently. And the money kept rolling in.

Christmas had less effect on our sales in Cambridge, where our upstairs showroom was mainly stocked with fine bindings from Paul Hirsch's library that we were selling on commission. Such books were hardly to be regarded as stocking fillers; in any case, at Gray's, tucked away in a side street, passing trade was not to be expected. But Percy was taking a long view, looking ahead to the time when Cambridge would once again be on the itinerary of private collectors, librarians, and trade buyers from across the Atlantic.

Chapter 6

Not long after Christmas we had a visit from our friendly local builder,
Mr. P., who had come to our rescue many times during our years at
Taylors. He had come to tell us that under the post-war re-training
scheme he had just taken on a couple of young demobbed soldiers who
had opted for the building trade. They were willing lads, he said; all
they needed was a bit of experience. So if we'd like some redecorating
done in the house, he'd put them on the job and charge us at half the
usual price. As we learned later, the government was paying their wages,
so he was doing quite nicely from the scheme.

Up to then all our redecorating had been a matter of do-it-yourself, or
rather myself, for Percy was not and never wished to be a handyman. I
reckoned that Mr. P.'s willing lads couldn't be any worse at the job than
I was and would probably make less mess.

"We'd better have the whole place done at that rate," said Percy, who
never could resist an offer that looked like a bargain. I was delighted. I'd
usually ducked doing the ceilings, and they were murky from smoke
from the oil lamps lit during air raids and electricity cuts. Jolly for Esther,
too, I thought, to have a couple of young men around the place. This was
largely a selfish thought, for I was concerned that her usually glum countenance might mean she was contemplating leaving us.

The two young ex-soldiers duly turned up with their pots of destemper
paint (no emulsion paint then) and brushes. Thankfully, no transistors,
either, later part of every building worker's equipment. They were, as
Mr. P. had said, willing lads, fit and lusty.

As I'd expected, Esther was almost at once a target for winks and
chatting up. But it was all one way. Overtures were met with a disdain-
ful nose in the air, a toss of her mop of red hair. She was not that sort of
girl.

"I'm sure the painters would like a cup of tea, Esther," I'd say encouragingly. Two mugs would be taken to wherever they were working and

dumped down unsmilingly on table or windowsill with a curt, "There's yer tea." Neither took offense, nor did they give up. Unresponsive though she remained, I suspected her of secretly enjoying the situation. For two weeks our meals became moveable feasts curiously flavored with the tang of turpentine. The chairs and tables, shrouded in old sheets like children playing ghosts, stood in huddled groups. Hours were spent in exasperated searches for concealed belongings.

At last it was finished; the apprentice painters packed up their pots of paint and brushes and were gone, leaving Esther undated and as glum as ever. They had worked well and cleaned up before they left. For a cut-price job, we felt we had had a bargain.

When everything was back in place, the rooms looked as fresh in the spring sunshine as they had the day we had moved in eight years before. It was as if we had turned over a new leaf.

Another improvement in our lifestyle came at about the same time, when Percy bought a 1936 eight-cylinder Lancia. She was beautifully appointed, with thick pile carpeting, leather upholstery, and polished walnut fittings. Our little workhorse Ford was worn out, and Percy, in one of his unpredictable impulses (when it came to motorcars) had fallen for this large, handsome vehicle just as he had fallen for the sporty touring Lancia we had bought secondhand in 1938 for £20 and sold for the same sum in 1941.

At the time, the chances of buying a post-war car were almost nil. We were told that the owner had laid her up throughout the war, hence her almost brand-new appearance. She was by far the grandest car we had ever owned and undoubtedly a status symbol. When she stopped and refused to start again the first time Percy drove her up to London, he was loath to blame her, even though she had stranded him in Epping, of all places, and I had had to come and rescue him late in the evening in the despised little Ford, fortunately not yet sent to the breaker's yard.

"She went beautifully all the way to Sotheby's. It wasn't until we got to Epping on the way home that she stopped and I couldn't start her," he said, more in sorrow than anger. The most unmechanically minded of men, he had handed over the problem to the nearest garage, which solved it the next day without much trouble — that time. It was the beginning of a love-hate relationship, which, like a shaky marriage, continues for years until one partner can stand it no longer; cars and marriages, I've sometimes thought, have quite a lot in common.

The first Parish Council elections since before the war were held in March 1946. Hardly an event to generate much excitement, one would have thought. But this time the Labour Party, riding high after their convincing general election victory, were going to attack Tory strongholds in local government right down to parish pump level. A post-war revision of parish boundaries had meant that our village was entitled to eight parish councillors instead of six as previously, and three representatives on the district council. Up to 1946 all had been men.

It was a time when women's organizations were urging their members not to allow themselves to be relegated to passive domesticity as had happened after the First World War. Instead they were being told they should play an active part in public life, put up as candidates in local elections, become magistrates, serve on governing bodies of school boards, and in general make sure the men didn't have it all their own way. That, in effect, was the message from the energetic, effective ladies in the top echelons of the Women's Institutes, in particular, an organization much given to boosting the confidence and morale of country women. As a member of my own WI, I took it to heart.

Who was putting up for our parish council, I wanted to know. Or for the district council, for that matter? When I asked that question at our WI's monthly meeting, I found that no one was sure. In any event, there didn't seem to be a woman among the likely starters.

"If you feel so strongly about it, why don't *you* stand?" suggested some of my fellow members. "Then we can all come and vote for you," they added encouragingly.

"I would have thought you had enough to do already with your home and your writing," Percy said, not unreasonably, when I told him I was going to put up for election for the parish council. It was characteristic that he did not try to argue me out of my rather shaky resolve.

I did little canvassing, an election address having been sent out on behalf of all the Independents. In any case, to canvas for a seat on a parish council seemed faintly absurd. Friends promised to come and vote for me, regarding it all as a bit of a joke. When nomination day came, the local newspapers found they had a story. Quite a few of the Essex candidates standing for Labour were nationally known personalities, Kingsley Martin, a frequent member of the BBC's brains trust being one of them, and the short story writer A. E. Coppard, another. Parish council elections had unexpectedly become News.

Percy, resigned to the situation, had promised to come with me to the village hall, where the annual parish meeting was to take place. Warned that a big attendance was expected, we were in our seats in good time to watch the hall filling up as it never had before for such a mundane occasion. The local Tories came streaming in, grimly determined to defend the village against "the Reds," a term used for anyone left of center. In keeping with our nonpolitical label, our group had decided not to sit together and was dotted around the hall. The nonpolitical came to see what would happen. If Reds were indeed present, they didn't advertise the fact.

The meeting began in an atmosphere of anticipation. The clerk, a slight, grey-haired man, was also the minister of the local Congregational church. He went through the agenda briskly in the manner of one who had done it many times before.

"Now we come to the election of the new council," intoned the clerk. "The names of the candidates will be announced in alphabetical order. Will they please stand up when their names are called and remain standing while the tellers are counting the votes."

As my name came in the middle of the alphabet, I was able to watch the reaction of the meeting to the first two of my group when their names were called. As first one and then the other rose and stood with assumed nonchalance, hands shot up from all parts of the hall. There was little doubt both had been elected.

Percy gave my hand an encouraging squeeze as I stood up in my turn, heartbeats quickening. Plenty of hands going up in front of me, and, yes, on either side too. Friends smiling at me. I longed to turn and look behind me but resisted the temptation. I could see the tellers still counting. Then a nod from the clerk, and I was free to sit down and watch someone else having to suffer.

Of the Labour candidates only Leslie Frost, the village school headmaster, got a respectable number of votes, but was still not elected. The Independents won by a comfortable margin.

Soon after the election I attended my first parish council meeting and was somewhat taken aback to find myself elected vice chairman. This compliment I took to be a chivalrous tribute to my sex rather than a show of confidence in my ability to step into the chairman's shoes if necessary.

For the honor of my sex, who were largely responsible for me becoming a councillor in the first place, I felt bound to accept. I could only hope and pray that the chairman was as healthy as he looked and that he stayed that way for the foreseeable future.

A week or two later Percy and I drove up to London for another annual meeting, a good deal more important from his point of view. The Antiquarian Booksellers' Association had been formed in 1906 and was thus in its fortieth year. Percy had served on the committee throughout the war years and had done stalwart work campaigning against the red tape imposed on the antiquarian book trade by what was then known as the Board of Trade. He was currently vice president.

"Come along to Brown's Hotel at about six," he said. "Meet me in the bar."

I had driven up with him for the ride, a very smooth one in our large new Lancia. I was not required to attend the meeting since I wasn't a member of the ABA (members were elected as individuals) so the day was my own and I intended to spend it entirely frivolously, shopping first, then standing myself, for the first time ever, to a beauty treatment at Elizabeth Arden.

When I went to find Percy at Browns Hotel, he was sitting at a table in the darkish, old-fashioned bar with half a dozen colleagues, all looking convivial and relaxed. As I came in, John Carter was the first to rise to greet me. He was one of the few intellectuals in the ABA at that time, and his background was very different from Percy's. This had made no difference to the friendship that had sprung up between them when John, an Eton scholar and a graduate of Trinity College, Oxford, first came into the antiquarian book trade as the London rare book representative for the firm of Scribner's in New York. He was some years younger than Percy, slim, and always impeccably dressed; with his bony face and thin, high-bridge nose, he had the air more of an aristocratic patron of the arts than of one who deals in them. He was married to a tiny live-wire of a woman, an American of Austrian extraction who was editor of the Woman's Section of the *Sunday Times*. It was one of those marriages in which mutual admiration reinforces affection and would last until death did them part.

"You should be proud of Percy, Barbara," John told me with assumed gravity. "This afternoon he was elected president of the ABA, an honorable office, where he will undoubtedly be highly effective." Percy chuckled. The celebration had obviously been going on for some while. When we drove up to London that morning I knew it was likely that he would be voted president and that he would not turn the job down. If he was pleased to have been elected, then so was I. That I would also have a part to play and that the day would prove to be a watershed in our lives never crossed my mind.

John bought me a drink, the party went on a little longer, and then we drove home. On the way I learned that the annual dinner, discontinued during the war, was to take place once again, never mind that the country was supposed to be committed to austerity, with restaurant meals restricted to three courses. We had never attended such ABA functions before the war, mainly because we couldn't afford it, and in any case Percy was not keen on large-scale junkettings. As president it was different, he would be expected to preside, and I must accompany him.

"All right, if you want me there," I said, not entirely averse to dining at the Mayfair, the venue for the dinner. "It won't be too difficult now we've got Esther."

"You'll have to stand beside me, you know, and help me receive the guests."

"Good heavens!" The prospect was daunting. "Must I really? I'll hardly know any of them . . ."

It was explained to me that the dinner was traditionally a formal affair with guest speakers from the literary world, a toastmaster, and the president and "his lady" receiving the guests as they arrived. It would, I could see, be more of an ordeal than a jolly evening out. And I'd have to mind my Ps and Qs, a prospect I found dispiriting. What was even more tiresome was the problem of something suitable to wear. My clothing coupons were all gone, and my only once-smart evening dress dated back to 1938. Everything else in my wardrobe was shabby or just wouldn't do. Perhaps, I was beginning to think, it might be best to have a strategic bad cold.

Percy had other ideas. "Why not ask Phil to lend you a dress?" he suggested.

This was Phyllis Calvert, a successful and very charming young actress who was married to the actor-turned-bookseller, Peter Murray Hill. Percy had known Peter since the days when he had sold books from a stall in one of the London markets between shows. By 1946 he was an established bookseller and an ABA member, one day to become president himself. The Murray Hills had come to my rescue once before, when, with remarkable generosity, they had taken part in a war-time concert I had organized in Takeley. By good luck, Phil and I were about the same size. A diffident plea for anything she could spare for the occasion to save me from letting Percy down brought a warmhearted response. I was welcome to borrow from her wardrobe, and she promised to find something really fetching for me.

The day came. I collected the dress, which was black, slinky, and far more sophisticated than anything I would have dared to choose for myself. I changed at the Edwardses' flat ("You *do* look smart!" said Olive encouragingly), hurried to the Mayfair, and took my place beside Percy at the top of the staircase leading to the banquet room, feeling far from confident.

There was no time for chat. As usual I had cut it fine, and the guests were beginning to arrive. The gold-braided major domo began booming out the names. A few were vaguely familiar to me; mostly their owners were not. Faces and more faces, mostly in couples, confronted me. Hands touched mine briefly; sometimes the grip was pleasantly firm, more often not. Sometimes there was a friendly squeeze from an elderly gentleman ready to linger, to tell me how well he remembered the first time Percy had come into his shop. The faces wore polite smiles, the women's glances flicked over me. Now and then there was a wink from an old friend to cheer me up: "Don't weaken, you're doing fine!"

When I had time to glance at my husband, the president, he gave every appearance of enjoying the occasion. He knew them all, the booksellers and their wives from the provinces combining the dinner with a jaunt to London, the cockneys from the suburbs, and the smoothies from the West End. His cordiality embraced them all, with sometimes a joke or a recollection thrown in. Although it was a role he had not played before, as a one-time actor he had the part pat.

I kept my smile going and waited for the flow of guests to come to an end, the last stragglers hurrying on into the anteroom, where the hands we had shaken were now grasping glasses.

"Come on," said Percy. "That's the lot, time we had a drink." And then, as he looked me over, "Yes, Phil's fitted you out well. You look very smart."

As such events go, the fortieth anniversary dinner could be considered a successful occasion. War-time austerity still restricted the menu, but the Mayfair knew how to get around rationing restraints, and the dinner was good. Glasses were kept filled, toasts were drunk, the guest speakers sung entertainingly enough for their supper; bonhomie prevailed.

Percy would not have accepted the presidency if he had not intended to bring about some changes. He thought the committee sluggish and inward looking, a club for the dealers at the top. It was too much a case of the London tail wagging the regional dog, in his view. With the war over, it was time for a change in outlook. Few of the committee were going to agree with him. As I would find with my fellow parish councillors, action was the last thing they wanted.

While I was becoming ever more deeply immersed in village affairs, Percy's commitments in London were multiplying. A new one was his membership on the council of the National Book League, which had just arisen, Phoenix-like, from the ashes of the National Book Council. The NBC was a worthy, non-profit organization formed between the wars to encourage reading and promote the wider sales of books. This was mainly done by publishing book lists for educational establishments. A wartime casualty, it was being revived with the support of the literary establishment, with plans to widen the membership and increase its influence.

From a modest office near Covent Garden the National Book League had recently been set up in an elegant eighteenth-century house in Albemarle Street, once the home of Fanny Burney, whose friendly ghost, it was said, could occasionally be glimpsed wandering through the upstairs rooms. Maurice Marston, who had gamely kept the old NBC alive on a pittance, was appointed director; a librarian was engaged to take charge of the reference library; exhibitions, lectures, and discussions were planned; and, since culture is absorbed more easily when there is alcohol to wash it down, a license was obtained. Soon there would be a restaurant.

The idea of a center in London devoted to books from all points of view — author, publisher, printer, illustrator — where book lovers could meet socially for a drink or a meal, attend lectures and exhibitions, was new and exciting. At a time when book sales were buoyant and paper rationing being phased out, publishers like Geoffrey Faber, Michael Sadleir, Desmond Flower of Cassell, and Robert Lusty, chairman of Hutchinsons, were in the forefront of those willing to promote and nurture such a venture. In effect, it was a club open to anyone who wanted to join. For their guinea a year subscription (half a guinea if they lived more than thirty miles from London) members were free to use the reading and writing rooms and the bar, the book information bureau and the reference library. They could attend the exhibitions without paying an entry fee, and once a month they received a copy of the NBL journal, *Books*. It was remarkably good value for the money; too good, in fact, as finances became increasingly a problem.

Had Percy not been entitled to a seat on the NBL council through his presidency of the ABA, he would, in any case, have volunteered his services; it was just the sort of organization to attract his support. Asked to stage its first exhibition, "Children's Books of Yesterday," he willingly agreed, especially as he was, at that time, in a position to supply most of the exhibits.

It was not long since Elkin Mathews had bought on behalf of the

National Magazine Company, and for a considerable sum of money, a remarkable collection of children's books and juvenilia known as the Bussell Collection. Permission to display it was readily given, since it had been bought largely as a promotional asset and Percy was able to persuade the purchasers that the exhibition was a prestigious event and would be patronized by royalty.

Percy was also lending his own collection of Victorian educational games, puzzles, jigsaws, and some of the early nineteenth-century peepshows that had come from the A. J. A. Symons collection purchased in 1941. Among the publishers of children's books willing to cooperate was Warnes, which had promised him half a dozen of the rarest Beatrix Potter titles, including Peter Rabbit's first appearance in print. This was the edition Beatrix Potter had herself published in 1902 after failing to find a publisher. She financed the cost of publication by drawing some of her savings from the Post Office. The print run was five hundred copies, and she is said to have made a small profit by selling copies to friends and relatives at 1s. 2d. each.

Warnes was also willing to lend the exhibition Potter's final (undated) proof copy and a bound copy of *Peter Rabbit*, dated February 1902, together with the original manuscript and the original colored illustrations that Potter supplied for the first Warnes edition. In her privately printed edition only the frontispiece had been in color.

The catalogue of "Children's Books of Yesterday" (now a sought-after reference book) was a modest little paperback with pink paper covers designed by Robert Harling. It lists nearly one thousand items yet is small enough to fit easily into one's pocket. No glossy plates, no illustrations apart from the cover design incorporating a decorative alphabet.

"How about coming up to London with me for a preview?" Percy asked me a couple of days before the official opening. The children were on holiday, the weather was fine. We all piled into the Lancia, picked up my mother-in-law from her bungalow down the road, and drove up to London for a Muir family private view.

When we arrived at Albemarle Street, the preparations were nearly complete for the preliminary press show the following day. To display just over one thousand items so that each was clearly visible yet protected was no easy task. It had been achieved by using a number of cube-shaped all-glass cases in which the books (mostly small) were grouped and standing open, each with its own catalogue label. Around the walls were colorful pictures by well-known book illustrators and the decorative writing sheets used during the late eighteenth and early nineteenth

John Masefield opening the first National Book League exhibition.

centuries for teaching handwriting. Set out on tables were some of Percy's Victorian jigsaws, parlor games, and outdoor games, quickly spotted by my two with cries of recognition.

"What children seek in books is delight," Percy had written in his introduction to the catalogue. There on display were story books that had delighted and enthralled generations of children, mine included. The wonder was that so many of these fragile publications had survived: the Perrault *Mother Goose*, dated 1785; the flimsy little eighteenth-century chapbooks, with their stories of highwaymen and Robin Hood; the "moveable" story books with little tags that animated the illustrations; the early nursery rhyme books; and the adventure stories. Other sections showed moral tales, educational aids, and hieroglyphic books, including Dr. Franklin's *The Art of Making Money Plenty* . . . (1817), which must have once been universally popular.

A couple of days later I went up with Percy for the official opening. John Masefield, the president of the NBL, arrived soon after we did to make the opening speech. He was formally dressed in frock coat and striped trousers, presumably the de rigueur garb for a poet laureate, which he then was. With his fluffy white hair, white moustache, and air of

39

benevolence, he gave the impression of a kindly cleric who had absent-mindedly forgotten to wear his dog-collar. There was a twinkle in his eye when we were introduced, belying the formality of the occasion. We had all met upstairs in the library, and as we went down to the exhibition room where a select number of literary guests were gathering, Masefield paused on the landing by a window overlooking the rear of the house. "Look," he said, pointing, "a blue ladder!" I followed his gaze, and there, as he'd said, was a bright blue ladder propped up against a wall below us. The others had gone ahead; for a moment Masefield stood, smiling, enjoying the unexpected splash of color in the greyness of the back street. Irrelevant though it was to the occasion, the picture of the elderly poet standing by the window, perhaps finding some poetry in the scene, stayed in my mind for the rest of the day.

After the opening speeches — Masefield sonorous, Percy brief and explanatory — the assembled publishers, authors, and bibliophiles resumed conversations interrupted by the formalities; most of them, to my critical eye, were more concerned with exercising their egos than examining the exhibits. Several of the children's book authors had been already introduced to me, but while retaining their names I had quickly forgotten their faces.

"I don't think you know my wife?" Percy said to the large, tweedy individual who had come up to congratulate him, followed by a smaller, slightly built man whose face was faintly familiar. In the babel of conversation around us, I managed to catch one of the names of these two but missed the other one. After some congratulatory remarks addressed to Percy, the tweedy man moved on and Percy was drawn away to meet someone else, leaving me with the smaller man.

As Percy's wife, I accepted that my role was to stay in the background and make myself agreeable if required. Left face to face with a children's book writer, I began the conversation with the sort of remark that ought to go down well: "My daughter will be thrilled to hear I've met you," I said brightly. "You're one of her favorite authors."

He gave a slight smile, as if he had heard that opening many times. "And how old is your daughter?"

"She's nine."

"Ah, then she hasn't grown out of them yet?"

The clue was there, but I didn't spot it. "Oh, no. She's read most of them, and she hopes there will be more to come."

This was received in silence. Dutifully intent on keeping the conversation going, I pressed on: "I expect you've children of your own, you write so vividly about them."

40

"Only the one." He'd thrown me a second clue; there was that slight, amused smile again. Was I boring him? "I do hope there are going to be more adventure books. . . ." I was bent on doing my best even if the conversation was running into the ground, when, to my relief, someone I did know arrived to rescue me.

"John!" I exclaimed thankfully, "Do you know Arthur Ransome?"

"I expect he does," the man I'd been talking to said quietly. "But my name happens to be Milne."

My mortified apologies were accepted with that faint, cool smile. "Don't worry," said the author of *When We Were Very Young*, as the flowing tide of the party moved him on. "I'm sure you will remember me next time." But our paths were not to cross again. Arthur Ransome had indeed looked just as I might have expected, every inch an outdoor man. Alas, I never did get the chance to tell him that my daughter was one of his fans.

Not long after it was opened, the exhibition received the seal of royal approval with a visit from Queen Mary. Percy was told that he was expected to wait on Her Majesty, and that the poet laureate would be there to brief him on protocol. When I saw him off, I noticed that instead of wearing one of his usual brightly colored woven bow ties, he had managed to find a rather boring neutral one for the occasion. Years before, when on holiday in Innsbruck with Ian Fleming, both men had bought a number of handloom ties in a variety of colors. Ian had soon tired of them, handing over his collection to Percy, who had worn them ever since.

"She will expect a present, you know," said Masefield, as he and Percy waited for the arrival of the NBL's royal patron. "Perhaps you would be wise to decide now which of your treasures you're prepared to part with."

Queen Mary arrived punctually, wearing a feathered silk toque and, although the month was May, a long fur-collared coat and carrying a rolled parasol.

Percy soon found that this was to be no perfunctory visit. The contents of each display case were thoroughly inspected, individual items extracted so that they could be examined more closely. While he answered many apposite questions, Masefield and the lady-in-waiting trailed along behind. The tour finally completed, Percy expected to be released to mop his brow and relax. This was premature. Turning to Lady Alice of Athlone, the lady-in-waiting in attendance, Queen Mary said briskly: "I shall go round again with Mr. Muir, Alice. If you are tired, there is no need for you to accompany us; I'm sure Sir John will be glad to look after you."

The second time round took even longer, but by then Percy was beginning to enjoy himself, encouraged by the royal interest. Nor did he forget what was required of him when they came to the last of the exhibits, some early nineteenth-century peepshows from his own collection, by no means the least valuable of the exhibits. Would Her Majesty graciously accept a small souvenir of her visit, he asked?

Queen Mary hardly hesitated: "Thank you, Mr. Muir, that is very kind of you. I would like one of those." Her finger promptly indicated the best and oldest of the group of peepshows that she had already admired.

Later, when Percy and Masefield were recovering over a cup of tea, Masefield said with a twinkle: "Do you wonder they used to say George the Fifth and Mary the other four fifths?" Before she left, Queen Mary had promised to let the NBL have some of the royal family's childhood books, which would be on loan from the library at Windsor. These duly arrived a few days later and were given pride of place in a velvet-lined display cabinet. Several were inscribed, one bearing the inscription: "To Dear little George, from his loving Grandmother, Victoria."

Not long afterwards Percy was required to be on parade again for the visit of the royal princesses, Elizabeth and Margaret. The London season was in full swing, and the two girls had been at a dance the night before. Sent along by their grandmother, they politely tried to stifle their yawns as Percy took them round. The books from Windsor kindled a spark or two of interest, but little else did. At least their visit helped to bring further press coverage.

Everyone involved was greatly encouraged by the attendance figures and the increase in membership as a result of the exhibition, and a program of further exhibitions was put in train. For Percy, mounting "Children's Books of Yesterday" had been a labor of love. He wrote off the time he devoted to it ungrudgingly. The reward came, unasked; the exhibition had put him in the forefront of authorities on the history of early children's books. The little pink catalogue would one day blossom into a handsome, illustrated quarto.

That summer we bought the library of the late Sir Rider Haggard from his daughter Lilias, whose writings on Norfolk life were popular at the time. The Rider Haggards were a literary family; one brother, an army captain, wrote several novels (now all forgotten), the mother wrote poetry, and a David Haggard wrote a history of his family, tracing their ancestry back to 1438.

When Percy catalogued Rider Haggard's own books, thirty-five of them, all first editions and priced at around £1 10s., they sold like the proverbial hot cakes, leaving the writings of his mother and brother to languish unsold at giveaway prices. Haggard had also built up a remarkable collection of books on Africa and Egypt, which were heavily annotated in his own hand. Nearly all those went to eager collectors in the United States, where, rather surprisingly, his books were more in demand than in his own country.

After he had finished cataloguing the Haggard library, Jutro, our German Jewish cataloguer, who had lived with us for the last two years of the war and had by then returned to London, left the firm. Highly strung and obsessively tidy (nicknamed Mr. Fusspot by the children), he had been a careful and diligent cataloguer, with a wide knowledge of continental books. Inevitably there had been times when we got on each other's nerves, but we had grown fond of him over the years and understood his longing to return eventually to Paris, whence he had fled in 1940. Life with the Muirs must often have been bewildering for a man of his anxious, unconfident temperament, and I doubt that he ever really felt at home in Takeley.

He had been doing some work for Percy after returning to London, but in 1946 he found another job. I was still helping out when I could spare the time, grudged selfishly from my writing. But even if I had volunteered to devote my energies to the firm full time, I doubt Percy would have jumped at the offer. What he badly needed was a young, trainable second-in-command, preferably male, and I wouldn't have filled the bill.

At least I found him a packer, also badly needed. Dave Francis was a local man, decent and hard-working but without a trade. I met him one day when he was on his way home from his war-time job as a night watchman. "They've told me they don't need me any longer," he said gloomily. "Now I'll hev to find meself another job."

When I said we might have a job for him, he looked startled, then dubious. To work for an antiquarian bookshop was something that had never occurred to him, although he lived barely a stone's throw away from us. It took some persuasion to convince him that we could get along together. Pressed to put his doubts into words, he eventually confessed that "he wasn't much of a scholar." As we had not considered employing him in place of Jutro, we assured him that scholarship was not essential for packing up books. Relieved, he took the job and was to remain with us as packer, boiler stoker, gardener, and hen plucker for the next twenty-five years.

With the death of my bachelor uncle and godfather that year, I came

43

into money. Not that I was the only one in the family to inherit. Uncle John had made a will in 1914 leaving his estate to be divided between his ten nieces and nephews, with a £500 legacy to each as well, and had never altered it. So my aunts' hints that I was liable to be cut out of his will for leaving my first husband and going to "live in sin" (even though subsequently getting married) looked like wishful thinking on their part.

Divided by ten, this welcome windfall did not make any of us rich; it amounted to less than £2,000 apiece, and, as it was to come largely from the sale of the property and shares, the temptation was to start spending in anticipation. At least I did not have to wait long for my £500 legacy.

To my surprise, my idea of using this sum to pay off our mortgage of around the same amount met with instant disapproval from our accountants — though not from Percy. Their argument, that it was much better to continue with our mortgage and use any spare capital in some more advantageous way, was no doubt correct, but we were not to be persuaded. We went ahead, paid off the mortgage, and felt all the happier in the knowledge that we owned our home outright.

Holidays by the sea, especially along the East Anglian coast, had been out of the question during the war years. Beaches were mined, holiday hotels either requisitioned by the forces or occupied by the elderly well-to-do who had fled from London and other bombed cities. By the summer of 1946, seaside resorts were beginning to get back into business.

"The *Times Literary Supplement* wants me to do an article on the Holkham Library," said Percy, when the school holidays were approaching. "So while I'm working there, you and the children can have a seaside holiday at Wells-next-the-Sea. There's a sandy beach and it's only two or three miles from Holkham Hall." That it was going to be a busman's holiday for him was no hardship. Such holidays would be the pattern of our lives for years to come.

Wells, a picturesque little port at the head of a marshy estuary, then made little claim to being a holiday resort. It had been a working port in a modest way for several hundred years, serving sailing barges, schooners, and trading vessels from Holland and Scandinavia. Popular with artists and unsmart sailing folk, its yacht basin was once again in use for pleasure craft. The inevitable post-war plague of holiday caravans was yet to come. The Crown Hotel, where we stayed, was an unpretentious old inn standing at the end of a long, narrow green flanked by dignified Georgian houses. This was the superior part of the town, aloof from the quay, the old warehouses, and the fishermen's cottages. The church, too, stood well back from where the people made their living.

Our landlady at the Crown was a formidable matron who kept her staff on their toes. She fed us on steak-and-kidney pie, roasts, and gammon; we hadn't eaten so much good red meat for years and marvelled at how she managed, considering the ration for butcher's meat was less than it had been during the war. In the mornings, while I took the children to the beach, Percy worked in the Holkham Hall Library. Much of the house had been closed up during the war. With only a skeleton staff to keep the place going Lord Leicester, the fifth earl, and his family had been living largely below stairs, taking their meals in the big, old-fashioned kitchen under the glassy gaze of the family's collection of stuffed seabirds, preserved under glass cases and brought into the kitchen for safety from bombs or bombardment. The house was soon to be opened up to the public, with concerts of chamber music taking place once again in the beautifully proportioned music room at the top of the marble staircase.

As Percy worked, members of the family would look in for a chat, treating him rather as if he were a magician, conjuring up exciting rarities from shelves and boxes; some they swore they had never set eyes on before. He was soon on friendly terms with Lady Leicester, who on learning that Percy had his family with him, invited us all to tea.

"You won't mind having tea in the kitchen, I hope," she said as she led us downstairs. The long table, where in pre-war days a dozen or more servants would have sat down to a meal, was laid with a white damask cloth and a plentiful tea of scones and cakes. Somewhat overawed by the occasion, my children sat silently during the meal staring at the stuffed birds ranged around the room, including a huge, forbidding-looking great auk.

When we admired what was a remarkable ornithological collection, Lady Leicester, an elderly lady of character who had been entertaining us with tales of encounters with their royal neighbors at Sandringham (offered some apples when the Sandringham crop failed, Queen Mary had sent a wagon to pick up half the Leicester's crop), told us of the competition in the past between Norfolk families over who owned the rarest specimens of sea fowl. Stuffed though the birds were, there had been occasions when an osprey or some such rarity, shot on the marshes and duly stuffed and mounted, would mysteriously vanish from a much prized collection. As one of a large number of specimens, its disappearance might not have been immediately noticed, but when its twin was to be seen proudly displayed at a neighboring mansion, suspicions would be aroused and its absence discovered. With no proof that the bird in question had strayed to a neighboring home (the date on which it had been shot could have been changed), there was nothing to be done, but there would be dark talk of treachery by an upper servant bribed to smuggle it away by an opposite number in the rival household. Or even by a dastardly scion of a noble house bent on being able to boast that his family possessed a collection unrivalled in the county.

Had anyone ever been caught, I wanted to know. Lady Leicester doubted it but couldn't remember. In any case, she said, it was all a long time ago.

The cutlery at Holkham was heavy, old-fashioned steel, the kind that used to be kept polished and sharp by the "knife and boot boy" when such a servant was still employed. Offered an apple by Lady Leicester, David in slicing through it cut deeply into his hand. Blood spurted, bandages had to be fetched, the wound bound, and tears mopped up, which effectively brought the tea party to an end.

Back at the Crown Hotel, a bandaged, crestfallen David was asked by one of our fellow guests how he had hurt himself.

"I cut my hand on the Lord's knife," he answered solemnly.

"A judgement on you, David," said his father. Nor was it his only misadventure on that holiday. Among the surplus war supplies released on to the market that summer were rubber survival dinghies issued to the RAF. Children clamored to be given these dangerous little crafts, and there had been several incidents of hapless youngsters being carried out to sea in them. While resisting David's demand to be bought one, it hadn't occurred to me that he might pal up with a boy whose parents had been more indulgent.

One morning, while contentedly sunbathing on the Holkham sands, I raised my eyes and saw my son and his little boy friend some fifty yards from the shore, gleefully paddling out to sea in a rubber dinghy. When I set off in pursuit, splashing through shallow water, catching up with them didn't look too difficult. I was reckoning on reaching them long before they got into deep water. Presently, as I gained on them, my warning shouts took effect, and I could see them struggling to turn the dinghy round. But the tide was already running out fast, as it did on that stretch of coast, well known to be dangerous, and it was carrying them swiftly seaward. Nor had I realized that there were dips and deepish gullies in the sand.

By the time I reached them and grabbed the stern, I was waist deep. A moment later I was almost up to my armpits, barely able to hang on to the boat and at the same time keep on my feet. The undertow sucked at my legs and the dinghy dragged on my arms like a captive struggling to escape, but at least I had the crew on my side, valiantly using their toy paddles to help us struggle back shoreward.

Somehow, out of breath, with aching arms, I got them back into shallow water. We had won; the sea was gentle, no longer an enemy. For the two little boys it had all been good fun. They jumped out and splashed through the shallows above the tide mark, leaving me to pull the plug from the dinghy and squeeze it flat. As I did so, I glanced up and down the beach. There was no sign of David's friend's mother, and Helen had wandered off somewhere. The scattering of holiday makers were still dozing or reading unconcernedly, as they had been when I went after the boys. No one had been aware of the danger only just averted.

Chapter 7

"Do you think your mother would come and look after the children so that you can come with me to Scotland?" Percy asked one day in September when the school holidays were over. "Willie Maxwell says he has sorted out some books for me, and he and Ella would like us both to come up to Edinburgh and spend a few days there."

My mother had not long since returned from Kenya, where she had been living throughout the war years, teaching music in a girls' boarding school while my father served (and later died) in the Kenya Royal Naval Volunteer Reserve. I had met her boat at Tilbury, a lengthy, frustrating business. Hours passed with my mother and her fellow passengers standing beside the rails on deck looking down on those who had come to meet them, lined up on the quay below. Kept apart by what seemed to be endless red tape and formalities, we waved and smiled, and those with good lungs shouted greetings and news. Disciplined as we all were from war-time queuing, we grumbled and put up with it.

It was seven years since I had seen my mother off to East Africa, where she was going to join my father, who had taken a job there. Now she was home again, changed by the passing years and her bereavement into an elderly, anxious little widow, without a home. The War Department had requisitioned her house and was still, despite my intervention, refusing to release it to her, at least for the time being, even though she was a naval officer's widow. It all seemed very unfair, especially when she found that a much younger naval wife was living happily in her house and showing no inclination to go elsewhere.

England might be home, but what with nowhere to live, rationing, fuel shortages, and the winter coming on, it wasn't the best placed to be in 1946. At least there were affectionate reunions, a new generation to get to know.

She had already spent some days with us before going the round of relatives and old friends, and was equipped with ration book, clothing coupons, and identity card. She would gladly return to take charge while I went off to Scotland with Percy, she said, an arrangement accepted with enthusiasm by my children; a grandmother who had lived in Africa and could tell bedtime stories about wild animals had the edge on the grannie down the road, who had lived nowhere but in England.

William Maxwell, whom we were going to see, was head of the Edinburgh firm of R. & R. Clark, printers for many of the leading publishers. Willie, as he was known to his friends, was a proud Scot, heavily built and masterful but generous and good-hearted. He and Percy had known each other for some years and had done business together. Through his firm and his friendships with many of the authors whose books he printed, he had built up a fine library, with contemporary writers well represented.

He was particularly proud of his long association with Bernard Shaw, who had for many years insisted on dealing directly with the firm that printed his books and plays. The friendship between Maxwell and Shaw had lasted for some fifty years and become, according to Willie, a mutual admiration society despite a few stormy patches.

"Shaw wrote and I advised him on the typography and format of his books," Willie said when writing to me about their association. "He was the kindest, most appreciative of men and, for want of a better word, the 'goodest' of all the literary lights it has been my honour to count as friends. . . ."

Willie had the Scot's pawky humor and a wonderful fund of Scottish stories, which he told with relish and much hearty laughter. A widower for many years, when we knew him, he was living with his unmarried daughter Ella, also a strong character, who made it her business to "keep him in order," for Willie could be something of a problem to pretty young women if he got half a chance.

We set off for Scotland in the Lancia, which was then behaving quite well. It was my first trip to Scotland, but as I was to discover, Percy had only to drive across the border for his Scots ancestry to become apparent. Scottish words and phrases slipped easily into his conversation, his Rs took on a slight but definite burr. This was unconscious and meant that he felt thoroughly at home.

Impressed though I was with Edinburgh's granite dignity, I was depressed by the grime and longed to see someone give Sir Walter Scott, atop his memorial in Princes Street, a good wash. What with the trains from the Waverley Station belching out sooty smoke into the center of the city and hundreds of coal fires in homes and offices contributing their share of pollution, it was no wonder that the buildings were all begrimed. But I enjoyed riding in the trams clanking their way through the main streets; they at least did not add to the dirt.

Perhaps I was unfair in believing the city fathers too stingy to allow money for steam cleaning, the problem then being a shortage of manpower rather than cash.

While Percy and William worked together, I went sightseeing, walking up to the castle that stands grey and dominant above the city. With my fear of heights, I could hardly bear to gaze down at the Princes Street gardens, green and well kept so frighteningly far below. The gracious Georgian squares with their charming fanlights above the heavy panelled doors were far more to my taste, as were the dignified old established bookshops such as John P. Grant in Dundas Street, belonging to Percy's good friend Ian Grant, who would give him loyal support on the ABA committee. Another fine shop was that of James Thin.

The Scots are a hospitable people, and the English are welcomed kindly, but when I joined a tour of the State rooms at Holyrood, I was made aware that some old wounds never quite heal. Our guide had led us into the room where, he told us, Mary Queen of Scots had slept the night before she was taken prisoner by Elizabeth's men. A meaningful pause had followed before he added grimly: "to be murrderred by the English." I fancy I was the only Sassenach in the party, but had there been several of us I'm sure the guide would not have modified his comments.

It was on the second night of our stay that I awoke with a sense of foreboding from a disturbing dream. I had not been dreaming of actual disaster, rather I had a feeling of some sort of threat to my family. It was so strong that I couldn't keep it to myself, not that I expected Percy to take my fears seriously. Nor did he, but he did agree that I should telephone home to set my mind at rest and stop fussing. I put a call through and was reassured by my mother that she and the children were in good health and all was well.

"There you are," said Percy, when rather sheepishly I reported my conversation with my mother. "That's another of your forebodings disposed of . . ." I had to agree, but all the same a faint uneasiness lingered.

On the return journey we made a detour to visit Francis Thompson, the librarian at Chatsworth. Francis and Percy had become friends when Percy spent a weekend there working on the library for an article he was writing for the *TLS*, one of a series on fine libraries in private ownership. On this occasion we had called to pick up some rare books of poetry for

50

John Hayward's English poetry exhibition, to take place at the National Book League in 1947.

They were considerable rarities, two of them fifteenth-century volumes printed by Wynkyn de Worde, another a collection of poems by John Skelton (c. 1545), and it was largely thanks to Percy's friendship with Francis that they were to be loaned to the NBL. After Francis agreed, Percy had suggested that perhaps Lord Cavendish, the heir to the title, might be asked to bring the books to London personally, since he travelled up quite often.

Francis wouldn't hear of this. "No, Muir, most certainly not!" he said emphatically. "Lord Cavendish is a very agreeable young man. I've nothing against him. But I would rather see these valuable books wrapped in a single sheet of paper and entrusted to the parcel post than allow Lord Cavendish to take them to London. He would undoubtedly leave them either in the train or in a taxicab, or even in some restaurant. Now, if you yourself could find an opportunity to collect them, I could assure the duke that he need have no fear as to their safety. . . ."

Francis welcomed us into his cozy bachelor sitting room, where the dowager duchess used sometimes to take tea with him. He lived alone, looked after by a housekeeper named Grace — "my old Grace," he was fond of calling her, while the Duchess was "Her old Grace." He was by this time an old man and suffering badly from arthritis. While remaining librarian, or keeper of the duke's treasures, as he preferred to call himself, much of the work was delegated to the young assistant who would eventually take over from him, Tom Wragg.

We found him in good anecdotal form, and over tea he was reminded of the time when "the old duke" came to him one day and said a guest had told him he ought to read *Pride and Prejudice*.

"Fellow said I'd enjoy it. I suppose we've got a copy somewhere?"

"Yes, indeed we have, Your Grace," said Francis. "You have the first edition in the library, a three-volume set."

"Never mind what edition it is," the duke said testily. "Just get it for me."

So Francis fetched the set and reluctantly handed it to him. At that moment the duchess joined them. "Is that a valuable set, Mr. Thompson?" she asked, looking suspiciously at the three little volumes the duke was about to walk off with.

"Yes, indeed, Your Grace," Francis replied, "it is extremely scarce and valuable."

Whereupon she turned to the duke and said sharply, "Then you mustn't have it. You'll only get marmalade or butter on the pages and ruin it!"

51

The duke didn't give in without a fight. He protested that it was his set of *Pride and Prejudice*, and he didn't give a fig if it was a first edition. He wanted to read it, and he'd dam' well do so.

"That you won't!" said the duchess and snatching the set from him, she marched out of the room.

"Later, when the duke had forgotten all about it, she brought the set back to me," Francis said with a chuckle.

We returned home to find all well. The children had been good, my mother said, and there had been no problems. Relieved and grateful, I forgot my forebodings, and the next day my mother left us to visit a sister. It was a couple of days after her departure that Helen started a cold. Nothing unusual in that; I decided to keep her at home for a couple of days to be on the safe side, before letting her return to school. But that time it was not just a cold. On the third day she was feverish, and by the evening she had a temperature of 105°F. Horrified, I rushed to telephone our doctor. His voice sounded grave, but he assured me there was no need for panic. He was about to go on a call and would come and see Helen the first thing in the morning. In the meantime, aspirin at three-hour intervals should reduce the fever.

It was a long, anxious night; in the morning Helen was still feverish but seemed better. But when the doctor arrived and examined her, I knew from his grave voice that she was seriously ill. He spoke of tests, the possibility of a lumbar puncture. In any case, she must be admitted to hospital straight away. He couldn't or wouldn't give a diagnosis.

At the hospital she was taken from us and put into a side ward. I argued that I should stay at her bedside but was bossily discouraged. Those were the days when ward sisters regarded parents as a nuisance not a help, rationing them to twice-weekly afternoon visits.

It was 6 AM when the telephone awoke us the next morning. A voice said that our daughter had suffered a severe hemorrhage in the night and had been put on the danger list. "We would like you both to come and stand by to be ready to give a blood transfusion if it is considered necessary," said the voice.

It was still dark when we drove to the hospital through silent, empty streets. We didn't talk. The duty doctor was waiting for us.

"I'm afraid your daughter has had a bad nasal hemorrhage," he said. "We've stopped the bleeding now, but she has lost a great deal of blood." He advised us to go in to see her one at a time, so I went in first.

She was lying on her back, her face milk white, her eyes closed. One arm lay outside the bedclothes, a saline drip taped to her wrist. Shattered by the change since the day before, I sat down by her bedside, afraid to speak or even to touch her, unsure whether she was unconscious or sleeping.

Suddenly, as if she had become aware of my presence, she opened her eyes, sat up, and clutched at a glass of water on the bed table; she muttered "I must drink" and gulped down a few mouthfuls. When she had had all she wanted and I took the glass from her hand, her eyes rested on me briefly, vaguely, as if she was hardly aware of me. I smiled and murmured consoling words as she lay back against the pillows, longing to hug her. But her eyes were already closing again. When, after a few minutes, Percy took my place, she seemed to be sleeping peacefully.

Later we discovered that there had been only one nurse on duty in the children's ward during that night. Busy with several babies, she had not had time to check on the little girl in the side ward until the early morning. By then the hemorrhage had been in progress for some time and had reached danger point.

After we had waited at the hospital most of the morning, pacing up and down, alert for every approach by the staff, we were told we could go home. It had been decided that a blood transfusion might do more harm than good, said the duty doctor, that it could start up the bleeding again by raising her blood pressure. In reply to our anxious questioning, he would only say that he thought another hemorrhage unlikely. They were still unable to tell us what had brought on her sudden illness; they were doing various tests and would keep us informed.

We went home and spent the rest of the day keyed up for a call from the hospital, our hearts lurching every time the phone rang. The news that Helen was ill had circulated, and friends kept ringing up to inquire. But there was no more bad news that night, and when I arrived at the hospital in the morning with books and clean pajamas, I was told that she was definitely better.

"But I can't let you go in," said the nurse, barring my way, "it isn't a visiting day."

When I stood my ground, pointing out that my daughter was still on the danger list (when the rules were relaxed), she gave in grudgingly and let me pass. Once in the little side ward, it was as if my daughter had been given back to me. She was sitting up against the pillows, pale but alert, eager to tell me all that had been happening to her.

"They're giving me M and B *and* penicillin. Dr. Lucey, that's the pathologist, has been to see me twice. He's awfully nice. He writes books for children. . . ."

53

She could remember little of the hemorrhage that had nearly caused her death, only that there had been a lot of fuss in the night and a doctor at her bedside. The day after my visit she was no longer on the danger list and steadily improving. The tests for polio and meningitis had proved negative. But what *was* her illness, we wanted to know? What had brought it on so suddenly? No one was able to tell us.

A week went by. I was expecting to be told I could bring Helen home, when the duty doctor telephoned: "I'm sorry, Mrs. Muir, but I have to tell you that the news is not so good. Your daughter has been diagnosed as having typhoid. We shall be transferring her to the isolation hospital tomorrow."

When I demanded to be allowed to travel with Helen in the ambulance, the hospital authorities reluctantly agreed, with the proviso that I be wrapped from head to foot in a voluminous white surgical gown; otherwise, I was told sternly, the clothes I was wearing would have to be burned, as indeed Helen's pajamas were. As I had clothes at home that had been in contact with the patient before the diagnosis of typhoid, I couldn't see the point. In any case, I still only half believed the diagnosis.

It set wheels in motion, nevertheless. Within a very short time a public health inspector was on our doorstep with a lot of little bottles, explaining apologetically that samples were required.

"Water from your taps, some garden soil, and, er, some personal samples as well."

"Blood samples?" I hazarded. "Er, no — we need feces, I'm afraid. We also need the names of any persons who have had a meal at your house during the past six weeks."

The implications of this request did not immediately strike me. I produced my diary and helpfully gave him the names of some of the friends whom we had entertained to a meal during the period in question. Fortunately, there had not been many. It was disconcerting to be told a few days later by Rupert Cross, our blind lawyer friend, that dinner with the Muirs had brought an unexpected sequel.

"A man from the council called on us with two little bottles and a very personal request. We did our best to comply," Rupert said, "but the bottles were very small, and it wasn't easy, especially for a blind man."

The public health inspector was followed by our local doctor, whose duty it was to give us all, the office staff included, anti-typhoid injections, with the result that within twenty-four hours we were all going down like ninepins.

Barred from seeing my daughter, I established contact with the matron at the isolation hospital, who proved helpful and sympathetic. After Helen had been there a week, she gave me her own opinion of the case. "As far as I am concerned, your daughter has *not* got typhoid, Mrs. Muir. And I think it would be much better for her to be at home."

Not long after I had reported the matron's remarks to my own doctor, we were told that further tests having proved negative, our daughter would be brought back from the isolation hospital to Bishop's Stortford, and we could come and take her home. She was paler and thinner when we collected her, and, while happy to be home again, understandably annoyed that the books and toys I had sent her regularly had all been put in the incinerator when she left the isolation ward.

Whatever her mysterious illness was, no other cases occurred in the neighborhood, and after a short recuperation, she returned to school to learn that she had unwittingly caused much fuss there as well. The theory that some vicious African bug had somehow sneaked into our house in my mother's luggage was briefly considered, then diplomatically dismissed, especially as no frightening illness followed in her wake elsewhere. Years later I met Dr. Lucey, the Scottish pathologist, at a social function. He was then retired but well remembered the case.

"Was it really typhoid?" I asked him.

"You see, we were looking for a diagnosis," he said. "At the time it seemed a possible one; there were pointers to it being typhoid. But mind, I'm not saying it was or wasn't," he added with Scottish caution. "She made a good recovery, didn't she? So you can be thankful for that. A very bright little girl, as I remember her . . ."

Chapter 8

One of the depressing things about the early post-war years was that everything was shabby and worn-out, including public transport. It was exasperating to hustle the children out of the house in the morning to catch the schoolbus, which was supposed to stop outside the pub next door, only to have them returning five minutes later saying gleefully: "We can't go! The bus was full and wouldn't stop."

Since the closure of the single-track rail service into Bishop's Stortford, the bus service had been proving inadequate to cope with the consequent extra passengers. We had been promised larger buses, but they were presumably still on the drawing board. Such relief buses that were available were ancient and unreliable. Grumbles and complaints got us nowhere.

Determined not to have my morning's writing disrupted by chatter and probably squabbles, I would get out the car and drive my children and any others thus stranded to their respective schools. Other mothers suffered the same problem, and few had the use of a car.

This, I thought, was a matter to be taken up by the parish council, along with the village's need for street lighting, a speed limit along the main road, and a bus shelter — for a start. My belief that it was our job to galvanize the district council and the county council into providing the village with such amenities was not shared by most of my fellow councillors, least of all by our clerk. As the poor man was elderly and underpaid, I couldn't altogether blame him for his resistance to being asked to write letters that years of experience had told him seldom had any effect. To be fair, when I persisted, he appeared to bear me no ill-will.

Whether or not it was due to the parish council's representations, relief buses did start coming eventually, but several years would pass and a child would be killed by a passing car before the village was allowed a speed limit.

The winter of 1947 was beautiful and cruel. Snow began to fall heavily during the first week of the new year; large wet flakes drifted down ceaselessly for a whole day. The next morning we awoke to the stillness of a white countryside, with only the occasional shush, shush from traffic passing on the white carpeted road. This was a foretaste of the weather that was to freeze the countryside almost to a standstill for weeks to come. No sooner was the snow swept from paths and doorsteps and partly cleared from the roads than icy winds brought fresh falls.

"Transport strike still on. Very short of food, no bacon to be had at grocer's. . . ." I recorded in my diary on January 16th. Despite the weather, Percy and I risked the icy roads in order to attend the opening of the National Book League's Victorian fiction exhibition arranged by Michael Sadleir and John Carter. For once, John's habitual cool had deserted him when he greeted us. He had secured a scoop.

"We invited Anthony Trollope's daughter, and I've just been told she has arrived," he said. "I'm trying to track her down. She's as deaf as a post and about ninety, but at least she is here."

He hurried away in pursuit of his aged quarry, and later she was pointed out to me, a tall, spare, and upright spinster. Whether she was carrying the expected ear trumpet I can no longer remember. Communication was clearly proving difficult, and I gave up any idea of asking her to autograph my catalogue. Instead, I plucked up courage to approach Rose Macaulay, who was also thin and erect but by no means deaf nor noticeably elderly. As she scribbled her signature at my request, she remarked somewhat acidly to the woman she had been talking to that she never could see much point in giving autographs.

Victorian fiction was an excellent follow-up to Percy's children's book exhibition. Between them, Michael Sadleir and John Carter had brought together a remarkable collection of the work of Victorian novelists, famous, infamous, and anonymous, with "gothicks" from Michael's own collection.

February brought more heavy snowfalls; the cold was unrelenting, the main road to Bishop's Stortford perilous with hard-packed ice. "Still bitterly cold," my diary recorded despondently. "Kept children at home. In consequence no peace. Anthracite finished and little coal left."

Early in February the government announced "a national fuel emergency." The use of electric fires was forbidden between the hours of 9 – 12 AM and 2 – 4 PM. Paraffin was already in short supply, and although there were some oil-fired heating stoves in the office, these burned up oxygen and gave everyone headaches, owing to the poor ventilation. The alternative was to work in overcoats. Dissatisfied with their wages and their conditions of work, the workers in the transport unions remained stubbornly on strike.

Three days after the fuel emergency announcement, we were given an even sterner warning over the use of electric fires. To be caught toasting one's toes before one of those comforting foot warmers during the prohibited period could result in "heavy penalties" said a government spokesman on the nine o'clock news. Caught by whom, we wondered. Nor was the penalty spelled out. Bastinado, perhaps, to fit the crime? It all sounded very Gilbertian.

Shortly before the fuel shortage became a national emergency, Percy had been invited to appear on television as a result of an article he had written for the *Geographical* magazine on nineteenth-century board games and jigsaw puzzles in the form of maps and similar educational games. The article had appeared in the December 1946 issue and had caught the eye of the producer of an afternoon TV program. Percy was rather taken with the idea of showing some of his collection on the air, and Peter Jones, the producer, came to Takeley to discuss the proposed program. The result was that we were booked to show not only the board games but a selection of "dissolving views" of railway scenes, tin clockwork toys, and some of Percy's much prized automata: the monkey conjurer, the tightrope walkers, a white mouse playing the fiddle, and other ingenious Victorian mechanical entertainments.

"They'll make splendid television," the young producer cried in delight. "We've never had anything like them before!" By then Percy was having second thoughts. The automata in particular were fragile, he pointed out, and not easily portable (they had to be taken to Alexander Palace for the program); they could be damaged in transit. But in the end, as I backed up Peter Jones, who was determined not to take no for an answer and was promising complete insurance coverage, Percy agreed. He would introduce each item, and I would act as a sort of sorcerer's apprentice, handing over the exhibits and doing the winding up where necessary.

Our slot was only about fifteen minutes, but as usual with a TV appearance, it was the preliminaries that took up the time. Percy had known the old "Ally Pally" well in the days when he had lived in London and attended First World War dances there. Even in those days it had hardly lived up to the grandeur of its name as a center for local entertainment. The neighborhood had suffered badly in the blitz, and the building itself looked pretty dilapidated as we drove into the yard, well ahead of the appointed time for our preliminary run-through.

A notice directed us to a bare wooden staircase; mounting it, we found ourselves in a large barn-like studio with cables from several cameras snaking across the floor. Technicians in corduroys (forerunners of jeans) and turtle-necked pullovers stood around gossiping while an elderly man clasping a life-size baby doll was being taken through his act. This was one of our fellow performers; we were, we discovered, rather a job lot.

He was a thin little man of sixty or so, serious and humorless. He was sitting on a Victorian horsehair settee with a papier maché baby's bath on the floor before him, and he was about to demonstrate how he taught hapless husbands left in charge of a baby the right way to bathe it and put it to bed. This appeared to be his self-appointed mission in life, and he was proud of the way he carried it out. As he solemnly explained, a young father could never be sure that his wife might not be suddenly taken ill, go absent, get drunk, or whatever, leaving her husband on his own to cope with the baby. So he was doing what he could to prepare young husbands to cope with the situation if it should arise. And there were many to thank him for his trouble, he assured the camera team proudly.

The presenter, Stuart Macpherson, a chunky, breezy Canadian, knew just what he wanted from his performers. Genial but firm, he took them through their acts with easy professionalism. After the baby bather came a dark-eyed, bosomy Italian soprano accompanied by her husband who was about half her size and touchingly proud of her. His role was manager and interpreter.

While she tried out a few bars, he confided to me a problem they had found in coming to England. She had, he explained, a problem with support. In search of a bra that would fit her, he had tried many, many shops, but always they did not have one large enough. So now they must wait for a new supply to come from Italy, for, he added with pride, she would buy only the very best.

Our rehearsal went satisfactorily. The walking doll we had brought, demure in a lilac silk crinoline, stepped out without a fall, the automata, occasionally temperamental, did their tricks as required. I wound up and handed over the exhibits while Percy talked, and afterwards our presenter declared himself very satisfied.

There was a break for us to lunch in the canteen before the live program in the afternoon. I had noticed the camera crew eyeing the automata with interest, and as we left for lunch an admiring little group had gathered round where the exhibits we were showing stood ready. Half an hour later when we returned, one of the crew came up to me looking somewhat sheepish.

"Thought I'd better tell you," he mumbled, "but that monkey toy of yours doesn't seem to be working right."

"But he was going perfectly well at the rehearsal . . . ," I protested and wound up the spring to prove it. The musical box tinkled its customary tune, the magician's beard began to waggle, his hands hovered over the little table in front of him, and two white balls popped up through the tiny trap doors. So far, so good. Green balls should have followed, then yellow ones, and finally a pair of dice. None of this happened. The white balls disappeared then reappeared as the mechanism beneath the table swung back on itself instead of forward. "Yes, I see what's gone wrong," I said crossly. "His balls aren't functioning."

In the dead silence that followed I bent my head over the magician to hide my blushes. The camera man left me to it. To his credit he didn't snigger. In 1947 to have done so would have been very bad manners. Soon afterwards we were on the air.

"In Victorian times education was largely a matter of cramming," Percy began. "The minds of children were regarded as jampots; the object of education was cramming into them as much jam as they could be expected to contain. . . ." The board games and jigsaws were shown to illustrate the point, but many of the exhibits we had brought were pure fun. I was still cross about the malfunctioning of our star turn, the magician, silently cursing the technicians for tampering with him, but at least the rest of the automata was working properly, as sweating in the heat and mostly off camera, I wound them up and handed them to Percy.

When the show was over, Peter Jones declared himself delighted. Would we do it all over again for the evening program, he asked. But Percy had had enough of the Ally Pally for one day, and we packed up and left while most of our fellow performers remained.

We were on the way home when, reflecting on the way things had gone, Percy remarked that showing the collection in black and white hardly did it justice.

"What are you giggling for?" he asked, as I suddenly began to chuckle.

"Because I've just realized I needn't have fretted so much about the magician not working properly. Green balls, yellow balls, white balls — in black and white it was all the same. No one watching the program would have noticed any difference."

As the arctic weather continued, rail services became chaotic and the local coal merchant found himself everyone's best friend. From time to time, the radio weather man would foretell the beginning of the thaw, the thick thatch of snow that covered our roof would begin to drip, and great slabs of hard frozen snow would slide from the roof of my chicken ark. Then it would freeze again, and we would wake to see icicles as sharp as daggers suspended from the eaves, glittering cruelly in the pale sunshine. On such days the beauty of the white countryside would compensate for all the discomfort.

Across the road Hatfield Forest was a picture in black and white under the blue canopy of a cloudless sky. When it was not a schoolday, I would take the children to the lake to slide. As they ran across the open plain downhill to the frosted fringe of marsh, haunt of hungry coots and moorhens, they were like a pair of little steam engines, their breath condensing into white puffs in the icy air. Hatfield Forest was beautiful at all times; for me never more so than when soft, deep snow covered the trails and clung to the branches of the birch trees like cotton wool. Here and there would be the tracery of tracks of birds and small animals, left like messages on the snow. On my lone walks I seldom met another soul.

With the long-awaited thaw came the floods and more chaos. Then once again the countryside was green, greener it seemed than ever before, while here and there the last of the snow lay in ditches in dirty, crunchy heaps. In the garden long delayed daffodils triumphantly opened their trumpets, and along the hedges the blackthorn was suddenly in bloom.

Chapter 9

It never occurred to Percy that one of his relatives would be interested in becoming an antiquarian bookseller and joining him in the business. At that time he barely knew of the existence of Laurie Deval, the only son of a first cousin whom he had not seen for years. Laurie, on the other hand, knew all about "Uncle Percy," whose reputation as a writer and dealer in rare books was something of a legend in a family without scholarly or literary traditions.

As a lad, so the story went, Laurie and some of his mates had gone on a cycle ride one weekend and passed through Takeley on their way to the coast. He had known it was the village where we lived and had spotted our house as they went by.

"That's where my Uncle Percy has his business," he had told his friends, "and one day I might work there."

At the time it seemed an unlikely future for an east London boy whose father worked as a storeman. Nor did anyone mention this youthful ambition to Percy at that time. But Laurie was a bright lad, and after gaining a scholarship to a good London grammar school, where he did well, he joined a firm of accountants and stayed with them until his call-up. On joining the RAF, he quickly gained a commission and qualified as a navigator in 1944. After the war, accountancy lost its appeal for him. Far more attractive was the idea of working in a more personal kind of business where there could be the prospect of a future partnership. An additional attraction was that he and the girl he was soon to marry both wanted to live out of London.

Desperate to find someone he could trust to manage the office in his frequent absences on buying trips, attending book auctions, and ABA committee business, Percy was very ready to consider his young cousin for a job when he learned, through his mother, that Laurie was interested.

Their first meeting, at the Bath Club, where Percy had invited Laurie to lunch, proved a success. The young, newly demobilized airman made a good impression on the older man, who was already disposed to take him on as one of the family. A three-month trial period was agreed upon, and Percy told Laurie he could lodge with us from Mondays to Fridays rather than having to make a tedious daily journey from east London to Takeley. As he was still based with his parents, he would be able to go home for the weekend.

I was glad to hear that the lunch had been a success and Percy's staff problem looked settled but was not so happy to hear that once again our spare room was going to be occupied and by someone I'd never even met. After Jutro's departure, I had pleaded for no further lodgers and believed my plea accepted.

"Oh dear, must he stay with us?" I sighed. "Someone else to feed!" "It'll only be temporary," said Percy soothingly. "Once he's married, they'll find somewhere to live nearby. And I know you'll like him; he's a lively, attractive young man with a good sense of humor. Just your sort!"

He was right, of course; the whole family took to Laurie. With his fresh, healthy good looks and conversation larded with RAF slang, he brought a cheerful, youthful breeziness into the house and the office and was soon accepted by the locals at the Green Man down the road. As a lodger he fitted in so easily that I had no grumbles. Long before the three-month trial period was over, we knew that he would stay.

It was a help, too, that his salary for his first year with the firm would be paid by the government through their retraining scheme for former members of the armed forces. Laurie was married that summer and with his pretty young wife, Mary, came to live in Bishop's Stortford.

Percy's year as president of the ABA was drawing to a close. Pressed to continue for a further year, he agreed. There was some unfinished business that he wished to see through. The decision was made easier now that he could leave Laurie Deval to hold the fort in his absence. Like all exporting businesses we were enmeshed in the red tape of exchange control. Heartily disliking, as he did anything to do with forms and figures, Percy now looked to his young cousin who had had two years' training in accountancy to devise some way of straightening out the tangle of forms and papers that had been accumulating over the years and might, he feared, one day bring us into dire trouble with some government department.

Percy had always found it hard to understand how it was that although he carefully explained procedures and methods of working to his staff, they sometimes failed to comprehend what they were supposed to do. He believed the system he had devised for running the business was perfectly simple and thereafter assumed that his staff would follow it. But this was by no means what always happened.

Throughout the war years and for some while afterwards the Bank of England required that a section of a form known as a CD3, must accompany the invoices of all exported orders. When the payment for the goods came through, a copy of the appropriate part of the form was supposed to be attached to the check when it was paid into the bank, while yet another duplicate went into the firm's files.

It was not until a polite but puzzled inquiry arrived one day from someone at the Bank of England that Percy began to suspect that something had gone wrong. After his reliable, conscientious secretary who had seen us through the early years of the war had left, there had been a not so bright successor. It was after she, too, had departed that the inquiry came and Laurie discovered an embarrassing collection of CD3s that appeared to have no partners. Somehow the system had failed. Too late Percy realized what had happened. Failing to appreciate the need to attach the correct form to each payment before it went to the bank, the young woman had instead been in the habit of gaily pairing up checks with any forms that came to hand, thus leaving an unholy mess for someone to clear up when she left us.

The Bank of England was very helpful. They wrote to say that two of their exchange control staff would come to Takeley to sort things out. Shortly afterwards two civil servants arrived, and for the next two days they sat at a desk in the office going through several years' accumulation of forms and invoices. Finally, they packed them into two suitcases and prepared to take their departure. When Percy began to apologize, feeling thoroughly ashamed of the breakdown of his system, they assured him that it was all in a day's work. It had happened before, they said, and would no doubt happen again.

"Well, I am most grateful to you both," Percy said as he saw them off, much relieved that he was getting off with nothing worse than a polite request to try not to let it happen again. "But what will you do with those papers you're taking away?"

"Oh, they'll be shredded," was the answer. "There's no point in us wasting any more time on them."

To have asked, as he longed to do, why then had he been required to fill in and file hundreds of CD3s in triplicate over some six years would hardly have been diplomatic in the circumstances.

By this time most of those antiquarian booksellers who had evacuated from London early in the war to carry on from premises in a country town or from their own homes were back in town. Shabby and battered though London looked, its streets full of bomb damage, boarded-up buildings, and weedy gaps, there was money about. The "wide boys" (illegal street traders) were doing quite nicely supplying the hungry consumer market with so-called export rejects. Along Oxford Street there was always a row of hawkers, suitcases of nylons at their feet and a lookout to warn them if the law was approaching.

In the prevailing climate of austerity, the ABA settled for a luncheon at the Dorchester that year, rather than an evening banquet. Among the guests of honor were Michael Sadleir and Harold Nicholson, both witty, urbane speakers, but on that occasion it was Bernard Miles who stole the show. Not then a theater manager, he had, as an actor, played many parts at the Old Vic and elsewhere. Currently he was having a great success on the radio doing a comic turn as a crafty yokel in Will Shakespeare country. It was sly humor in the classic tradition, and at the Dorchester he had us all happily chuckling at gags in a broad Warwickshire accent. A few years later he would launch his brave venture for a theater — The Mermaid — in the cultural desert of the city.

Percy had been far from happy at the choice of the Dorchester as a venue for the luncheon. To his regret there was no gainsaying most of his colleagues on the committee who thought it entirely appropriate for the up-market image they felt the ABA ought to project. His own view was that to have chosen somewhere rather more suited to the majority of members' pockets would have been fairer and more suitable.

As it happened, the date of the luncheon coincided with the first day of the Chelsea Flower Show, an event that Percy, a keen gardener, was determined not to miss. Extracting ourselves from the proceedings as soon as we dared, we made for Chelsea to relax and breathe deeply among the profusion of blossom and fragrance. During the long, icy winter most of the exhibitors had been facing disaster and the hard choice of keeping the frost out of their greenhouses or out of their homes. Somehow it had worked out, and the displays and instant gardens looked as beautiful and enviable as ever.

I was able to linger at the show with Percy, confident that when we got home Esther would have given the children their tea and, if we were late, seen them off to bed. This wouldn't happen again, for the next morning she announced that she was leaving. She said neither why she was going nor where. Perhaps it was to a job where she would have a bathroom to herself as well as a bedroom — but she didn't tell me. She had been with us for two years. One winter's evening I had found her sitting by the slow-burning stove in the dining room after the children had gone to bed, reading one of my novels. It was unfortunate that a servant girl who appeared briefly in the book, a less than attractive character, was also called Esther. I did not ask her if she had enjoyed the book; she made no comment. With her family housed elsewhere, there was nothing to keep her in Essex. At the end of the week she left, and we did not see her again.

My family doubled in size that summer, although only temporarily. My middle sister, who had settled in Kenya before the war, had come to the conclusion that it was not a country in which to bring up her two children. The Mau Mau, an underground terrorist organization, had been killing white settlers in a particularly nasty way, and the atmosphere of fear and mistrust was such that many of the British were leaving. The Channel Islands were a popular choice for Britishers disenchanted with post-war life in parts of the shrinking British Empire, and it was in Jersey that my sister and her husband were looking for a new home.

The last time we had been together was in 1937. As with many families, the war had separated us for a decade. In the intervening years we had both had families, so as well as the pleasure of our reunion (tinged with some curiosity as to how faces and figures had withstood the passage of time), we were each meeting for the first time a niece and a nephew.

Suddenly I was an aunt, with an eight-year-old pocket-sized nephew, very neat and tidy, with my sister's eyes; beside him was a pretty little six-year-old niece. Both were very self-possessed children, summing me up, I felt sure, as I studied them.

My sister was looking at me hopefully. Three years my senior, with a peach-bloom complexion, blonde hair, and a Marilyn Monroe figure, she was being pursued by lovelorn youths when I was still a skinny, mousy-haired schoolgirl. As working girls in London, the three-year gap lost significance, but our paths soon diverged as she landed in Shanghai, married, and went to Kenya, while I remained in England.

"Phyllida hardly changed," I recorded in my diary later. "Still very attractive and smartly dressed. Agreed to have her children to stay while she and husband go house-hunting. . . ."

"I'll arrange for them to go to your village school," said my sister confidently when she arrived with the two children a few days later. "It will just be a temporary arrangement to get them out of your way during the day, and they will, at least, be learning something."

The summer term had already begun, and although I was much in favor of the idea, I couldn't believe that Frost, the headmaster, would be willing to slot two little strangers into the school for a couple of months just to suit our convenience.

"I doubt if he'll agree," I said dubiously. "After all, it isn't as if you were going to come and live here."

"Oh, I expect I can persuade him." Undeterred she set off for the school. She had always been good at getting her way, especially with men. Sure enough she was soon back to tell me that there was no problem. "He was very kind and says he'll take them both. They can start tomorrow."

It was a great relief. I had just begun working on a new novel and had been somewhat unnerved at the thought of having a couple of lively children about the place all day.

My sister having departed, it was up to me to see that her two children set off each morning on their mile walk to the local school, after my own two had caught their bus going in the opposite direction to their schools in Bishop's Stortford. The little Hargreaves accepted their transition to an Essex village school remarkably well. At first I watched them trotting hand in hand up the road with some uneasiness, fearing tears on their return. To my relief they settled down quite happily, their Kenyan background giving them a status not enjoyed at their East African boarding school. To the local children the puzzle was that they were not black, especially when they jabbered away together in Swahili.

My own two regarded this habit of lapsing into an outlandish tongue with suspicion, but on the whole the four cousins got on well enough together. The boys, much of an age, would disappear into the woods in search of adventure, returning with muddy clothes and wet feet; the girls, more sedate, would play at dressing up or pick wildflowers in the fields. To spare Percy from chattering little voices at mealtimes, there was nursery tea upstairs, with Helen as the eldest keeping order. Fond as he was of children (the younger, the better), Percy had much on his mind just then. Apart from the normal routine of getting out a midsummer catalogue — that year it numbered one hundred pages — the bookshop in Stortford was still taking up much of his time, and he was revising his paperback *More Letters to Everyman*, which Cassell was to publish as a hardback. As well as all this, there was the extra work and responsibility of his second year as ABA president.

He had known when he accepted the presidency that in the post-war climate some change was inevitable. Yet for many of his committee it was change that they would by no means welcome. He had never been much in sympathy with the attitudes of some of his colleagues on the committee. It was no secret that several took part in auction rings while paying lip service to the association's rule that members should not participate in illegal settlements. In Percy's view one of the most unpleasant aspects of the so-called Ring was the bully-boy tactics used by some of the leading participants, who were not above making life difficult for the small, independent-minded dealers unwilling to join "the boys" at country house sales and provincial book auctions. Nor had he any great liking for those successful merchants, both in London and abroad, who were in the business of paying unrealistically high prices at auction in order to gain publicity or as a ploy to establish a high price for future dealings in some scarce item.

His sympathies lay with the not so prosperous bookseller trying to make an honest living in the provinces. They were the ones, he believed, who should be looked after by a trade association; the big boys were well able to look after themselves.

The ABA was proud of the fact that it was the first national association to be formed. It was also proud that it had become, more recently, an international association. Reputable dealers operating in other countries were admitted to membership, provided they could find the necessary sponsorship and were approved by the committee. This was not difficult for those who regularly did business in the UK, and although it was usual that such dealers were members also of their own national associations, the ABA had never insisted upon that. In any case, in some countries, including the United States, no national association existed. For this reason a number of American dealers had found it helpful to join the ABA — and had been warmly welcomed by their British colleagues.

That this right to grant membership to foreign dealers might be challenged was certainly not a possibility the ABA committee had ever contemplated. Nor could anyone have envisaged that its international standing might become a stumbling block to good relations with continental colleagues. Which was why the arrival of a letter from Mynheer Menno Hertzberger, president of the Netherlands Vereeniging van Antiquaren was something of a bombshell.

As Percy wrote later: "The letter suggesting that the suffix in the ABA's title [i.e. international] might be questionable aroused the committee from its normal lethargy. He [Menno Hertzberger] suggested that it would be profitable for representatives of all the existing associations in the trade to meet and discuss post-war problems. The Dutch Association would gladly act as host; as the oldest of the associations it would be fitting for the ABA to preside."

"The ABA committee," Percy continued, "was largely composed of elderly gentlemen with even one of the founding fathers of 1906; an overwhelming majority of them represented the leading London firms. Almost immediately after the Secretary had read the letter one of these expressed the view that we should have nothing whatsoever to do with the suggestion. This aroused general hearty expressions of approval from other members. . . ."

Percy, as president, had already read the letter and was in thorough agreement with the proposal, but he knew from experience that he was going to have to proceed very warily if there was to be any chance of getting the idea accepted, or even seriously considered. In the first place it was an entirely new proposal and therefore suspect. Then it came from a foreigner and meant meeting other foreigners on an equal footing. Even worse, it might lead to the removal of the one qualification, apart from the ABA's seniority, that allowed it to call itself international.

Percy felt strongly the importance of the British presence at Amsterdam. The insularity so promptly displayed by many of his committee was anathema to him. At heart a European, never happier than when he was travelling abroad, he had immediately perceived the long-term value of an international organization to widen horizons and bring closer co-operation between the members of the different associations. Mynheer Hertzberger had, he felt sure, rightly judged that the time was ripe for such a meeting. It was a time when there was the will to pull down barriers. Nationalism had become a dirty word, too closely associated with Nazism.

After a lengthy and sometimes bitter discussion, Percy gained a grudging agreement that the Netherlands president should be invited to meet the committee at a future date in order to enlarge upon his proposals. The invitation was accepted, and, although Hertzberger did enlarge on his ideas with passion, they were, as Percy wrote afterwards, "discussed in very short order, the most vocal member of the committee dismissing the subject as hardly worthy of discussion."

This led Percy to declare that he would attend the meeting in any case. At which a majority of the committee declared that he should then go on his own responsibility and, although he had been invited to preside, pay his own expenses. Fortunately, the committee did not consist entirely of Little Englanders. There was support from Dudley Massey and from Winifred Myers, whose father had been one of the founding fathers, and also from two other good friends, Stanley Sawyer and Harold Edwards.

The Amsterdam meeting was to be in September, and Percy proposed that we should travel in company with the Edwardses. The hospitable Dutch had made the point that it was to be a social as well as a business meeting, so wives of delegates would be welcome. With Esther having left, I had the problem of finding someone to look after the children in my absence, my mother not being well enough to take on the job. Determined not to be left behind, I found a comely widow of a jockey who was prepared to "help out" on a temporary basis. She was a motherly soul who took to David on sight, and he to her. He was then small for his age, and she was soon telling me what a fine little jockey he would make and offering to put me in touch with a good stable where he could train when the time came. A kind offer that we never did take up.

At the end of the school term I handed over my little nephew and niece to my sister with a mixture of regret, for they were endearing children, and relief that I was returning them as sound in wind and limb as when they had arrived. It wouldn't be so long before I would see them again, for they would soon be settled in a home in Jersey.

Before going to Amsterdam we took our children back to Wells in Norfolk for a holiday with no work-strings attached. This time we found all the war-time sea defenses gone, twice as many holiday visitors, and a regatta to cater to the sailing fraternity.

I had done some sailing in coastal waters with my father when he had kept a yawl on the Blackwater. It was not a sport that appealed to Percy, whose preference, if one had to travel on the water at all, was to go in as straight a line as possible to a set destination. There was no question of my taking part in the regatta, but a couple of days beforehand I sneaked off, hired a sailing dinghy, and put out to sea on a rising tide with a brisk offshore breeze.

I should have known better. Happy and relaxed, delighted to be on the water, my hand confidently on the tiller, the dinghy cleaving through the sparkling little waves, I was making a good speed with a following wind that was already freshening as I left the harbor behind and headed out to sea. The canvas was at full stretch, when unexpectedly the wind veered. The sail slammed across in a vicious jibe, and it could have been only my lucky star that saved me from capsizing as the dinghy heeled and rocked like a horse determined to unseat its rider. The tiller was wrenched from my hand, and a lot of water came sloshing over the deck around my feet. For a frightening moment she floundered out of control, canvas flapping.

"Bit breezy fer yew, wor' it?" asked the boatman with a grin as I returned his dinghy half an hour later, sooner than I had intended. Once I'd got back in control, much chastened by my folly, I had come about and headed back to the safety of the harbor. There was, as the boatman had observed, a good deal of water slopping about in the bottom of the boat when I clambered out.

"Well, yes, it was rather," I admitted.

"Ar. They did say it was like to blow up later." But I hadn't thought to listen to the weather forecast. "Had a nice sail?" asked the family when I rejoined them on the beach.

"Lovely," I said. For the second time the sea off Wells had let me off with a caution. It was a salutary lesson and taught me, when I had my own sailing dinghy on the Norfolk coast some years later, to treat the sea with more respect.

Chapter 10

On a mild September evening we set off for Holland, Percy and I and Harold and Olive Edwards. As we came thorough the Harwich port customs and currency control to the half dark quay, the well-remembered tangy ferry port smell met us; rotting fish, fuel oil, seaweed, tar. And there alongside the quay was the *Queen Wilhelmina* looming high above us, a dependable matron who would carry us safely and, we hoped, comfortably across the North Sea to the Hook of Holland.

In the harbor the sea looked reassuringly calm. We were all in holiday spirits and in no hurry to go below. For a while we stayed on deck while the ferry got underway, watching the lights of Harwich fade. Soon we could see the shoreline of Felixstowe, picked out in a twinkle of lights (the container port that was to bring the town prosperity had yet to be built) quickly left behind until there was nothing ahead but the dark sea — calm, thank God. Then it was time to go into the bar to celebrate our first channel crossing for seven years.

Percy and Harold Edwards had made their first trip to the continent in 1926, when they had travelled to Berlin from Ostend at the height of the German inflation, with hardly a word of the language between them. Their hope of making a killing in rare books did not quite come off, but they did well enough to get a taste for buying abroad. For Percy there had been a frustrating if fascinating trip to Russia not long afterwards, followed by many more visits to Germany and Austria for holidays and book buying, with friendships developing along the way. Like most Scots he liked nothing better than "to be up and awa'."

Neither he nor Harold, who was one of the small British delegation, was sanguine about the outcome of the Amsterdam conference, but to be going there at all was agreeable and could be profitable. For Olive and me it was pure holiday.

"There's Menno!" said Percy as the boat train drew into Amsterdam station the next morning. He had spotted a small, wiry little man hurrying along the platform, peering through horn-rimmed glasses at the descending passengers.

"He looks worried," I said.

"He always does," said Percy.

Menno Hertzberger was both a bookseller and an auctioneer. Clever, highly strung and always on the move, he dealt in the international market. Since the end of the war he had successfully rebuilt the business he had had to abandon when, as a Jew, he had gone into hiding. Percy had done some business with him (he was also a member of the ABA) and had met him in London.

The conference we were to attend was very much Menno's baby. As Percy was to write later: "Five long years put up extra barriers between nations. There was no consultation. Menno had 'a dream' for bringing countries closer together. The best common ground, he believed, was 'the book.' Therefore, it was for the antiquarian book trade, dealing as it did in the works of great writers from many countries, to lead the way in international cooperation. He was a man with a mission, at least in his own eyes."

But there was a more mundane aspect. With dealers from a number of countries coming to Amsterdam for the conference, business should follow. It was an argument to counter the doubts of some of Menno's Dutch colleagues, not all of whom shared his enthusiasm for hosting a conference at a time when Holland was still struggling back to its feet. While he had won over the majority, a few remained aloof.

Like most of his countrymen Menno was a good linguist, fluent in English, French, and German, with a somewhat idiosyncratic pronunciation. Hurrying us all away in his car to the Pay Bas Hotel, where the British delegation were staying, he lost no time in briefing Percy and Harold as we drove along the clean, tree-lined streets, the houses all with their flower-filled window boxes, cyclists outnumbering cars. Enraptured by the beauty of Amsterdam in the mellow autumn sunshine, I gazed in delight at the tall, long-windowed houses mirrored in the still waters, transient pictures broken by the passage of laden barges, to take shape again as the waters stilled.

That first evening was spent with Menno and his second wife, Dora, in their tall, canal-side house in the city. When the Germans invaded Holland, Menno had become separated from his first wife, and they had never been reunited. He and Dora had not long been married. She had a young child, for whom Olive had brought a jar of peanut butter at Dora's special request. She told us, somewhat to our surprise, that it was highly valued as a baby food in Holland and was almost impossible to find in the shops.

She was much younger than Menno; with her round, small-featured face and straight blonde hair, had she worn a winged white bonnet, a full striped skirt, and sabots, she could have stepped out of an old Dutch painting.

As we women talked of domestic shortages, comparing notes, Menno was telling Percy and Harold that the conference was likely to be embarrassed by the presence in Amsterdam of a certain Mr. Hans Goetz, who had settled in Copenhagen before the war and become manager of the biggest antiquarian bookshop in the city. During the war he and his family had taken refuge in Sweden, where he had understandably kept a low profile. After his return to Copenhagen, unproven rumors of his collaboration with the Nazis had begun to circulate, and he was now persona non grata with the Danish antiquarian booksellers association. He had for some while been a member of the ABA and he was now proposing to claim his right to participate in the Amsterdam conference and in any future international organization. If he did so, Menno said, the Scandinavians might well walk out.

As far as the British were concerned, this was not their quarrel. The ABA had nothing against Mr. Goetz, and the members were perfectly willing to do business with him. All the same, Percy realized that it would be a disastrous start to the conference if the Scandinavians were seriously upset when good will all round was needed. As he already knew Goetz slightly, Percy promised to have a talk with him and if possible persuade him not to attend. In return, Percy would try to mediate with the Danes on Goetz' behalf.

There was to be a good deal of mediating between countries and factions in the years to come. The case of Hans Goetz versus the Danish association was not going to be settled easily, but at least Mr. Goetz did agree to stay away from the Amsterdam conference, much to everyone's relief.

Percy was sympathetic to his problem but had only time to see him briefly before the conference opened. So the unhappy Hans Goetz lowered his sights and approached me on our second evening in Amsterdam when I was returning to the Hotel Pay Bas.

"Mrs. Muir, please forgive me. I would like to speak further with your husband if it is possible. Things are very difficult for me in Denmark, but I must stress that there is no truth in these accusations which are being made against me . . . ," he spoke quietly, with dignity, in German-accented English, a well-dressed middle-aged man with expressive dark eyes. His voice, though controlled, held the underlying passion of the falsely accused.

I listened to him in helpless sympathy. I did not, then, know a single Danish bookseller (we would soon become good friends with several) and did not see what I could say or do to help. When I did, some time later, mention his name to one Dane, the only response was a shake of the head and an unforgiving comment: "Mr. Goetz is a werry bad man," with no further elucidation. All I could do was to assure Hans Goetz that Percy had his situation in mind and would do his best to resolve it. As he refused to come into the hotel with me, I could only wish him luck, which seemed miserably inadequate in the circumstances. The situation of the unhappy Hans Goetz was not unusual in those early post-war years. That a German Jew would lie low in Sweden during the Danish occupation seemed to me only to be expected. Now he was doing very nicely in business, especially with the trade in other countries, which suggested that jealousy might be a factor in the Danes' reluctance to embrace him as a colleague. Many accusations of collaboration were being hurled around in the late 1940s.

Olive and I found the Amsterdam shops poorly stocked, with most goods still rationed. Only the brilliant variety of flowers, the fruit and the vegetables in the street markets were plentiful. We had been invited to a mid-morning coffee with Dora and told which tram to take. Along came the right number, and we climbed aboard, only to be met with an angry but incomprehensible torrent of Dutch from the driver-conductor as well as unfriendly stares and mutters from the seated passengers. Abashed and baffled by this reception, we could only plead: "We don't understand. We're English!"

It worked like a charm. Instantly the atmosphere changed. Disgusted looks became smiles. The conductor shook hands with us; several of the passengers followed suit, even though by boarding the tram as we did we had jumped a queue. One English-speaking passenger, who insisted on paying our fares, explained that our crime had been to get on the tram at the wrong end, thus breaking the regulations and dodging the queue. But anything could be forgiven the British by the Dutch in 1947.

Our bookseller hosts, the Netherlands Vereeniging van Antiquaren, organized various outings for us — a round trip of the canals is almost obligatory for visitors to Amsterdam, and a visit to a working windmill is not to be missed either, or to a polder, for much of the drowned land was being brought back into cultivation. Soon most of us were carrying souvenirs of *klompen,* or clogs, the footwear of the population during the war, we were told. The trick to make them comfortable was to wrap one's feet in the thickest kind of socks. I took mine home and for years used them for stumping around the garden in winter on our heavy Essex clay.

While the social side of the conference was jolly, the business sessions brought national differences to the surface. It was soon clear that Menno Hertzberger was deeply suspicious of British intentions. As an international association with a large membership, including a number of Americans, the ABA could continue to accept nationals from other countries as before, thus making a new international organization appear superfluous. The French, in principle approving the idea of an overall organization to link national ones, were making it clear that they had no intention of being told how to run their affairs by such a body.

Though Percy believed, as Menno did, that the time was ripe to form a genuinely international body, he could see the danger of going too far too fast. While Menno was impatient to have his baby christened and suitably clothed, Percy, as chairman, was concerned that the conference should go no further at that stage than giving it their blessing. Points had already been raised regarding the status and acceptability of countries that might want to be affiliated. There was the tricky subject of former enemies and of suspected collaborators, like Hans Goetz, who was to haunt this and future conferences like Banquo's ghost. And what about countries that as yet had no national association?

All these problems, he told the conference, could be sorted out at a later date. So were they in favor of going ahead and forming an international body to be a link between the existing national associations? As a start, its executive could be the presidents of those associations who would be empowered to speak on behalf of the members they represented.

This neat, encapsulated proposition was what he had hoped to achieve as a first step. It was carried unanimously. The good will was there. But there were still questions to be answered, not least that of whether any association should be allowed to accept members from countries other than its own, as the ABA had been doing for some forty years. This, Percy foresaw, could be the sticking point for his own association when he went home to report to his committee. For, as he told the conference bluntly, "I can assure you, that if a condition of forming a new international body is that the British are not entitled to accept American members, you may take it that we should not agree to any such suggestion."

There were plenty of other matters to be aired. In the aftermath of the war, trading between countries was bedeviled. Arrangements from country to country were frequently changed. In Holland there was a ban on the importation of novels from the USA and from the UK; only the biggest companies could obtain a license to import, complained a Dutch delegate. Someone else proposed that libraries should be prohibited from buying private collections direct, instead of through a recognized bookseller. A sore point, it appeared, for both the Danes and the Dutch but regarded as one of the facts of life by the British. The *Clique*, too, was under attack for accepting advertisements from non ABA members, a practice roundly condemned by Menno, despite the fact that the journal was privately owned and the owner and editor was present at the meeting.

At the final session the venue had to be fixed for a conference in 1948. Someone proposed a Scandinavian country. This brought the hitherto silent Swedish delegate to his feet.

"Please do not say Scandinavian countries," he pleaded. "Copenhagen must be the place. The Danish people are in a better position to hold a conference in their country."

The Danes having generously agreed, it would be Copenhagen in 1948. "There was much speechifying," Percy wrote later. "It made me nervous because I was well aware that there would be much opposition in one quarter and any attempt to dictate terms for an international body's formation might well be self-defeating."

As he knew very well, the acceptance of any proposals for the formation of an international league would depend on the answer to the question: What's in it for us?

The Dutch brought the conference to an end in style with a banquet at the Vondel Park Pavilion, one of the best restaurants in Amsterdam.

"It's going to be a lengthy affair," Percy warned me as we got dressed. "Menno says the Dutch association will be there in force, and a good many of them are going to want to make speeches. And by the way, you're going to be sitting next to the mayor of Amsterdam."

"Oh, lord," I said, depressed by such a prospect, anticipating being bored to tears by a pompous, overweight dignitary hung about with chains of office. This, as I was already learning, was one of the disadvantages of being the chairman's wife. No giggles with friends, enjoying private jokes, no letting the side down by easing my toes out of my smart but constricting party shoes. My Ps and Qs must be carefully minded — which wasn't quite my style once a party got under way, or hadn't been in the past.

The Dutch, unlike the British, were not restricted as to the number of courses a restaurant could serve. The menu at the Vondel Park generously offered us five.

No one had warned me that in Holland oratory takes precedence to gastronomy, so when Percy rose to announce that Mynheer X would address us just as my soup plate was whisked away, I thought some very important announcement was about to be made. A royal death? A Russian invasion — or something equally grim?

Annoyingly, the Dutchman was speaking in his own language and was therefore incomprehensible to me. Baffled, I sought enlightenment from my dinner partner, who had turned out to be a charming gentleman who spoke excellent English and had already assured me that he was not going to make a speech.

"He is saying how happy he is that you have all come to Amsterdam, and he is sure that from now on there will be much friendship and co-operation between colleagues of the countries represented," he translated, sotto voce.

I thought the speaker must be saying rather more, but I didn't press for a further translation. When that speaker sat down, another Dutchman was on his feet almost before the token applause had died away. Shortly before the banquet was due to start, Percy had been warned by Menno of the democratic Dutch custom that allowed those who wished to speak the opportunity to do so. All they had to do was to send up their name to whomever was presiding, in the knowledge that they would sooner or later be called upon to make their contribution. No one had told Percy of this curious custom when he was asked to take the chair. With no idea of how many Dutchmen would feel impelled to have their say, he decided to be on the safe side and hurriedly arranged with the maître d'hôtel for the speeches to be interspersed with the courses, as an alternative to a spate of Dutch rhetoric boring all the guests to tears after the last course.

At least we were able to talk to our dinner partners during the hors d'oeuvres and while we were actually eating the subsequent four courses, but with good manners inhibiting talking with one's mouth full, conversation could only be spasmodic. And to lay down knife and fork for only a minute was to risk having one's half eaten plateful whisked away by a hurrying waiter as yet another worthy *burger* rose to his feet. A risk I preferred not to take, because the food was delicious.

I was sorry to see the mayor slip quietly away while I was still eating my *glace fantasie*, murmuring apologetically to me that, alas, duty called

78

him to attend some other function. I had thought we were getting along rather well, even though we had hardly exchanged more than a few sentences.

Percy had kept the speeches of the visiting delegates until coffee time. One of the last to address us was the president of the French association, a man of Percy's age with expressive brown eyes, grey hair, and a well-trimmed grey moustache. A Frenchman to the core, for whom Paris was the hub of the world, passionate in his beliefs, loyal and generous to his family and friends, shrewd in his judgements of people and events, André Poursin was a man after Percy's own heart, a man of vision whose love of France never prevented him from being able to look beyond national boundaries.

His speech was exactly what we needed, passionate and sincere. Reduced to somnolence by what had gone before, we were roused to enthusiasm by a torrent of French oratory. He persuaded us that we were at the beginning of a new era of international brotherhood and cooperation. As dealers in books, we could lead the way. In company with most of those present I understood only snatches of what he was saying, but I got the drift and thought it splendid. Had he ended by calling on us to stand and sing the Marseillaise, we would all have joined him with a will. When he sat down, he was applauded to the echo. The dinner over, Percy came down the table to congratulate the Frenchman, and they were soon deep in conversation. It was the beginning of a friendship that was to last until André's death in 1970. The two men were as alike in outlook and attitudes as it is possible for a Frenchman and an Englishman to be. Both enjoyed the good things of life, shared the same sense of humor and had little patience with stupidity, while ready to show sympathy to the underdogs in life. But where Percy's emotions were always kept in check, André's were on a looser rein.

On our last day in Amsterdam Percy went round the bookshops without much hope of the other delegates having left him any bargains but still managed to find enough to pay our fares. That evening our small British delegation celebrated the successful conclusion of the conference with an all-British dinner party at our hotel. The Pay Bas had a Hungarian pianist playing in the restaurant and a plump, not-so-young vocalist. Perhaps tipped off by the head waiter, they were soon acknowledging the presence of the British with well-known cockney songs. By the time we had finished our dinner, we had dined and wined well enough to have no inhibitions about joining in the choruses.

It was Saturday night; the restaurant was full. Middle-aged Dutchmen and their wives smiled and nodded tolerantly as our party belted out "Bicycle Made for Two" and other old favorites. Presently the waiter came to Percy with a note from the pianist: If the gentleman would care to sing a solo, he, the pianist, would be happy to play his accompaniment. "Tell him I'll sing 'The Old Folks at Home' if he can play it," said Percy.

"I think he can play anything," said the waiter.

As we learned later, the blonde singer was a Londoner and had taught her husband all her favorite cockney songs during a thirty-year marriage. Never mind that Percy had chosen an old American favorite; they, too, were both far from home.

The other diners fell silent as Percy, sitting beside me at the table, sang the poignant, familiar words in his warm, strong baritone. When he finished, there was applause from the whole room. The pianist bowed, his wife wiped away a tear. Then we all went to bed.

We were less happy the following morning as the ferry ploughed through a grey, choppy sea back to Harwich. When we came ashore, our wan looks awoke no sympathy in the stony hearts of the British customs men. Not only did they open up all our suitcases, but they took my handbag from me and searched it thoroughly, while ignoring Olive's.

What could they be expecting to find? I wondered crossly. Diamonds? Drugs? Subversive literature? All we had brought back to England were two bottles of Dutch gin and some happy memories.

Chapter 11

In November there was the royal wedding of Princess Elizabeth to Prince Philip of Greece, an event to make us all forget, temporarily at least, Crispian austerity. Households with television sets were in a minority; parts of the country were still out of reach of the BBC's single transmission service. As far as Percy and I were concerned, television was a luxury we could do without. Nor did we want our children to become addicts and neglect their schoolwork, this being a prevalent reason given by intellectuals and many professional people for resisting the lure of the Box. Those who admitted to succumbing were likely to explain that it was there for the benefit of their au pair or babysitter. Not that Percy's refusal to buy a set prevented our children from viewing; all they had to do was trot down the road to a neighbor's house. But I did make sure that they saw the royal pageantry by taking them to our local cinema, where we queued to see the wedding film on the British Movietone News.

With London en fête for such an important and romantic event, the National Book League put on a fashion book exhibition, which was opened by Phyllis Calvert in a dual role of star of the London theater and antiquarian bookseller's wife. It was a glamorous event, and, I recorded in my diary, "Phyll looked as pretty as a picture." The exhibition was arranged by James Laver, keeper of the Department of Illustration and Design at the Victoria and Albert Museum and the author of a great many books, one of which, *Nymph Errant*, was a bestseller in the 1930s and now, sadly, completely forgotten.

The tide of enthusiasm for the NBL was running strongly, with many more exhibitions in the pipeline. As one of the aims was the encouragement of excellence in book design, an annual exhibition of a selection of a hundred books submitted by publishers from their current lists for adjudication by experts had become an established competitive event. The judges of the entries did not pull their punches. In their catalogue of the chosen books such comments as "Ill-fitting initials on a stately book"

(A History of Chatsworth) and "The case is unworthy of the book" on a new edition of *The Compleat Angler* were not unusual. Still closely involved with the NBL and on friendly terms with Maurice Marston and the librarian, Miss Edmonson, Percy was finding his advice and help regularly sought, both of which he continued to give freely for many years to come.

The year 1948 saw the birth of the Welfare State — almost universally welcomed in Britain at the time. No more doctor's bills to add money worries to the misery of illness; for up to then when the breadwinner was "on the club," as the saying went, which meant that his insurance would cover his basic wage, his dependents had not been covered. No more quizzing hospital patients (or their relatives) on their ability to pay for their bed and treatment; free prescriptions, including the bitter-tasting iron tonics that were supposed to put the roses back into one's cheeks. And no more "ten-shilling widows," those elderly unfortunates widowed too early to qualify for a National Health Service pension and thus granted only the basic ten shillings a week, dating from Lloyd George's Insurance Act of 1908.

Some changes were greeted with dismay. Up to this time our village had had its own district nurse. And it was not long since the local nursing association, run by a committee of public-spirited ladies, had bought her a nice little runabout car. They had worked hard to raise the money to pay for it and were justly proud to see the nurse driving in comfort around the village instead of peddling to her visits, frequently in the rain, on a much used push-bike as district nurses had always had to do in the past. When they learned that under the NHS Takeley would in future have to share its nurse with three other villages, they were highly indignant. Insult was added to injury when they learned that the Area Health Authority was commandeering her car without paying any compensation to their association.

As the only female member of the parish council, it was not long before I found myself drafted on to the management board of our village primary school. One of the other managers was a diehard Tory former Home Guard CO with whom I regularly clashed on the council. This gave me another opportunity to counterbalance his Colonel Blimp utterances. While taking his membership on the board for granted, his interest in the running of the school was minimal — except for one item on the agenda, the entries in the punishment book.

"Any beatings?" he would ask with anticipatory relish when the book was passed round the table, it being obligatory for any corporal punishments to be written into the book, together with the nature of the crime. Usually there would be at least one culprit (more often than not the same one) who had received a couple of "strokes on the hand from the cane."

"Ah," Mr. C. would say with satisfaction. "Well merited, I have no doubt."

As one particular boy's name cropped up pretty often, it could hardly be said that the punishment had much deterrent effect.

Although situated on a main road not much more than thirty miles from London, the school was still making do with a row of smelly little huts in the playground, where the children would perch their small bottoms on bare wooden seats over buckets emptied at infrequent intervals. Some, starting school for the first time, were so terrified of suffering the awful fate of falling through the hole that they would hold out (not always successfully) until release from school came at the end of the morning and they could run home or be collected by Mum; or so I was told by the infants' class teacher.

Despite such problems and the protests of newcomers arriving in Takeley with school-age children (the village was expanding fast), "the installation of flush lavatories" was an item on the school managers' agenda for several years.

From the age of four and a half our daughter had been going to the junior school at the Bishop's Stortford High School for girls. I felt no guilt in paying the £5 a term instead of supporting our own free village school. It was a perfectly normal thing for better-off parents to do and the teaching and amenities were excellent. However from 1944, with the introduction of the so-called Butler Act (it had been devised by our MP, R. A. Butler), entry to local authority high schools and grammar schools (high schools were usually girls only, grammar schools boys only) was to be by selection. The junior sections (up to eleven years) were being phased out and fee paying came to an end.

The Butler Act was a watershed in the British education system. To gain entry to a high school or grammar school it became necessary to pass a written examination generally known as the "Eleven Plus" because it was taken in the boy or girl's eleventh year. Success in this exam soon came to be regarded by ambitious working class parents as the road to a brighter future and possibly a professional career for their children. This sometimes led to the unfortunate children being pressured to pass. One day I would write a novel on this theme.

For children in their final year at primary school the Eleven Plus became a hurdle on the road ahead. If you cleared it you were one of the clever ones and took the fast lane with the clever kids. If you failed you were sent down the slow lane with the not-so-brights and the thickheads to the "Secondary Modern" school intended for the non-academic who were not expected (at that time) to leave with any academic qualifications.

When the time came for Helen to sit the selection exam she sailed through and gained a place at the Bishop's Stortford High School, as we had hoped and expected. At our village school only two made the grade that year, one of them being the headmaster's daughter.

In the early post-war years, the verb "to squat" took on a new meaning. Not only had hundreds of homes been destroyed by enemy action, many others had fallen into disrepair through lack of labor and materials. And all domestic building had ceased. Desperate for somewhere to live, families reunited after war-time separation began moving into empty Nissen huts and war-damaged buildings, refusing to be moved out. With local authorities hard put to offer any alternative accommodation, there was no quick solution.

The unappealing word "squatters," a label adopted by the press, made these unfortunates seem social outcasts. It was true that they did often look bedraggled and unwashed, but given the conditions in which they were living, they could hardly be expected to look otherwise, and I felt that they should be helped rather than harassed.

The government's short-term policy to ease the housing situation was a rash of factory-made, matchbox-like, one-story buildings with a life, it was said, of ten years, popularly known as "pre-fabs." Since they were intended only as temporary homes, their lack of architectural charm was shrugged off. In fact, they did have a certain cheerful, toy-town appearance and were said to be warm and cozy, with the modern conveniences many of their occupants had never previously enjoyed. When we took the train up to London, we would spot them on cleared bomb sites, sprung up, it seemed, like mushrooms almost overnight.

Takeley had been promised a new council housing estate, which was good news. But when the first houses were built and the parish council was asked to recommend tenants from our depressingly long list of applicants, I found it an agonizingly difficult task. No points system ever works fairly, but going to visit the hard cases, as I felt duty bound to do, made the choice even harder. Often they were families from London, squatting unhealthily in makeshift accommodation, the breadwinner having found a job locally in one of the light industries that were appearing around the periphery of what had been the USAF base at Stansted

Airport. Their need of a home might be desperate, but inevitably the council's inclination would be to favor the local applicants, known to everyone, instead of some wretched newcomers who had arrived uninvited from heaven knew where.

The village had begun to expand and was no longer the agricultural community it had been before the war. Soon there would be a couple of private housing estates with another still to come; we would have a new school and a thirty-mile speed limit that few motorists would bother to observe.

As Percy had expected, Mrs. I., who had stayed on for the time being when he took over the bookshop, had decided to retire. He replaced her with a much younger woman with experience in the trade. Nesta Morris (not her real name) impressed Percy as intelligent and trustworthy. She was a bright, attractive brunette, and we both liked her.

"I may let her take over eventually," he said. "I fancy that's her aim, and it really is taking up too much of my time. I'll have to see how she gets on." Business was still good, and the shop had also brought Percy the opportunity to buy some valuable private libraries in the neighborhood. Nevertheless, his initial enthusiasm for the retail book trade was beginning to dwindle as the antiquarian business, which was our bread and butter, steadily improved. By this time Elkin Mathews' staff had increased to five, Percy having engaged another former member of HM forces, this time a woman, whose job was to send out our monthly duplicated lists of inexpensive secondhand and out-of-print books, which mostly sold to the trade. Our quarterly catalogues of antiquarian books were going well; the first one issued in 1948 was something of an experiment, listing a collection of trade cards collected by the Marchioness of Hastings and her family over more than a hundred years, as well as some enchanting Victorian valentines and Christmas cards. Some of the prettiest of these Percy couldn't resist keeping himself to add to his private collection of Victoriana.

It was the libraries of private collectors that had been coming our way during the 1940s that put jam on our bread and butter. There had been A. J. A. Symons' books and Victoriana from Finchingfield, Holbrook Jackson's extensive collection, and the library of Sir Wilfred Meynell (husband of the poet Alice Meynell), which had come to us through Percy's long friendship with Francis Meynell, the typographer, Wilfred and Alice's son. Among the plums in the Meynell library had been the manuscripts and letters of Francis Thompson, the young poet they had befriended when he was a penniless drug addict. Nearly all of these had gone to a Catholic institution in the States.

Through the good offices of another friend and one-time bookseller, Douglas Cleverdon, a BBC drama producer, we had been able to buy a number of books written and illustrated by Eric Gill, as well as many of his engravings and some personal correspondence. Percy had long been an admirer of Gill's work, and, while normally our catalogues were issued in plain white or cream covers, Number 110 containing the Gill collection bore a reproduction of his engraving of Eve reaching up for an apple while the temptress snake's sinuous body slides between her thighs. Printed in bright red, beautiful and erotic, it was the firm's most spectacular cover design.

There were some curiosities in the collection, including a diagram for an ice house and various devices for gravestones. There were also several portraits, as well as a large number of engravings. Catholic though he was all his life, Gill was a law unto himself. On one postcard to a friend in 1927 he had written: "If I say according to Canon Law ' I am not married' and you say ' According to English Law you are,' I retort ' Well, I don't care for your English law, it's all a jumble' . . . ."

Much of this catalogue went to institutions. Private collectors who bought the Gill items did well, for they were buying in a rising market. The majority of the engraved blocks were priced in single figures. Two or three noughts could be added to those prices now. With the collection was an album of wood engravings bound by Gill and issued to a few friends with the title *Eroticagraphica.* It was, indeed, highly erotic. As the star item of the catalogue, it instantly sold for £300.

Through this catalogue we came to know Evan Gill, who was working on a Gill bibliography. Some years younger than Eric, he was a devoted admirer of his brother. We found him a friendly, likeable but unremarkable man. He had a fairly mundane job with a manufacturer of animal feeds. I suspect that he had rather envied Eric's sexual drive. His visits to Takeley were apt to lead to some dodging on my part.

As the summer of 1948 wore on, newspaper and radio reports on the situation in Berlin grew more and more worrying. The Russian bear, so much admired during the siege of Stalingrad, had become a beast to be disliked and mistrusted. Meetings of the four occupying powers were getting nowhere. Were we really on the brink of World War Three?

"If war does break out again, we'll emigrate to Canada," Percy said, and meant it.

When the Russians cut off all access to Berlin by road, the American and British forces combined to fly in supplies to the beleaguered Berliners along a dangerously narrow and congested corridor. It was a remarkably well-organized operation, glumly supported by most people at home, despite ominous warnings in the press of the likelihood of "an incident" occurring to trigger a full-scale war.

There was little stomach in Britain for another war, especially among the young. "Would you rather be dead than Red?" was a question they were fond of posing to their elders, who generally preferred to dodge the issue rather than admit to any readiness to sacrifice the country's youth once again. Nevertheless, there was no question but that National Service should continue, as it would do for another nine years.

Chapter 12

At the end of his two-year stint as ABA president, when Percy stood down, he was replaced by Dudley Massey, an old friend who had loyally supported him in committee over his determination to attend the Amsterdam conference. There was no question of Percy retiring from the committee, for there was no tradition of past presidents doing so. Following the decision taken at Amsterdam to hold a further conference at Copenhagen, he intended to do his utmost to ensure that the ABA became a part of the international organization that he felt sure was going to be formed whether or not the British were in favor.

Ten countries would be taking part this time, including Italy. No one had raised objections to the presence of a former enemy country, but feelings were still running far too strongly in the countries that had been occupied for Germany to be invited to join.

Percy knew very well that he was up against the old guard on the ABA committee. While claiming to be in favor of trade cooperation in Europe, they were maintaining their stance that since the ABA was already an international association and had been one for forty years, it was quite unnecessary to form a new one. If there was a desire among these other countries for some form of overall organization, then all they needed to do was affiliate to the existing British association, which would be happy to welcome them. So ran the argument. Meetings could take place in London, the ABA's secretary would be available, and costs would be saved. What could be more simple or practical?

This, more or less, was the proposition the British delegates were asked to take with them to Copenhagen, and they knew before they started they were in for trouble. This time Dudley Massey would lead the British delegation. Dudley, who followed his father into the antiquarian book trade, was a shy, thin-faced man with the look of a consumptive poet. A director of the old, established firm of Pickering & Chatto, like Percy he was one of the inner circle of bibliophiles, self-named "the Biblio Boys," who met monthly to dine and talk books. Other members were John Carter; Michael Sadleir; Frank Francis, director of the British Museum; Richard Jennings, journalist and book collector; and Simon Nowell-Smith, librarian of the British Library.

For Dudley to have accepted the presidency showed considerable courage, for his nervousness when he was required to speak in public was painful to behold. At the same time he had a certain tenacity of purpose, combined with natural charm and a whimsical sense of humor, qualities that would stand him in good stead as he became more involved in committee work and the league.

Winnie Myers was the only woman on the ABA committee at a time when women antiquarian booksellers were rare. She had inherited a well-established antiquarian bookshop from her father but before long switched to dealing mainly in autographs. A plump, soft-spoken woman, her easy-going manner concealed considerable expertise and shrewdness. She had been one of the small British group to attend the first Amsterdam conference and was on good terms with Menno Hertzberger.

She had never married, mainly because after her parents' death she had taken on the burden of caring for a mentally retarded sister, a task she accepted without complaint. Although she was in agreement with Percy and Dudley Massey on the question of the formation of an international league, she had friends in the other camp in the ABA whom she was anxious not to upset. As vice president, she was expecting to follow Dudley when his year of office was over and was hoping for a trouble-free term, for she was by no means a natural fighter. Nevertheless, she had agreed to be one of the three British delegates at Copenhagen.

The Danish invitation to the conference was issued to any members of the various associations who cared to attend. "We will be happy for you to bring your families, too," they wrote.

"Good," said Percy. "We'll all go. We'll make it our holiday," and he booked rooms for us at a seaside hotel on the outskirts of the city, recommended by our hosts. We would sail on the ferry from Harwich to Esbjerg. Never having been abroad before, the children were thrilled.

It was the last week in August when we set off for Denmark. We had booked on a Danish ferry, and once aboard the children rushed around enjoying its foreignness. The evening was warm, with a light breeze. No one said anything about seasickness. We were still in calm waters when I settled the children down in their cabin, tired out after the excitement of our departure.

When I joined Percy, I was conscious of a movement of the boat that

I didn't much like. "This can sometimes be quite a nasty crossing," remarked a jovial character at the bar. "Never worries me, though," he added with a hearty laugh. Nasty crossings didn't worry Percy, either. But I well remembered some unhappy journeys from Dover to Calais and said I thought I'd turn in early.

Experience has taught me that it's a mistake to watch the sea rushing up to the portholes. Better to shut one's eyes and turn to the wall. I had just managed to drop off to sleep amid alarming bangings and creakings as the ferry ploughed on through the night, when a miserable little wail from the next-door cabin broke urgently into my dreams.

"*Mummy,* I want to be *sick!*"

Almost at once came news from another voice, cross and sleepy. "He's *being sick!*"

In the morning the wind had eased, but not enough for David and me as we turned pale faces towards the horizon, longing for the sight of land, while the other half of the family tucked into a hearty meal of bacon and eggs. It wasn't fair, David said, as we left them to it and went up on deck.

Denmark was green, watery, and flat. Our train journey took us through lush pastures dotted with well-kept homesteads, with glimpses of neat red-roofed little towns. The older houses made me think of Hans Andersen.

Our hotel stood close by a sandy bay free from beach huts and other seaside clutter. The children were eager to paddle. I warned them that this was the Baltic Sea, and the water would be cold even by Norfolk standards, but they were not to be deterred. Percy had gone into Copenhagen to contact the Danish association president; the day was sunny, so off we went to the beach.

It was still early, and there was no one about. As the children raced across the sands, a woman appeared in a long toweling robe. She was no longer young but was slim and tanned. She strolled down to the water's edge, took off her shoes, dropped her robe and a towel onto the sand, and walked stark naked into the sea.

The children stopped in their tracks, gazing after her in wonderment. Never before had they seen a naked adult. And in full public view! Denmark was evidently a very strange country. It would not be the last time that we encountered unashamed nudity while we were there.

The conference opened the next day. Not to be outdone by the Dutch the Danish booksellers (that they were known as "boghandlers" was an irresistible joke for the British) had arranged a full program of social and cultural events with part of the hospitality courtesy of Carlsberg Breweries. There was a tour of their delightful not-too-large city, gayer than Amsterdam with its painted houses along the waterfront; a coach trip to Elsinore, where Hamlet is regularly performed in an open-air theater; and a visit to the Tivoli Gardens theater to see a performance by the Danish Ballet Company.

The Gardens, an extensive amusement park slap in the center of the city, combining all the fun of the fair with a children's theater, concert hall, and other cultural entertainments, seemed to me typical of the Danes' outgoing attitude to life. Nor was there apparent disapproval for the evening parade of the ladies of the night wearing the latest fashions, while the law turned a blind eye.

I fell in love with Denmark and the cheerful uninhibited Danes, feeling more at home in their company, despite a minor language problem (one can get by pretty well with *tak* and *skaal*), than in any other European country. The weather was fine, the air clean and invigorating, the people quick to smile. Out in the harbor the sculptured figure of Hans Andersen's "Little Mermaid" reclining on her rock summed up the endearing quality of the people and the country that had charmed me almost as soon as we arrived.

When the conference opened for its first business session, Percy found himself once again elected chairman. He had half expected that this would happen and had decided he would accept the chairmanship in the belief that it would be the best chance of preventing the assembly from dissolving into acrimony when the ABA's proposal came up for discussion as the second item on the agenda. That the British would be opposed by Menno Hertzberger he had no doubt. Nor did he expect the proposal to be accepted by the French or the Swiss. The best to be hoped for was some form of compromise.

The preliminary formalities had been prolonged with flowery introductory speeches and the need for translations into French and English, so that when the time came for item two on the agenda, lunchtime was approaching. Glancing at his watch, Percy decided to adopt the well-known ploy of British judges, who will often find it expedient to adjourn for lunch when a tricky point of law crops up. The afternoon session would inevitably be difficult; there was nothing like a break for a drink and a meal to sustain good will.

"We have very little time before lunch, and I think the second item on the agenda, the British association's proposal, will be difficult to dispose of," Percy said. "In order that delegates may have time to think it over, I should like to read to you the full resolution as it was sent out from our association."

This he proceeded to do. It was a lengthy resolution, couched in would-be diplomatic terms with a tongue-in-cheek preamble praising the Dutch for their initiative in calling the 1947 conference. Then came the nub of the matter: The ABA believed that the international spirit shown by the participants at Amsterdam could best be fostered by the affiliation of the other national associations to the British, "thus preserving the continuity of international service we have hitherto offered. . . ."

The resolution went on to explain that the ABA was willing to reconstitute its existing advisory council to include two delegates from each of the other national associations and coopt accredited dealers from countries without national associations, such as the United States. Voting powers would be based on the number of members of the different associations. The council would have its headquarters in London and would share the expenses of secretarial services with the ABA. To provide the necessary funds each association would contribute £20 per hundred members.

In effect the message from the British was: "We have been running the show for the past forty years and doing it without complaints. If you want to join us, we'll be happy to welcome you and give you a vote, so long as you pay your dues."

As soon as he had read out the resolution, which was listened to in silence, Percy proposed the adjournment for lunch, remarking that it would give everyone the opportunity to talk over the proposal before the afternoon session.

As he had half expected, Menno Hertzberger was instantly on his feet amid a chorus of protest and disbelief from the rest of the delegates, insisting that he had five questions to ask before any discussion of the proposal began. Was it possible, he demanded vehemently, for one association to be both national and international? And if the advisory council was truly international, why was it left to the Dutch to take the initiative in Amsterdam? He had been a member of the ABA for twenty-eight years, he said, and never had they consulted the Dutch. . . .

There was more on the same lines; Percy heard him out, not unsympathetically, for basically both men wanted the same thing, then replied briefly and declared the meeting adjourned before anyone else could intervene. He knew that over the smorgasbord washed down with Carlsberg there would be much lobbying. The British were not without friends; the Danes more than anyone wanted their conference to succeed. But the mood of the meeting was clearly against the British, and, while Dudley felt that he had a duty to put forth the ABA's resolution, and that all three of the British delegates must fight their corner as well as they could, an impasse was the likely outcome. This Percy was determined to avoid if he possibly could. In any case, they were on a sticky wicket.

When the conference resumed after lunch, Hertzberger's previous tactic of attempting to put Percy in the position of apologist for the ABA, thus undermining his impartiality as chairman, was thwarted by Nic Tulkens, the Belgian association's president.

"We feel the point of view of the British association ought to be put by the president of the ABA," he said diplomatically.

Deflected but not deterred from his determination to torpedo the British case, Hertzberger turned his guns on the unfortunate Dudley. He had not forgotten his cool reception by the ABA committee in London in 1947.

"Speaking for the Dutch association, we think you do not fully understand the other nations' point of view . . . ," he said with some truth. "At Amsterdam plans were made for an international association and were agreed upon by all countries present. Why," he asked bitterly, "should the British obstruct these plans?" Somewhat nettled by Hertzberger's tone, Dudley replied that although the British delegates had wide powers, they had to reserve the right to refer some decisions to their own association for further discussion and ratification. As for the ABA's advisory council, it was already representing a number of American members who had no national association of their own. But a reconstituted council would be very different, with a membership representing all the other associations.

It was no good. International though the ABA's advisory council might claim to be, the French could not conceive the British accepting a president chosen by another country. Such a new organization, Monsieur de Nobele, the French president believed, would remain essentially British. Neither did the Swiss care much for the British proposal. Their representative, William Kundig, was a well-known auctioneer of antiquarian books and manuscripts in Geneva, with considerable standing internationally. When he stated firmly, "Our association objects to any form of affiliation such as that suggested in the resolution," it was clear that he was expressing the majority view.

There was more disagreement over the question as to whether delegates to an international body would have a free hand to vote, or whether they would be obliged to refer to their national associations. While

Hertzberger for the Dutch maintained that majority decisions should prevail, the French took the British view that delegates must reserve the right to refer to their associations any matters likely to effect their own rules.

André Poursin, as immediate past president of the French Association, intervened forcefully on this point, as Percy had expected, knowing that the French were not going to be told how to run their own affairs by anyone. While not prepared to support the British proposal, Poursin was forthright in insisting that there must be no interference in the internal affairs of the affiliated associations.

"We make a great point not only of the independence of the national body, but also of the independence of individual associations," he declared. "Each must, in our view, remain master in its house."

As the possibility of arbitrary decisions being enforced on an unwilling ABA had been one of that body's main objections to joining an international organization, Percy felt he was at last getting somewhere. After a few more points had been made, it was a relief to see Poursin, rather than Hertzberger, rise to sum up.

This he did with skill and diplomacy, stressing the points on which there was general agreement — the independence of each country, the proposed international body to have its own budget made up of contributions from each national unit, with a president elected from any country represented. After making his final point, that the international organization "will thus be a completely independent body," he paused and then addressed the British delegation with some emotion: "In this connection we would like to ask our British colleagues, why, since we are in agreement on most points in setting up an international organization, should they wish it to be linked up with the British association? We think in view of the good will . . . we all have towards one another, that it should be possible to reach an agreement."

It was the right moment to call for an adjournment. This Percy promptly did, proposing a short interval for general discussion. It might then, he suggested, be possible to frame a resolution acceptable to all.

"Unanimity is of the utmost importance here," he told the delegates, some of whom had taken no part in the debate. "And I hope and believe it can be arrived at. We are not really so far apart. . . ."

The point had come when the British had to choose between two options: whether to withdraw their resolution, agree to an entirely independent organization, and hope the ABA would accept a *fait accompli* on their return; or to stick to their guns, put the ABA resolution to the assembly, and see themselves out-voted, as Percy knew they undoubtedly would be. The independent body would then be formed, leaving the ABA out in the cold.

Percy had no doubt that it had to be the first option, despite the known views of some of his colleagues at home. The adjournment allowed time for a consultation between Dudley, Winnie, and himself. The result was a unanimous agreement that the time had come to give way as gracefully as possible. The decision was then passed on to the other nine presidents, and an entirely new proposal was quickly framed to be put before the assembly.

When the meeting was resumed, the word had gone round that the British had decided to be *raisonable*, as the French put it. The atmosphere had become cordial; there were smiles and nods of approval as Percy once again took the chair.

"The interval has proved exceedingly helpful," he told the assembly. "The British delegates have agreed to withdraw the resolution which is on the agenda in their name, and I think I can now put before you a resolution upon which you can agree unanimously. . . ."

The proposal was that the conference should at once adjourn to allow the presidents of each national association to draw up a constitution and rules for a new international body. A saving clause for the ABA was that the powers of the new international body "shall in no way infringe the independence of any national organization." As Percy had forecast, this proposal was promptly agreed to without further discussion. Hertzberger, who had gained most of what he had fought for, did not dispute the clause safeguarding the right to national independence. It only remained to decide when and where the presidents should meet to carry out their task.

William Kundig, who was soon to be elected the first international president, was all for wasting no more time and at once proposed that they should meet *immediatement!* Once again no one disagreed.

After the conference had been adjourned for the presidents to get to work, André took Percy's arm: "Allons, mon cher. Les deux présidents limogés vont prendre une verre," he said and led Percy off to the hotel *terrasse*.

Percy, tired but thankful to be released from his labors, was only too willing. But the word *limogés* puzzled him. What did it mean, he wanted to know. André gave his deep, infectious laugh and explained. Limoges was where the HQ of the French army was traditionally based. There, high-ranking generals of the French 12th Army Corps were sent when superseded by subordinates. Now he and Percy had both, like the generals, been replaced by younger men as presidents of their respective associations. They were now, as the British might say, "put out to grass." Not that this meant that either intended to take a back seat in the running of the organization that was about to be formed.

Chapter 13

The International League of Antiquarian Booksellers — ILAB to English-speaking members, LILA to the French-speaking — came into being the following day. Its constitution, drawn up by the ten presidents, was approved by the general assembly, its officers and executive committee duly elected. Its birth had not been easy, the labor had been protracted, and it would suffer growing pains for years to come; but it was a wanted child, and the Danes saw to it that its christening was suitably celebrated.

When Menno Hertzberger proposed William Kundig for president, it was Percy who seconded. He believed that Kundig, a man with authority, position, and money, from a neutral country, was the right choice. He certainly had no wish to take on the job himself. As he wrote some years later: "I did not take to Kundig. He was a boaster . . . and he enjoyed bullying. He boasted that he was King of the Black Market; but it is fair to say that the laws he broke were not Swiss laws and his good humor was impenetrable. . . ."

Despite reservations about Kundig's character, Percy got along with him pretty well, not least because he was a good host and a first-class raconteur. His election as president was unanimous and was followed by the Dutch proposal for Percy as vice president. Hertzberger was then elected honorary treasurer, with André Poursin and Einar Grónolt Pedersen making up the executive, the latter representing the Scandinavian countries.

The fact that the league was starting life with no money in hand had largely been ignored in the discussions. That funds should be provided by member associations (those with memberships of more than 150 would pay double) had been agreed, but that did not mean that funds were instantly available, especially in view of the stringent currency regulations then operating in many countries in Europe. Switzerland, without such problems, was clearly the best place for the funds to be held, as Kundig pointed out. He followed this with a typically grand gesture: So that the work of the International League could begin straight away, he would personally loan it the necessary funds.

Meanwhile, the Danes, anticipating a happy conclusion to the morning's discussion, had tipped off the press. Informed by a Danish delegate, Mr. Friis, that they were waiting to hear the good news, Percy announced an adjournment "to mark this great occasion," both to celebrate and to see that the press was fully informed of what had been achieved. "Spread the news in your own countries," he told the delegates. "Governments can do a lot for us if they will, and governments are very sensitive as to what appears in the press . . . we hope, too, that one result of this conference and the formation of the league will be to persuade the booksellers who have no national association to form one."

Ten associations, including the reluctant ABA, made an excellent start. Percy had no doubt that more would be formed and would join. There had, in fact, been an American observer at the Amsterdam conference.

There had already been some coverage of the conference in the Danish press; with the formation of the league we found ourselves a media event. Not only was Percy interviewed at the conference hall, the following morning an eager young reporter turned up at our hotel and insisted on talking to Percy while we were breakfasting in our bedroom, not a time when I was keen to be photographed. There had been a party the night before; I felt far from my best, but there was no escape from the press photographer.

"He's made me look like Eleanor Roosevelt," I grumbled crossly when the story appeared the next day above a lot of unintelligible Danish from which I disentangled something about novelist wife of conference chairman, Mr. Percy Muir. But our Danish hosts were delighted with all the publicity and even more so with the increased volume of books sold during the conference week.

Among the various invitations and publicity material awaiting us (and all the other delegates) when we arrived in Copenhagen had been one for a soirée at Branners, the bookshop under the direction of that same Hans Goetz who had haunted the Amsterdam conference and was still being cold-shouldered by the Danish association. While diplomatically refraining from embarrassing the British by turning up at the conference as a member of the ABA, he was not going to be overlooked on his home ground.

"I think we should go," Percy said. "I don't want to upset the Danes, but after all we've nothing against Goetz; in fact, he has behaved very well. It will be interesting to see who else is there."

The first ILAB executive committee. From left to right: Percy Muir;
Einar Grønolt Pedersen, William Kundig, Menno Hertzberger and André Poursin.

The party took place in the large and elegant showroom of the Branner premises. Looking around, it was clear that apart from the Scandinavians, pretty well all the other countries were represented, their delegates feeling, as we did, that it was not their quarrel. Suave and smiling, Hans Goetz and his vivacious wife moved among their guests murmuring their appreciation of the support of so many friends and colleagues. "We have been so looking forward to meeting our friends from other countries. It is a difficult time for us, you understand. . . ."

Glasses were filled and refilled. The atmosphere was cordial. Surrounded as we were by fine books, some of the guests were moving purposefully along the shelves. No reason, their stooped backs suggested, as they pulled out a volume here and there, that sociability and business should not be combined.

As Percy's wife I had been introduced to most of the delegates and such wives as were accompanying them. Many of the ladies at the "soirée" seemed to speak only French. All were dauntingly well dressed. As to who was French, or Belgium, or Swiss I had no idea. The few Danish phrases I had managed to memorize had gone down rather well with our hosts and hostesses, who, in any case, mostly spoke good English. In fact, I would have done better to have smartened up my inadequate schoolgirl French, which was going to need considerably more than a brush-up in the years to come.

One morning during our stay, badgered by the children to take them to a swimming bath, I took them to one along the coast. In view of the Danes' uninhibited attitude to sex, I was surprised to find males and females strictly segregated, with separate baths. I thought this rather illogical, since both baths opened into the sea at the far end, where, presumably, the sexes could mingle as they liked. But perhaps, as by then they would be in deepish water, it was thought unwary females would be safe enough.

Entry into the baths was guarded by a stern dragonwoman who spoke no English. David, small for his eight years, was scrutinized closely before being allowed (something of a concession, I gathered) into the women's section. The reason for the segregation was clear once we went through the barrier. There, sunning themselves along the side of the bath opposite to the changing cubicles was a group of naked females, disposed on sunbeds and deck chairs, gossiping and nibbling at Danish pastries. None being exactly slim, the scene had a Rubenesque quality.

My children were inclined to stand and stare. Hurrying them into a cubicle, I told them that in the circumstances they could forget about their swimsuits, which would save me having to dry them later. After all, when in Rome . . .

Helen modestly demurred, said she would wear hers anyway, while David, less inhibited, ran out naked.

I had not reckoned on the dragonwoman. No sooner had he left the cubicle in his birthday suit than she appeared, waving her arms and gabbling indignantly in Danish. The words were incomprehensible, but I got the drift; it was okay for the ladies to display their bodies in the seclusion of the females-only bath, but for even an eight-year-old male it was strictly *forbudt*. So it was into the cubicle again and on with his bathing trunks.

Back on the edge of the bath at the shallow end, he decided that he wasn't so keen on a bathe, after all. Having put in a tentative toe, he protested that it was cold. Too cold. My efforts to persuade him that it would be lovely once he was in were to no avail. Exasperated, my patience gave way and, dumping him in the shallows beside the steps, I swam off to join Helen, leaving him yelling lustily in two feet of water.

I had been aware of some hostile glances from the far side of the bath even before I got my son into the water. When I glanced back at him, he had already scrambled out and was being led away by one of the Rubens ladies to join her friends, oiled and gleaming like basking female seals.

"We don't need to bother about him," said his sister in superior tones, as I wondered aloud if he would join us of his own accord when it was time to leave, or if I would have to go over and wrest him from his lady friends. "I don't care if they want to keep him."

From time to time I glanced to where David was clearly having a splendid time being fed sweet cakes and petted by jolly naked ladies. The dolce vita, indeed. Would he ever forget it? More to the point, would he come away willingly?

When we returned to our cubicle to dress, I called across that it was time to go.

"Farvell, David," said the lady who had enticed him away. "Now you must go to your mother."

Smiles and farewells sent him on his way. Someone gave him an apple. He didn't hurry. As he rejoined us, there was a glint of triumph in his eyes.

"The lady who was bare was very nice to me," he said.

The business sessions of the conference lasted three days. As well as the actual formation of an international organization, the agenda dealt with problems of payments among countries bedeviled in the aftermath of the war by exchange control laws that inevitably created a black market in currency deals. Then there was the matter of an international black list of bad payers or defaulters, long-windedly termed "a confidential information service concerning solidity." An international directory was to be published, a mammoth task to be shouldered jointly by Percy and André Poursin. This had its plus side, for it would lead to many agreeable Anglo-French meetings, usually in Paris. Those who worked with André could expect to be lunched or dined very well indeed. Unless he decided they were *casse-pieds*, his term for bores.

It was also agreed that it would be helpful to have an international dictionary of trade terms and descriptions. It was Menno Hertzberger who first put forward this idea, and, as often happens with proposers of bright ideas, he found himself lumbered with carrying it out, which he accepted with no great enthusiasm, although he was promised Danish cooperation. Other problems surfaced, several to crop up again at future meetings, but with most the prevailing atmosphere of good will ensured general agreement.

At the end of the final session, Dudley Massey, with Percy's and Winnie Myers' approval, rose to propose that the 1949 conference should be held in London, a proposal accepted with enthusiastic applause. With this invitation the three British delegates had put the ball well and truly in the ABA's court.

The farewell banquet was a jolly affair, typical of the Danish preference for informality. Instead of having to listen to long speeches, we were invited to sing a song in praise of eggs and bacon, the words of which were printed on Carlsberg beermats. As a gesture to the French, we belted it out to the tune of "Frère Jacques."

I was agreeably placed beside the Danish president, Einar Grónolt Pedersen (Percy's partner was Einar's attractive wife). Einar was tall, wore horn-rimmed spectacles, and spoke English and French with an engaging disregard of grammar. In English the French *mon cher* became "my dear" irrespective of which sex he was addressing. His sense of fun was as irrepressible as his fondness for women, leading André to describe him as *pas sérieux*. Which was perhaps not altogether fair, for his wholehearted support of the league had been instrumental in bringing in the rest of the Scandinavian countries. Percy had taken to Einar from the beginning, for he was a lovable man. It was a friendship that time would not dim.

When I read the dinner menu, I was aghast at the amount of food we were being offered. Dutch herrings, lobster, prawns, smoked salmon, eel — just for starters; followed by roast duck, turkey, and lamb, with cheese if we were still hungry. To wash it down, there were the Danish national drinks, Carlsberg or Tuborg topped up with aquavit and finally liqueurs. To my apologetic murmur that I would never manage it all, Einar replied, "Eat slowly, my dear. Eat slowly, and you will manage." Somehow I did.

As was to become the tradition at league farewell banquets, the presidents of each country's association were asked to say a few words in their maternal tongue, once they had paid tribute to their hosts and hostesses in one of the official languages.

Most memorable of the speeches in Copenhagen was one from the grey-haired, rather solemn Ilmari Jorman, who let himself go in a torrent of passionate Finnish oratory. It hardly mattered that none of us understood a word; it sounded splendid. But I did notice that the French were chortling behind their hands as Ilmari sat down to prolonged applause having brought his speech to an end with a ringing cry that sounded like "Kee-piss." A salutation, I supposed. But André, catching Percy's eye, was heard to murmur: "Quelle question indiscrète!" It was, in fact, the Finnish form of *skaal.*

Chapter 14

When we got home, the news from Germany was worse, with no sign of a breakthrough in the discussions between the USSR and the Allied powers. As the airlift to supply beleaguered Berlin built up, the narrow air corridor, the Berliners' lifeline, was becoming dangerously congested. Aircraft bringing in vital supplies had a bare three minutes to land and clear the runway. One serious incident, the media warned us, and we might once again be at war.

It was a golden September. Day after day the sky was cloudless blue. As I picked blackberries in Hatfield Forest, the sunshine glinted through the slender birch trees and Keats' lines ran in my head as they always did in early autumn: "... to set budding more, and still more later flowers for the bees, Until they think warm days will never cease. ..." But the provident squirrels busily harvesting "the plump hazel nuts" for their winter larder weren't fooled by the Indian summer. Disturbed by my passing, they would whisk up into the trees ahead of me. There were so many of them in the forest that at one time there had been a price on their heads (or rather on their long bushy tails), a method of control that had soon proved too expensive.

When I walked in the forest in such weather, the threat of nuclear war seemed to me like science fiction. Yet district and urban councils, on instructions from the government, were appointing civil defense officers to recruit teams of local volunteers who were to be instructed in what to do in the event of a nuclear attack. Those who, like me, had served in the ARP during the war were an obvious recruitment target.

Heaven knows why I allowed myself to be dragged in, along with a job lot of worthy middle-aged citizens who had served the locality dutifully as air-raid wardens or at first-aid posts. We were, I suppose, all compulsive volunteers. We met in a bare room at the top of a narrow staircase in a house in Great Dunmow, hardly an ideal place from which to make a quick exit if duty called. Our instructor, a keen, conscientious young man, was soon bemusing us with technical jargon designed to persuade us that we really could be of some use should the worst happen.

There was a so-called drill once a week. For the first three or four sessions I almost kidded myself that I was needed to play a part in saving my fellow citizens from death from radioactivity. It was after a month of turning out on dark and foggy evenings that I began to wonder if I would really qualify as a potential heroine in the Third (presumably nuclear) World War.

"I can't think why you ever wanted to join," Percy said one evening when I was reluctantly preparing to attend another tedious session of drill and instruction.

"If I drop out now, some of the others might, too," I said lamely. "And then the poor young man could lose his job."

This was not an argument to convince Percy, who suggested, not without reason, that I already had quite enough commitments without wasting my evenings playing at nuclear defense. On reflection, I decided he was right and became a civil defense dropout. How much longer our instructor remained on the district council's payroll (at £700 per annum) I can no longer remember.

Percy, Dudley, and Winnie's assumption that the ABA would endorse the decisions they had taken in Copenhagen proved correct. When Dudley made his report, the opposition had little option but to agree that the British were now committed to membership of an organization in which they would be on the same footing as all the other member countries. For London members the pill was sweetened by the prospect of foreign dealers arriving with their checkbooks for the September conference. There was the predictable nitpicking over the constitution of the league fuelled by in-built suspicion of interference by foreigners, despite the fact that the independence of all associations in running their own affairs had been agreed.

Percy had no sympathy with Little Englanders. He also felt that it was high time the association put its own house in order now that it was pledging itself to accept a set of international rules of conduct. It was well known throughout the trade that many ABA members, including some of the committee, regularly took part in auction rings and that the practice was winked at if not openly condoned by most of the committee, despite the fact that the rules required members not to indulge in such illegal practices.

During the early post-war years, a number of important privately owned libraries had been coming on to the market through country house sales, attracting the antiquarian book trade in considerable numbers. That the big boys would see to it that local dealers, provided they were willing to fall into line, got a share of the pickings, had become widely known. Given that the local men (hardly any were women in those days) were seldom willing to fall out with their more prosperous colleagues, there was little local opposition to the "ring," especially when keeping out of the bidding brought a cash and tax-free dividend at the settlement following the sale.

It was, after all, easy money. A local dealer might make a token bid or two during the "knock-out," when the books bought on behalf of the ring were put up for sale, usually in a private room booked for the occasion at a local pub, but by and large he kept quiet. If it was an important library, the difference between the total "hammer-price" in the auction room and that realized in the subsequent knock-out could run into many hundreds of pounds, paid out in cash. The dividend on this, divided among those present, less the hire of the room and any other expenses the "ringmasters" might see fit to include, was sometimes as much as £50.

There were always some dealers, usually those interested only in specialist lots, who could afford to ignore the ring and bid as they saw fit. While not much liked, they would usually be tolerated, since they did not represent serious competition. For the rest, even if they disapproved, few thought it worthwhile to protest.

"A waste of time," they would argue. "You never will stop it. It's the same in all the fine art trades — endemic."

J. E. was not one of these. It had happened that after moving his business out of London to a rural area, he had found himself drawn in to a ring operating at a country house sale, by a local colleague. The experience had been thoroughly distasteful, the company not at all to his liking. Noting that many were members of the ABA he had wanted to know if the association (to which he belonged) was doing anything to prevent it happening. And if not, why not?

It was a question he put to Percy, among others. The answer he got was that there was, indeed, a movement to tackle the scandal of auction rings operating in the antiquarian book trade, for Percy and a small group of anti-ringers, which included John Carter, had decided that the time had come for action.

A strategy had been worked out by which a spy would be infiltrated into one of the larger settlements following an important auction and would secretly note down the names of all those taking part. Subsequently, the ABA would be confronted with the evidence and informed that it had been enclosed in a sealed envelope and deposited with the editor of the *Times*. This envelope would be opened and the names it contained given full publicity — unless all those named were willing to pledge themselves to comply with their association's rules, which specifically required members not to participate in auction rings and illegal settlements.

Letters complaining about rings operating at book auctions and other fine arts sales had been appearing from time to time in the *Times'* correspondence columns; for this reason, a member of the editorial staff, known to John Carter and Percy, had already been recruited into the plot. Should it happen that the named ringers lapsed into sin, having earlier appeared as repentants, the story would be allowed to break.

On learning what was planned, J. E. volunteered to play the part of the infiltrator. He had come to bookselling relatively late, he was not well known in the trade, and he ran his own business from his home in Buckinghamshire. The possibility of being unmasked as a spy did not worry him. He was a tall, well-built man, and, as he remarked with a smile when he came to see us in Takeley, he was well able to take care of himself. He had no scruples about the part he was to play. As far as he was concerned, it was perfectly justified in its aim of bringing to an end a conspiracy to defraud vendors.

On the day of the chosen sale, he arrived in good time, having been to the view the previous day and made his presence known to some of the dealers. He took a seat beside the local colleague who had previously introduced him into the ring, kept quiet, and marked his catalogue with the prices realized and the names of the buyers. When the sale ended, he joined the other dealers at the nearby hotel where he had learned the knock-out would take place. He had no trouble in being admitted. There were some forty or so dealers present, including a few locals.

A large number of lots had been bought by the ring, mostly the more expensive items. When put up for auction, the bidding between half a dozen or so of the best-known dealers was keen. J. E. bid a few times but was always easily outbid as he had intended. Shortly before the end he slipped away quietly, a complete list of all the participants and buyers of the lots in his pocket.

The strategy worked as planned. The secretary of the ABA received a letter informing her that the names of the members who had taken part in the knock-out had been sent to the editor of the *Times*, who would release them to the public unless the paper was assured that no further infringement of the law would be countenanced.

Caught red-handed, the ringers of Charing Cross Road and their fellow culprits talked furiously of treachery and betrayal. But huff and puff as they might, faced with a witness who was not going to be intimidated, they had no option but to agree to mend their ways from then on and either respect the law (the Auctions Act of 1927) or resign from the ABA. No one resigned.

The identity of the "traitor" soon circulated within the trade. Threats to "teach him a lesson" were made by certain characters who had been doing very nicely with regular "divvies" from knock-outs. But it all came to nothing. J. E. cheerfully rode out his unpopularity in some quarters and continued in business.

No one was naive enough to believe there would be no more rings at book auctions — or for that matter at fine art sales in general, where they occurred just as often. As it was frequently pointed out by ABA members, dealers outside the association could "settle" among themselves. But this was to dodge the point. As far as Percy was concerned, and those who supported him in the action taken, they had, at least for the time being, put an end to the scandal of illegal practices on a large scale being blatantly carried on by some of the most prominent members of the trade, who had been (as Percy and John saw it) for long bringing the antiquarian book business into disrepute.

The furor soon died down. The supposedly reformed gentlemen were still to be seen self-importantly attending the larger provincial auctions and country house sales but with a somewhat lower profile. If two or three dealers did come together for a coffee or a drink after a long day at an auction sale, that was natural enough. And supposing a bit of business was done between friends and a book or two changed hands, well, there was no law against that. Leopards do not change their spots; there are times when they lie low in the jungle, hidden by their protective coloring.

In November Percy and I were off abroad again. This time it was to Geneva. William Kundig had called his first committee meeting, the venue being his own city. It would be essentially a business meeting, Percy said. If I came with him, as he hoped I would, I'd have to amuse myself during the daytime while he was in committee.

It was term time and not too difficult to make reciprocal arrangements for the children. Cats and hens could be left in the charge of Francis, our packer. We flew Swissair. Percy was relaxed about flying. I was not. Irrationally I could never get rid of the feeling that just because I was on board an aircraft and mistrusting its ability to take me safely to my destination, it would prove my fears justified by falling out of the sky. Nevertheless, I took the risk and sat in the plane fidgeting uneasily, longing to be back on the ground again.

Geneva! I had never been there before. After grey, battered London, with its bomb sites full of weeds, Geneva glittered with prosperity. There behind the smart plateglass windows were the luxury goods we had learned to do without: jewelry, expensive furs, perfumes, jewelled watches, clocks of every description. In the patisserie shops pyramids of whipped cream topped the cakes and pastries. When I looked along a rail of dresses in a department store (not that I could afford to buy), half of them were carrying British labels with the "kite mark" that was stamped on our export orders; smart suits and dresses that we looked for in vain in our stores at home, if we had the necessary coupons to buy them.

André Poursin arrived by road from Paris soon after us and booked in to our hotel, the Astoria, with a view of the lake. It was large and comfortable rather than grand. That evening the Kundigs took the three of us out to dinner. William was a genial, expansive host. His wife smiled thinly and said little. She was said to be a good businesswoman and usually sat beside him on the podium when he was conducting an auction, acting as his clerk. At such times William would be in his element, turning the sale into a one-man performance. Lots that did not reach their reserve would be "pour ma petite femme!" Poor Juliette, tall, long-nosed, and no beauty, hardly fitted the part. Her devotion to William brought her little kindness in return. In public he largely ignored her, concentrating his attention on any younger woman present who happened to take his fancy. To my embarrassment, I found myself cast for this role while we were in Geneva. I suspected it was done to annoy her. To Juliette's credit, she showed no sign of holding it against me.

As we walked back to our hotel past the brightly lit shops, André paused to gaze at a window display of Fabergé watches and other pretty trinkets for the rich. In an adjoining window the light glinted on cutglass bottles of perfume from the top French fashion houses.

"Ah," he sighed, gesturing at the windows, "Regardez, Barbara. Les Suisse, ils ont tous!"

We were like children with empty pockets gazing into a sweet shop window. Well, I consoled myself, I could at least take home some Swiss chocolate, hideously expensive though it was. With sweets still rationed, it would be a treat for the children.

The other members of the committee arrived the next day, Menno and Einar, neither of whom had brought his wife, and the Tulkenses from Brussels, together as usual. They were long-standing friends of the Kundigs, and Nic had been co-opted to the ILAB committee.

When the committee was not meeting, it stayed together under William's patronage for drinks, lunch, and dinner at the restaurant of his choice. That Denise Tulkens and I should join them was taken for granted. At no time did the Kundigs invite us to their home.

The weather was clear and frosty, the lake stretched away to the misty horizon, calm as the sea in summer, with a backdrop of snow-clad mountains. The view delighted me; window shopping soon lost its charm. I enjoyed exploring on my own, wandering through the winding streets of the old town, turning into alley ways and courtyards with darting cats and little workshops. The Grand Rue, where we had been told there was an antiquarian bookshop, turned out to be narrow, winding, and far from grand, its shops mostly small, not aiming to be smart. The bookshop was a one-man business owned by a Monsieur Bader, a small, friendly character, ever ready for book chat. It was the sort of shop that beckoned the diligent searcher willing to spend time penetrating its cluttered recesses.

For Percy, quickly on excellent terms with Monsieur Bader, it was the only shop in Geneva where he could find books within his price range. The snag was that one might call on Monsieur Bader only to find the shop locked. On the door would be a note with the message "Gone Fishing!"

Before we left Geneva, William had set his committee members their homework. Percy and André were jointly enjoined to go ahead with the international trade directory of members projected at the Copenhagen conference. It was a task that might have wrecked their blossoming friendship but would, instead, cement it. To my delight I learned that this meant a visit to Paris early in the new year.

Chapter 15

Americans who before the war had been regular spring or summer callers at Elkin Mathews' premises in London were now finding their way to Takeley, or at least some were. The fact that we were on the direct rail line to Cambridge made it convenient for those going there by train to stop off on the way. As an encouragement they would find transport awaiting them at Bishop's Stortford station and be invited to a home-prepared lunch once their business was concluded.

Dealers who booked in at the Dorchester or the Cumberland with a tight schedule, combining London auctions with going around the bookshops, found it handy to propose themselves for a Saturday visit to Takeley when there was no business to be done in London. If this meant the sacrifice of Percy's precious gardening time, business had to take priority. But in most cases these would be colleagues we were happy to see again; many were good friends.

Freddy and George Staak, Danish by birth and American by inclination, were dealers in children's books. They were usually the first to arrive, often with the swallows. It was Freddy (Fredrika), squarely built and mannishly tailored, who did the selecting. A careful buyer, she was not to be tempted into new fields. After she had made a pile of the books she wanted, George, an amiable character, would be called over to approve — largely as a matter of form. He would then wander off to find me and be regaled with a tea of hot buttered scones topped with homemade jam. This he would consume with so much enjoyment that I felt in honor bound to provide the same tea each time they came to visit us.

Saturday and Sunday customers making the journey from London would often linger after lunch for the rest of the day. Mercifully, none came to breakfast. When a couple visited, as they frequently did, it would be my job not only to provide lunch and often tea, but also to look after the partner who had come along for the ride. As my own inclination on a spring or summer afternoon was for a healthy tramp in Hatfield Forest,

I would sometimes persuade one or the other to accompany me. "Perhaps you'd like a country walk?" I would say hopefully. "It's very beautiful in the forest. We could go to the lake. . . ."

In the family it became a joke that luckless visitors were likely to be returned to their spouses with mud-caked shoes, bramble scratches, and a bunch of unwanted wildflowers. Defending myself, I would declare that they hadn't complained, at least not to me.

When Phil and Fanny Duschnes from New York came to see us, my much-loved half-Siamese cat had to be temporarily imprisoned in the spare room, for Fanny was terrified of cats. Both were tremendous anglophiles, loved London, and were almost embarrassingly uncritical of British shortcomings: poor public services, industrial disputes, and the like. I used to fear that the day would come when their rose-colored spectacles would fall off. As far as I know, that never happened.

Happily, their anglophilia did sometimes bring rewards. On one occasion they strayed by mistake into the Leander Club. Unaware the club was for members only (upper-crust ones, at that), they sat down at a table and ordered strawberry teas. "When someone came up and asked if we were members, were we embarrassed," said Phil, recounting the episode to Percy. "We explained how much we loved England and how we'd come to Henley because we'd heard it was so typically British. Of course, we apologized and were getting up to go when this fellow came up, I guess he was the club secretary, and said he'd be delighted if we'd look on ourselves as the club's guests. And they wouldn't even let us pay for our tea!"

Phil Duschnes was a big, overweight man with a jovial manner who spent freely, smoked large cigars, and enjoyed life. His wife, Fanny, was a smartly dressed, well-corsetted lady who always looked as if she had come direct from her hairdresser. She had a good head on her shoulders and helped her husband in their up-market business, where they dealt in fine printing and quality illustrated books. It was a happy partnership — they always seemed ideally suited — ending sadly with Phil's premature death from a coronary in the 1960s.

We enjoyed the Duschneses' visits. It would have been hard not to respond to their warm-hearted enthusiasm for all things British. Phil did have just one small grumble on one of their visits to London. Booked in at the Ritz, he discovered he was being charged ten shillings extra for iced water in their bedroom. So next time they booked in at the Dorchester, where the American insistence on water having ice in it was better understood.

When it came to doing business with Percy, it was the Staaks in reverse.

Fanny left Phil to do the buying and stayed chatting with me. Bearing in mind her smart urban clothes and expensive nylons, I did not suggest a country walk.

When Kitty Gregory paid us a visit, accompanied by her tall, rather silent, artist husband, it would be she who disappeared into the book room with Percy. Kitty, who looked as dainty as a porcelain shepherdess, owned a boutique in New York and would be in search of flower prints, tinsel pictures, miniature books, and other such frivolities. She was a good businesswoman and knew exactly what she wanted. Her husband would be left to me to entertain and, as far as I know, was content to join me on a forest ramble. We both liked him and were sad for Kitty when one year she arrived widowed, on her own.

Between mid-June and August we could expect visits from librarians buying for special collections in American or Canadian universities or for prestigious cultural foundations. The Houghton Library at Harvard, the Lockwood in Buffalo, the Newberry in Chicago, the New York Public Library — such names crop up in the files over and over again. It was and still is a market much wooed by the British antiquarian book trade. Thanks to his skill in building up a good working relationship by the judicious use of his pen, coupled with his scholarly investigative attitude towards book collecting, Percy had the edge on many of his competitors in this field, although mainly in the lower price ranges.

During the war, with visits to the UK suspended, a number of trans-atlantic friendships were established and maintained by correspondence — more often than not handwritten on Percy's part in his favorite green ink, for he had never been happy with the impersonal typewriter or got further than a slowish hunt and peck. Some of these bibliophile pen-friends eventually found their way to Takeley. Others we were able to meet when we visited the United States in 1951.

It was always a red-letter day when Bill Jackson, chief librarian of the Houghton Library, came to see us. His way of securing the most desirable archives on offer by preemptive bids had earned him the reputation of a tycoon among the book-dealing fraternity. A tough negotiator, had he chosen a career in industry, he undoubtedly would have been equally successful. He once told me he had earned part of the money to go to college through expanding a paper route until he had half a dozen lads working for him. Forceful though his personality was, with friends he was warm and generous. He and Percy were very much on the same wavelength, and it was thanks to him that we would make the trip of a lifetime.

Percy Muir with a customer in the bookshop at Takeley.

While we would normally have notice well in advance of the visits of librarians and trade buyers, private collectors on combined book-buying and scenic tours of Britain were liable to turn up in Takeley at any time during the holiday season. Given an hour or so's notice, hospitality would normally be offered, at least if it was a first visit. This was the way that Percy liked to do business. As for me, warned at short notice to expect two extra for lunch, there was nothing for it but to abandon my type-writer and get down to work in the kitchen.

There was both pain and pleasure to be had from this exercise. To leave the current novel suspended between chapters could sometimes be an almost physical wrench. At other times, when perhaps I'd be trying to get through a writer's block, my mentally lazy self would be happy for an excuse to exercise my wits on the much less taxing occupation of cooking some acceptable "pot luck" for our guests. Not that some ingenuity wasn't required in the days before domestic freezers and when butcher's meat was still rationed.

It was enjoyable, in any case, to meet the customers (at least as a rule), and if I lost some writing time, it had to be acknowledged that the royalty checks my novels brought to the family coffers were little more than a smear of jam on the bread and butter earned by the firm.

The bookshop in Bishop's Stortford had been making a satisfactory profit since we had taken it over in 1945. It had also, as Percy had expected, brought him some useful purchases, as it became known that he was in the market to buy as well as sell — the spinoff that comes to the High Street secondhand book dealer. But after three good years he began to feel that it was taking up too much of his time. The novelty had worn off; he had new and absorbing commitments. The bookshop had become expendable.

Nesta, the young woman who had been running it for him for a year or so, was eager to buy him out. This sounded like an excellent idea. With relief Percy agreed to assign her the remainder of the lease with the stock and allow her to buy him out over a period, forming a limited company in which he would hold the debentures.

We had never known Nesta well and knew nothing of her private life. She was single, had a pleasant manner, and was not bad looking, with short, chestnut brown hair, a good complexion, and a slim figure. I had noticed that publisher's reps enjoyed chatting her up and had assumed she had a boyfriend. During the months following the changeover, Percy would call in from time to time to see how things were going, and I would stop to glance at the window display when I passed by. As far as we could tell, the business was going much as it had done while we were running it.

It was not much more than a year after the formation of the new company when our accountant rang Percy up one morning. "I wonder if you've heard about your former bookshop," he said. "I hope that girl who is running it doesn't owe you any money, because I'm told the sheriff's officers will be going in next week."

We had not heard, and it was a nasty shock. It turned out to be the old story — the woman with a nice little business and the bad hat who volunteers to help her run it and lives the life of Riley on the takings. Poor Nesta! She had fallen for a moneyless Irishman whose wedding we had attended not so long before, when he had married a friend's daughter in the Catholic church. After ditching his bride in less than a year when he discovered her family did not intend to support them, he moved in on Nesta and began helping himself from the till. As the debts mounted, the rates and the rent went unpaid, time ran out for what had been a very nice little business, and the bailiffs moved in.

It was a melancholy occasion when Percy and I watched the stock being auctioned on the premises, going for the most part at giveaway prices. It did not take long. A few bargain hunters and a few ghoulish spectators stood around on the bare floorboards in the dusty empty premises. The shelves had been cleared; there were books stacked in cartons and others tied in bundles, unwanted merchandise that had once looked so bright and saleable on the shelves. The windows were dirty, and most of the fittings had gone, as had the owner and her Irishman (they had left town together). Only the shell of the business remained. Over the scene hung a depressing smell of failure.

We bought a few lots. I rescued a few children's books for my own two — Dr. Doolittles and E. Nesbits. With hindsight I should have invested in the A. A. Milnes and put them away to appreciate tenfold. In vain I looked for my own novels. Secured by the debentures we held, we eventually recouped the money we were owed.

"A great pity," said Percy regretfully as we came away from the auction. "There was no reason why it should have failed. . . ." It was the epitaph of many a small business left in the wrong hands. Alas, it did not open as a bookshop again.

Paris still smelled as it had in 1934, of bad drains, Gauloise cigarettes, and alcohol on the breath of men in berets lounging nonchalantly in doorways. During that brief visit I mostly walked, paying my respects to the great cathedral of Notre Dame, climbing up to the church of Sacre Coeur, its architecture too sugary for my taste, delighting in the mellow Palais Royal; walking, gazing until my tired feet demanded that I rest them in a pavement café.

Luncheon would be with André and Percy at André's favorite restaurant in Les Halles, Paris' equivalent of Covent Garden market before it moved out of town. With no music, poor lighting, and tables crowded together, it was an unadorned temple to gastronomy and always busy with its patrons tucking in for all they were worth — fruit and vegetable merchants, for the most part, who had been building up an appetite since the early hours.

The choice of the meal was a serious business; André gave it the same concentration that he gave to a catalogue of rare books. A debate with the table waiter often led to a further discussion with the "captain" or even the maître d'hôtel before a decision was taken. I had to learn to accept that the meal would last a couple of hours at least.

When it came to the choice of wines, which needed as much or more deliberation as the choice of food, Percy's opinion would be sought, from courtesy, but never mine. In André's view, this was a subject my sex was not capable of understanding. Not that I was bothered by such blatant discrimination; I drank whatever was poured into my glass, enjoyed it, and was grateful.

The French, it is said, are not given to inviting friends into their homes. The Poursins proved an exception. André was the soul of kindness and hospitality to those to whom he took a fancy; happily, this included the Muirs. In his home he was a benevolent autocrat.

The Poursins lived in a big family villa in the 16 arrondissement, a prosperous residential area of Paris. To be invited to an evening meal *chez Poursin* was an experience. As André habitually had his main meal at a restaurant near his shop, in the evening it was supper, a fairly simple one of cold meats, cheese, and fruit. We sat at the long mahogany dining table *en famille* — grandparents, the two grownup sons, a dark-eyed, well-developed daughter of Helen's age, and our host and hostess. Everyone talked at once. There was a television set in the salon next door, a recent acquisition, and at some stage of the meal someone would glance at his watch, jump to his feet, and cry: "Toute la monde au TV!" At once, all the family except Edith, our hostess, would leave the table and hurry into the salon to gather around the set and watch a program of all-in wrestling. There would be derisory comments on the merits or demerits of the contestants, much argument between the younger members of the family, with an accompaniment of tut-tutting from the older generation, who watched just as avidly. Once the program was over, the set would be switched off, and everyone would return to the table.

Television was then a novelty in French homes. On a later visit to Paris we found that the novelty had worn off and all-in wrestlers had become casse-pieds. André had some English. "I speek Eengleesh, Geeniss is good for you!" was a favorite greeting to the likes of me with little French at their command. He would roar with laughter at his joke and quickly lapse back into his own language. As Edith could not or would not speak any language but French, there was nothing for it but for me to communicate as well as I could with the aid of a pocket dictionary. Soon I was referred to by the grandparents (too correct to call me by my first name) as Madame La Dictionaire.

117

I was interested to know how the Poursins had survived during the German occupation. Like most comfortably-off French families, they had a house in the country to retreat to and enough land to provide them with basic food. André had kept his car on the road by using methane gas. They had managed and had no wish to dwell on the past. One of the many deprivations that still rankled in Edith's memory was, she admitted, the lack of coffee.

"So what *did* you drink?" I wondered.

She laughed and grimaced: "Mauvais café."

It was a brief visit, but it would not be long before we returned. Meanwhile, I had the proofs of my sixth novel to correct, and Percy was once again working on translating traditional fairy stories. This time he had been commissioned by the Limited Editions Club in New York to translate two favorites, *The Sleeping Beauty in the Wood* and *Beauty and the Beast*, fables first printed in French in the seventeenth century. With both he went back to the original text, that of Charles Perrault for the former and of Madame Le Prince de Beaumont for the latter. Both the new editions were oblong-quarto publications and imaginatively illustrated in brilliant colors by well-known illustrators, Henry Pitz, an American who was to become a good friend of Percy's, and Sylvain Sauvage, a French artist. The editions were limited to 2,500 copies and soon sold out, few copies ever reaching this country. The work brought Percy a useful fee and a commission for another translation, *Hansel and Gretel*, which was to follow after an interval.

The reception of these two publications was gratifying. It was work that Percy had labored over with love as well as meticulous scholarship, as he had done when he translated from the Danish of Hans Andersen. He believed he had no gift for story telling (one or two attempts at fiction had convinced him of this), so to translate stories that had survived for generations was the next best thing.

Published as *The Evergreen Tales*, these delightful books were subtitled "Tales for the Ageless," which maybe is how collectors of children's books see themselves. It seems unlikely that those who bought them ever allowed children to get their hands on them.

By 1949 the Labour government was beginning to run out of steam. With an unassailable majority, they had pushed through most of their nationalization program without public protest. First it had been the Bank of England (many people had thought it already nationalized), then it was the turn of the coal industry, followed in 1948 by the railways and the main road haulage companies. All of a sudden, so it seemed, we had

British Rail and British Road Services, and no one, bar a few diehard conservatives, was greatly dismayed. War-time rules and regulations had conditioned the British public to governmental *diktats*, and in any case there was general approval of a welfare state.

Electricity and gas had long been monopolies, so it was regarded as perfectly reasonable for them to come under public ownership. Only when it came to the nationalization of steel was there a sustained protest, ending in a thumbs down in the House of Lords, which caused a big row and prevented the bill from becoming law before the government ended its term of office.

Apart from domestic problems, there was plenty of news to alarm people during the years 1948-49: traitors on trial in the United States; the beginning of the nuclear arms race, with reports of the first atomic bomb test in the USSR; a communist government in China. In Europe hundreds of men, women, and children were still rotting in displaced persons camps. But there was a brighter side to the picture with Marshall Aid helping to rebuild economies ruined by the war, and the formation of NATO to bring some assurance of future peace in Europe. In Britain rationing had been eased somewhat, and although we didn't know it when we made our plans for a European holiday, we were in for a really scorching summer.

This time it was not to be a busman's holiday. Our friends and neighbors, David and Anne Sachs, were joining us; we would drive through France and Switzerland into Austria, taking Helen with us as far as Geneva, where she was to stay with a family and, we hoped, learn French.

Percy's love affair with Austria, begun on a holiday in Kitzbuhl with Ian Fleming in 1929 and continued through the 1930s, had of necessity lapsed during the war years. Now he was determined to return, even though our stay would be strictly limited by the meagre travel allowance.

We set off towards the end of July in the Lancia. At Dover there was the usual catechism by po-faced officials as to the purpose of our journey and the amount of money in our pockets. Were we aware that we were not to take more than £25 worth of sterling each out of the country? Yes, that was all we had with us. But Percy did have a wallet crammed with French francs and a few Swiss francs saved from our Geneva visit. We knew Switzerland would be expensive, but we planned to spend only one night in the country before crossing into Austria. That was what we thought . . .

Once across the channel, we sped along the straight, almost empty roads of northern France, through somnolent villages, the houses shuttered against the afternoon heat, the scars of war still evident. The towns we drove through, Rheims, Epernay, Chalons-sur-Marne — battle-grounds of two world wars — had been patched up, more or less, but were still depressing. Even the sight of fields of champagne vines hardly cheered us. But the Lancia was running sweetly, and our spirits rose as we pressed on southward into the wooded hills and vineyards of Lorraine. In Nancy, where we spent our first night, the Place Stanislas took our breath away with its splendor. Once part of the Duchy of the dukes of Lorraine, the city had been rebuilt and richly embellished by Stanislas, the ex-king of Poland. Fortunately the Hôtel de Ville, the Grand Hotel, and the Civic Theater, all part of the Place and linked in a beautifully proportioned unity, had suffered little war damage. Graceful twin fountains played, and the gilded railings of the palace gleamed in the evening light. Not far away is the triumphal arch built by Here, the architect of the Place (and of many fine houses in the surrounding countryside), in honor of a visit from Louis XIV.

The one antiquarian bookshop was not to be passed by, holiday or not, especially as it had been recommended by André. This kind of call, we had already discovered, cannot be hurried in France. First the formal greeting, the handshakes followed by an exchange of pleasantries. A few remarks on the state of the trade before a polite inquiry as to the caller's special interests. Books would then be brought for inspection, lovingly displayed and discussed. If Monsieur was determined to browse for himself along the shelves, he would be courteously maneuvered towards the most expensive stock with a dismissive gesture towards the rest as not being worthy of his attention. Business having finally been concluded, preferably in cash ("Monsieur doit comprendre nous avon une taxe systeme unique"), a bottle of wine and glasses would be produced from a cupboard.

The Sachs were tolerant of this sort of delay and happy to wander off sightseeing. There was much to see in Nancy, and we promised ourselves we would return. Our route took us through Strasbourg, less fortunate in the war than Nancy, one bomb having destroyed the transept of the cathedral, famous for its perfect gothic nave and its astronomical clock. This we had to see, but little else, for Austria beckoned, and Percy was intent on pressing on into Switzerland, from where we would cross the border at Bludenz.

It was a brilliant afternoon as we came within sight of Switzerland. In the blue distance the range of white-capped mountain peaks was more like a mirage than reality. I happened to glance at my daughter and saw that she was staring rapt at the unfolding view. "Look," she breathed, "mountains!"

120

It was love at first sight, and it would last. Brought up in East Anglia, she had never seen mountains before. From that moment onward, they would continue to exercise a pull, fascinating her with their mystery and majesty as they had always fascinated her father. I was different; mountains oppressed me. Plagued by vertigo on drives over high passes, I was happiest at sea level.

Nor was the Lancia happy on long ascents. On some of the steeper ones, she began to steam like a kettle. This was ominous, for there were many more ahead. By the time we reached Geneva, cooling-down halts and the need to quench her thirst had put us behind schedule.

I was, therefore, firmly discouraged from lingering at the house at which we deposited our daughter with Madame R., a French teacher recommended by Madame Kundig. This had been Percy's idea, and Helen, out-going and ever ready for new experiences, had gone along with it without protest. Belatedly, I was smitten with misgivings, not, I was thankful to see, shared by my daughter. As we drove off, looking back to wave goodbye, there was that same mixture of guilt and relief (no tears, thank goodness!) that parents feel when the school train takes their child off to boarding school and they can walk away down the platform freed from responsibility for the care of their little darling until half term at least.

Lucerne was green and white, a smart picture-postcard lakeside resort basking in the late afternoon sunshine, agreeable as a pretty woman with money is pleased to make herself agreeable. Spick and span and prosperous, it welcomed tourists blandly, so long as they had money, plenty of it. Our trouble was that we were running short.

We had planned to be comfortable, in a modest way; we had booked for an overnight stay accordingly. The hotel we had been recommended to looked grander than we had expected; our bedrooms were large and well appointed with fine views. There was an excellent restaurant. After the long drive and the tiresome halts, we were ready to relax and dine well. "How much have you got in Swiss francs?" Percy asked me as we were changing for dinner. He had been turning out his pockets and counting up coins and paper money.

"Sorry, I've none left. I gave what I had to Helen for pocket money."

"Well, I hope the Sachses can help," Percy said, "because I've barely enough to pay our bill, and we'll need more petrol before we cross the border."

Finance was David Sachs' job. He had been at the Bretton Woods conference; he worked in the city and advised people how to take care of their money. None of this meant that he was any better supplied with Swiss francs than we were. The dinner menu looked good. With the bill in mind, we chose carefully. The next morning, breakfastless, but with the bill paid, we dodged the porter, carried our suitcases out to the car, filled up the tank, and spent our last few francs on coffee and rolls at the cheapest café we could find.

"We'll be all right when we get into Austria," Percy said. "We should make it before the evening." An hour later the Lancia caught fire. We had been climbing towards the Klauser pass, with frequent halts and tricky scrambles down to mountain streams for water to quench the car's continuing thirst. The scenery was magnificent, but we all were too concerned over our progress to appreciate it fully.

Percy was driving, and Anne Sachs, a non-driver, was sitting beside him. Her feet, she remarked, were getting hot. A moment later there was an ominous smell of burning. We were out of the car in quick time, throwing our luggage on to the roadside. Flames were flickering from the engine. Doused with a bottle of soft drink and chunks of damp turf from the roadside, they hissed and soon subsided. A mechanic from a nearby village replaced a burnt-out cable and got us going again, with a warning that more work was needed.

It soon became clear that the Lancia was not going to take us into Austria that day. There was nothing for it but to drive into Chur, the principal town in the Grison Canton. It was off our route, but it was a question of finding a good garage and handing over the limping Lancia to experts.

Somehow Percy got her up the two-thousand-foot climb to where the old town of Chur overlooked the rugged surrounding countryside and got her on to the forecourt of the main garage. There we presently learned that major surgery was required, including organ transplants. We would have to spend not one night in Chur but two. It was a nice old town, off the normal tourist track, standing at a meeting point of routes from Italy and the Engadine. A pleasant gabled hotel offered us double-bedded rooms for £2 sterling a night, but we still needed Swiss francs for the garage bill.

"I'll have to ring William Kundig," said Percy, putting his pride in his pocket. A call to William's office in Geneva brought the information that the Kundigs were on holiday at San Moritz, a couple of hours by rail from Chur. A further call to the Silvaretta, one of Switzerland's most expensive hotels, brought William to the telephone: "How are you, my dear Percy?" he boomed, "Good to hear your voice. Where are you speaking from?"

Percy told him. "Our car's broken down. We're stuck here for two nights, and we're broke."

"Ah, so you want money. How much?"

"Say five hundred francs, to be on the safe side."

"Sure that's enough? Okay, go into the bar and have a drink, and you'll get the money in five minutes."

Percy had intended to ask for a credit guarantee. "I know you're a miracle worker, William, but I don't see how even you can send us cash in five minutes," he said.

William was enjoying the situation. He told Percy to do as he was told, put down the phone, go into the bar, and wait for the miracle to happen. Percy didn't argue. We gathered in the bar and waited. Within five minutes the hotel manager came into the room and with a little bow and a smile handed Percy a bundle of crisp Swiss notes — "With Monsieur Kundig's compliments," he said.

The Kundigs and Tulkenses were staying together at the Silvaretta. As the next day was my birthday, Percy and I were invited there to lunch. The car being in dock (it wouldn't have made the trip in any case), it meant travelling by train on the narrow-gauge track that ran through the high mountains. To me, a terrifying journey. When we were not snaking through tunnels or running along ledges cut out of the sides of mountains, we were crossing bridges strung across gorges so deep that I couldn't bear to look down. Percy was in his element. I controlled my vertigo by gazing up into the deep blue sky when I wasn't shutting my eyes in terror.

William was at San Moritz for his health. He was overweight and had been warned that he was heading for a coronary. He was on a strict regime, Juliette told us, that excluded spirits. Our arrival was welcomed as a diversion. Celebrating my birthday was an excellent excuse for William to abandon his boring regime for the day. Percy was slapped on the back and led off to the bar while I joined Juliette and Denise on the terrace to enjoy the view of the snow-clad mountains. The air was thin and cool, the sun brilliant. Drinks were ordered, followed by a lunch rich in cream and buttery sauces, the finale being a bombe surprise in my honor.

William was in great form and as usual monopolized the conversation, telling his best stories. As nurse might have said, so much excitement foretold tears before bedtime, but they wouldn't be William's. The lunch over, Percy and Nic were led away by William to the manager's office to drink a bottle of port. For Juliette this was the last straw. She retired weeping to her bedroom.

123

"Never does he listen to me," she moaned to Denise and me as we sat at her bedside attempting to console her. "He is killing himself, and I cannot stop him." Which was true, but at least he was enjoying the process. Loving but unloved, poor Juliette was cast in the role of spoilsport.

Primed by port and brandy, Percy organized a special birthday treat for me. It was, I suspect, William's idea. It turned out to be a hired car to take us back to Chur. The journey was perhaps a degree or so less terrifying than going by train. In gratitude I felt it behove me to keep my eyes open and admire the spectacular ever-changing view. This I managed to do, for I too had had plenty to drink. Altogether it was an unforgettable birthday.

Although we had never intended to go to Chur, it was certainly well worth a visit. One of the oldest towns in Switzerland, with an eleventh-century cathedral, a fine fifteenth-century town hall, and many of its streets still cobbled, one felt the twentieth-century had made little real impact and its citizens got along very nicely, as they had done for generations, without bothering about the tourist trade.

The Lancia was ready for the road as promised on the morning after our trip to San Moritz. It was blazing hot as we headed for Liechtenstein and the Austrian border. With still some climbing ahead, we didn't push our luck and force the pace. Along the route were castles, mostly ruins, perched above the green valleys with a dramatic backdrop of mountains merging into the misty blue sky. It was beautiful, but it still wasn't Austria. Then we were in Liechtenstein, a country in its own right that guards its independence proudly and had a good record in caring for asylum seekers at the end of the war, including many deserters from the German army. Once, before the war, Percy had contemplated emigrating to Vaduz to set up in business there. That had been a pipe dream, but he looked around with a touch of "what might have been" as we passed through the peaceful, prosperous principality.

This time we reached the border and crossed into Austria without incident. The contrast with Switzerland struck us almost immediately. In Bludenz the shops were poorly stocked, nearly everything more expensive, clothes especially. The people looked tired and discouraged. We had booked at a hotel in the then little-known ski resort of Gargellen, perched on a mountainside. To reach it meant driving up a very steep winding track buttressed with pine logs. Halfway up, it looked as though the Lancia was not going to make it.

"Perhaps if we were to lighten the load," Percy suggested. So, we, the passengers got out and walked (as passengers did in the old days to help the horse pull the carriage up a steep hill). Relieved of our weight, the Lancia struggled on to arrive at boiling point at a wide clearing where the hotel stood, a long wooden chalet-type building, cozily niched into the protective lower slopes of the mountain range with a view of the wide green valley below. Inside it was light and airy, smelling deliciously of pine. Walls, ceilings, floors, and furniture were all golden unpainted pine wood.

We soon discovered that we were the first British guests to stay at the hotel since the war. The tall Austrian proprietor, his thin face nut-brown, wearing worn leder hosen and green embroidered jacket, welcomed us with touching pleasure. Life had been hard, he said, but now they could, perhaps, look forward to better times.

The five blissful days that followed persuaded us that the journey had been worthwhile. Each day we awoke to sunshine and the tinkle of cowbells. Picnic lunches were prepared for us, and we idled away the time with easy walks on the gentler slopes or lazing amid wildflowers beside mountain streams where, if we kept still, families of marmots would pop up and stand on their hind legs to inspect us, their furry heads cocked inquiringly before they vanished as suddenly as they had appeared. All around us cicadas chirped unceasingly. Harmless little creatures I took them to be until one day, when I had stripped off my shirt and bra, dropping them onto the grass while I drowsed and sunbathed, I awoke to find they had made a meal of my bra, leaving it full of tiny holes.

The menu at our hotel was limited, the food good but simple, the coffee atrocious. We were to find wherever we travelled in Germany or Austria in the late 1940s that good coffee was the most acceptable present one could bring from England. The Austrians were very ready to talk of the bad years of the war; the blame for their sufferings was put squarely on Hitler and the Nazis. The country people were bitter at having been involved in a war not of their choosing; never had they regarded the British as enemies, they assured us. The owner of a shop in Gargellen where we bought charming local-made dirndls, had once worked as a tailor in Saville Row in the years before the "Hitler Zeit." "Ah, the war — it should never have happened!" That a sizeable proportion of the Austrian population (antisemites for the most part) had welcomed the Anschlus was never mentioned.

Our journey home was uneventful. We took an easier route, and the Lancia, like a horse heading back to the stables, gave us no trouble. We collected Helen from Basle, very pleased with herself for travelling alone from Geneva. She had made a good start in French and enjoyed a great deal of delicious Swiss ice cream, never to be forgotten for its superiority over the English variety. We passed through Luxembourg, where the trains still ran through the main streets, and through the battle-torn Ardennes. Bastogne, a center for wild boar hunting, deep in the Ardennes Forest, where the Germans had made their final, desperate counterattack against the American forces, displayed its war wounds as a tourist attraction and told the story in a diorama of how General Patton and his troops had stopped the enemy.

And so back to Essex, refreshed and ready to play our part in the ILAB conference, to be held in London during the first week of September.

Chapter 16

The ABA was now on its mettle. Never should it be said that the Dutch and the Danes could put on a better show than the British. Although the number of countries participating would be the same, many more members of the national associations would be taking advantage of the chance to come to London. Hotel accommodation was relatively cheap, and no one was being asked to pay for the outings and entertainments offered by the host country.

The anti-leaguers, a minority but still vocal, predictably complained at the cost, for all ABA members were invited to make a contribution. It was all very well for the big dealers operating in London, said some sourly; they could look forward to increased business, but what about the provincial dealers with no London shop window to attract those foreign buyers? What about a book fair or exhibition to run concurrently with the conference? This was before the days of proliferating book fairs, and the prospect of organizing such an event as well as the conference program was too much for the committee, or anyone else involved, to contemplate. In company with other out-of-town booksellers, we had no expectation of our foreign colleagues finding time to come book hunting in Takeley. As far as Percy was concerned, the benefits from membership of the league were long term and not necessarily financial — not a view shared by some of his colleagues, especially those who had never forgiven him for the part he had played at Amsterdam and Copenhagen.

As the preparations for the conference got underway, a small group of wives, of which I was one, decided to do their share by forming a ladies' committee. The question of how to make our female guests feel happy and welcome was discussed at length. On the probably unwarranted assumption that wives of delegates would want us to entertain them on their one free afternoon while their husbands were in the general assembly, we mulled over the possibilities. The zoo? Too hot and smelly. The houses of parliament? But the houses were not sitting. Why not ask one of the top fashion houses to put on a dress show? This idea was promptly vetoed by Ernestine Carter, with the authority of her position as fashion editor of the *Sunday Times*. To expect Messrs. Worth or some other London fashion house to invite a random group of antiquarian booksellers' wives (hardly likely buyers of model gowns) to their Mayfair showrooms for a special display of fashions was naive of us, to say the least. Ernestine had not then met Mesdames Kundig and Tulkens, nor the beautiful Ingelese Blaizot, one-time Danish cabaret star. But she had a point, and in any case none of us dared to argue with her.

In the end we settled for a tea party at Dickens and Jones, then one of the most staid of the London stores. This was greeted by Percy with a dampening: "Is that the best your ladies' committee can do?"

Well, we were offering our services, via the official program, as interpreters and shopping escorts, I said defensively. In fact, we were volunteering to be problem-solvers in general, even if we might fall short in the provision of accomplished linguists. Our committee was not, we had to admit, much good in Finnish.

Percy had booked a room for us at a small West End hotel for the duration of the conference. Our foreign guests had been found accommodation in half a dozen central hotels ranging from the Ritz, where the Poursins were staying, to the Regent Palace. Important as we all thought it, a conference of antiquarian booksellers, even if it was an international one, was hardly the sort of event to grab press headlines in England, although it had certainly done so in Denmark. But at least we could rely on a preview in the *Times Literary Supplement*.

Under the pseudonymous cloak of "Special Correspondent" Percy was allowed three columns to recount the how and the why of the league's formation, its program for the London conference, and its hopes and aims. His reference to the ABA's initial reaction to the idea and subsequent attempt at a take-over was an exercise in diplomacy. "The divergence of view that had emerged both at Amsterdam and more strongly at Copenhagen," he wrote, "was overcome by the common sense of the delegates" and "the intense desire of all those present" that an international body should come into being.

One basic assumption in the formation of the league, he believed, "was that the antiquarian book trade was becoming increasingly conscious of the dignity and high standing of its calling and of the existence of a code of ethics. . . ." Whether those who took part in the ring subscribed to this high-minded approach to trading is open to doubt. Percy had them in mind when he continued: "Indeed by encouraging the observance of high ethical standards . . . it will help to further the community of interest between booksellers and collectors which has become almost demonstrably the best hope for the future of the trade itself."

Years later, recalling his two years as ABA president, he would write of his revulsion at having to read out the British resolution that had nearly torpedoed the Copenhagen conference. Nor could he ever quite forgive the ABA committee for insisting that it be put forward. "They [the committee] had largely become a self-perpetuating body . . . consisting mainly of old heads on old shoulders. They were all strongly conservative in the reactionary sense and as a natural consequence, xenophobic. The scholarly bibliographical approach to the trade shown by the German refugee booksellers [who had arrived in England shortly before the war] was a shock from which they were only just recovering. . . ." Many of these scholarly booksellers from Austria and Germany had become personal friends of ours and were firm supporters of the league, participating enthusiastically in the 1949 conference.

My own efforts to get some coverage of the conference in the popular press were well intentioned but did not work out quite as I had planned. The social part of the conference would also go off the rails at one point during the week.

We had hoped for fine weather but had not bargained for a heat wave. On the Sunday when most of the delegates arrived, London was sweltering, and it was just as hot for the official reception at the Mayfair the next morning, prior to the general assembly getting down to business. By this time most of us knew each other from the previous conferences and meetings of presidents. This meant that there was much embracing, on both cheeks by the French-speaking contingent and one cheek by the Scandinavians (I was always getting this difference confused and either drawing back too soon or proffering the other cheek unnecessarily), amid a chorus of multilingual greetings.

William Kundig was in good form and took center stage with his usual aplomb. Since it had been agreed in Copenhagen that the league should be a bilingual organization, the two languages being English and French, it fell to Percy to do much of the translating. Later, to his relief, a trilingual Dutchman, an imperturbable character called Franco, became official interpreter, a task he performed for several years with skill and humor.

There was some good news for the delegates on that first day. The black list of bad payers was in the process of being drawn up and was already having its effect. Debtors were paying up. On the other hand, the honorary treasurer was having his own problems with getting in the subscriptions from some member countries. The reason for this was not reluctance to pay but bureaucratic regulations on the transfer of currency, which had been bedevilling international trading since the war. This was a problem the league was hoping to tackle. Meantime, sources of income apart from the subscription would have to be found.

The international directory, by then nearing completion, was one of these. While sales were not expected to do much more than cover the cost, a useful profit could be made if dealers were allowed to advertise in its pages.

Rather surprisingly, this seemingly sensible idea met with some opposition, especially from the French, on the grounds that it would make the directory "a commercial" publication, and that, M. de Nobele maintained, would not be ethical. It would, he said, mean that those booksellers who could afford to buy space would be making a profit from the directory where others did not. Some would be more equal than others.

The British took a more down-to-earth view. Put succinctly by John Carter: "This is one way in which the richer bookseller can make a contribution . . . there is nothing undemocratic in someone taking a larger-size advertisement — if they pay for it." As far as most of the delegates were concerned, this pragmatic attitude made good sense, and the British view prevailed.

There was other news; the dictionary of trade terms was going ahead but was likely to prove a longer and more complicated task, said Menno Hertzberger, who was, in fact, rather regretting that he had taken it on. Looking outward, William was happy to tell the delegates that there had been some useful contacts with UNESCO.

After being given lunch at the Mayfair, with grouse as the main course (a novelty to many of the guests), the delegates were free to take up warm invitations from British colleagues to pay them a visit. The option of a sightseeing tour of London was taken up mainly by the wives, the ladies' committee opting to go along in the prevailing spirit of intercontinental camaraderie.

To invite the delegates and their wives to a dinner in the library of the Guildhall had seemed like a splendid idea. To have hired the big hall would have been too expensive; the library was a most appropriate venue and a more intimate setting for the hundred or so guests, who would surely be impressed to find themselves dining in such dignified and historic surroundings.

So it was against a mellow, softly lit background of ancient tomes in somewhat dried-out leather bindings that Dudley Massey and his charming wife, Sheila, stood formally shaking hands with the arriving guests. The one snag was the dinner itself. This had to be provided by the official Guildhall caterers, Messrs. X & Y, who, perhaps discouraged by years of rationing, were by then resting on their inedible laurels. The turtles that had given their name to the soup had given it little else. The portions of aged hen masquerading as the chickens they presumably must once have been were tough and smelly; the sweet, unsweet and best forgotten. It was a travesty of a meal, and we could only sit and hope that the wine (which was rather better; it could have hardly been worse) was being poured in sufficient quantities to wash away the taste of the food for our unfortunate guests and that it would be the memory of the tender little lunchtime grouse that would remain.

On the first day of the general assembly, Laurence Gomme, the president of the newly formed American association (the ABAA) had been formally welcomed from the chair as an "observer." The following day, during a break in the business of the meeting, Laurence was invited by Kundig to say something of the formation of his association and its aims and objects.

In no sense a great bookseller in the Dr. Rosenbach tradition, Laurence had for many years been in charge of Brentano's New York antiquarian book section. On retiring from the job (rather sooner than he had intended), he had been working as an assessor from an office in New York and was, therefore, in no sense a competitor in the business of buying and selling books.

Laurence was British born, a kindly man whose eyes looked on the world benignly through thin-rimmed spectacles. Unassertive, small of stature, he liked to think well of his fellows. When his wife left him, after many years, he told his friends without rancor that the marriage had been one of "two nice people who couldn't get along together."

Up to 1948 the United States had no national association of antiquarian booksellers. There had been some attempts to form one from time to time, but it was not until January of that year that a small group of dealers had come together to test the water and found sufficient enthusiasm for them to call a general meeting, when a constitution was drawn up and governors appointed, as required by Federal laws. This somewhat lengthy legal process resulted in the birth of the ABAA, with a membership of sixty dealers. As one who had warmly supported the project, Laurence, a well-liked and noncontroversial member of the trade, willing to do whatever was necessary, was elected president.

Their association's main aims and objectives, he told the assembly, were to further friendly relations and cooperation among members, stimulate interest in book collecting, uphold the status of the trade, and maintain professional standards. They wanted to promote exhibitions of books and related material and cooperate with other organizations in similar fields of interest at home and abroad.

"We have a great sense of our organization's possibilities," he said with some pride. "We wish to be of value to and receive the value of association with European organizations. That was something very close to my heart and that of most of the members of our board. . . ." The word "most" was significant, for as with the ABA, the Americans had a xenophobic element.

There had not been time, he continued, to put the question of joining the league to a general meeting of the membership, but it was his fervent hope that it would be accepted when he reported back.

Called upon to reply, Percy took the opportunity to underline the message he wanted Laurence to take back, that the conferences held by the league were very much business meetings, as well as social events. Each affiliated association had shown that morning that it had its own point of view. "We are called together here to say . . . exactly what we think about the future of the league and the possibilities of what the league can undertake . . . or cannot undertake." It was, Percy knew, important to make clear to the Americans that the league was not run for the benefit of a few of the important European dealers, such as Kundig, with the small countries and smaller dealers sidelined. "Everyone states his opinion perfectly freely. . . . This is a democratic institution and every man is as good as the next."

He might have said "and woman," for there were, in fact, several woman dealers present, including Winnie Myers, the ABA's next president, but it was still very much a man's world in the antiquarian book trade at that time.

One item on the agenda of much concern to everyone present was the black list and whether the league could make a bob or two from running a debt-collecting service. "Send me your debts, and I will do my best to collect them," Kundig boomed, having told the assembly that he had already collected some eight thousand Swiss francs for members who had applied to the league to chase their slow payers. Much of this money had been wrung from dealers in the Argentine, who had become notorious for ordering books knowing full well that their country's insolvency could hold up payment almost indefinitely.

"When does a debt become a bad one?" asked someone from the floor.

"After one year," Kundig replied. And how had the president succeeded in collecting so much from slow payers, another delegate wanted to know.

William was not telling. "I have a little secret I cannot divulge," he said with a chuckle.

When the session ended, Percy made it his business to look after Laurence Gomme. Welcomed as Laurence had been as an ambassador from the ABAA, the London dealers, with some honorable exceptions, saw no point in making a fuss of someone who was unlikely to become a customer. But Laurence was happy to be in London, in any case; although he had lived more than forty years in the United States, he was still at heart an Englishman.

As the week wore on, London continued to swelter. While we had all been hoping that the weather wouldn't let us down, we hadn't bargained for oppressive heat, nor had the Scandinavian contingent, who complained: "In such weather we would be by the sea in our countries, away from the hot streets and so many people. . . ." At the Copenhagen conference, one of the high spots had been the convivial Carlsberg Brewery party; happy memories of unlimited lager lingered, especially in London's thirst-provoking heat. Unable to find a London brewery willing to open its arms and vats to visiting foreign booksellers, the ABA entertainment committee turned to the British Council, who responded by offering a "reception and cocktail party" at 56 Portland Place, with the proviso that it was strictly limited to the "overseas visitors." An exception was made for the members of the league executive. So Percy and I went along dutifully to be received by Sir Stanley Unwin, the publisher, who was by then very much an establishment figure. It turned out to be a low-key event, with most of our guests somewhat weary after spending most of the afternoon being escorted around the British Library.

Restrained was not a word that could be applied to the party the following evening. There was no general assembly that day; instead, a day's outing had been arranged, with a sightseeing visit to Cambridge, lunch at the University Arms, followed by a drive through Essex to Beeleigh Abbey, home of William Foyle, who had invited us all to drinks and to see his personal book collection.

Practically everyone opted for this outing, the British dealers being eager for the chance to see what was said to be Willie's remarkable library, built up from his extensive secondhand and rare book business in Charing Cross Road over some fifty years. The expedition had been carefully planned and timed, with a steward on each of the three coaches to see to it that no one went missing. Time for sightseeing was limited, let alone

133

for forays into Cambridge bookshops. It was a longish cross-country drive to Maldon, and we were supposed to be back in London around eight o'clock.

Some doubts had arisen about such an expedition (too long a day, little chance to buy books) but had been brushed aside. With an early enough start, all would be well, said the optimists. This never had much chance of being achieved, what with guests having to be picked up from hotels here and there and morning traffic building up on the eastward route out of London. By the time our convoy arrived in Cambridge, we were already more than an hour behind schedule.

Polite requests for everyone to arrive punctually at the rendezvous for lunch fell on inattentive ears. Assuming that they had been brought to Cambridge to see and admire a beautiful university town, our guests quickly dispersed in all directions, with cameras at the ready. Groups had to be photographed against backgrounds of dreaming spires, postcards had to be bought. By the time the complete party sat down to lunch at the University Arms, we were running even later.

Luncheon for a party of a hundred or so, all in holiday mood, was not an occasion to be hurried. By the time the anxious stewards had rounded up straying guests and got everyone, so they thought, into their seats on the coaches, the afternoon was half gone. Heads were counted. But where was Monsieur S? . . . "Dans une librarie, bien sur," volunteered a compatriot. A steward scurried off in search of the missing passenger and presently Monsieur S. was to be seen hurrying towards the coach, a parcel of books under his arm, having been run to earth at Deighton Bell's.

There was little of scenic interest to keep the passengers awake as the coaches headed for Essex, past fields of bleached stubble, newly turned ploughland, little hills, little villages. Drowsy from sightseeing and the luncheon wine, heads nodded, the chatter became a murmur: "Where have we got to? . . . Oh, there's a long way to go yet. . . ."

Unexpectedly, the three coaches turned off the road on to a forecourt. This was an unscheduled stop as far as the stewards were concerned — but not the drivers. "Twenty minutes!" they announced and disappeared. The passengers began to rouse themselves. An English pub? One could buy a drink? Bon! An opportunity not to be missed. Nor were the British averse. They had missed their afternoon "cuppa" and built up a thirst during the long drive.

Considerably more than twenty minutes later and nearly two hours behind schedule, we were on our way again, driving endlessly, so it seemed, through the darkening, flat countryside. As our guests peered through misted-up windows, they were obviously beginning to wonder if the journey was ever coming to an end.

At last, we turned through a wide entrance, and there was the Abbey, high-gabled, timbered, impressively medieval in the dusk, lights flooding out of mullioned windows. Headlong Hall? Nightmare Abbey? Thoughts of Thomas Love Peacock stirred.

The heavy door stood open; silhouetted in the entrance was the small elderly figure of Willie Foyle waiting to greet us. Beside him was another, larger figure in heavy, red-trimmed mayoral robes, a chain of office around his neck. The mayor of Maldon had come to welcome us to his borough.

Seen close up, it was clear that both gentlemen had filled in the time agreeably. His Worship, beaming with cordiality, was ready with a prepared speech. It was too bad that he was given no chance to make it. The buffet luncheon had been good of its kind but not substantial. Protocol went for a burton. Eager to get at the Foyle hospitality (not to mention the loos), the less inhibited of the British led what was practically a stampede into the house, most of them bypassing their host and the mayor in their haste. In no time, the plates of dainty canapes were cleared, drinks were downed, bottles emptied. Willie had been warned by telephone that we would be late, but he could hardly have expected such hungry hordes.

To do him credit, he rose to the occasion. Bottles were brought up from the cellar, servants quickly appeared bearing plates piled high with sandwiches. By then a lot of drink had gone into a lot of empty stomachs. It had been a long drive but, as everyone agreed, well worth it. Dinner dates in London were forgotten. It was a good party, and no one wanted to break it up, least of all Willie's British colleagues.

"Come and see Willie's books," Percy said to me. "He's put out an exhibition for us."

The books were displayed in the part of the Abbey that had once been a small, private chapel. There under the vaulted roof, laid out on a refectory table almost as long as the room, were the rarities that Willie had bought for himself — fine bindings, incunabula, early travel books, three-decker eighteenth- and nineteenth-century novels, among many other desirable acquisitions. Willie was already there, giving a commentary in his high-pitched voice that sounded like a rusty hinge. It was just as well he was too deaf to overhear some of the comments of the British in the party as they moved along the table with knowing shakes of the head. "That's not right, y'know. He's bought a dud there. No use telling him, though. He wouldn't listen." While others were gleefully pointing out the books they had sold him years before at a very nice profit.

I fancy the food and drink must eventually have run out, or perhaps our coach drivers, who had been well entertained in the kitchen, had decided it was time to get on the road. No one bothered about returning to their original seats, and Percy and I, getting into the first coach we saw, found ourselves in the company of a lively French-speaking group travelling through the darkness back to London to the strains of such Gallic favorites as "Alouette" and "Frère Jacques" rendered with such gusto that my own attempt to introduce "Down at the Old Bull and Bush" as a British contribution to the musical medley didn't stand a chance. Dropped off, eventually, at our hotel, all we wanted was to flop into bed.

Through a contact at the *Evening Standard* I planned to get at least one social event in the papers by asking for a reporter to come to the ladies' tea at Dickens and Jones. We would, I explained, be entertaining wives from ten different countries, including Finland, and among them would be Madame Kundig, wife of Switzerland's foremost rare book auctioneer, who was chairing the first international conference to be held in London. Surely this was newsworthy, I urged. Worth a paragraph in the Diary feature at least and perhaps a photograph?

"Well, maybe we'll try to get a reporter along if there's nothing much else doing," said my contact without great enthusiasm.

A fair number of the wives turned up, to my relief, including Madame Kundig, looking like a grande dame as usual. The tea was a predictably sedate affair. Attempts by our committee to mix up the different nationalities were politely resisted. The Dutch had no problem with English and could communicate quite easily with the Scandinavians, but these two groups mostly steered clear of the French and Belgians. As for the French, they had no wish to converse with anyone who didn't speak their language.

We did have one bridge between the French-speaking ladies and the Scandinavian group in the young, glamorous person of Ingelese, the Danish wife of Georges Blaizot, a distinguished Parisian bookseller. With her wide blue eyes, neat figure, and Nordic coloring, Ingelese could fairly be described, and often was, by the French word *ravissante*.

Her marriage to the scholarly, reserved antiquarian bookseller, many years older than herself, was an unlikely one. She knew no French, he no Danish, but both had some English. I can no longer remember how they met, but it had been love at first sight, and soon after the end of the war Georges had married her in Denmark and carried her off to France. A

Georges and Ingelese Blaizot.

natural, fun-loving girl, she was doing her best to turn herself, with Georges' help, into a chic, sophisticated Frenchwoman.

Our ladies' committee passed cucumber sandwiches and little cakes, chatted in "franglais," and did our best to make the party go. Eventually a reporter from the *Standard* turned up with a photographer. I hurriedly introduced him to Juliette Kundig, who graciously agreed to answer a few questions. He was a sharp young man, and, as he talked to Juliette, I could see him surveying the field. Presently, we were lined up for a group photograph, with Juliette in the center and other wives of presidents in the forefront, all smiling brightly into the camera. This brought the party to what I hoped was a happy conclusion. The reporter seemed in no great hurry. As our guests were leaving, I noticed he had lingered to have a chat with Ingelese, for which I could hardly blame him.

"Seen the *Evening Standard*?" one of our ladies' committee asked me the following day.

"No, are we in it?" I asked hopefully.

"See for yourself!"

I looked at where she was pointing. There on the Diary page was a smiling, full-length photograph of Ingelese, with an accompanying interview. Not one other of our guests appeared in the picture. The conference did get a brief mention, but that was all. In the circumstances there didn't seem much point in presenting Juliette Kundig with a cutting. No doubt someone else did.

The conference social program included a promenade concert conducted by Sir Adrian Boult and, perhaps the high spot of the week for many of the delegates, a visit to the Royal Library at Windsor with the king's librarian, Sir Owen Moorshead, as our guide. The bibliophilic perambulation was an opportunity for some British one-upmanship not missed by Sir Owen, who had put out for our guests' inspection such priceless treasures as the Mainz Psalter, dated 1457, a masterpiece of early printing "laboriously brought to completion for the service of God by Johann Fust . . ." according to the catalogue description. I was to see this same volume at close quarters many years later at the "Printing and the Mind of Man" exhibition at Earls Court when Percy was chairman of the Impact Committee that organized it.

As well as the rare books, our guests were shown some historic documents, among them some memorabilia of the Battle of Waterloo. Perhaps Sir Owen lingered somewhat over this bit of our history, as the Dutch, Belgians, and Scandinavians gathered around him and the French drew back without comment.

The conference came to an end with what was becoming the traditional finale, the farewell dinner, which took place at the Mayfair. The menu made up for the debacle at the Guildhall with braised baby turbot, Kent chicken, and pêche Melba, all beyond reproach. Dancing was a welcome relief after the obligatory speeches from each association president (most of whom would have been happy to have been let off the task), and, while the ladies wore the party dresses they had been saving for the occasion, it was, I thought, Ian Grant, a Scot from Edinburgh and a future ABA president who stole the show when he took the floor resplendent in kilt and sporran.

The league's committee had been given plenty of work to do before the 1950 conference, to be held in Paris. The number of member countries had gone up to eleven with the admission of Austria, and, as Kundig put it, "Germany was now knocking at the door."

Chapter 17

Ian Fleming's idea of building up a collection of books that "started something," or, as he later liked to describe it more grandly, "marked the milestones of human progress," was a shrewd one. He was moving into a market that had hardly been tapped. In fact, Percy was doing it on his behalf, which suited them both: Ian because he could not be bothered to do the necessary research, and Percy because he thoroughly enjoyed it.

The friendship between Ian and Percy began during the mid-twenties when Ian became a customer of the firm of Dulau, the rare booksellers in Bond Street, where Percy was a partner. Ian had strolled into the shop one morning and got into a conversation with Percy. They had carried on the conversation over lunch together and the friendship that began continued until Ian's death in 1964. When Percy joined the firm of Elkin Mathews (then in an elegant, double-fronted shop in Conduit Street) in 1930, Ian had continued to come to Percy for the books he wanted. By then, they had taken a holiday together in Austria, and Percy would often play bridge with Ian at his club, Whites in St. James Street.

Ian told Percy he was prepared to invest £200 a year in his new collection of books and agreed that it should include documents and ephemera; one such item would be Mussolini's discontinued passport. The sum sounds small enough by present-day standards, but at the time it enabled Percy to acquire for Ian "milestone books" in medicine, science, philosophy, photography, and social history, including the first appearance of the Communist Manifesto.

The scope was wide enough to include sport (Ian had been a Victor Ludorum at Eton) and pastimes. One of the rarest items bought for the collection was a first edition of Baden Powell's *Scouting for Boys*. Ian accepted Percy's advice over the purchase of this modest little paperback rather dubiously. Years later he was agreeably surprised to find his copy featured as one of the showpieces of a prestigious book exhibition.

After Ian joined Naval Intelligence in 1939 his interest in collecting waned. No further books were added, and the collection was boxed up and stored away safely for the duration. This made no difference to his friendship with Percy, and his directorship of Elkin Mathews continued; not that he did anything more than lend his name to the board.

The two men continued to meet fairly frequently, and Ian would pay us occasional visits. On these occasions I would remind him of his duties as Helen's godfather, usually to no purpose, for he was not interested in other people's children. It was a different matter when his son Caspar was born.

When the war ended and Ian left the navy, Percy had hoped his interest in book collecting might revive. This did not happen. Nor had he any desire to return to stockbroking; he had grown used to power, action, and travel. The position of foreign manager for Kemsley Newspapers gave him all three. He became Lord Kemsley's favored young executive, with a salary of £5,000 a year and two months' annual leave (one of his conditions for taking the job), which he would spend idling or writing novels in the sunshine of Jamaica, where he had his second home, Goldeneye.

While Ian's collection stayed largely unregarded in London, Percy continued to buy "milestone books." He was finding an increasing sale for them, especially those in social history, many of them going to the States. Once or twice towards the end of the 1950s Ian considered selling his complete collection, but by then he was not in need of money and was rather enjoying the prestige of owning so many increasingly valuable books. Each item was boxed in black buckram and color-coded according to subject, his own idea. After his marriage to Anne Rothermere she would complain, with some justification, that it was impossible to fit them into any decoration scheme. Thus they remained in their sombre black boxes, largely unread, ranged along one wall of the drawing room in the big riverside house Ian and Anne bought at Sevenhampton, until Ian's death in 1964. How they were eventually bought by Indiana University for the Lilly Library is another story.

In the autumn of 1949 the *Sunday Times* staged its first post-war book exhibition. Percy had been involved in the 1938 exhibition and agreed to arrange an exhibit for the National Book League's stand. His choice of a subject, "Books You Never Read," enabled him to borrow two-thirds of those he needed from the Fleming collection, much to Ian's gratification.

Probably it was the first-ever exhibition of first editions of those familiar invaluable books that everyone takes for granted. Bradshaw (railways), Crockford (clergy), Debrett, Roget's *Thesaurus*, *Who's Who*, Whitaker, and many other household-word books were there in the form in which they had made their first appearance.

141

"Most of these now portly and occasionally portentous ancients were no longer in their first youth, and becomingly slender and humble . . . ," Percy wrote in his introduction in the exhibition catalogue. I was delighted when he included the only rare book I had ever managed to buy, a first edition of the popular nineteenth-century reference book *Enquire Within*, 1856, for which I had paid one shilling in a Chelmsford second-hand bookshop. It was, as Percy noted in the catalogue, "the first of the handy home guides, full of pious exhortations." One example was "What maintains one vice would bring up two children," a reference to the cost of the demon alcohol.

By arranging for the presentation of their £1,000 Literary Award to Winston Churchill for the first two books of his *History of the Second World War*, the *Sunday Times* cleverly assured Churchill's presence on the first day of the second week, when the presentation was made, thus pushing up the attendance figures. Two other authors whose names are still remembered won £100 apiece: Alan Paton for his novel *Cry, the Beloved Country* and Spencer Chapman for *The Jungle Is Neutral*.

"There were no teething problems" (at the "Books You Never Read" stand), wrote Leonard Russell, literary editor of the *Sunday Times* in a preview of the exhibition, "Mr. Muir's massive calm would not permit them. . . ."

We had continued to extend the firm's premises in Takeley over the years in a piecemeal way, which was all that our local building and planning regulations would allow. When we added a seventy-foot storage shed (it had once housed battery hens), it seemed as if we had unlimited space. But, in the way of bookshops, it soon filled up, and before long another shed had to be added to house the duplicator needed for printing our monthly trade lists. Part of the big shed had been partitioned off into a small office for the secretarial staff, but they were still without toilet facilities and central heating.

It was a time when patience and perseverance were needed to obtain permission for any kind of building work. You took your place in a queue as for nearly everything else from public transport to oranges. Eventually we were allowed the necessary plumbing work and the daily trek, when nature called, from office to the house mercifully came to an end.

When it came to being granted permission for central heating for the firm's premises (the house had to wait), we finally won our case by demanding an inspection from the fire control authorities. On seeing our free-standing, unguarded electric fires and oil heaters, the inspector threw up his hands in horror. The place was a shocking fire risk, he told Percy,

142

and should never have been allowed, never mind that we had been keeping warm (more or less) that way for six or seven years. So we got our central heating with the installation of a massive coke-burning boiler. Known as the Janitor, it normally provided adequate warmth, but had its moods comprehensible only to Francis, our packer, who now had to combine his jobs of packer and gardener with that of boilerman. Sited at the rear of the garage, between house and bookstore, it was intended to supply heat to both when planning permission came through for the installation of our domestic central heating.

For Francis, tending the Janitor became a challenge. When it labored over delivering a particularly large clinker, as it sometimes did, he would act as midwife and proudly display, for anyone interested, the burned-out mass of coke he had managed to drag from its innards. "That was a real big 'un I got outer 'er this morning," he'd say in triumph.

When the Labour government called a general election in February that year, the Liberals were rather better organized than in 1945, although in the Saffron Walden constituency we were still fairly thin on the ground. Undaunted by his previous lack of success, George Edinger put up again. This time he had the official blessing of the Liberal Party, for which he was not noticeably grateful. Percy and I, by this time, were both serving on the constituency committee and subscribing to the *Liberal News*, a lively little news sheet that had Nancy Seear (later Baroness Seear) as one of its regular contributors. The party was claiming the long-awaited Liberal Revival and the probability of being in the position of holding the balance of power in a hung parliament, a recurrent pious hope never quite fulfilled. They could at least boast that they were contesting some 475 seats.

To try and maintain a middle-of-the-road (marginally left of center) position during an election campaign is likely to irritate travellers both to the left and to the right. "All you're doing," I was accused, "is getting in the way." As I hated pestering people, I dodged doorstep canvassing, and Percy was too busy even to consider it. Supporting George at public meetings was another matter; this Percy did with some zest. Public speaking was an art Percy had mastered as a young man when employed by the Christian Evidence Society, an organization he had worked for briefly before joining the army in 1914, which would send him to Speaker's Corner in Hyde Park on Sunday mornings. There, standing on his soap box amid the Sunday strollers, scoffers, and oddballs, he had learned how not to lose your audience to a more entertaining speaker nearby and how to make hecklers wish they had kept quiet.

143

We were both interested enough in the outcome of the election to sit up until the small hours as the results came through on the radio. A close race had been forecast, with Labour tipped to win. This they did — just — scraping home with a majority of six. For the Liberals it was once again a sad story of lost deposits and only nine seats to show for all their campaigning and hopeful forecasts. George Edinger did manage to save his deposit, but, as the local party had been boasting he would push Labour into third place, it was hard to know whether to congratulate or commiserate with him.

Black Market Green, my seventh novel, was published in June of that year. My sales had been steadily rising with each new title. Number six, *Pleasant Burden*, part autobiographical and set in the 1930s, had achieved a satisfactory sale of six thousand. I was hoping for a modest increase on that figure with my latest book.

It was a story of village life, as were most of my books, a love story with a bit of villainy to add excitement. I had enjoyed writing it, perhaps more than any of my previous novels, and I believed I had written a workmanlike piece of fiction. Nor had there had been any adverse criticism from my publisher. Had I strayed outside their guidelines (no sex outside marriage and no swear words stronger than "damn" or "blast"), there undoubtedly would have been.

I had long since given up hope of literary acclaim. Serious newspapers seldom if ever noticed books published by Hurst and Blackett; equally, they were ignored by the literary journals, and I had little hope of being promoted by my publishers as bestseller material, with all the accompanying razzmatazz. If I had been published under the Hutchinson imprint, as was Percy's friend Dennis Wheatley, it might have been different. To be on Hurst and Blackett's list meant some ninety percent of one's sales were to the big lending libraries, chiefly Boots and W. H. Smith, which had branches all over the country, and to the public libraries. By and large Hurst and Blackett's readers were borrowers, not buyers of novels.

My six free copies duly arrived the week before publication. As always, when I tore open the parcel to see my dog-eared, corrected typescript metamorphosed into a shiny dust-wrappered hardback smelling of printer's ink, it was as though it had been written by someone else. Was it really my book, dressed up so smartly? In the past I had disliked most of my dust-wrappers, usually run-of-the-mill jobs turned out by underpaid artists. For a change I found the rather cozy village scene depicted on my latest wrapper quite acceptable, if something of a rural cliché.

I had labored over the book for nine months, and now there it was,

144

the navel string cut. There was little more to do than wish it luck. Percy was given his inscribed copy, which he would read, as he read all my books, disconcertingly quickly; my mother would be sent hers, which would be shown to her friends and neighbors, all of whom would be urged to ask for it at the library.

There was worrying news in the papers at the time, for war had broken out in Korea, a place that for most of us could well have been described in Neville Chamberlain's never-to-be-forgiven phrase about Czechoslovakia, "a far country of which we know little." Told that this was a just war to check a communist take-over, the British public, bewildered but resigned, accepted without much protest the idea that British forces must be involved. We still had National Service, which meant that young men answering to their call-up were liable to find themselves dispatched to a place few of their families could have located on a map.

"Have you seen today's *Daily Express*?" asked a friend over the phone one morning soon after the arrival of my voucher copies.

"No, is there some fresh war news?" I replied, the war being more on my mind than anything else just then.

"Nothing to do with the war," was the reply. "It's your new novel. I thought you'd like to know there's a review of it — a good one, with a headline!"

I hurried off to buy the paper. It was true; *Black Market Green* had made the headlines. The review was by John Betjeman, who had put my book at the top of his new fiction column, praising it warmly. "Truthful, humourous and much more like country life than most country books," he had written under a heading featuring my title.

It was a generously long review, the kind to gladden any novelist's heart. Greatly encouraged, I wrote at once to thank him, signing my letter with my own name instead of my pen name, Barbara Kaye. A day or so later I received a reply on a postcard: "Well, well! You must be the wife of biblio Muir," he wrote. "I did enjoy your book. . . ."

Naively I assumed that other reviewers would follow Betjeman's example. When, a few days later the book won praise in the BBC's "Woman's Hour," I was even more encouraged and rang my publishers to find out if they were geared up for a big surge in demand.

Geoffrey Halliday, the Hurst and Blackett manager, responded calmly. Yes, he had seen Betjeman's review and knew about the "Woman's Hour" mention, but I should remember that "one swallow, or even two, don't make a summer." Sales were satisfactory, and the reviews were certainly helpful, but it was too soon to talk about a new print run. However, they were arranging for a window display in the Bishop's Stortford stationer's shop (which also sold a selection of hardbacks), and perhaps I would like to go along and sign a few copies.

A display in a local stationer's plus an invitation from the Bishop's Stortford Rotarians to give a talk at their monthly luncheon club hardly amounted to razzmatazz. No one rang up from the BBC to ask me to take part in a "chat show," nor were any American publishers competing to buy US rights. No Hollywood film mogul cabled for the film rights. Nor did literary editors of the *Sunday Times* and *Observer* feel they should follow Betjeman's lead. During the weeks following publication a trickle of favorable reviews from provincial newspapers helped to boost my flagging morale, but I knew by then that bestseller status was not for me.

A year later *Black Market Green* was to attract interest somewhat disconcertingly from quite a different quarter when we were preparing to leave for the United States.

It was not long after the book's publication that it was necessary to put my would-be career of successful novelist to one side in order to play hostess to our friend André Poursin and his young daughter. Percy had already made a couple of trips to Paris to work with André on the International League directory, one of them on his own, when the Poursin family had taken him into their home and their hearts. This time André had volunteered to come to Takeley and proposed bringing Anne-Marie, his thirteen-year-old daughter with him to spend part of her school holidays with us and improve her English.

"She's about the same age as Helen, so they ought to get on together," said Percy. Which I knew did not necessarily follow. "Then we'll take the two girls with us to Paris when we leave for the conference at the beginning of September."

This was in effect an exchange visit, for the Poursins had invited Helen to stay at their country house in the Puy-de-Dôme district while we attended the conference. David, who was not invited, would spend the time at a children's holiday center.

The prospect of devising acceptable menus for a gourmet Frenchman was daunting. Game was out of season, butcher's meat still tightly rationed. A sacrifice on the altar of friendship had to be made — the slaughter of one of my capons. Caponizing chickens by the injection of hormones had recently come into use. Once I had mastered the technique of inserting a tiny pellet under the loose skin just above one of the bird's wings, I was not to be deterred by dark hints from the men in our

Barbara Kaye, holding a copy of her latest novel, at a book promotion event.

circle of friends about loss of manhood through eating "Barbara's emas-culated chickens." Our man Francis, who had to hold the squawking cockerel while I performed the operation, clearly disapproved of such interference with nature. The effect of the injection within two or three weeks was a fat, silly-looking bird with a small pink comb and no interest in life, bar eating.

André and Anne-Marie arrived at the end of July. André's affectionate greetings and pleasure in coming to our home encompassed us all. Anne-Marie, five feet of Latin femininity, just budding into womanhood, was dark-haired, dark-eyed, and in complete contrast to our tall, fair daughter, whose figure was slim and boyish. As Percy and André laughed and joked together, delighting as always in each other's company, the two young girls shook hands guardedly, taking stock of each other. Completely different in character as well as in looks, the daughters were not to repeat the friendship of the fathers, although they got on well enough

147

during the visit. Rather, it was our eleven-year-old son whose interest was aroused in this pretty nubile French guest so different from his sister. From Anne-Marie's point of view, his undisguised admiration could hardly be taken seriously, and mostly she dismissed his eager glances with a Gallic shrug. Communication was, in any case, difficult, David having no French and Anne-Marie not wanting the bore of employing her limited English in conversation with a boy two years her junior. For poor David the gulf was unbridgeable.

The ILAB directory was finalized for the printers during André's visit. For much of the time the two men were closeted together in our living room, as many years later Percy and John Carter would be when they worked on the final proofs of their magnum opus, *Printing and the Mind of Man*. From time to time I would hear André's chortling laughter as they chuckled over some of the dealers' names and specialities. "Maintenant Monsieur Dieu. Et son spécialité? Comment? Sexology!" Followed by a shout of laughter from André: "Nom de Dieu!"

To my relief, my fears about the quality of my cooking proved groundless. André ate everything I offered him with apparent relish, my meringues Chantilly bringing me a special accolade. He was the only one of our guests who would break off his conversation and turn to see what was coming out of the kitchen as I brought the main course to the table.

During that visit we took André and Anne-Marie to Beeleigh Abbey for a more decorous session with Willie Foyle than our previous visit. After visiting the library, Willie invited us into the drawing room, where he poured drinks from a glass decanter of a very special brandy. He had taken down both decanter and glasses to match from the marble mantle-shelf above the fireplace. He watched us respectfully sipping the brandy, waited until our glasses were empty, and then remarked, with his high-pitched giggle: "I've had those glasses fifteen years, and they've never been washed once in all that time."

148

Chapter 18

One of the Danish booksellers at the Copenhagen conference had made the interesting suggestion that members of different associations should be encouraged to "exchange their children." This, he suggested, would bring about better "international understanding." Had some of us taken this proposal literally, the result might, I fancy, have been the reverse of his hopes. If swaps were not quite what parents were looking for, the idea of arranging exchange visits for their young through the league was an attractive one. Although it has to be said it was taken up by only a few of us at that time.

Anne-Marie was the first of a number of young people who came to stay with us in Takeley through Percy's involvement with the league. Her two brothers were to follow; Hans Goetz would send his daughter, Maria; there would be an Austrian boy from Salzburg. An auctioneer from Marburg would send us one of his sons, and two sisters would come to us from Munich.

Mostly these boys and girls fitted well into our family life. I was no disciplinarian; our regime, I discovered, was considerably more relaxed than theirs at home. The Germans were diligent in improving their English, the French took it easily, lapsing into their own tongue as far as possible. Maria Goetz was ever ready to try her vocabulary on the opposite sex; the Austrian boy was confident that he had little to learn.

Percy, busy as always, saw these youthful guests mainly at meal times. Because he enjoyed using his French and German, he would talk to them mostly in their own language, while I would stick to English, since that was what our young guests were supposed to be learning. Thus, meals would be bilingual, with my children and I picking up some German or French perforce. They, after all, were going to be in a like situation on the return visit.

Occupied as he was with the never-ending search for interesting stock, cataloguing, attending London book auctions, ABA and league committee meetings, as well as meetings of the National Book League and the usual bibliographical functions, Percy somehow found time to contribute to a series of lectures the ABA was sponsoring for young newcomers to the trade, known as the "Bibliomites."

Our spring catalogue in 1950 ranged from Americana to books on ale and wine, with many diverse subjects in between, including a French work on, of all things, monkey glands. As a novelty, the catalogue contained an intriguing supplement — a dessert course, as it were.

The last time he had been in Paris, Percy had been attracted by a collection of small copper engravings, both plain and colored. They were made, he had been told, for inserting into sweetmeat boxes. Many were accompanied by verses. Printed in the early nineteenth century, none of the engravings had been used for the purpose for which they were designed. Some were still in sheets, others had already been cut out and shaped. Such charming trifles, Percy decided, surely deserved to be collected. Known to the French as *bonbonnières*, so far as he knew they were unknown to British collectors of ephemera. Taking a chance, he bought the lot.

In the supplement to the catalogue, offered at under £2 for a set of eight, they sold as quickly as the sweetmeats they had been intended to accompany. It was an encouragement to Percy to buy more of such novelties. Increasingly our catalogues would include ephemera and such printed collectibles as engraved letter headings, Victorian valentines, and harlequinades, some of which Percy put aside to appreciate in his private collection of Victoriana, favorite books, and presentation copies from writer friends with their letters.

August went swiftly. The book to follow *Black Market Green* was put aside as I strove to ensure that Anne-Marie enjoyed her stay in England, making trips to the seaside, to Cambridge to punt on the Cam, and to Whipsnade to spend one long hot day at the open-air zoo. It was an afternoon for lazing in the sun, which was what the lioness was doing when we came to the lion enclosure. But her mate had other ideas and after some rather charming preliminaries persuaded her to comply with his desire. As my two country-bred children stopped to watch with undisguised interest (to see copulating lions was a novelty), Anne-Marie looked away primly, urging us all to hurry past. "It is not nice," she told us reprovingly. "We should not look." But my two still lingered, and in a minute the little love scene was over.

We set off for France a week before the Paris conference was due to open. Percy had been over-working and was badly in need of a few days' rest before the stress and strain of the usual meetings and social events.

On André's recommendation, we had chosen a hotel in Barbizon for a brief holiday. Kundig was already staying in Paris and was known to be in poor health. His heart condition was worsening, and Percy knew he might be called upon to deputize for William some of the time.

This was a task Percy was willing to undertake; to accept the presidency, if it came to that, was another matter. It meant giving a good deal more time to the business of the league, at the expense of his own business. He was doubtful if he could or should do that. Earlier that year there had been a meeting of presidents in Brussels. Some useful work had been done and consensus achieved on some of the items for the conference agenda, but several tricky problems remained, including Germany's request to be allowed to send an observer to the 1951 conference. And the Danes were still objecting to Hans Goetz continuing membership of the ABA. As Percy would write later, "This was a hardy perennial that came up on every ILAB agenda for years."

Once back in France, it was amusing to see Anne-Marie become a confident little mademoiselle, while Helen was now in her turn the learner. In the restaurant car on the train to Paris Anne-Marie clearly enjoyed translating the menu for us all and then conducting a serious discussion with the table steward. It was probably the high point of her holiday.

We did not linger in Paris. Helen was left at the Poursins' (the two girls were to leave the following day for the country), and André drove Percy and I to our hotel in Barbizon. We were staying in a pretty, timbered auberge with swags of wisteria falling around the windows, harboring, as we were to find out, myriads of mosquitos, for we were close to the forest of Fontainebleau. It had a certain cachet, boasting patronage by royalty, Princess Margaret having recently dined there with a party of friends. Not that André, a true republican and no snob, had recommended it to us for any such a reason. Far more important was *la cuisine*, which he had sampled and approved. The village itself was associated with the group of nineteenth-century landscape artists who had once lived and worked there. Some of their studios remained and had become picture galleries, although most of their names no longer carried much glamour.

Under André's tutelage we dined well that first evening. We had planned this brief holiday as a mini second honeymoon. The evening was warm, and no one had told us not to leave our windows open. We had gone to bed happy and relaxed, looking forward to the morrow. After an hour or so asleep, I awoke to a sinister high-pitched hum and the realization that we were under attack. For the rest of the night an army

151

of mosquitos zoomed over and around our bed. There were no mosquito nets in the room and nothing to be done except pull the sheets over our heads and wait for the dawn. When it came and I dared to look in the mirror, my face was splodged with red lumps, itching like mad. Percy had escaped more lightly but declared that he felt totally exhausted and couldn't face even coffee and croissants. As he was hardly ever ill, I was alarmed and without consulting him ran downstairs and asked the hotel manager to call a doctor.

When Monsieur le Médecin arrived, he was brisk and jovial. A brief examination was followed by a predictably French diagnosis. Monsieur's trouble was undoubtedly *une maladie du foie* — a liver disorder. But fortunately not serious. A prescription was scribbled, monsieur was advised to be *raisonable* with his diet, drink less wine, and he would soon recover.

As the doctor was leaving, I raised my bitten face and begged for advice to assuage the damage and avoid further assaults. His answer as he hurried away gave me no comfort: "Eh bien, Madame, il faut chasser les moustiques."

After the doctor's departure Percy at once felt better. A few restful days spent pottering about Barbizon, enjoying the formal gardens at Fontainebleau, and resisting the restaurant's lusher specialties as well as its wine card, were enough to restore him to health for the rigors of the conference. Back in Paris we learned that William and Juliette Kundig were installed at the Hotel George V, and William was apparently prepared to preside as usual. With some 240 booksellers and their families expected, it was going to be an even larger conference than that of London. Among those who had already arrived was Laurence Gomme, this time with his association's application for membership in his pocket.

Britain was well represented, with Dudley Massey in his second year as president leading the ABA delegation. Winnie Myers and the Sawyers had come as usual, and Kenneth Maggs and his wife were attending for the first time.

A pile of correspondence awaited us when we booked in at our hotel. Among it was a postcard from David. We had taken it for granted that he would be happy at the children's holiday center where we had left him in Broadstairs (it had been warmly recommended by Percy's uncle), and I had not been worrying about him. The card was blotched with what could have been tears. "I hope you are having a nice time," he had written. "I am very unhappy here. I think I shall run away."

"I know it's very worrying for us both," Percy said as I sat reading and re-reading this pathetic little communication. "But I expect it's only

152

some minor upset that has got out of proportion. We can't possibly go home to sort it out now. Certainly, I can't, and I don't want you rushing back to England either."

After talking it over, we decided the best thing to do was to telephone the center, find out the situation, and make sure that David hadn't carried out his threat and disappeared, heaven knew where. So I put in a call to Broadstairs.

"The children are all on the beach," said a woman's voice cheerfully. "Your son? Yes, he's with the rest of them. He's very well. They're all having a splendid time."

Another call to Percy's uncle in Broadstairs brought a reassuring promise that he would go and see what the trouble had been and if necessary take David home with him.

"Now you can stop magnifying the problem," Percy told me, which was exactly what I had been doing.

There was little time for sitting and worrying. The usual eve of conference momentum was building up. Because this was Paris, much time was spent in restaurants over protracted meals, with the original party of four or five snowballing into a dozen or more. Despite the general bonhomie, there were, as always, undercurrents. X was said not to be on speaking terms with Y, and Monsieur A had brought his mistress with him, having left his wife at home, and so on. . . .

First names were used far less than in England. Between the French wives and the rest of us, formality prevailed. Hats were worn for most daytime occasions. As far as I was concerned, that useful form of address "Madame" saved much memory searching for names I quickly forgot or never knew.

News soon came from Broadstairs to allay my fears. We need not worry, there would be no running away. Kind Uncle Horace had sorted out the trouble. Some more pocket money had helped, and all was now well.

To Percy's relief William Kundig turned up for the opening session. He was looking somewhat thinner but was as confident and in command of the assembly as ever.

There were compliments all round in his opening speech, including a tribute to the ABA for its "impeccable organization" of the London conference. This was somewhat offset by a flowery reference to Paris as "the capital of the intellectual world" and his own joy in presiding there.

His chairman's report was lengthy. Much had been achieved since the

London conference, including a meeting of all the affiliated associations' presidents in Brussels, where a revised set of rules had been drawn up for the approval of the general assembly. The adoption of these was to lead to much lengthy discussion, especially as the aim of one of them was to disqualify the unfortunate Mr. Goetz.

More delayed payments had been collected, a code of practice had been drawn up, and negotiations with governments had been taking place on the question of currency problems over the export and import of books. Percy would report later that he and André had the proofs of the geographical section of the directory ready for circulation. Although Menno could report that more work had been done on the dictionary of terms, it was still a long way from being completed.

It was somewhat shaming that the ABA was among the countries reproved for laggardly payment of their subscription, but then so were France, Italy, and Austria, not to mention Holland and a couple of the Scandinavian countries, while the Americans got a pat on the back for sending in their contribution even before their association had been accepted as a member.

Early on the agenda, while Laurence Gomme and several other members of the ABAA waited in the wings, Kundig put the American application to the vote. Its acceptance was, of course, a foregone conclusion, as it was that Laurence would become a member of the committee. When the vote had been taken, William, who liked to do such things with a flourish, summoned Laurence and the other ABAA delegates into the chamber, announcing: "I am delighted to inform you that you are invited to take part in the league by thirteen votes against none. Mr. Gomme is now a member of the committee. So, Mr. Gomme, come and take your place here!" gesturing to the platform to which Laurence duly mounted to general applause.

The task of saying the appropriate "few words to mark the occasion" was given to Percy. Never one to indulge in long eulogies, he declared that his task was completely unnecessary. Nonetheless, his response was sincere and heartfelt. "I have only to say one word to our American colleagues in the person of Mr. Gomme," he said, "and that word is 'Welcome'!"

When he replied, Laurence would have loved to tell the assembly that the decision to join the league had been unanimous. As it was, he could claim that the ABAA had a "coast to coast" membership represented in the delegation he was leading. It was, he said, more than he had expected that they would become affiliated to the league so speedily. At the general meeting the vote had been "almost unanimous." They had, he added rather obscurely, "resolved our differences by reducing the lack of unanimity." This was something of an understatement. The ABAA, like the ABA, had its share of anti-Europeans, and, as Percy would write later, a good deal of credit was due to Kundig for forcefully putting the case for joining when he was invited by Laurence to attend the ABAA's annual general meeting.

As the conference wore on, interspersed with receptions and cultural visits (the Louvre, Montmartre, Versailles) and a considerable consumption of alcohol, Kundig continued to preside at the business sessions, but he relied increasingly on Percy to deputize for him at the social events, sometimes at very short notice. On one evening, the French had arranged a six o'clock reception at somewhere rather grand at which the minister for the arts, a formidable woman politician, would be present to receive the delegates. This was the kind of obligatory function that has nothing to do with pleasure. Speeches are likely to be either perfunctory or platitudinous or both, drinks tepid and limited, canapes uninspired. There are invariably too many people making too much noise and seldom the chance to sit down. Back in our hotel room, after a tiring day, Percy and I had planned to put in no more than a token appearance, when the telephone rang. It was a message by someone speaking for Kundig. He regretted he did not feel well enough to attend the reception, and would Monsieur Muir kindly take his place?

Percy groaned. We had been lying relaxed on the bed, putting off the moment of getting dressed for this boring reception. The request couldn't be ignored. Duty called. Scrambling into our clothes, we rang down for a taxi. By then it was the worst of the evening rush hour. "Il faut attender, M'sieu," said the hall porter, his voice disclaiming all responsibility. As in England, taxis in 1950 were mostly ancient and in short supply. By the time we finally arrived at the reception, Madame the Minister had been waiting half an hour to deliver her prepared speech of welcome and was not amused.

"You'd better keep out of the way," Percy said to me, as he went forward to make his apologies. If a man has to placate a lady, it is just as well for his wife to be out of sight. Keeping well in the background, I watched the ice begin to melt. Soon the lady was smiling. Her delayed speech was delivered in French, and it was for Percy, standing in for William, to respond in the same language, and of necessity off the cuff. That he could do so, and throw in a joke or two, owed something to those long ago Sunday mornings at Hyde Park Speaker's Corner, as well as to his

155

friendship with André, which had brought a limited knowledge of French to a fluency equal to his easy conversational German. This was not the last time during the Paris conference that Percy had to step into Kundig's shoes.

There was no meeting of the assembly on the fourth day of the conference. Instead, we were driven in coaches to be shown Versailles — the state rooms, impressive and at the same time oppressive, the Hall of Mirrors, le Petit Trianon, the statue of Le Roi Soleil bewigged and mounted, his charger about to step off the plinth into space. The sun shone, we climbed up endless steps, took photographs, and absorbed snippets of French history. We were due to dine with the Kundigs at their hotel that evening in company with the other members of the committee and their wives. There had been both a morning session and a long afternoon session ending at six-thirty the previous day. William, pressing ahead with the agenda, had then seemed his usual self, although Percy had thought he looked tired. He did not show up on the outing to Versailles, and it was assumed he was taking the opportunity to rest.

We arrived punctually, to be greeted by Nic and Denise Tulkens, grave faced, who told us that William was seriously ill. Nevertheless, Juliette was insisting that the dinner party go ahead. A few minutes later she appeared, pale and distraught but in a smart evening gown, her hair newly coiffeured. When we inquired after William, she replied dolefully, "Malheuresment il est très malade. C'est encore son coeur." He had been working too hard, as usual. He should never have agreed to chair the conference. He was killing himself!

The other guests were arriving, and soon we were all sitting sombrely at a long dining table in the Kundigs' private suite. It was as if the funeral had already taken place, and we, the mourners, had been invited to eat the funeral bakemeats. There was some desultory, low-key conversation as the guests recalled other friends and colleagues suddenly struck down. Refusing to eat, Juliette sat silently at the head of the table through the first course; then, murmuring an apology, she got up and hurried from the room.

Released from the strain of her sorrowing presence, her guests' tongues at once began to wag freely, William himself being the only possible topic. But Juliette was soon back, to sit silently as before, but now with the tears running down her long, pale face.

When the meal had dragged to its end, Nic Tulkens went along the passage to William's bedroom, at Juliette's request, returning presently to say that William wanted to talk to Percy, and I was to come, too. We found him in bed, propped up against a pile of pillows, looking smaller than I remembered him, his face thinner, a pink flush on his cheekbones. Frightened though he clearly was, he was going to extract some drama from his situation.

"I have shouldered my share of the league as long as I can, Percy," he said heavily, when we had paid our respects and offered sympathy. The room was not large and was lit only by the bedside lamp; there seemed nowhere for us to sit. He was addressing Percy, and I had only a walk-on part. "Now the time has come to hand over the reins," he continued. "You must take my place, my friend. You must take the last session of the assembly, and you must tell them that the state of my health makes it imperative that I rest. Tomorrow I will have my letter of resignation ready for you. You can explain that I am too ill to read it personally."

We did not stay long by his bedside, for Juliette came to ask us not to tire him, a request that clearly irritated him. Some of the other guests were then granted an audience. There was no doubt he had enjoyed his presidency and regretted having to resign it on his doctor's advice. A powerful personality with the will and the means to get things done had been needed in the first years after the league's formation. In Percy's view, William had been the right man at the right time. Without his determination and forceful character, the league could well have foundered before it was truly launched.

Juliette told us that he was to see a heart specialist the next day. As it happened, there was a conference of cardiac consultants meeting in Paris that very week, and one of the most eminent would be examining him in the morning. We left as soon as we decently could. Poor Juliette was inconsolable. It was not a party at which anyone wanted to linger, and Percy would have much to do the next day and to think about that night.

I believed that he should accept the presidency. He was the obvious man for the job, and I think he knew it. His doubts lay in whether he could afford to give it the time it was going to demand. All the same, I could not see him turning it down.

In the morning, when the committee met prior to the final meeting of the assembly, Percy had decided that if he was to become president, he must have André (who was adamant that he would not accept the presidency) as his vice president to share the burden. He was ready to step into the breach, he told the committee, but only for as long as it took to find an acceptable successor.

Hertzberger, although owed a debt for having set the ball rolling in the first place, was regarded primarily as an auctioneer, and therefore, by many of the delegates as not a genuine bookseller. Nor was he popular in all quarters. Einar Grónolt Pedersen was a delightful character but would have lacked the necessary authority, nor did he want the job; Tulkens, the Belgian president, was needed as treasurer, and Laurence Gomme was too new a recruit and not well enough known to the Europeans.

One unexpected problem that Kundig's resignation had uncovered was that there was nothing in the rules for dealing with such a situation. Rather oddly, when drawing them up, no one had envisaged one of the executive either dying or retiring. A new rule had therefore to be devised and put to the assembly. This stated that if a member of the executive was unable to continue in mid-term, then he must be replaced by an election held at the next general assembly, with the new member elected to serve only for the unexpired period of the mandate of the committee member he was replacing.

Percy had been to see Kundig in the morning and found him somewhat better. His letter of resignation was written, and when the general assembly eventually met, having been delayed until the late afternoon, Percy read it to the delegates, prefacing it with his own tribute to "a very great president, who established the league, who carried it through periods of extreme difficulty . . . and on more than one occasion prevented it from shipwreck by the strength and force of his character." His successor, he added, would have a hard task to perform.

The news of Kundig's unexpected retirement was a considerable shock to the conference. Not only had he been admired and respected, his international standing in the trade had been an asset, bringing status to the presidency. As he said in his letter of resignation, addressed to Percy as vice president, "I have done all that I could do and my thoughts have been increasingly directed towards [the league's] prosperity. . . ." This was certainly true. He had been generous with both his time and his money, allowing the league to operate from his Geneva offices and providing financial backing in the early days when funds were short. After the ABA's ill-advised resolution to the Copenhagen conference, for the league to have been based in London would have certainly been unacceptable to the majority of the delegates.

Although Kundig had resigned the presidency, his withdrawal was to be only partial. For, as Percy told the assembly, the presidents of the twelve associations had unanimously agreed that he should be made president of honor, a proposition promptly endorsed unanimously. In this new guise he would be entitled to attend future committee meetings.

After Kundig's elevation to the status of elder statesman and the adoption of the new rule to the constitution, the choice of who should be the new president was a foregone conclusion. It was Nic Tulkens who was first on his feet with the proposal: "I think it would be wise for the assembly to request Mr. Percy Muir to continue the mandate for Mr. Kundig."

Percy's reply had been carefully prepared. He told the delegates that he was grateful for the honor but would accept it only as a matter of convenience for the league. He would, he stressed, in no circumstances be persuaded to continue after the end of Kundig's mandate. Should the conference decide to elect him, he would accept only on the conditions that between now and the next conference they prepared to replace him with a new president and that he was their unanimous choice.

By then the delegates had already made up their minds. They were not worrying about what would happen in a year's time. It was Captain Cohn, a forceful member of the American delegation, who put the matter to the vote (declaring that Tulkens' proposal had been a suggestion not a motion): "I move that this body elect Mr. Percy Muir to complete the term of Mr. Kundig."

His election was unanimous, as was that of André Poursin to the position of vice president. Nic Tulkens was confirmed as honorary treasurer, and his invitation for the conference to be held in Belgium the following year gratefully accepted. After this, Percy was ready to declare the business at an end.

The one item that remained unresolved was the choice of a design for the emblem everyone thought the league ought to have. A number had been submitted, and Percy called a recess so that they could be passed around to the delegates for a choice to be made. This was bound to be difficult, and, when no agreement on any one design could be arrived at, it was the gallant Captain Cohn who saved the meeting from the anticlimax of drawnout discussion by coming up with the sensible solution of handing over the selection to the committee. They were perfectly capable of doing it, he said crisply. The Captain's contribution to the league debates would be always very much to the point. So it was that the neat little logo — a book encircled by the words "Amor Librorum Nos Unit" (love of books unites us) — became the league's emblem, approved by the general assembly in Brussels in 1951.

At the farewell dinner the following evening, held at the Restaurant du Pré Catalan, the six-course menu might have been described as an exercise in gastronomic one-upmanship. We were offered consommé or iced melon, lobster with port, roast partridge (trumping the British grouse), foie gras, salad, cheese, and pêche Melba as the finale. All this was accompanied by two excellent wines, Pouilly Fuissé and Nuits St. George.

The week of continuous hospitality had been something of a challenge to British livers and hardly what the doctor had ordered for Percy. To my relief he stayed the course with flying colors. When, during this sumptuous meal, I glanced along the top table to where he was sitting between two pretty ladies, Edith Poursin and Lorette de Nobele (wife of the French president), he looked to be bearing up remarkably well.

As the president's lady, there was no way I could escape my duty of making a grateful speech of thanks on behalf of the female guests. My dinner partners on either side also had bits of paper at which they would peer between courses, their faces, like mine, abstracted. Should I dare to say a few words in my schoolgirl French? It was all very well to have been told by one or two Frenchmen, mellow after dining well, that my accent was "charmante" or (not quite so pleasing) "amusante." I was sure it was neither. Unlike Percy, I was no linguist.

I needn't have worried. By the time my turn came, after a dozen other speeches, no one was paying much attention to what was said, or in what language. A gratefully phrased "merci" was all that was required.

The next day André drove us to his country home in the tiny, medieval village of Beauregard l'Eveque, perched on a hillside, a few miles from Clermont Ferrand, where we were to stay a couple of nights and retrieve Helen, whose French, we found, had improved considerably, for the two Poursin sons, Jean-Marie and Jacques, were also on holiday and had been making a fuss of her.

After dinner on our first evening the young people insisted on a game of Monopoly. This, naturally, was the French version of the game. André promptly withdrew to his study, taking Percy with him. The rest of us settled down around the dining table, Anne-Marie and her brothers eager to outdo each other in acquiring paper fortunes. I had noticed, when we played the game at home, that it was seldom conducive to harmony, but aggressive acquisitiveness was discouraged. It was very different at the Poursins; in the battle for possession of such desirable properties as the Rue de la Paix, or the Faubourg St. Honoré, all restraint was abandoned, as shouts of J'achete! J'achete! drowned my own, or Helen's modest bids. Soon the two brothers were putting up houses and hotels on most of the best streets in Paris, while Anne-Marie, with the luck running against her, stubbornly clung to the down-market Gare du Nord, yelling that she was selling to *no one*, however much they offered. More skilled at the game, or luckier, the two brothers gleefully built up their holdings, demanding their rent from the rest of us.

Outbid and out maneuvered, Helen and I were soon broke. Edith Poursin, smiling serenely through the hubbub, was still in the game, retaining a modest property or two, when, faced with bankruptcy, her daughter hurled her last few francs at her brothers, burst into tears, and rushed from the room.

None of the family seemed at all dismayed. The two young men merely grinned and continued to challenge each other. Edith, calmly picking up a card to take her turn, caught my eye, smiled, and shrugged. "J'ai l'habitude," she said. "I'm used to it."

It was the time of the village grape harvest. Nearly every house of any size had its own small vineyard, where it was the women, in wide cotton skirts, bright colored scarves around their heads, who did most of the picking. In the morning, after André had declared that the time had come to harvest their crop, we spent the day amid the low-growing vines on the stony slope behind the Poursins' house. The September sun was hot on our backs as we worked our way along the rows, crouching down beside one vine after another, the juice from the squashy-ripe grapes staining our fingers. Edith, like the two peasant women hired to pick for the day, had tied a cotton kerchief over her dark hair and worked as steadily as they did. When our containers were full, we tipped their juicy contents into the big basket strapped on to Jacques' back as he came up and down the rows to collect from the pickers. As soon as this was full, it was emptied into one of the tubs standing on an old wooden handcart, which from time to time he trundled along the village street to the communal press house.

André, handicapped by a game leg damaged in a car accident, took no part in the harvesting, leaving it to his sons, but he would not have missed the evening session when the grapes were pressed, the "most" tasted, their quality debated. For me, the day had been golden, a day of utter peace and contentment. When my knees ached from unaccustomed crouching, I would stand up and stretch and watch Edith and the two peasant women picking neatly and swiftly, chatting the while. The two girls picked, too, but not for long. After the tensions of the conference, the lobbying, the fuss, the dressing up (although I enjoyed most of it), the overeating, the protocol, my day as a grape picker was bliss.

We all gathered in the old, stone-built press-house in the cool of the evening. There we were greeted by a leathery-faced humorous character rather in the manner of mine host welcoming customers to a wayside

161

inn. Already the greater part of the crop had gone through the press. By the light of a hanging oil lamp, cloudy glassfuls were drawn off for us to taste, holding them first to the light to show the color. The "most" had a fruity sweetness that clung to the tongue, its taste lingering in the mouth. Watching Percy and me drink, a twinkle in his eye, the man in charge made a remark to Jacques that had them both laughing robustly. His French accent was hard for me to understand. It was Edith who enlightened me that to drink a glassful was a splendid cure for constipation.

There was a delicious scent from the pulped grapes as they gave up their juice under the weight of the wooden press. As we stood watching, our shadows tall on the whitewashed walls in the soft lamplight, it was if we had travelled backwards in time, and I wondered how many hundreds of wine harvests the little house had seen. Only later did I learn that it was already condemned and would soon give place to clever new technology.

Chapter 19

Elkin Mathews now had a new recruit to the staff. Reg Read came to work for us in 1950 and would stay with the firm for the next eighteen years. When he left in 1968, it was to take charge of Foyle's secondhand book department in Charing Cross Road. A cheerful, willing young man, he had left a safe, if dull, job as a clerk in the Bishop's Stortford town council offices for the totally unfamiliar world of antiquarian book dealing. It meant a daily cycle ride of four miles there and back, a packed lunch (no pub lunches in Takeley in those days), and sharing a cramped little office, partitioned off from the long, draughty stock shed, with a series of juniors, or part-timers. The view was of our vegetable garden, and the boss's wife would pop in and out to borrow stamps or stationery.

As jobs go, there was not much pressure. Tempo would speed up when the quarterly catalogues went out and the response came in telephone calls and cables ("Please keep off the phone," I would be warned at such times), for most of our customers were heard rather than seen, with some privileged exceptions.

After the closing down of the Bishop's Stortford bookshop, we had lost our outlet for inexpensive books of the kind that accumulate from bulk purchases. With the steady rise in printing costs, cataloguing books worth less than £4 had become uneconomic. Reporting them to the trade through the *Clique*, as I had done, was time consuming (my time had been given free), while the solution adopted by some dealers of dumping slow-selling or unwanted stocks in Hodgsons book auction rooms in London was a nuisance when one's business was thirty miles away. To use the local salesrooms was, in those days, tantamount to giving books away. The answer was office technology, such as it was then. This, for us, was the latest power-driven Gestetner duplicator. With the aid of this machine, Reg Read doubled as secretary and compiler of our monthly book lists. By no means were all of these inexpensive books.

Our quarto-size Christmas 1950 list, with an appropriately pictorial cover (a kiss, eighteenth-century style, beneath the mistletoe), offered first editions of both Kate Greenaway and Beatrix Potter. The price for the extremely scarce first issue of *The Tale of Peter Rabbit*, privately printed by the author in 1901, was £20 — a remarkable bargain (a presentation copy of this little book recently sold for £60,000 at auction). So also was the peepshow of the opening of the Great Exhibition by Queen Victoria, in six hand-colored sections for four guineas.

Percy had grown up at a time when it was usual for an employer to address his staff formally, no matter how long they had been with the firm. It was a convention he maintained and approved of, seeing no reason to differentiate between the office staff and Francis, our packer and gardener, who was "Dave" to Laurie, but addressed as "Mr. Francis" by Percy during the twenty or so years he worked for us. So that while Read was "Reg" or "Reggie" to Laurie and everyone else, to Percy he was always "Mr. Read." Mateyness, as far as Percy was concerned, was out of place in any office.

Laurie Deval, belonging to a generation not given to formality, thought this attitude old hat. Naturally gregarious, he had no wish to be "mistered" by Francis, who was old enough to be his father, or by anyone else. Very different in character though he and Percy were, they worked well together on a basis of mutual affection and respect for each other's point of view. There would be the inevitable occasional disagreements between the younger man, full of energy and new ideas, and the older man, with more experience and more caution, but these would be resolved without rancor. Fortunately, they had a similar sense of humor. By 1950 Laurie was already establishing his own specialities of modern typography (he had his own handpress), press books, and books on arts and crafts. These would stand him in good stead when, many years later, the partnership of Deval and Muir came into being.

My own part in the running of the business had become peripheral, mainly meeting customers at the station and playing hostess as required. This was my own choice, for as well as writing novels (I was trying to squeeze in an extra one in 1950-51) and looking after my family, I was becoming ever more enmeshed in village affairs. No longer a small agricultural community, Takeley was growing fast. There was light industry in the area around what had been the USAF base to the north of the village, the demand for houses for commuters was being met by a developer who had wangled permission to build a small private estate on wasteland near the disused railway station, and we had been allowed a dozen houses on our first post-war council house estate. Compared to our pre-war houses, these were very "desirable residences," and families were queuing for them.

My self-imposed task of gingering up the parish council came into action in the autumn of 1950, when our parish clerk received a letter from the welfare committee of the county council. Whitehall, it appeared, in its guise as a benevolent universal nanny, had been telling local authorities that they should encourage parish councils to set up so-called Evergreen Clubs in their village for the benefit of their old-age pensioners. The welfare committee was therefore nudging us to take the appropriate action.

The flat tone of our clerk's voice as he read out this communication clearly indicated that he did not expect us to have anything to do with such nonsense. He was not far wrong; the first reaction of my fellow councillors was resentment that any bureaucrats should think they had the right to tell us how to look after our old people.

"That's not something old folks want. If we were to set up a club, they wouldn't come to it. They're a lot better staying by their firesides, specially in winter time. Any road, for those that want to join clubs there's the Legion and the Women's Guild and the Mother's Union and all. And the Women's Institute, too, for that matter. . . ." That was the general tone of the objections, regardless of the fact that the organizations mentioned catered for either men or women, but not for both.

"I move we leave it on the table," said Mr. C., the councillor with whom I usually clashed, with a challenging glance in my direction. Leaving an item "on the table" was a convenient way of dealing with a matter that the council felt it better to ignore, rather than vote against.

I reacted as he had probably expected. "But how can we be sure our senior citizens would not want a club of their own?" I protested. "Surely we ought not to turn down the idea without first consulting them, especially as we're being offered a grant to help finance it."

My intervention brought about the discussion our clerk (himself a senior citizen) had clearly hoped to avoid. Well then, said my fellow councillors, if such a club was formed, who would run it? It was certainly not a job for the parish council, but someone would have to be responsible for getting it started.

"I'm sure we could find someone willing to take it on," I persisted, with an uneasy feeling that they were all looking at me. "At least we could try out the idea," I said. "Ask around and see how much interest there is . . ."

"Well, may we leave that to you, Mrs. Muir?" said the chairman briskly, seeing his opportunity to move on to other matters. "I'm sure we all agree that it will be in good hands."

Once again I was lumbered. I had already said too much to wriggle out of such a challenge without loss of face. The only woman on the council, I had fallen into an obvious trap.

The idea of Evergreen Clubs was new. One had started up recently in a village not far off, but I knew of no others. Would our old people really want to leave their firesides on a winter afternoon for tea and cake in the village hall, with maybe some amateur entertainment or a game of whist? I asked myself dubiously. Even if a few women turned up, would any men?

If anyone knew the views of our old-age pensioners, it was Isobel, the post-mistress (she'd know who had bad legs and would need transport and who got on or didn't get on with her neighbors), so to Isobel I went for advice.

Six weeks later we held our first meeting. Although the four old men who turned up were heavily outnumbered by sixteen women, they didn't seem to mind, and within three months the membership had doubled.

There was no way I could dodge being the first Madam Chairman, but we were not too ambitious. It was just a pleasant afternoon with old friends, a game of cards, a good tea, and a gossip, with a party at Christmas, a visit to the pantomime, and an occasional outing. After the club had been running for a year, I deftly shifted the burden of the chair onto the shoulders of the vicar's wife. By then, Evergreen, or Over Sixties, Clubs were springing up all over the place.

Chapter 20

Personally, I would not have chosen February for a visit to Norway and Denmark, but that was the way it worked out. Whether it was the idea of the British Council's UK headquarters or their man in Oslo to mount an exhibition of British books first in Oslo and then in Bergen in the coldest month of the year, we never discovered. It was, it seems, just one of many projects for waving a cultural flag in Scandinavia.

Percy's association with the British Council had come about through the National Book League, which at that time was publishing a series of useful little bibliographical booklets on behalf of the council, as a supplement to *British Book News*. Later the series would become *British Writers and Their Work* under the general editorship of Bonamy Dobrée. Among the many contributors would be such distinguished writers as T. S. Eliot, Edmund Blunden, and Kathleen Raine.

The selection of the books for the exhibition was largely left to Percy; he was also to lecture on the theme of illustrated books and fine printing in the UK. He would, of course, be paid, though as usual with the chronically underfunded British Council, not generously. But apart from the fact that it was the sort of commission he enjoyed, he intended to kill two birds with one stone.

A league committee meeting was required to be held early in 1951; what better place, therefore, than in Oslo? Although their association was too small to host a conference in Norway, the Norwegian antiquarian bookseller's president, Jorgen Cappelen, was ready to offer hospitality to the league committee if they would like to meet in Oslo. When Percy took Cappelen up on this offer, a further even more attractive one followed. After the committee had finished its business we were all invited for a weekend, as Jorgen's guests at the ski resort of Jeilo, halfway between Oslo and Bergen. Apart from Laurence Gomme, who couldn't manage it, the committee members were happy to accept.

As Percy had some business to attend to in Copenhagen, we took the ferry from Harwich to Esbjerg once again. This time the sea was calm enough for me to enjoy my Danish egg and cheese breakfast. I was delighted to be back in Copenhagen — that beautiful, lighthearted city, where I felt instantly at home despite knowing only a few words of the language, and already we had some good friends.

To my mother I wrote, "Despite Copenhagen being a port I've seen no squalor. Away from the shops the people all appear to live in bright, neat homes and the houses are built with cellars for their central heating boilers. Indoors it's beautifully warm and cosy. The boys wear a kind of plus fours with thick woollen stockings, which I must say I envy. Football, the national game is sensibly played under cover. . . ."

It was snowing when we left on an overheated train for Oslo, via Sweden, the next morning, in company with Einar Grónolt Pedersen. The train, I noticed, was fitted with a snowplough. Snow drifted down steadily. With the countryside all white, the journey was boring until we stopped at a station and I looked out of the window and saw smoke pouring from beneath the coach adjoining ours. With no idea what the word was for "fire," I could only shout and point, which I did vigorously. The response of the nearest station official was phlegmatic. I was waved back from the window. Someone came ambling along the platform to inspect the trouble and conferred calmly with another official. Presently, the coach was uncoupled, and we pulled out of the station without it. What happened to the occupants, if any, I never discovered. Sweden was clearly a country where no one got in a flap.

When we arrived in Oslo, it was dark and still snowing. At the big hotel in the center of the city where we were staying, Norway's licensing laws were explained to us. It was forbidden to serve guests with wine or spirits after 3 PM, we were told. But if we wished to drink lager, that was permitted at any time.

"But no one obeys this law," Jorgen Cappelen said. Sure enough, the two elderly ladies dining at a table near ours had a shopping bag on the floor beside them from which from time to time they would discreetly refill their glasses.

Jorgen had invited us to dinner that first night. He was a splendid-looking man; well built, fair-haired, and blue-eyed, exactly fitting my idea of a Viking. This was a word he taught me to pronounce correctly as "Weeking" when, the following day, he took me to see the famous Viking long boats on display in an Oslo museum. Now that they had been restored, they looked, he assured me, just as they had in the days when Norwegian oarsmen braved the North Sea to raid the coast of East Anglia.

Cappelens were publishers as well as owners of the largest retail bookshop in Norway. The antiquarian side was only a small part of their business, but Jorgen had been one of the first to support the idea of the league and had attended the Paris conference. The Norwegians, we quickly discovered, were not only a hospitable people, they were also highly literate. To make the point, we were told proudly that Churchill's *History of the Second World War* had sold more copies per head of the population in Norway than in any other European country. The British still had a stock of good will left from our stand against Hitler. It was very pleasant to find ourselves liked and admired as we had been in Denmark. I was therefore disconcerted and rather hurt when, as I was walking alone back to our hotel after a stroll around the city (handsome, but rather stark in its clinical modernity), two young men, who looked like students, glared at me as I passed by and shouted something incomprehensible but certainly abusive.

"Oh, they will have been socialists," said Jorgen dismissively, when I told him of the incident.

The books for the British council exhibition had arrived before us and had been already set up by the council's Oslo representative, so that after Percy had delivered his lecture to a respectful, rather solemn audience, he was free to turn his attention to the business of the league. This was the first committee meeting since Kundig's retirement. The tricky question of the German's application for membership was on the agenda and likely to prove controversial, for not surprisingly the Dutch and the Scandinavians were not enthusiastic. But with diplomatic handling, Percy did not allow it to wreck the atmosphere of general accord.

By great good luck our visit to Norway coincided with the Norwegian national ski-jumping competition held every February on a steep hillside on the outskirts of Oslo. There, in open country an almost vertical jump had been constructed, with stands on either side for paying spectators equipped with their footmuffs, thermos flasks, and fur-lined rugs.

Jorgen had seen to it that we had the best seats, from where we watched the tall, grave figure of King Haakon arrive to the strains of the national anthem. Never having watched competitive ski-jumping before, I spent the time catching my breath as one intrepid young man after another leapt into the air from the little wooden platform at the top of the jump and became briefly airborne before landing not always as neatly as he had intended somewhere down the lower slope of the narrow, roped-off corridor. The weather was clear, and while the older people sat sedately in the stands, wrapped up in their rugs and furs, the brightly clad youth of Oslo, in their woolly caps and blue or red anoraks, milled around on the hard-packed snow at the foot of the jump buying hot dogs and hot drinks and shouting encouragement to the competitors.

A couple of days later, Percy, André, Einar, and I travelled by train with Jorgen to Jeilo, the Tulkenses having had to return to Brussels. As neither André nor Einar had brought his wife, nor had Jorgen, I was the only woman in the party. Jeilo was just south of the Arctic circle, a bleak and empty enough place to have been the location for the making of the film of Scott's ill-fated polar expedition, *The Worst Journey in the World*.

"The mountains are werry high," Jorgen said as we gazed out of the windows at the frozen, unfriendly landscape, comfortably insulated from the cold in the well-heated train. "Jeilo is a place for serious skiers, but the hotel has some not so difficult slopes." I said I had never learned to ski, much to my regret, and added rather unwisely that I would love to try but supposed I was too old to start.

Gallant as well as generous, Jorgen promptly disagreed. I was still a young woman; I would learn quickly, he was sure, especially as I was able to skate. The hotel had a resident ski instructor; he would book a lesson for me for the next morning. The ski shop would fit me up with boots and skiing clothes.

The hotel was snug and well appointed. We had an enjoyable party the first evening, much enlivened by the bottles of wine Jorgen kept producing like a conjuror from under the table. Afterwards there was dancing, and much to my surprise a total stranger sitting at a table on the opposite side of the room with another man came over to our table and in good English invited me to dance, despite the fact that I had four male companions.

He was a nice-looking fellow with an engaging smile. My four companions had shown no inclination to lead me on to the floor up till then. I looked at Jorgen for guidance. He nodded, so I took the floor with the bold, blond young Norwegian, who danced well, conversed politely, and, when he returned me to our table at the end of the dance, clicked his heels and thanked me with a courteous bow. After he had returned to his own table, Jorgen explained that in Norway it is perfectly in order for a stranger to ask a lady in another party to dance with him. For her to refuse if she is not already about to dance with someone else would be regarded as discourteous. The young man did not return to claim me again, but by that time the men at my table were not going to give him the opportunity.

André Poursin, Percy Muir, Nic Tulkens and Einar Grónolt Pedersen
at the Norwegian national ski-jumping competition.

The next morning, with the temperature subzero and the sky leaden, the prospect of a skiing lesson had less appeal. But the instructor had been booked and chickening out was not my way. Jorgen was taking Percy, André, and Einar up into the mountains to see the site of the Scott film, and I was directed to the ski shop to be fitted out for my ordeal.

To leave the warm hotel was like diving into a chest freezer. To my relief, all the experienced skiers were already black dots in the white distance, and there was no one around to watch my flounderings. The instructor fixed me up with skis and helped me put them on. Young, sunburned, and smiling, he wasted no time. A few encouraging words: "Vee ski togedder. It is not zo difficult . . ." All I had to do, he said, was to relax and keep my knees bent. Poised on the top of the nursery slopes, a firm arm around my shoulders, a voice murmuring in my ear, "Plees, yust relax . . . ," then suddenly, incredibly, I was actually skiing. Or rather, my instructor was carrying me along with him, holding me so that we moved smoothly in unison. Together we swooped down the slope with a satisfying shush of skis cutting a path in deep snow. It was

171

rather like waltzing in the old days with a really good dancer whom one followed automatically. I wanted to go on and on. Then we were back where we had started, and I was being told: "Now plees, you go by yourself."

Ah, that was a different proposition. My belief that I could stay upright with two long bits of wood strapped to my feet began to waver. The slope we had just skimmed down so easily looked steeper than I had thought. I flexed my knees, gripped my sticks, sucked in an icy gulp of air — and stayed where I was.

One thing about learning to ski in subzero temperatures is that it's a poor idea to stand still for long. "Now, plees," repeated the instructor, no doubt thoroughly bored with me. That time I went. Somehow I was still semi-vertical when I reached the bottom. It was where the ground rose again that I collapsed untidily, skis crossed, arms waving. The instructor had seen it all many times before. He stood there waiting for me to pull myself upright, clinging on to him like a drunk hanging on to a street lamp post.

"Now vee climb up and you must try again, plees."

Joy and frustration alternated. Sometimes the skis behaved themselves, pointing the way I wanted to go; sometimes they slithered and pointed all ways. "Yust a leetle more practice, and you will ski werry good," encouraged my instructor each time he rescued me, retrieved my lost sticks, pulled me up, dusted me down, and set me off once again, and again, until he'd earned his fee and I'd earned a hot drink.

After the men returned from their trip and we had lunched, our party with one accord retired to our bedrooms for a siesta. Percy had been less than enthusiastic about my sudden eagerness for learning to ski, being convinced that I would ruin the trip by breaking a leg or even my neck. Relieved to find me relatively unscathed after my morning session, he expressed a fervent hope that I was now satisfied and would take no further risks.

He was asleep when I crept out of the room, collected my skis, and made my way back to the nursery slopes. There was no one else in sight. After the revelry of the night before, most guests were sensibly enjoying a siesta in their rooms. It was ridiculous, but I felt committed to ski just once more, on my own, to prove to myself I could do it. Poised on the top of the beginner's slope, I felt as if I was standing on a diving board telling myself to jump.

The first run went well, better than I had expected. I stayed upright, confidence grew. A clumsy turn, but I still managed not to fall. It was on

172

the way back for another go that I came unstuck. One stick stuck in the ground and was at once out of range as I tried to grab it. I felt a muscle in one leg pull sharply, and I was floundering helplessly, skis in the air. My problem then was how to stand up without a tall, solid man to haul me to my feet. The answer my brain, spurred by the cold, proposed was simple enough. Remove those wretched pieces of wood, pick up my sticks, and with their help limp back to the hotel before I froze to death. At least, I told myself, there had been no audience.

At dinner that evening I boasted to André that while they were all snoozing, I had been out on the nursery slopes skiing on my own.

"Mais oui, Bar-ba-ra," he replied with a chuckle. "I had a fine view from my window. It is not so easy to rise when one falls, n'est-ce pas?"

A couple of days later we arrived in Bergen, where it was even colder than in Oslo, a damp, vicious cold that nipped my nose and earlobes. I quickly bought a pair of earmuffs and decided that they were rather becoming. There was nothing I could do about my nose except mop it frequently, or sniff. Mostly I did both.

The resident British Council representative took us under his wing, cheerfully breaking the news that the books from the Oslo exhibition had only just arrived and were still in their packing cases. If it was to be ready in time, Percy had better take charge of the setting up without delay. To this end I was promptly recruited for the fetching and carrying. Not that I objected; by then I had little enthusiasm for pottering about Bergen in clothes I had thought adequately warm but that were definitely not.

As we went up and down, to and from our hotel room, I tried to improve my tiny Norwegian vocabulary by reading the day's menu pinned up in the lift for the guests' inspection. It was possible to guess at some of the dishes, but what, for heaven's sake, was a "forlorn egg"? Both words were near enough to English, given the odd oblique, to be recognizable. Yet the dish was not.

Was it some curious Norwegian delicacy, I asked Mr. Thomas, the British Council's man in Bergen, an amusing Welshman who spoke the language fluently.

"You can order it quite safely," he said. "It's a single poached egg."

Most evenings, during our stay in Bergen, Mr. Thomas would join us in our bedroom, where he would regale us with a repertoire of mostly unprintable (at least for those days) Welsh stories while we drank the brandy he had smuggled into the hotel in his briefcase, together with three wine glasses. "It would be a shame indeed to drink this from tooth glasses," he rightly declared.

With some last-minute improvisation, the exhibition was set up and opened on time. Percy gave his accompanying lecture, and as in Oslo translation was unnecessary — the audience all understood English. We had arranged to stay on for a couple of days, and one of the academics who attended the lecture volunteered to show us the old town, where fourteenth-century Hanseatic League merchants had lived and prospered in fine gabled, timbered houses, many of which were still standing, beautifully preserved. Through the power of the league the ships of such merchants enjoyed special privileges in many European ports.

Our guide showed us the oak-panelled bedroom in one merchant's house, with a cupboard in the wall on one side of the bed that opened into the passage. It was through this aperture that the housemaid was expected to make up her master's bed, thus rendering it unnecessary for her to enter the room. As the merchant would frequently be there alone, attending to his business, while his wife remained with the children in the family home in the country, this device was, no doubt, her idea.

To have visited Bergen without making a pilgrimage to Greig's home beside the fjord would have been like going to Rome and not seeing St. Peter's. The fjord was hard frozen when we drove out to the modest house where the composer had lived and worked with a wide stretch of water at his doorstep. From the house we walked along a path to a simple wooden hut on the very edge of the fjord. The interior was bare of furniture save for a grand piano, a stool, and a plain wooden table. A wide window ran along one side, framing the view of a range of high, snow-clad mountains, the dark green of the pine trees, and the hard white of the frozen water.

Trolls? Mountain kings? Easy to believe they were somewhere not far away. Greig's music seemed to seep out of the walls of the little room. The insistent beat of his *Peer Gynt Suite* was hammering its rhythm in my head as we left.

I was constantly struck by the similarity of the Norwegians, at least the ones we encountered, to lowland Scots. They were hospitable and friendly, if a little guarded. We were invited into several homes, and always there were well-filled bookcases. At one dinner party, given for our benefit, I received a lesson in how to observe the Norwegian drink ritual on a formal occasion.

No one had warned me before the party that guests were supposed to restrain their thirst until their host raised his glass, made eye contact with everyone at the table, then gave them the go-ahead to drink, with a hearty cry of "skaal!" And that was not all. My neighbors at the table on

174

either side of me were waiting courteously to salute me personally, again with eye contact, raised glass, and the inevitable "skaal."

Oblivious of all this ritual, I had begun my dinner and taken a sip of my wine, when the learned professor sitting opposite caught my eye and raised his glass to me. My normal British response, a smile and a sip from a briefly raised glass, failed to satisfy him.

"No, no," he said severely. "That is not the way we do it in Norway. I will teach you. First we raise the glass. So! Then we look at each other," his eyes met and held mine solemnly and together we chorused "skaal!" "Then we drink." I took a mouthful of wine and was lowering my glass, but the lesson wasn't over. "Now you must look at me again, still with your glass raised," said the professor. "Good! We smile, and it is finished. We may lower our glasses and eat our food. Perhaps, we turn to greet another fellow guest as you and I have done. This is our custom."

It was a lesson I kept in mind. From time to time I would practice on surprised Scandinavians met in pubs in England by responding to their automatic cry of "skaal" in the way the professor had taught me. "Ah, so you've been in our country," they would say in pleased tones.

Much as I had enjoyed our visit to Scandinavia, I was glad to see the green and brown patchwork of the East Anglian countryside again. It was March, time to collect my usual batch of day-old chicks — eight yellow pullet chicks and their eight little golden-brown brothers, all peeping plaintively, downy to the touch as I popped them one by one into my do-it-yourself brooder, heated by a jumbo-size electric lightbulb.

As usual, no sooner had they settled down and begun to feed, than a pecking order developed. Fluffy and endearing they might look, but pushing and shoving for food was the way to survive; weaklings were soon trodden underfoot. Rearing chicks every spring had become part of my routine ever since 1940, time consuming though it was for the first six weeks. Hens were part of our establishment and fresh eggs for breakfast taken for granted.

April saw the ABA elect a woman president, the second in its history (the first, Miss Evelyn Banks, was president in 1932). In becoming president, Winnie Myers was following in her father's footsteps. She was forty-two and a successful dealer in autographs and documents, working from an upstairs shop in New Bond Street. A slight facial tic rather endearingly suggested a good-humored wink. There was usually a cigarette between her lips. Soft-spoken and easy-going, she must have felt somewhat daunted by the prospect of taking over the ABA presidency, but to have ducked her turn when it came round would not have been in character. Not for nothing was she a member of the Fawcett Society, an organization dedicated to equality for women.

Winnie and I had become good friends during the league conferences; all the same, I had not reckoned on being asked to reply to the toast to the lady guests at the ABA dinner that year (we were back to evening banquets once again), the thought of which terrified me. When I appealed to Percy to get me off the hook, suspecting that it was he who had got me on to it in the first place, he replied that it was Winnie's own idea to ask me, adding, "If you're not prepared to speak, you must tell her so yourself."

The toast, I learned, was to be proposed by the biographer Hartford Montgomery Hyde, whose biography of Mrs. Beeton had just been published. An Irishman with an even larger fund of anecdotes (which he told extremely well) than Percy, his *Who's Who* entry gave as his recreations the unlikely combination of hunting and music. During the war he had at one time held the job of assistant passport controller in New York, something of a bypath along the route to being a member of the Allied Commission for Austria when the war ended. He was witty and good company, and, although by no means good-looking, women took to him.

He was an occasional customer of ours, and once he turned up at our house with a wild and beautiful Irish girl. No sooner had they arrived, than she set off on a foraging expedition on her own (it was a time when rationing was tight), returning triumphantly with a dozen new-laid eggs. How had she done it? Simple! She had seen some hens in a cottage garden, knocked on the door, asked if they had any eggs to spare, and offered a better than market price.

To have to follow such a practiced performer as Montgomery Hyde with most of the trade there and many of our friends was tough. I knew Percy's views on after-dinner speeches; they could be clever, informative, or even an ego-trip, so long as they entertained. As someone who had once been part of a double act on the musical hall circuit, he never had any problem living up to such a dictum.

With much hard thinking, I contrived a speech of a sort and declaimed it in the bath out of earshot of the family. A few bits made me giggle, so they stayed in when I rewrote it. Another bath, more declaiming. I thought of going sick, a victim of a mysterious twenty-four-hour bug. But that was chickening out and letting Winnie down as well. At least I had an excuse for buying a new morale-boosting evening dress.

To the novice in public speaking, the first chuckle of amusement from an audience is a delicious, heartening sound. The adrenalin flows, suddenly the faces all around are friendly, ready to chuckle again. It's all right, it doesn't matter much what you say (but don't outstay your welcome) because they're on your side.

When I sat down to the sweet music of applause, Percy, who was a few places away, came along the table to give me an approving pat on the back. Had he been uneasy lest I let the side down? If so, he had not showed it.

Winnie had no doubt been as nervous as I was. As Madame President she had managed very creditably, her easy-going personality lending the occasion a good-humored informality. When it was all over, we congratulated each other with sighs of relief. Ahead of us both was Brussels, where Winnie would be leading the British delegation, and I would be endeavoring to behave with the decorum suitable to the president's consort. After that it looked as if our long-planned trip to the States might actually come about.

The Festival of Britain, opened in May 1951, was the exciting outcome of an idea first conceived in the grey days of 1948 to mark the centenary of the 1851 exhibition. It was an imaginative and courageous concept considering our parlous economic state at that time. Apart from its main purpose of boosting our tourist trade and exports, it was intended to boost our flagging morale and show the world that we were by no means a spent force.

While the transformation of London's south bank of the Thames was the focal point of the festival and the main attraction during the summer and early autumn, there were many regional festival events throughout the country. For anyone with ideas, merchandise, or services to sell, it was a bandwagon not to be missed.

In 1950 it had occurred to me that I too might scramble aboard. I had just delivered the last book of my current contract with Hurst and Blackett. Normally, I took a couple of months off from writing before beginning a new book. Instead, I decided to forego this break in order to write a suspense novel with a Festival of Britain background. A topical, right-up-to-the-minute "whodunit" should, I thought, catch the reviewers' eyes and prove a seller. Nor was I bound to offer it to Hurst and Blackett, since I had not then signed a new contract.

An idea for the story was already developing in my mind, and by denying myself my two-month break, I thought I could just about fit in a book in time for publication during the festival. My plot was a variation on an old theme, romance combined with some dirty work at a country house party. In my version there would be no body in the library.

Instead, the mystery would be the disappearance of a valuable family heirloom. To add glamour, the story was set in the family home of hard-up aristocrats hoping to make a bob or two from a mixed lot of foreign guests over in England for the festival.

A number of writers of detective novels and suspense stories have tried their hands at writing other kinds of fiction. My father had, for a time, written light romance under one name and "blood and thunders" (as they were then called) under a different pseudonym for the magazine serial market. To turn from the former to the latter was, after all, in the family tradition; except I would use the same pen name.

The wish was enough to sow the seed. It was early summer when I began *Festival at Froke* and therefore not too hard, even for a sluggard like me, to get out of bed a couple of hours before breakfast and settle to work while the family slept. In four months the book was finished.

"Hurst and Blackett aren't going to like you selling this book to another publisher," commented Innes Rose, my agent, when I gave him the typescript. "You know they are expecting you to sign a new contract."

My reply was that I would think about that when he'd found a publisher for the new book. I was pleased with it and still riding my usual wave of optimism after the delivery of a completed typescript. A few weeks later he wrote to say he had sold it to a subsidiary of John Murray's for their Gryphon Books imprint to appear in their 1951 spring list. Good news, I thought. My bright idea had come off.

It was too bad that J. B. Priestley should have had the same idea and chosen almost the same title for his new novel, *Festival at Farbridge*. This was a heavyweight of nearly six hundred pages, and it was published the same month as *Festival at Froke*, completely stealing my thunder. In the event, it proved to be one of his least successful novels. In his preface to his publisher, A. S. Frere, he wrote that he had returned "to the old comic tradition of story telling" and "it has been fun to do but by no means easy." The letter continued that if it will "light up a few evenings for you and Pat . . . and the boys in the office and on the road . . . I shall be satisfied." He added in parenthesis "But this doesn't mean I don't want any royalties, for I am collecting them for the Inland Revenue." There are one or two barbed references in this prefatory letter to the literary establishment, with whom he was clearly disgruntled.

The National Book League was brought into the festival program of events early on. Their brief was to mount a retrospective exhibition of British Books, illustrating the influence of the printed word on five centuries of British character and achievements, a challenging assignment

178

that, apart from being limited to the writings of the British, could be called a forerunner of the famous "Printing and the Mind of Man" exhibition held at Earls Court in 1963.

The overall design was of fourteen aisles, each one expressing "a particular facet of the British character," as stated in the NBL catalogue of the event. These were the Artist, the Bible, Children, the Poet, Science, Sport, and so on. Percy was asked to take charge of one section. I had expected him to choose Children; instead, he opted for Science — and found himself a member of a high-powered six-man panel, all, except himself, with a string of letters after their names. Four were fellows of the Royal Society. But as the introduction in the catalogue to the Science section points out, "The emphasis is on the book rather than on the scientist," and Percy was on the committee as a bookman with considerable knowledge and interest in scientific books. It was a field of collecting in which he had already a good deal of experience through his research during the building up of the Ian Fleming collection. Once again Ian's name would figure in the list of distinguished lenders.

One member of the panel was a customer of ours. This was Geoffrey Keynes, eminent surgeon and bibliophile, the brother of Maynard Keynes. A tall, handsome man who gave the impression that he had little time for those who did not share his interests, he and his wife lived not far from us in the village of Brinkley, near Cambridge, where, in his retirement, most of his time was spent working on his remarkable and extensive book collection, which was to be left to the Cambridge University Library. He would sometimes drive over to Takeley on a Saturday morning if Percy had something of interest to show him. But he was not a sociable man and seldom stayed longer than necessary to buy what he wanted. Some years after we had left Essex, I wrote to ask him if he would contribute to a small memorial volume in honor of Percy's eightieth birthday. His was the only refusal of the thirty-four friends and family members from whom I sought contributions.

If no woman's name appeared on the Science panel, my sex was well represented on some of the others, with Marghanita Laski and Kathleen Lines as joint advisers for the Children's Corner, Vita Sackville-West for the Countryman panel, and Rebecca West for the Free Citizen. In overall charge was John Hadfield, a charming man who got on well with everyone, best known as the editor of that attractive and long-running miscellany *The Saturday Book*.

Percy's loan of a Byron letter to the Lion and Unicorn pavilion at the South Bank exhibition brought us a joint invitation to the private view.

By good luck it was a fine summer's day. As we neared the exhibition our gaze was caught and held by the "Skylon" glinting in the sun like a fantastic elongated metal pencil pointed at both ends and stretching high into the sky, balanced above the exhibition site as if on air.

Once in the festival grounds, the dominant sound was the rush of cascading water as an enormous scoop tipped hundreds of gallons back and forth. My first and lasting impression was of gaiety and innovation. Gerald Barry, the festival director, had recruited a brilliant team of artists, architects, and industrial designers — Hugh Casson, Osbert Lancaster, Rowland Emett, John Piper, and Ruari McLean, to mention some of the most talented. Between them they had created a multifaceted exhibition, sparkling with wit and vitality. The message from this mixture of culture, fantasy, technology, inspired gadgetry, and fun was clear. We were telling the world (and reminding ourselves) that we were neither dull nor boring. Rather we had a culture we could be proud of, and at the same time we were bursting with talent and inventiveness. The dreary post-war period was over; it was time to do a bit of showing off. That, at least, was how I felt when we left at the end of a crowded day, with still much that we had had no time to see.

Next time I would bring the children and take them as well to the newly created Festival Gardens and the fun fair, reminiscent of the Tivoli Gardens in Copenhagen. Memorable among the many attractions that delighted them both was the Festival Clock, as full of surprises as a conjuror's box of tricks. Another was the Roland Emett mini-railway that carried visitors round and round the gardens, slowing down to a snail's pace but never actually stopping. Like the South Bank Festival Exhibition, it was all tremendous fun.

Chapter 21

"Why don't you two come over and pay us a visit?" our American friends kept urging us. "There's nothing we'd like more," we would answer truthfully. "We really will one of these days . . ."

There was only one thing that held us back: the cost of financing the trip. Percy had no intention of going without me (I couldn't disagree with that), and the price of the return fare for two people on the *Queen Mary* or the *Queen Elizabeth* was beyond our means, even if we travelled second class. We never considered flying. Most of the American dealers who visited us in Takeley in the fifties made the sea crossing, which normally took around five days and, given reasonable weather, was considered an agreeable and civilized way to travel.

It was Bill Jackson who solved the problem for us. "Why don't you let me fix up a lecture tour for you?" he suggested to Percy. "The fees will cover the cost of your passage; you'll get your travelling expenses paid while you're in the States, and there will be plenty of hospitality. Donald and Mary Hyde are sure to want to have you both to stay at Four Oaks Farm, and you'll be the guests of Harvard when you come to Cambridge. The fall will be the best time. All you have to do is to give me the dates that suit you, and I'll look after your itinerary."

It was an opportunity not to be missed. It meant being away from home for about a month, but Laurie would keep the business ticking over, David would be at his boarding school, and Helen could stay temporarily in her high school hostel, which catered for a small number of girls whose parents were abroad. As for my commitments, I would hurry on and finish the novel I had in hand and make my excuses to my various local committees, blaming Percy's need for me at his side for my absence from any meetings.

Visas for our visit were necessary. It was a time when McCarthyism was panicking Americans into a communist witch hunt, creating mistrust of all foreigners, especially those suspected of being left wing. To be a Liberal meant one was likely to be labelled "red," or at least pink. It was in this climate that one fine day Percy and I went along to the American Embassy in Grosvenor Square to be vetted for our visas.

We were interviewed separately, presumably so that there could be no colluding or prompting between us. The interviews took place in a large, multiwindowed room with a number of small tables where the applicant sat facing an interrogator. I had expected nothing more than a brief bureaucratic formality. A glance through my passport, a question or two about the purpose of my visit and its length, after which my visa would be stamped in.

Not so. My female interrogator's curiosity as to what I did and had done throughout my adult life was unnerving. And why on earth did she need to know where my grandparents were born, something I didn't even know (or care about) myself? It was tempting to say Timbuktu, but she didn't look as if she had much sense of humor. Besides, I was already under suspicion, having admitted that I wrote novels.

"I need to know the titles of all your books," she told me sternly. "Please repeat them to me."

I obeyed and watched her write down each title and the name of my publisher. "They're not all still in print supposing your embassy wants to buy them," I volunteered. "Perhaps they would like to buy a copy of my latest, so that you can read it? It's the one about the Festival of Britain — very topical," I added, getting in a plug. "And there are a couple of American characters." Unsmiling, she ignored this suggestion. I had a feeling I was not making a good impression. But after all, it was her job to be mistrustful. When the interview was over, we parted coldly. I can no longer remember how many questions I was asked; several seemed pointless. Reunited (Percy's interrogation had been even longer than mine), we joined a queue of disgruntled fellow Britons in order to have our fingerprints taken. This was done in a cubicle where a man sat at a table with a black pad in front of him, containing a substance that looked like boot polish. Seizing my hand, he pressed my thumb and forefinger down hard on the pad, then immediately transferred them to my visa form. A paper tissue was offered to wipe off the black stuff, and I was free to go. Our visas, we were told, would be sent to us in due course, as we devoutly hoped.

Not long after this, my publisher, Geoffrey Halliday, rang me.

"The American Embassy wants to know if you're a communist," he said, chuckling. "They seem to think *Black Market Green* might be subversive literature. I told them I had no idea what your politics were and suggested that they read the book to see what they made of it."

182

We decided not to tell our liberal-minded American friends about the fingerprinting. They were embarrassed enough over McCarthyism as it was. It would have been unkind to rub it in.

Presumably, my novels were not regarded as a bar to my entry to the United States, for our visas presently arrived. The next step was to book our passage. This Percy did on a French one-class boat, the *de Grasse*, quite a bit cheaper than either of the *Queen's* but slower, taking eight days for the crossing.

"The longer crossing will give us a rest before we begin the lecture tour, and we shall enjoy the French cooking," said Percy, the good sailor. Myself an indifferent sailor, I was not so sure.

We were leaving at the beginning of October, not long after the ILAB conference in Brussels, where Percy would be presiding. Most of the leftover business from Paris had already been sorted out by the executive committee. The work on the directory was finally done (the dictionary of terms was still lagging behind), the design for the emblem had been chosen, and the books were balanced. The one item on the conference agenda likely to prove controversial was the German application for membership.

There had already been some diplomatic lobbying. To the British, it seemed unreasonable to refuse the German application when the Italians and Austrians had already been admitted. The application was considerably helped by Helmuth Domizlaff being at the time president of the German association (which included fine arts auctioneers as well as antiquarian booksellers). Domizlaff was known to have been an anti-Nazi with a record of courageously helping a number of Jews to escape from Germany before and during the war.

Percy had first met Helmuth in the 1930s on his first visit to Munich. He had been given the name as someone with whom he might do business, but when he called at Domizlaff's apartment, there was never anyone there. Determined to track down his quarry, he sought help from another Munich book dealer.

"It is easy to find him," he was told. "There is a small *weinstube* not far from where he lives. I will write down the name for you. If you go there any morning between ten o'clock and midday, you will find Herr Domizlaff sitting at a table at the far end on the left. Opposite him will be his friend Herr —— and they will be playing chess."

Percy followed this advice, and there, just as he had been told, was Helmuth Domizlaff engaged in a game of chess. After this first meeting, Percy called on Helmuth whenever he came to Munich and was always

183

a welcome guest at the Domizlaffs' apartment near the Englische Gartens after Helmuth and Irma were married. It was a friendship easily renewed when they met again after the war.

Helmuth was a quiet man with a gentle, philosophical manner. He spoke excellent English and had built up a scholarly antiquarian business, which he ran from private premises. The atmosphere in the spacious, high-ceilinged room where he kept his stock was always calm and orderly. Percy invariably found books he was glad to buy (Helmuth specialized in early children's books), and business would be conducted in a leisurely way over coffee or a glass of wine. The outcome was always satisfactory to both parties.

We flew to Brussels a couple of days before the opening of the fourth league conference. Nic and Denise Tulkens were at the airport to welcome us; heavy rain was not allowed to dampen the warmth of our welcome. Dull and drowsy from the anti-travel-sickness pill I had taken, I had forgotten that we were arriving as VIPs, with press photographers focusing on our descent from the aircraft. Fellow passengers, scuttling for shelter under their umbrellas, shot us curious glances, no doubt wondering what kind of celebrities we were. Encumbered with a large bouquet, kissed on both cheeks, protected by Nic Tulkens' umbrella, I found myself lined up beside Percy at the entry to the arrival lounge for what is now known as a photo call.

We had arrived on the eve of the seventh anniversary of Belgium's liberation from the German occupation. This was celebrated on the Sunday in the beautiful, gilded, medieval Grand Place, beflagged for the occasion and crowded with sightseers. Thanks to the Tulkenses, Percy and I and other early conference arrivals had an excellent view from an upstairs window overlooking the Place. From this vantage point we watched the arrival of King Baudouin, who had recently replaced his father on the throne, King Leopold having been forced by civil disturbances to abdicate in favor of his eldest son. The royalist Tulkenses, both French-speaking and Catholic, were delighted to see their personable young king play his part in the ceremony.

After the arrival of the royal party and the triple rendering of the Belgian national anthem, came the diplomatic corps, identified by national flags on the bonnets of their large, chauffeur-driven limousines. The British ambassador, whom we were assured by the Tulkenses was very popular, was one of the last to arrive. It was something of an anticlimax to see him drive himself into the Place in a modest, by no means new, Austen. Could it really be our chap, we wondered. But yes, there was a neat little Union Jack fixed to the bonnet and the Belgium military band was playing "God Save the King." On the whole, we rather enjoyed this unpretentious appearance.

I found the ceremony moving. Disabled war veterans marched in the procession with their able-bodied comrades. Some, rather surprisingly, had pipes or cigarettes in their mouths. We were reminded of how much the Belgian people had suffered during the war. And in the early years following liberation there had been difficult times with great unrest at one time threatening to plunge the country into civil war. Now with a new king on the throne, Belgium was at last returning to stability and a growing prosperity.

No sooner was the procession over, than the stilt-walkers, who had been waiting their turn, took over the center of the Place with their traditional "Dance of the Tall People." It had rained steadily throughout the celebrations, but the dancers, in Flemish, Scandinavian, French, and British teams, grotesque and jolly in their colorful costumes, stumped about in their clumping dance routines, towering over the applauding spectators, damp but undeterred.

It was not so long since stilts had been in practical use in parts of the low countries, mostly by farmers needing to cross marshy or flooded land, so we were told. Namur, in particular, had been famous for its stilt-walkers. Stilt-racing was a popular local sport, and rivalry between neighboring towns was sometimes settled by stilt fights.

"Our hotel is luxurious and far too expensive for us," I wrote to my mother on the Hotel Metropole writing paper stacked in a rack on the mahogany desk in our bedroom (rather horrid actually, buff colored and red bordered), "but the Tulkenses *would* have us stay here. Outside our window there's an electric sign that keeps reminding us that Guinness is good for us." Apart from paying the hotel bill, we were barely allowed to put our hands in our pockets. As on our previous visits to Brussels, the Tulkenses overwhelmed us with hospitality. We were often in their elegant shop in Rue du Chêne, where the shelves gleamed with bound sets of French literature. Fine bindings and the beaux-arts were Nic's specialities, and the shop was right at the top end of the market.

Alas, it was only rarely that Percy could buy anything from Nic, much as he would have liked to, for we operated in a very different, less exalted market. Percy's determination that Elkin Mathews should never again be in hock to the bank meant that he bought only stock that could be paid for without recourse to borrowing. He was not looking for a pot of gold or a gamble. The spectacular books that brought £1,000 bids at auction were not for us. So our visits to the Rue du Chêne were mainly social and were understandingly accepted as such. But there were other bookshops in Brussels where Percy could buy profitably.

Original drawings by nineteenth-century artists was a field he had recently begun to cultivate, together with the books they had illustrated. These could sometimes be found relatively inexpensively in Belgium. Eventually, there would be a distillation of the knowledge acquired by dealing in these when he wrote *Victorian Illustrated Books*. But that was some years ahead. Not so far ahead he would travel to Brussels for some very special business.

Largely unscarred by the war, Brussels had an air of solid, middle-class prosperity; its citizens, mostly shortish and squarish in build, lacking the stylishness of the French, went stolidly about their business, seldom showing much animation. Food was taken seriously, and helpings were, to me, dauntingly generous. There were plenty of smart restaurants and smart shops with Parisian fashions. For a capital city, Brussels then seemed small after London and Paris. It was easy enough to explore its orderly thoroughfares on foot. Its many fine medieval buildings and churches were still undwarfed by the post-war developers' take-over bid of the skyline, with their steel and concrete many-windowed office towers. In the older parts of the city there were many narrow streets, winding uphill, where one came upon street markets. Not far from the Tulkenses' shop I found one market where they sold caged birds, including wild ones. This should have put me in a rage, but the song chorus was so pleasing that it failed to do so.

In Belgium one quickly became conscious of being in a country of two nationalities, the French-speaking Walloons and the Flemish, who sounded like the Dutch (the two languages are very similar), both peoples fiercely guarding their identity while pragmatically (or so it seemed to us) accepting the status quo. The conference program was in French, English, and Flemish. "Du Syndicat Belge de la Librarie Ancien et Moderne" became "Het Belgisch Syndicaat voor oudere en Moderne Boekhandel," and the association's committee was evenly balanced between Flemish and Walloons.

The Brussels conference went smoothly and with little controversy. Waiting in an anteroom while the German application for membership was debated, Helmuth Domizlaff need not have worried (he had been shaking with nervousness, he told us later), for Percy and André had seen to it that the ground was well prepared before a vote was taken. The result was eleven out of twelve associations in favor.

186

*André Poursin, Barbara Kaye, Laurence Gomme and
Menno Hertzberger at the 1951 ILAB Brussels conference.*

Percy Muir proposing a toast at the 1951 ILAB Brussels conference.

In the album of photographs sent to us by the Tulkenses when we returned home (treasured to this day), Percy is shown warmly welcoming a smiling Helmuth to the league. The photographer, an amusing émigré Russian, who was also a bookseller, had a sly sense of humor, which only became evident when the conference was over. A photo of the top table at a formal lunch on a hot day shows the men sticking it out in their jackets and ties, the women in formal dresses and hats, all politely conversing with their table companions — in my case, William Kundig. This is followed by a close-up taken at lower level, showing a line of feet, just visible beneath the drop of the white tablecloth. Some are half eased out of their shoes, some twisted in discomfort. Unaware of the camera's intrusive eye, I had secretly freed my toes from one constricting white shoe and partly from the other. The photographer had clearly found the picture irresistible.

William Kundig, apparently recovered from his illness in Paris, attended the conference with Juliette. As President of Honor, he was an ex officio member of the committee and had every intention of continuing to influence events. One of the early items on the agenda, added at his insistence, was for a code of practice to be drawn up, to which all the associations would be expected to adhere. It was a proposal with which Percy agreed but which he also knew would be bound to cause much controversy. With some adroit footwork he had the assembly agreeing to give the task of drawing up the code to an ad hoc committee, which would naturally include the President of Honor. The ball was thus left in Kundig's court, though, as it turned out, not for very long.

The Brussels conference left Percy in no doubt that everyone wanted him to continue in office for the following year. In Paris he had said that he was prepared to carry on only until someone could be found to replace him. At the end of the year no obvious candidate had appeared; to resign would have left the league without the leadership it needed. The year had gone well, the committee had carried out the tasks required of it, the trade directory was on sale and bringing in funds. Although the office of president took up time he could have given more profitably to his business as well as entailing much travelling, Percy, I knew, did not regret having taken it on. Nor did he dislike the prospect of continuing to keep the reins in his own hands for one more year. His commitment to all that the league stood for was still total. In this he knew he could count on André's support.

Loyal to the league from the start, Winnie Myers had attended every conference and made many friends among the delegates, establishing rapport with the Americans in particular. She was heading a strong

British delegation that included several past and future presidents who gave her good support, while Dudley Massey kept at her elbow to retrieve the presidential handbag that inevitably kept going astray. Easy-going though she was, Winnie was no fool and could be relied upon not to let the side down.

Our Belgian hosts showed us many treasures — their Memlings and Bruegels in Brussels and a fifteenth-century printing press at the Plantin Museum in Antwerp, which ran off charming mementos for us all. And there was a day's outing to Bruges with a visit to the St. John Hospital, where old ladies in white starched caps sat in the garden, little cushions on their laps, fingers swiftly manipulating their bobbins as they created dainty lace doilies and hankies for admiring tourists. We ended the day in an immaculately clean and tidy sixteenth-century farmyard, sitting on three-legged stools at long oak trestle tables, supping on home-cured bacon from wild boar, served on wooden platters by mob-capped wenches and men-servants who looked as if they had stepped out of a Brueghel painting. After the bacon and home-baked loaves, we filled up the crannies from bowls full of gooey rice pudding served with treacle, the meal washed down with home-brewed ale of surprising potency.

The evening was fine and warm, and we feasted against a background of painted hay wains. Soon the party became hilarious. While the guests flourished their wooden spoons, abandoning table manners, scooping the pudding into their mouths from the communal bowls, swigging down tankards of ale, our host and hostess, the owners of both the farm and a fine book collection, a handsome, smartly dressed couple, stood a little apart, enjoying the show they had organized in such elaborate detail. As for the Russian photographer, it was a splendid occasion for him to exercise his wit. Decorum might have gone for a burton, but it was certainly the high spot of the week's entertainment.

We returned to Takeley relieved that all had gone so well. There was less than a month before we set sail for the States and much still to be done. We had never been away for so long before. I was suffering from feelings of guilt for abandoning my family, my hens, cats, and hamster, not to mention the Parish Council and the Women's Institute, of which I had become president in 1950.

"You'll be able to forget about your village problems for the next six weeks," Percy said with some satisfaction as we packed. We were both greatly looking forward to our first visit to the States. Novices to the lecture circuit, we had hardly considered how much stamina we were going to need to sustain the tight schedule Bill Jackson had arranged for Percy.

Chapter 22

From the quay at Southampton, the brightly lit French liner, the *de Grasse*, looked impressive. In fact, she was elderly, slow and creaking in her joints. Salvaged by the French after being sunk by the British Navy off the African coast, she had been refitted and put back into service. According to a fellow passenger, it had all been rather a waste of time. She was out of date, no longer up to the job, and this was her last transatlantic crossing, after which she was due for the breaker's yard.

I wasn't too happy with this news and couldn't quite dismiss an uneasy feeling that the ill-fated *de Grasse* might take her revenge on the British passengers she was carrying, not that there were many of us aboard compared with the numbers of Americans returning from continental holidays and the French GI brides who had been home to display their offspring to Mama and Papa.

Wrapped in rugs, for it was October and cool, we lazed on deck while children rushed around playing shuffleboard and shouting "faites attention!" Transitory friendships formed, for us mostly with anglophile Americans on their way home from a stay in the UK. The ship did not boast a cinema; there was some desultory dancing in the evenings and a table-tennis tournament that called for some adjustment to one's game, especially by the third day out, when the *de Grasse* began to roll like a sailor on leave. That evening as I watched the nippy little Filipino crew making everything fast on deck, there was no doubt that a storm was blowing up.

"Teefoon, teefoon," said one cheerily, when I asked what we might expect. By then half the passengers were lying around doped with dramamine, the dining room half empty.

It was a pretty nasty storm that night, almost convincing me that my earlier unease (now physical as well) had been well founded, and that the ship was going to opt for a grave on the ocean floor rather than suffer the indignity of the breaker's yard.

"Well, if she does go down, at least we shall die together," Percy said at one point, as we clung to each other in the noisy darkness, listening to bangs and crashes. I doubt if the ship was in any real danger of foundering, but as she pitched and wallowed, sometimes nearly throwing us out of bed, I knew that I was neither brave nor philosophical enough to accept with equanimity the possibility of drowning, even with my spouse sharing the same fate.

By the morning the storm had abated somewhat, though the poor old *de Grasse* continued to roll in a turbulent sea and the passengers to grumble or stay below. Luckily, it had mercifully blown over the day we were due to arrive, and, as we came in sight of Long Island, the sky was clear. Passengers began gathering along the deck rails pointing to where, silver grey through the haze, Manhattan's famous skyline could be seen towering into the blue sky like a promised land, as it had been to so many travellers from Europe and the East.

As everyone told us then and later, there is no better introduction to New York City than to sail up the Hudson on a fine day to be confronted with the view of massed skyscrapers and thousands of windows glittering in the sun, with away to the left the massive green Statue of Liberty dominating the entrance to the dock. The scene was familiar because we had seen it so many times in American films, yet this did not lessen its almost overwhelming impact and the sense of national power and affluence it conveyed.

Almost as soon as we came alongside the quay, we spotted Laurence Gomme, a small, bespectacled figure in a grey suit, waiting to welcome us. We were to stay at his home in Westchester County, half an hour's journey into New York Central Station by commuter train. It would be our base while we were there.

"I'm afraid you'll have to queue for quite a while before you're through customs," Laurence said apologetically after greeting us warmly. "Too bad you haven't a babe or toddler with you. They give mothers with babes and small children priority."

Did we do the same with foreigners in Britain? I had no idea. Babyless, we took our place in a long queue of restive British and French nationals and were kept sternly in line by a hefty port official with the manner of a Nazi gauleiter. My inbuilt dislike of being ordered about strongly tempted me to disobey this character when he marched up and down the queue shouting at those who attempted to stray to "keep in line."

"For heaven's sake, don't," said Percy sensibly, "or we'll be here all day."

191

When the customs men finally reached us, we were asked to open all our four cases, each of which was thoroughly searched. Did we look like drug smugglers, gun runners, or maybe purveyors of communist literature, I wondered, when they let us go with a curt okay.

"Well, Percy's passport says 'bookseller' so maybe they were expecting to find an unexpurgated copy of *Ulysses*," said Laurence with a grin as we loaded our cases into the car. "Don't forget you came off a French ship."

An old friend of Laurence's, Russell Cook, had come along to take us for a lightning tour of the city in his middle-aged Ford ("a cook's tour, of course," he punned) before we set off for the Gomme home in Scarsdale. Russell and his wife, Clara, were staying with Laurence during our visit, invited, we gathered, to help him out in looking after us.

"Fifth Avenue first," said Russell and when we got there pulled up and made us get out and stand on the sidewalk, in order to gaze up with the expected gasp of amazement at the distant summit of the Empire State Building. We were then only a few blocks from Laurence's office on the fourth floor of the Rockefeller Center, with heaven knows how many floors above it.

"Where are the stairs?" I asked after Russell had parked, instinctively looking around for them as we headed for the elevator. "Don't worry, there are stairs," he said, "but it is an offense to use them." I thought this odd. It was odd, too, to see the notice: "To the Air Raid Shelter." In London we had long since stopped worrying about air raids.

No one had told me about the ice rink in front of the Rockefeller Center. To see skaters circling around in the open air right in the middle of the city surprised and delighted me. I would have lingered to watch them, envying their skill as they skimmed over the ice making their turns and figures so confidently. But I was urged back into the car.

"Come on, the tour's barely begun . . ."

So off we went along streets like caverns, shut in from the October sunshine by the tall buildings that lined them, to stare at other even more impressive monuments to trade and industry: the Woolworth Building, the Chrysler Building, the Bank of Manhattan, the eccentric Flat Iron Building, and then Wall Street, with an unflagging commentary from Russell. A son of the city, he was happy to show it to us. Laurence, born in England, was only a stepson and kept quiet.

To me New York was as I had expected from the movies and magazines, yet at the same time there was so much that was unexpected. Fifth Avenue, Park Avenue, the Waldorf Astoria, the yellow cabs — I recognized them all. But the movies had not (at that time) shown us the sleazy side of the city: streets with garbage piling up in the gutters just a stone's throw from Fifth Avenue (there was a garbage collector's strike on); the tawdriness of Broadway in daylight, hung about as it was with a spider's web of overhead wiring, tatty shops squeezed in between the theaters and movie houses; the ramshackle elevated railway, looking as if it had been designed by Heath Robinson.

"It's the only one left," said Russell. "They'll be tearing it down any time now."

Not only the elevated. I wondered to see so many streets had gaps like missing teeth where a building or block was being "torn down" to be replaced by one more steel and concrete tower. I was used to gaps in London — bomb sites still waiting for development permits, but these sites had nothing to do with bombs. Impressions crowded in on us; the sidewalks were wider than at home, the streetcars all single-deckers, the traffic zipping along straight-running streets moved faster, the George Washington suspension bridge was unexpectedly beautiful.

Fascinating though our cook's tour was, after eight days of sea and wide horizons, its effect soon became claustrophobic, and we were both glad when Russell headed the car out of the city for the wooded hills of Westchester County. There in a comfortable, modern detached house, one of a small residential settlement perched on a rocky hillside, Clare Cook, a comely, kind-hearted woman and a devoted wife, was waiting to make a fuss of us and feed us on home-cooked American fare.

After the meal the men were content to sit and talk, Clare to have a nap. But I, ever restless in new surroundings, wanted to be out, take a walk, stretch my legs before the last of the daylight was gone. It was a short descent from the house to the main highway. With a sense of adventure, I came down to the road and set off along the narrow footpath beside it, with the rockface of the hillside looming above me. Cars whizzed by; one or two slowed for the occupants to stare at me curiously. Now and then, as the cars speeded up again, I would see a head turn to look back at me. Twice I was offered a lift. Clearly, there was something about me that puzzled people.

After a while, tired of the highway and the swish-swish of its continuous traffic and failing to find a side turning that might lead me to fields and farmland, I gave up and made my way back to the Gomme home, where the men were sitting smoking and yarning just as I had left them.

Laurence hoped I had enjoyed my walk. "Not much," I told him.

193

"For one thing people in the cars that passed me stared at me as if I was a nutcase. It almost made me feel like one. Do I really look odd?"

Russell and Laurence roared with laughter. "You look fine," said Russell. "But you were on foot. No one here goes walking along the highway, not unless they've broken down, or they're hoping to hitch a lift. The folks going by in their autos didn't know what to make of you. Probably wondered if you were hoping to hitch. We don't expect to see a woman on her own walking for pleasure along our highways."

For the few days of our stay in Scarsdale we became commuters, travelling into New York City with Laurence on his usual train, crowded but not uncomfortably so. Grand Central Station did not make me sit down and cry; it made me sneeze. No sooner did we step down on to the platform than I began to sneeze and kept right on until we came up from the track to the station concourse. "How sensible," I recorded in my journal, "to run the trains on a lower level. Why had we not done the same in London when we built the main stations?" And how clean New York Central was and how bright and lively with its shops and quick food bars. And I thought with shame of our American customers who came by train to Takeley, doing so from grimy, gloomy, soot-festooned Liverpool Street.

While Percy visited Dave Randall at Scribner's and called on other colleagues, I went to see my literary agent's opposite number. I had had no luck with Putnam, once my father's American publisher, but I hadn't given up hope of selling the American rights of my festival novel. The agent, who had been sent a copy, quickly dashed my hopes.

"Sorry, but it won't sell over here. Waste of time to offer it. Too British." I said I'd been told that that was just what the American reader liked, and what, in the past, my father and some of his contemporaries had supplied.

"Maybe, but you're talking of before the war. Sure, there are British writers that sell well over here." He cited one or two: Agatha Christie, Marjorie Allingham. . . . His tone made it clear that he didn't see me as one of them. No harm in letting him see my next book, he said, as he saw me out. But he hardly sounded enthusiastic.

Percy was being dined at the Grolier Club that evening, and Laurence was going along with him. "You're not included, I'm afraid," said Percy. "It's a stag evening; no women."

"Never mind," said kind Russell Cook, "while Percy's with the boys, you and I'll go on the town, Barbara. We'll start with clam soup at Grand Central Station; there's no place where they make it better. Then I'll take you down Broadway."

194

I'd never eaten clams. We sat at a circular bar; big bowls of milky-white soup, thick as buttermilk were brought to us, with warm bread rolls. The soup tasted delicious, so long as one dodged some odd bits of rubber. Afterwards I didn't want anything else but the experience of seeing Broadway at night, with all those tags of twenties and thirties songs about "the Great White Way" running in my head.

Russell parked the car, and we walked, drawn like moths towards the flashing, ever-changing patterns of the lights of Broadway, I with my head back, dazzled by the colorful, relentless commercialism of the night sky, my gaze captured and held by the ingenuity of this advertisement and that, the enticing signs for the many different entertainments, the variety of the display, so far in advance of Piccadilly Circus and Shaftesbury Avenue. Poor old London, I thought, left behind after six years of black-out. Would we ever catch up?

Movies, theaters, cabaret shows, hotels that people strolled through as if they were shopping arcades — that was new to me then. Restaurants, street vendors, everyone busy selling something, the sidewalks crowded as people jostled and gawped. "C'mon, c'mon," said the lights. "Take your choice, have fun." But Russell and I had only come to stand and stare.

Percy gave his first lecture of the tour at the Pierpont Morgan Library to an invited audience. He had chosen to recount his experiences in Russia in 1928 when he was working for Dulau in Bond Street. He had gone with a colleague at the invitation of the Russians to visit some of the great private libraries taken over by the Soviets, with a view to making an offer for their contents. It had looked like the chance of a lifetime, but doing business with a committee of commissars proved impossible, and the two men returned empty-handed. As Percy recounted the trip, it made a splendid story, humorous and rueful, with some bibliographical tidbits to titillate an audience largely made up of book collectors. I had heard most of it before, but he told it so well that I never minded hearing it again. In any case, I enjoyed watching his audience hanging on his words and chuckling at the humor that always salted his talks and lectures.

The Morgan was the most magnificent and extensive of all the private libraries we saw. Yet it had been founded only in 1924, not long before Percy's aborted Russian visit. Had he been successful, some of the treasures he had vainly sought to buy might well have come to rest in one of the Morgan's fabulous special collections. Nevertheless, some additions had come to the library from Elkin Mathews now and then, and Fred Adams, then chief librarian, had been known to Percy for several years.

He was a friendly, likeable man who wore his considerable erudition lightly and had one of those youthful countenances that never seem to age. After he left the Morgan some years later he settled in France, from where he and Percy kept up a spasmodic correspondence.

To lecture at the Morgan was a splendid start for the tour. The "Russian Adventure" went down well — enjoyed by an audience probably accustomed to rather drier diet. As was to happen at all Percy's lectures, no sooner had he finished than a little congratulatory group gathered around him of those wishing to shake his hand and say their personal thanks. Invariably, it included one or two voluble adulatory ladies. Expensively dressed, fingers beringed, hair well lacquered, they were eager to add another visiting celebrity to the list of VIPs they had met, chatted with, shaken hands with. They just had to say how they had loved the talk and wouldn't he please tell them how many books he had written so that they could read them all . . .

Courtesy required that should the visiting celebrity have been so misguided as to bring his wife with him, some attention must be paid to her. I soon grew accustomed to smiling ladies coming up to introduce themselves and take a look at my interesting husband's choice of a wife. As an appendage to the speaker, I quickly realized that little was expected from me other than normal civility.

I did have one problem. If the lecture was in the afternoon, tea would be served when it ended. This was usually a token cup that in the American version of the Marriage at Canaan very soon metamorphosed into a dry martini, if not bourbon on the rocks, a drink unfamiliar to me until then. As I thought I knew what went into a dry martini, at the Morgan I settled for the safety of the known rather than risk the unknown.

My first mouthful from an unexpectedly large glass of a pale, ice-cold liquid, a squiggle of lemon dangling from its frosted side, took my breath away. From then on my startled tonsils were so stunned that they hardly noticed what was going past them. Dick Wormser, president of the ABAA and soon to replace Laurence Gomme on the league committee, had brought me the drink, and, as we stood chatting, I drank it down, when my glass was quickly refilled. Soon I was feeling remarkably carefree. We were being taken out to dinner, and Percy came over to tell me it was time to leave.

"Okay," I said happily, took a couple of steps, and found the floor was moving up and down as if we were back on the *de Grasse*. It was my first experience of the great American martini ("ninety percent gin," Laurence said later), and it was beginning to dawn on me that it was very different from the British version. I made it to the door somehow and with the help of Percy's steadying arm got out and into a taxi without falling over.

"If you can't take it, you'd better stick at one in future," said Percy, who had been sticking to bourbon, a drink I came to like, in moderation. The rest of that evening remains a blur.

The next lecture date was at the university library in Philadelphia. On our way, we stopped in Princeton to be shown the new university library there, not long since completed, large and impressive, its functional modernity made pleasing to the eye by finely grained wooden panelling.

From Princeton we caught, by the skin of our teeth, a train to Philadelphia. We were getting our breath back when the pullman car attendant, a colored man, came to check our tickets. As he did so, Percy made some remark that aroused his curiosity.

"Where you-all come from?" he asked in a soft southern accent. "Not American, is you?"

"No, we come from England," Percy said.

"That so? Well, you suttenly speak good English."

Much amused by this compliment, Percy couldn't resist repeating the incident to some of our American friends during the tour. From their politely concealed incredulity we gathered that it was one of those classic traveller's jokes often told but usually regarded as apocryphal.

On our arrival in Philadelphia it was something of a cultural shock to find that our taxicab driver had no idea where the university library was. Never having been to the city before, we were unable to direct him. It was a relief when he managed to find his way there with no more than forty-five cents on the meter. Percy's lecture was fixed for mid-afternoon. This allowed time for us to be taken out to lunch by the university librarian, who looked so boyish (this seemed to be a characteristic of American librarians) that at first I took him to be one of the students.

We had noticed that New Yorkers ate well; Philadelphians, we found, didn't lag behind. Accustomed as we were from the war years and ever since to miniscule helpings of butcher's meat, our stomachs recoiled from the enormous (to us) portions of beefsteak put before us. A pause for digestion after the meal would have been welcome, but this couldn't be allowed, since our youthful host believed he was in duty bound to drive us around William Penn's city for a lightning tour. I had taken overlong chewing my steak, so the poor young man had to rush us around at speed that allowed us little more than a glimpse at the historic buildings and fine architecture. But at least we would be able to say we had seen

Independence Hall, saluted the statue of William Penn, briefly paid our respects to the Friends' Meeting House and enjoyed a much too brief glance at the elegant Georgian frontages in Rittenhouse Square — before our schedule took us on to New Jersey.

Among the audience at Percy's lecture was the ebullient Edwin Wolf, associate for many years of the legendary Rosenbach brothers, a name as famous in the antiquarian book trade as Duveen was in pictures. The opportunity to meet the Rosenbach who was living in Philadelphia in his retirement was not to be missed. Nor was "the Doc," as he was known in the trade, loath to grant us an audience.

When his lecture was given and Percy could decently escape from his fans, Ed took charge and whisked us off in his car to the beautiful eighteenth-century house in Locust Street where Dr. Rosenbach lived. There we squeezed into a basketlike contraption that served as an elevator and rode up to the first floor, entering a long room with the dual role of dining room and aviary. Disturbed by our entry, tiny, brilliantly colored birds took wing, whirring around in their wire enclosure. Parrots, chained to their stands, cocked their heads and favored us with malevolent stares.

"The Doc likes birds," said Ed, "and he keeps terrapins on the roof. He's fond of terrapin stew."

I wondered about the parrots, but it appeared they were there purely as decoration. "He just likes to see them around," said Ed. We ascended one more floor to the library, where the Doc, a small stout man with a choleric complexion, was waiting to receive us. He was then an old man in poor health, diabetic and with a dicky heart. Hence the lift. In the room with him was his very pretty resident nurse wearing a becoming blue uniform.

We were greeted genially, our host being not at all averse to showing his fabulous collection to an English member of the antiquarian book trade. During a long life spent supplying wealthy collectors and important institutions with rare books and manuscripts, he had built up a collection of his own that few of his customers could have rivalled.

"Take a look," he invited expansively, gesturing at the surrounding dark wood shelving packed with books from floor to ceiling. "Ed'll take them down for you."

Ed, in the role of the Doc's impresario, was already going along the shelves.

"This is the Eliot Indian Bible," he said, passing a thick, well-used volume over to Percy, "the Natick, with the English dedication." The date was 1661.

"What's that you got there?" Rosenbach broke in. "An Indian Bible? Aw, c'mon, Ed, show 'em a rare book." The Eliot Bible at that time was worth around £3,000. Ed, accustomed to his boss's ways (he had joined the firm of Rosenbach as a young man in 1929), grinned and continued to pull out incunabula and other rarities guaranteed to make any bookseller's mouth water, while Rosenbach, his eyes twinkling with enjoyment, kept up a running commentary of how and where he had bought each one, his memory undimmed by age. Meanwhile, Ed kept our glasses filled.

Since leaving New York that morning, we had not had a moment to ourselves. We were going on to a dinner given in Percy's honor by the Philadelphian Antiquarian Booksellers Circle, and we still hadn't checked in at our hotel, but the Doc was in no hurry to lose his audience. The pretty nurse had stayed in the background as we talked, obviously with no interest in the books. Longing for a chance to freshen up before our next date, I caught her eye, and she led me to her own bathroom, right out of a glossy magazine.

"What a fabulous library," I said. "Do you have a lot of people coming to see it?"

"Sure. The doctor likes company. His books keep him happy," she said tolerantly, as a children's nurse might say of her little charges and their toys.

Eventually Ed got us away. We left with the impression that what with his library, his terrapins and aviary, his pretty nurse at his elbow, and Ed Wolf at hand when required, the doctor's declining years were not without their compensations.

Primed with the Rosenbach bourbon, we'd got our second wind by the time we arrived, somewhat tardily, at the Greenwich Village, the restaurant where the Antiquarian Booksellers Circle held its dinners and meetings. Most of the wives had come along as well, perhaps to keep me company. It was an informal, convivial evening, the first of several of the same kind given for us during the tour.

After the meal we were invited to sit in on the business meeting that followed. "Very different from the British equivalent," I recorded in my journal. "Plenty of jokey exchanges and wisecracks aimed at raising laughs rather than at making serious points. . . . Percy, asked to speak, put in a plug for the league."

It was rather like playing to the second house, following the formal, decorous fixture at the university.

Bill Jackson had booked us for two nights at the Hotel Bellevue

Stratford. In the event, we were to be there only one. Totally exhausted, we fell into bed that night, hardly aware of our surroundings. I had not even noticed that we were on the fifteenth floor. A peek out of the window when I got out of bed the next morning, and I drew back with a squeal of horror. I had never slept at such a height before.

"Well, just don't look down then," said Percy sensibly as I retreated, whimpering, back to bed. But even if I kept away from the window, that ghastly drop was still there, waiting for my body to go hurtling down to smash on the concrete below.

On our second day in Philadelphia we met, for the first time, two collectors who had become customers and then friends through correspondence. Before that there were courtesy calls to make at the bookshops of the colleagues we had dined with the night before. While Percy was in one of their shops, I went into a nearby Woolworth store to buy some postcards. The salesgirl who served me recognized my accent right away. "You sound like you're from England," she said. When I acknowledged that I was, she asked perfectly seriously if I happened to know her aunt. "She's called Rarbinson, Mrs. Mildred Rarbinson, but we kids always called her Rarbie." Politeness required a response, so I asked where the aunt lived.

"Last time we heard she wrote from a place called Durby. I thought maybe you might've run across her."

Another allegedly apocryphal story.

The first of the two customers we were due to meet was a passionate collector of Keats, and for some while Percy had been helping him to build up his collection. He could afford to pay for what he wanted and was clearly a young man to be encouraged.

"He lives with his parents on the thirtieth floor of a new apartment block," Percy said. "So if you think you can't face it, you had better say so before we get into the elevator."

I groaned inwardly but said I thought I could. Up we went in a steel cage smoothly enough, to a brand new apartment, glossy with fresh paint and near enough the top to make me feel that the building was gently swaying. There we were greeted by an elderly couple and a thin, shy young man keyed up to meet the understanding English bookseller and show off the treasures in his collections (Percy had sold him a number of Keats' letters), while I was invited to enjoy a bird's-eye view of Philadelphia from one of the city's tallest skyscrapers. Backing away from the wide windows framing a view of empty sky, I pleaded to be allowed to give all my attention to the Keats letters and first editions laid out for

Percy's benefit. When the visit ended, it was wonderful to be back on street level once again.

During our visit the young man's mother had shown me her fitted kitchen, gleaming with gadgetry. When I admired it, saying that it looked as if it had everything any woman could want, she shook her head. "I know, everyone says that. But I used to bake my own bread and make cakes before we moved here. Now there's no place to do it. It's a smart-looking kitchen," she said with a sigh, "but it wasn't meant for home baking, so I've given up." I didn't ask if the view from thirty stories compensated for no home baking. Somehow I doubt if it did.

Chapter 23

Our next date was with the artist Henry Pitz. Percy knew him as a book illustrator, although, as we soon discovered, his work was by no means confined to that field. For a couple of years or so he had been buying from our catalogues the work of the nineteenth-century book illustrators (Charles Keene in particular), and, as was apt to happen between Percy and customers he knew to be dedicated collectors, a correspondence developed that ranged wider than buying and selling. Like Percy, Henry was a letter writer who seldom left a page unfilled. When he learned that we would be in Philadelphia that October, though briefly, he was eager to meet Percy.

"Met Henry Pitz, the artist," I recorded in my journal, "a small, slight man, talkative and friendly. He took us to see an exhibition he had arranged at the Art Museum — contemporary work full of vitality if not greatly to my taste. Instant rapport between him and Percy. . . ."

After we'd had a meal together, Henry asked if we had anything more to do in the city. On hearing that there was nothing pressing and that in any case we were due in Somerville, New Jersey, the next day, he insisted we cancel our second night at the hotel (I needed little persuasion) and go back with him to his house at Plymouth Meeting. Whether or not his blonde, good-looking wife, Molly, had been warned to expect a couple of guests, I never knew, but she took our arrival in good part and welcomed us warmly to the hundred-year-old converted farmhouse in the still predominately rural part of Pennsylvania that had been settled by German immigrants during the nineteenth century.

"House beautifully warm," I noted approvingly in my diary. Warm bedrooms in private houses were a novelty for us. And it was a great relief to sleep only one story up.

We found ourselves much in sympathy with the Pitz family, for we had a lot in common: two children of the same ages, a love of books and classical music (Molly played more than one stringed instrument), and a

Four Oaks Farm, Somerville, New Jersey.

shared dislike of the rush and noise of urban life. Percy always enjoyed the company of artists, especially if they were genuine professionals (rather than dilettantes), and he instinctively recognized quality in crafts-manship, although totally without artistic ability himself. Specializing as he was then in the work of nineteenth- and twentieth-century book illustrators, meeting and getting to know Henry and Molly was one of the unexpected bonuses of the tour.

The next morning, refreshed by our overnight stay, we were driven by Henry to Trenton, through wooded, hilly country burnished with the golden browns and reds of the fall. There we were met by the Hydes' chauffeur, who drove us in considerable comfort to Four Oaks Farm, Somerville, where the library had become in just a few years the mecca of Boswell and Johnson addicts and bibliophiles galore.

We knew from hearsay that it would be a memorable visit. All the same, when George, the chauffeur, drew up before the front entrance with its classical columns supporting an arching pediment, I was some-what taken aback by the size and grandeur of what, from its name, had sounded like a comfortable farmhouse, stylishly modernized perhaps, but not particularly grand.

There was no need to be daunted by first impressions. When Donald Hyde came hurrying out to greet us, his genuine smile of pleasure was enough to banish any doubts as to whether we really were welcome.

Bill Jackson had assured us that the Hydes would be happy to put us up. He would be coming to dinner that evening, Donald told us, to see how we were making out.

In Mary Hyde's book, *Four Oaks Farm*, the two-volume story of the house and the development of the library, which she published in 1968, Gabriel Austin, the editor, writes that for Don "the chief purpose of Four Oaks was to serve, in Johnson's phrase, 'to keep friendship in constant repair'." Certainly it was a house where guests felt instantly at home, uninhibited by formality — as the Hydes had intended they should. At the time of our visit they had been living there for eleven years. They had built on a library for their extensive and increasing Boswell and Johnson collection, so that it appeared as an integral part of the house itself, which was comfortable and spacious and had the warm atmosphere of a house loved by its owners. Festive parties were held and some very special ones devoted to the famous doctor and his biographer.

The timing of our visit was unlucky, for a few days before we arrived, Mary had suffered a miscarriage and was still in hospital. It was typical that despite the disappointment, she was prepared to see us, and, when Donald drove us over to the hospital, she chatted to us cheerfully, looking very pretty, though fragile.

How were we standing the pace, Bill Jackson wanted to know when he turned up that evening. We had no complaints. We were in five-star accommodation in good company and with every comfort and temporarily off duty. We were not quite halfway through the tour, with seven more lectures to go.

That our fellow guests at dinner that evening were all book collectors went without saying. For Percy their names rang instant bells; for me not a tinkle. That they were anglophile to a man — and woman — equally went without saying. It would have been a help, though, if Percy had thought to brief me, because it was not until much later that I learned that the agreeable lawyer called Streeter who was my dinner partner that evening owned one of the finest collections of Americana in the States. By then I had no idea what we had talked about or whether I had shown my ignorance of his bibliophilic eminence.

The next morning the butler brought a breakfast of waffles, sausages, and coffee to our bedroom, a civilized arrangement, which allowed me to linger in bed in the company of Nancy Mitford's latest novel, *The Blessing*, just published and thoughtfully put by our bedside for light entertainment. Meanwhile, Percy, very sensibly, made the best of his time in the company of James Boswell and Dr. Johnson and Donald.

The Four Oaks Farm Library was unlike any I had ever visited. It was light and airy, light streaming in from a long bay window that looked out on to the garden; the large workmanlike desk and the filing cabinets were white; the bookshelves, running from floor to ceiling were of shining steel topped by a white cornice. The effect was spacious, cool, and elegant.

Much has been written about the library's treasures; many more were to be added as the Hydes' interests widened into other fields of literature. Scholars came to study texts; the redoubtable Dr. R. W. Chapman, whose eminence as a bibliophile was matched by his eccentricity, had not long preceded us. Oblivious (perhaps deliberately) of a polite request to guests to extinguish their cigarettes before entering the library, he had sat at Mary's desk chain-smoking while studying the priceless texts. Too daunted by his scholarship to remind him of the library rules as they worked together, the only solution she could think of (as she records in her book) was to pick up the half-smoked cigarettes strewn about on her desk and finish them off herself. "So by the end of that week-end there were two chain smokers in the house."

On our second day at Four Oaks Farm Donald drove us over to call on Lila Tyng, first wife of the publishing tycoon, Henry Luce, who welcomed us by running up a Union Jack on the flagpole at the entrance of her large and imposing mansion. Her name, I thought, suited our slim, smiling hostess, who lived surrounded by an enviable collection of objets d'art set against wallpaper, which, she told us, had been specially imported from China. At lunch we were waited on by a butler who could have been cast for James Barrie's Admirable Crichton. This was the second of a count of five butlers encountered on our tour.

Afterwards I saw my first polaroid camera deliver its instant (black-and-white) snaps, as Donald took photos of us in the garden with this new toy. Alas, in a year or two the pictures had faded away. But the happy memories of a brief but delightful visit remained undimmed.

From Somerville it was a four-hour train journey to Washington. Once again we were given VIP treatment. A chauffeur-driven car from the Library of Congress met our train and drove us to the Dodge Hotel, where I noted in my journal that "the maids change the bed linen each day but they don't bother with dusting or tidying. Service is slow. Breakfast comes with hot water in a jug to pour on teabags. Horrible." Why didn't we order coffee instead of tea?

The weather was warm, the government buildings an unrelenting white in the October sunshine, the Capitol immense, as if swelled up with self-importance. It was not until I found my way into a residential street of mellow Georgian houses not yet torn down in the name of progress that I felt I could learn to like Washington if ever we were to return.

We were there for two reasons: to visit the Library of Congress, where Percy was to have a talk "canned" for broadcasting at some future date, and for the lecture he was to give at the Folger Hall, a replica of the Globe Theater of Shakespeare's time. Before this we were taken on a tour of the "stacks," where, as in the British Library at the time, millions of books are preserved for posterity, of which the greater part of the population neither knows nor cares but pays the bill nevertheless.

I was curious to see how well the system worked. "I'll show you," said the librarian deputed to look after us. "Any book you would like to see?"

"How about *Daddy Long-Legs*?" It was the first title that came into my head, hardly an erudite choice. In a couple of minutes I had it in my hand, a modest cloth-bound book that I had once read, re-read, and loved in my romantic teens.

"Does anyone read it nowadays?" I asked.

"They certainly do. It's still in print."

This time I had been briefed about the Folger Library before we met the director. Not that Dr. Wright, a genial character, was going to leave us in any doubt as to the worldwide fame of its Shakespearean collection, or of the fact that it held the largest number of the original editions of the plays anywhere in the world, as well as innumerable reprints. Nor was the library concerned only with Shakespeare; it was equally strong, we were told, in the English Renaissance. As for the Elizabethan Age in general, if I had a mind to study it, the Folger, with some 100,000 books on the subject, was the place to come to write my thesis. And if I wanted some light relief, I could look through the quarter of a million old playbills.

As the Folger had been in existence less than thirty years, we had to agree with Dr. Wright that it had done pretty well. "Rogues and Vagabonds in the Book Trade" was the talk he had chosen from the three or four Percy had offered. Perhaps it was appropriate. As a rich foundation, the Folger could well have had experiences of such characters.

Too few hours later, for we had sat up drinking, listening to Dr. Wright's repertoire of anecdotes, all told deadpan, we dragged ourselves out of bed to catch a south-bound train on the Chesapeake-Ohio line. We were due that afternoon in Charlottesville, where Percy was to deliver a lecture

206

at the University of North Virginia. We would be shown around, dined, and would then catch the night train back to New York. At least we were travelling in comfort in a brand-new twenty-four-seat railcar, fitted with adjustable footrests, antiglare windows, and deep-cushioned upholstery. But it was going to be a long day. Lulled by the gliding, almost noiseless movement, we caught up on lost sleep.

"You'll be crossing the Mason-Dixon line," a New York friend had said, rather as if we would be travelling into a foreign country, when we had mentioned we were going to Charlottesville. I thought I knew what she meant. But when I looked out of the train window as we passed through wayside stations and saw separate waiting rooms, labelled "Non-Whites" and "Whites," it was a shock just the same. I felt a mixture of anger and depression.

Probably it would have been self-indulgent to have aired my social conscience while we were briefly "south of the Mason-Dixon line." Percy had caught my eye when we saw those labels, and I knew he felt as I did. But we were guests and had not come on a mission to change an established if repulsive way of life. To protest would have been only to embarrass our hosts and change nothing.

Seen through a veil of rain, the university building looked old and mellow. Designed by Thomas Jefferson, it was brick built, the color softened by time, and stood surrounded by green lawns. An unusual and attractive feature of the campus was a long red-brick wall. Instead of being supported by buttresses, it was built in a winding line and had stood (we were told) for some hundred years. It was called, I learned, a crinkle-crankle wall. Alas, it stands there no longer.

It was correctly assumed that we would want to visit Monticello, the beautiful home of Thomas Jefferson, that most admirable of American presidents. Preserved for posterity, it was as it had been in his lifetime, his many ingenious inventions — doors that opened as one approached, for example — still working. Another more eccentric device was the hammock suspended from the ceiling over the table in the dining room, which served as a bed for his manservant, who would haul himself up at night by means of pulleys. This unusual sleeping arrangement was, apparently, cheerfully accepted by the devoted servant.

Before Percy's lecture we were invited to dine with Dr. Fredson Bowers, a member of the faculty, and his wife, Nancy. The rain had cleared, and we sat on the terrace in the warm evening air eating the typical southern meal that Nancy had promised us — southern fried chicken followed by strawberry shortcake. Percy already knew Fred as a bibliographer. I should have known his wife, Nancy Hale, as a successful American novelist. Popular though she was in the States, I had never come across any of her books in England.

The Bowerses were good company; American academics, I had already discovered, far from being intellectually arrogant, were as human and friendly as everyone else we met. I had always been somewhat in awe of academics, my own education having been sparse and sporadic. Before meeting Percy, the nearest I had come to academic circles in England was when I was invited by hearty unacademic undergraduates to May balls in Cambridge.

The Bowerses were liberals, but book talk was more rewarding (and safer) than talking politics. Nancy, a buoyant, confident lady, discussed current fiction with me. She had written more novels than I had. "I'm terribly old," she said cheerfully but did not reveal the date of her birth. To my regret, I never did catch up with any of her novels.

Even in the short time that we were in the South, it was easy to be seduced by its soft-speaking charm, warm climate, and the gracious way of life for well-off whites. But Bill Jackson's schedule allowed for no loitering, and after Percy had delivered his "Rogues and Vagabonds" talk at the university, the Bowerses saw us off on the night train.

We slept fitfully ("a bumpy ride," I noted, "old rolling stock, noisy and jerky"), snatched a hurried breakfast at New York Central, and caught the next train to Scarsdale to dump our luggage, shower and change before returning to the city for yet another long day. Percy had various business calls to make. Lazaire, the editor of *Book Auction Records*, was giving us lunch, and in the evening Percy was being dined at the Grolier Club by Philip Duschnes, while Fanny and I went to *The Four Poster Bed*, an economically staged play with two characters only, then running to full houses. We were not yet flagging, but the pace was hotting up.

That day for the first time since I had left home, I felt homesick. It was October the 15th. After struggling along for twenty months with a majority of four, Clement Attlee, the prime minister, had called a general election. I longed to be back in Takeley, if only for the day, taking people to vote, showing the flag for the Liberals, and sitting up into the early hours to listen to the results coming through on the radio. The prediction was that it would be a close race, quite probably a hung parliament with the Liberals holding the balance, as I hoped.

Philip and Fanny Duschnes took it for granted that we would be eager to know the result as soon as possible and promised to take us to Times Square to watch the news coming through on the electric newspaper outside the Flat Iron Building. When the play ended, the two men came to the theater to collect Fanny and me and drive us to the square. When we got there, a small crowd had gathered. In England it would have been the early hours of the morning. We stood staring up as the lights spelled out the news items, impatient to see what, to us, was the most important news of all. Then it came: "Churchill victory almost certain," flashed the lights, bringing an "Ah . . ." of relief from our little group. Beaming with pleasure Phil and Fanny shook our hands.

Had Percy and I been at home, we should certainly have voted Liberal, although not for George Edinger, who had been replaced for Saffron Walden by Oliver Smedley. Oliver, whom we both liked, was another eccentric (would anyone else have stood?) who, although declaring himself a convinced Liberal, in the event, turned out to be a good deal more to the right than our sitting MP, Rab Butler.

Liberals though we were, we were not unhappy to see Winston Churchill once again prime minister. His defeat in 1945 had bewildered our American friends, looking, as it did, like ingratitude. Rather, it was disenchantment with Conservatism and all it had stood for in the past that made my generation and those too young to have voted before opt for change. After six years of a Labour government, the pendulum had swung back. "The Nanny State" had probably been good for us during the immediate post-war years, but the disciplines imposed had become irksome. All the same, it hadn't been a walk-over for the Conservatives; as we left the square, the electric newspaper was announcing: "Strong opposition front bench assured. . . ."

Percy's next lecture date was at Yale, and our host for the next three days would be Wilmarth ("Lefty") Lewis, a friend since he first began coming to London as a budding collector and sought advice from Percy's chief, Dr. Evans, in the days when Elkin Mathews had elegant premises in Mayfair.

"A young American who was consumed with zeal for the works of Horace Walpole was an object of interest to Evans," Lewis wrote in his autobiography, *Collector's Progress*. His book tells the story of how an obsessive collector went about gathering a collection of books, manuscripts, and miscellanea, by and about Horace Walpole, that became legendary in the world of book collecting and one of the most distinguished libraries ever centered around the life of an eighteenth-century writer.

It is also a most engaging book, reflecting Lefty's own engaging character. The copy he gave Percy was inscribed "To Percy, who has been a

209

companion in the Progress." The three of us were travelling to Connecticut together the day after our return to New York. We had arranged to meet on the platform at New York Central, and Percy and I were there in good time. As we stood waiting for Lefty to turn up, a group of youthful GIs were standing near us with a pile of luggage. I paid them little attention, and soon most of them had wandered off in search of refreshments. It was a warm day, and we were, as usual, short of sleep, hoping for a nap on the journey to Newhaven. Presently Lefty turned up in a rush just as the train came in, grabbed my suitcase, and shoved it on to the rack in the coach as I settled into my seat. I was a little surprised to see him carrying in three more bags and wondered sleepily why he had brought so much with him.

It was a somnolent journey; even Lefty, an eager conversationalist, lapsed into silence part of the way. On our arrival at Newhaven, he took charge, handing out the luggage through the window to a "red cap" (porter to us), that now extinct species still to be found on American stations in the 1950s. As he took the last piece down from the rack, a rather shabby canvas bag, Percy queried: "Is that yours, Lefty? Because it isn't ours."

"No, I thought it was yours," said Lefty, surprised. "Oh dear, well, I'd better just leave it there."

His chauffeur was waiting for us with the car; the red cap loaded the luggage into the boot, and off we went to Yale University, where Percy was to lunch with Professor Tinker, a distinguished elderly member of the faculty, of whom everyone seemed in awe. The invitation to lunch did not include the lecturer's wife. In the 1950s, Yale, like Harvard, was strictly a male preserve, so I was handed over to a pleasant young woman to be entertained at the "Ladies' Club."

Mercifully, there was a breathing space between luncheon and Percy's lecture. Lumbered with us during the interval, Jim Babb, the university librarian, invited us to his home. There, his sensible wife took one look at our pale, hollow-eyed faces and offered us her spare room for the rest of the afternoon. No gesture could have been more welcome. It was a pretty, chintzy room, but all we saw were the twin beds. Gratefully, we flung ourselves down (sex was far from our thoughts), and for two blessed hours we were allowed to sleep undisturbed.

It was a pity there was no opportunity for us to see more of the university. My general impression was of spaciousness, with none of the enclosed, monastic aspect of Oxford and Cambridge colleges. As for the remarkable and extensive library, I had no more than a glimpse of it in advance of Percy's lecture.

210

The home of Wilmarth "Lefty" Lewis, Farmington, Connecticut.

It was as well that we'd got our second wind, for the dinner party arranged for us that evening was a lively affair. Our host, Fritz Liebert, assistant keeper of the rare books, was a large, exuberant young man, who was to become Beinecke Librarian at Yale. The usual drinking session that we had learned to expect before we sat down to the meal was so prolonged that, apart from Lefty, the names of our fellow guests, selected no doubt for their bibliophilic track record, had mostly faded from my memory by the time I wrote up my journal. Some would certainly crop up in the years to come in the pages of that yet unborn journal, *The Book Collector*.

Thanks to this generous hospitality, we were feeling pretty carefree when Lefty decided that in fairness to his chauffeur it was time to set off for Farmington, where he lived in a gracious New England house, set in a formal English garden with lawns sweeping down to a replica of Horace Walpole's library at Strawberry Hill.

"You shall see it all tomorrow," Lefty promised us. "I do three different tours. There is one for people who are not bookish but feel they ought to please me by having a quick look at the library. I do a few tricks for them, such as showing them a painting that once hung in the dining room at Strawberry Hill in 1750, or telling them the name of the head housemaid employed by Walpole in 1760. They enjoy that, and it doesn't take long. The second tour is for people like you, Barbara. You shall see some of his books and manuscripts, and I'll throw in one or two of the tricks if they amuse you. As for Percy, he is going to get the whole works. I'm warning you now, Percy, it will take all day."

211

We had been given the ground-floor guest suite, a large twin bedroom with bathroom, shower, and a door leading into the garden. Adjoining was a dressing room with a bed in case Percy wished to desert me, or I him, something that rarely happened during our long married life.

As Lefty was outlining the next day's program the chauffeur brought in the luggage and departed. "Well, I'll wish you goodnight," said Lefty, ambling to the door.

"Hadn't you better take your bags with you?" Percy said, pointing to two cheap canvas grips on the floor beside our own three suitcases. "Aren't those yours?"

"No, they certainly aren't mine!" Lefty said, gazing at them doubtfully. "I supposed they belonged to you and Barbara when I put them on the train. Are you *sure* they aren't yours?"

"Positive," I said. *"These* three are ours. I remember you putting those two and one other on the rack just before the train went."

"Oh dear, oh dear, how dreadful!" Lefty sat down on one of the beds, looking at us in comic dismay. "I do remember thinking you had rather a lot of luggage. And there was the one we left on the train. Oh dear. . . ." He began to giggle. "I wonder what's happened to that?"

I zipped open one bag. Inside was a toilet holdall, shaving gear, a cotton singlet, a pair of Y-fronts, and a photograph of a young woman in a cheap metal frame.

"Well, I did think some of your luggage looked a bit like GIs' bags," Lefty said, as we recalled the group of young soldiers who had been standing on the platform shortly before the train came in. "Poor boys, they must be in a state. And I could have been caught for stealing their bags, couldn't I? A luggage thief, that's what I am. How shocking!" He looked from one to the other of us, his face crinkling into a rueful grin. "What *are* we to do with the booty?" On top of Fritz Liebert's generous hospitality, it was all too much. In a moment all three of us had collapsed on to the beds in helpless laughter.

"I think I'd better take away the evidence," Lefty said presently, mopping his eyes. "I'll see you both in the morning, if I'm not arrested first." Still chortling, he went off to his own quarters, a misappropriated GI bag in either hand.

In the morning a butler came soft-footed into our bedroom with a breakfast tray. Mr. Lewis, he said, wished us to know that he had telephoned the railway authorities, and the two canvas bags had been put on a train back to New York.

We had, in fact, slept well with untroubled consciences and were ready for whatever program Lefty had arranged for us. Once again we had a host whose wife was temporarily absent. "Annie Burr is in Washington, being Madame Connecticut," he told us. We never did gather what this actually entailed, but it sounded impressive. It was disappointing not to meet her, and, alas, I never did, for when Lefty came to see us in Takeley, she had already died of cancer.

Lefty was a lovable man, small of stature, sociable, a great talker. The collecting bug had bitten him early. Philately and coins had eventually led him into collecting books and very soon to concentrating on Horace Walpole. By the time Dr. A. W. Evans, his mentor at Elkin Mathews, retired, the habit of turning up regularly at the Conduit Street premises (at first it had been Cork Street) in search of nuggets of Walpoleana was established. From then on whenever he came to London, Lefty would be among the select few to be invited to stay on for sherry and book talk after the shop closed. Thus, a friendship between him and Percy grew and was kept warm by regular correspondence during the war years.

Before my introduction to Horace Walpole, Lefty told me he had an invitation for me. "There is to be a football game this afternoon in the Yale Bowl, which is Yale's term for its football ground. It is supposed to be an important match. I know nothing about such matters, but if you think you would like to join the spectators, some friends of mine have said they will be happy to include you in their party. As for Percy, he has already assured me that he prefers to spend his time in the company of his namesake." (Percy's middle name was Horace.)

As I hesitated, wondering if by accepting I would be written off as a hopeless philistine, Lefty said with a twinkle, "Don't worry, you are not going to escape seeing the library. If you really would like to watch this football game, there is plenty of time for both."

As it turned out, Lefty's middle-brow tour proved so entertaining that I tore myself away with regret when the party of football aficionados came to collect me, Jim Babb and his wife among them.

"Well, Barbara, I hope you have an enjoyable time," said Lefty courteously as he and Percy came to see me off. Then added wickedly: "But personally I think you're *mad!*"

As I had never seen a game of American football, I felt it was an experience I ought not to miss, a view endorsed by the jolly party I had joined, who assured me that I was going to find it thrilling. When we came to the ground, the "Bowl" turned out to be a gigantic amphitheater. All around, parties were picnicking beside their cars, beating off the wasps whose spies had brought news of a supply of tasty food. Vendors of souvenirs, flags, and cans of drink were shouting their wares, including "weenies," a traditional snack at American football matches, I was told. My unfamiliarity with this mini form of hot dog caused surprise. Surely we had them in England? Not so far, I admitted, wondering why not, since we had long been eating the full-sized variety.

No, we didn't have majorettes, either — well, not so far as I knew. But no doubt we would. And then as we took our low-level seats, looking down on to the green pitch, there appeared a lot of pretty young girls dressed in frogged jackets and mini skirts, tight across neat little bottoms, who began limbering up for their half-time performance. They made, I thought, a pleasing contrast to the enormous, helmetted young men about to do battle in the Bowl.

When the game began, any likeness to either British soccer or British rugger seemed to me purely accidental, with the players hurling themselves at their opponents more like Roman gladiators than our footballers. They all looked about eight feet tall and were clad in some sort of armor. As bodies piled on to bodies in a melée of beefy entangled limbs, I held my breath in alarm, half expecting to see a flattened corpse at the bottom of the pile when play was halted. Instead, they all leapt up unscathed.

All the same, from time to time one or more had clearly had enough and could be seen limping off the field to be immediately replaced by another courageous warrior who had been awaiting his turn on the sidelines. As a spectacle, the game certainly had its moments. When it ended, I was no wiser as to the niceties of play, and I have no recollection of whether or not Yale triumphed.

"I hope you are not too exhausted by your experience," said Lefty when I was returned to Farmington. "Percy has shown remarkable endurance. Tomorrow, being Sunday, you shall both have a day of rest."

He was as good as his word. Bliss it was to laze the day away, reading, talking, eating delicious meals prepared by unseen hands and served by the Lewises' Jeeves-like butler. First Yale, then Harvard was the schedule, with Bill meeting us in Boston ("You'll find it very English," everyone kept telling us) and showing us the city. The journey through wooded scenery was delightful, New England at its most colorful, splashed with the golds, browns, and crimsons of the fall. We were more than halfway through the tour.

"You'll be staying in Dana Palmer House as guests of the university," Bill said, as he drove us to Cambridge. "And as we've got C. S. Roberts arriving tomorrow, you'll be in good company." Roberts, a Cambridge academic and bibliophile, was also on a lecture tour. A modest man who was fond of describing himself as a middle-brow book collector, he had been somewhat overwhelmed (as he told us later) to hear himself paged on his arrival at Idlewild and to learn that the wealthy owner of a famous private library who was to be his first host had sent a private plane to fly him to where he was to stay. This certainly put Mr. Roberts into a class above us.

Guests of Harvard University though we were, we saw little of the campus during the five days we stayed in Cambridge, Massachusetts. Percy's center of interest was the Houghton Library of Rare Books and Manuscripts. If the tour had one high point for him, it was being able to spend a morning there in the company of its chief librarian, our good friend Bill Jackson. For years cables from the Houghton, coming to us over the telephone via our local Post Office (during war-time) had rung sweetly in Percy's ears, helping to keep us in the black. To enter its portals with Bill as his escort was as exciting as for a jewel merchant to be invited into a maharajah's palace.

As for me, I was delighted to be taken to Concord by Dolly Jackson, Bill's kind and devoted wife, who had visited us more than once in Takeley and was a great favorite with my children. The frame houses were so clean and white, the unfenced lawns so green and trim; it looked almost too orderly and peaceful for real human beings to be living there. In Louisa Alcott's house the clocks had stopped sometime in the 1860s. Meg, Amy, Beth, and Jo were still around somewhere; one could almost hear their voices, the swish of their skirts.

A little deprecatingly Dolly wondered if I would like to visit the historic site "where the embattled farmers stood. . . ."

I thought it was the least I could do, so there we stood, Dolly and I in amity, reading the words on the Concord Memorial, monument to the fallen in the fight for independence that told of the firing of "a shot heard round the world." So many shots since then, all over the world. Ruefully we exchanged smiles.

Earlier we had been taken to see Paul Revere's house in Boston, old, small, narrow; it looked as if it was being elbowed out of existence by the big twentieth-century buildings that towered over it on either side. There had been much else to see, the Back Bay, fine architecture, and, inevitably, George Goodspeed's bookshop, but the one picture my mind retained after we left was of the little timbered house of Paul Revere, a folk hero, who, though he lived to be a prosperous silver and gold merchant and the Grand Master of the city Masonic Order, is remembered only for one patriotic exploit.

215

Throughout our stay in Cambridge, the Jacksons took care of us from breakfast until bedtime. We saw Emerson's house, two other libraries, and were even taken to a performance of *Macbeth*. Each night we would fall into an alcohol-induced sleep. If there were bibliophiles in Massachusetts who couldn't put away generous amounts of bourbon or dry martinis, we never met them. On the eve of our departure, Bill told us that there was no staff to serve breakfast at Dana Palmer House on Saturday mornings, so we must make do with the students' cafeteria.

The thought of being the sole woman in this male enclave unnerved me, but Bill was reassuring. "Don't worry. The students are all in the middle of exams this week," he said. "I doubt if they'll notice you're there."

The following morning as I walked sedately into the canteen beside Percy, it looked as if he was right. All around were silent young men munching cereal with textbooks propped up beside their plates. No one even bothered to glance in our direction as we made our way to an empty table. The canteen catered for hearty, youthful appetites. The breakfast cereals in individual packs were large enough, in my eyes, to satisfy a whole family. As I helped myself to fruit juice and a cereal packet, I saw that I was not the only female in the room. Two colored women were dispensing coffee and dishing out hot food.

While we ate our breakfast, students came and went, heavy-eyed with pre-exam gloom; few were talking. After eating a third of my cereal, I went to the food counter for coffee, carrying my cereal packet with me.

"There's more than half left," I said as quietly as I could, proffering the packet to one of the colored women. "It was rather too much for me."

She glanced at me without interest and snapped: "Puttit in th' trash bin."

I peered into a large plastic-lined tub standing beside the counter, full of a disgusting mixture of part-eaten food, bits of cardboard, cigarette stubs, and other detritus. All this was clearly going into an incinerator rather than to feed livestock. At home, where war-time disciplines still prevailed, institutions were expected to separate the edible from the inedible for the benefit of the swill man who came daily to collect pig or chicken food.

Was I really meant to junk good food? My social conscience rose up in revolt at such waste. "But there's such a lot left. Look! . . ." I waved the packet at her. "Surely it could be used? . . ."

"*Put it in the trash bin!*" The exasperated bellow broke through pre-

216

occupation with the last-minute absorption of learning. Heads were raised all around the room to see what the fuss was about. Suddenly I had become the center of attention. Mortified, I hastily dropped the rejected packet into the bin and slunk back to our table — without my cup of coffee.

Later that same day we took an afternoon flight to Buffalo. The weather was suddenly much colder. Heavy rain threatened to turn into sleet. As we came into land at the airport, snowflakes like tiny pieces of iridescent cotton wool whirled around in the runway lights.

"I'm afraid we've got a fifty-mile drive to Pavillion," said Dr. Charles Abbott, who had come to meet us. "That's where we live. But don't worry, we're used to snow in Buffalo."

We were used to snow in Essex, but to be driven in the dark through a snowstorm to an unfamiliar destination and by a stranger, albeit a friendly one, was a disorienting experience. If we did hit a drift, there was a spade in the back, Dr. Abbott assured us. But Percy and I were not dressed for snowdrifts.

In the event, the spade was not needed, and we arrived safely to find a roaring log fire awaiting us in the Abbotts' book-lined living room. Once again we were being welcomed into the family circle by people we had never met before and instantly made to feel at home. Like the Pitzes, the Abbotts lived in an old farmhouse, homely but comfortable. This time there was neither butler nor cook; there were young people in the house, and the big kitchen was where everyone gathered to chat and drink coffee. It was just like home.

"You'll be staying with my wife's Aunt Mildred tomorrow night," said Charles. "She lives in a large house and has plenty of money. She likes giving hospitality to visiting VIPs, so you'll be well looked after. We're very fond of her, but, as you will find, she's a lady who expects to have her own way."

The next day, after an enjoyable and all too brief stay, we returned to Buffalo through roads banked high with ice-encrusted snow. It was no weather to trudge around slushy streets exploring the city. Instead we gladly accepted Charles' invitation to make ourselves at home in the welcoming warmth of the Lockwood Library, where not a few of the collection of author's manuscripts and "work sheets" had come from Elkin Mathews.

The Lockwood Collection really did get down to basics and for that reason had a special appeal to me as a writer. There were the first scribbled thoughts of authors and poets, many of them contemporary, plus second thoughts, jottings, heavily corrected manuscripts, and drafts of work later abandoned or entirely rewritten by such writers as Wilfred Owen, Siegfried Sassoon (who had sought Percy's advice before sending MSS to the Lockwood), T. S. Eliot, and many others. As I pored over them, totally absorbed, Percy said teasingly: "If Charles writes to ask you for some of your own work-sheets, you'll know you've arrived."

I thought of all my rough drafts that had gone in the waste-paper basket, the notebooks of jottings I'd thrown away, the pages of screwed-up abandoned typescript. Had I thrown away literary treasures that might have proved exciting to future researchers? I thought it highly unlikely.

At Aunt Mildred's we were again to enjoy American gracious living. Aunt Mildred was elderly, bright-eyed and unbowed. She was also witty and well informed. In England she would surely have been made a dame. She was a widow and lived alone but was not without one or two faithful beaux (as I fancy she might have called them) on call to help with the entertainment of VIPs. Her house was in the best residential quarter of Buffalo, large and well staffed. In her self-appointed role of hostess to the visiting VIPs she was able to amuse current guests with stories of the behavior of those who had preceded them, not all of whom had come up to her expectations.

"Of course, they all insist on going to see Niagara Falls," she said, as we sat drinking tea in her drawing room. "I tell them that it's a long and tedious journey with nothing to see on the way, and not worth the trouble of going. But they will go just the same."

I was no exception. I had arrived eager to see the falls; she must have seen my face fall.

"I expect *you* want to go, too, don't you?" she said, looking at me somewhat accusingly. "Well, I suppose it can be arranged, so long as there isn't any more snow. My chauffeur can drive you part of the way, then you'll have to take a bus. I can't spare him to drive you all the way there and back." She turned to Percy. "What about you, Mr. Muir? Do you also want to see the falls?"

Percy hastily disclaimed any such desire, thus putting himself into the class of sensible guests. Aunt Mildred then gave me a stern warning. I was not on any account to cross over to the Canadian side, where the falls were more spectacular. "If you do, you will have no trouble in entering Canada, but you will not be allowed to re-enter this country without a re-entry permit, which you probably do not have. I warned Sir Malcolm Sargeant not to cross into Canada, but he didn't listen and in consequence nearly missed conducting his concert here when the immigration people refused to let him through. It caused a lot of bother, and he had to be rescued by the British Consul, who only got him to the concert hall in the nick of time. Sir Malcolm seemed to think regulations would not apply to someone like him."

Percy was giving his lecture the next day in the early evening. We were then due to catch the night train to Chicago. The sky was leaden when I set off for Niagara in Aunt Mildred's car, after she had given us lunch at her club, the Garrick, a woman's club very different from its London namesake, full of smartly dressed young matrons all on first-name terms, but, I noted, not as far as Aunt Mildred was concerned.

The previous evening there had been a formal dinner party given by Aunt Mildred, the table set with heavy old-fashioned silver on a white damask cloth and lit by a silver candelabra. Two scholarly elderly gentlemen had been invited as our fellow guests for Percy's benefit. Aunt Mildred was a lively hostess and her gentlemen friends courteously attentive. Again I felt that we had slipped back fifty years.

"Some opposition from P. to my going to the Falls," I recorded in my diary. This was an understatement. Percy, always inclined to train fever, like Somerset Maugham's Ashenden, was convinced I would run into some kind of disaster and fail to turn up in time for the train.

Fortunately, there had been no further falls of snow. Aunt Mildred's chauffeur was glum as we sped along the drab exit from the city, the slush dirtying the Cadillac's shiny chassis. His instructions were to take me no farther than the place where a through bus left for Niagara, and he was not going to exceed them. The journey on a half-empty bus through flat, featureless country masked by snow was indeed boring. As we neared the town, I was unprepared for the heavy industrialization on the outskirts. Naively, I had expected to see a picturesque little township, making its living from the tourists who came to gaze at its famous natural phenomenon. Instead, the town was making the best of Nature's prodigality with free power to turn the wheels of industry. Souvenir shops there were in plenty, but no one was expecting much tourist trade in November.

There were icicles hanging like daggers from the roof of the building that I was told on the bus was the place from which to view the falls. No one got off with me. On the door was a notice to say that an elevator was available to take sightseers down to the viewing platform.

"Ten cents," said the man selling the tickets. There was only one other taker, an elderly woman who acknowledged my comradely smile ("We're both a bit crazy, aren't we?") with a curt nod. Down we went with the elevator all to ourselves, the roar of the falls increasing in volume as we descended. When we stepped out on to the viewing platform, it was like standing in front of a giant bath tap turned full on by God. Staring at so much water crashing down from such a height into the pool below stunned the senses.

I can't remember how long we stood there, huddling in our overcoats, icy spray stinging our faces, growing colder, yet hypnotized by such a spectacle of overwhelming natural forces. The elderly woman turned away first, muttering that it was too cold to stay long. In a minute or so I followed her. The great volume of water would keep on falling; there was nothing more to see unless I was going to risk crossing over to Canada to gaze at the even more impressive Horseshoe Falls and have to be igno-miniously rescued by the British Consul. But would anyone bother about the likes of me?

I had no problem with the return journey to Buffalo, despite having to change buses and find my way to Aunt Mildred's house on foot. Which no doubt served me right. Thankful to be back in the warmth and thaw out my frozen toes, I found that Percy and our hostess had been getting along famously in my absence. Ladies of advanced years with literary leanings usually took to Percy and were not averse to a tête-à-tête with a handsome man. When we left to catch our train, we were both invited to come again, but I couldn't help feeling that the invitation was aimed at Percy, the sen-sible guest, who did not wish to be taken to Niagara Falls in November.

It was snowing again when we boarded the train for our all-night journey. We had booked a "roomette," a novelty to us both, and we found it wonderfully compact. Everything anyone could possibly need for the night was provided: wc, washbasin, wardrobe, shoe cupboard, electric shaving socket, drinking water. Everything, that is, except fresh air. The snag was that by mistake we had been given a single. We squeezed into the bed too tired to make a fuss. Percy dropped off first but was soon awake, alternately sweating and shivering with an attack of claustropho-bia, complaining that he had awoken feeling as if he was in his coffin. I began to feel we were both buried in the same box. In the end, desperate for sleep, we left the door open into the corridor. The sleeping car stew-ard presently came along to protest against such eccentric behavior (did we want to be robbed, or maybe murdered?), but we paid no attention and finally slept fitfully until daylight.

Heavy snow on the track made us two hours late in arriving in Chicago, where Jim Wells of the Newberry Library and his assistant and girlfriend, Mabel, were patiently waiting to meet us. This was one more occasion

220

when friendship established through correspondence paid dividends. The shared interest of the two men was the Newberry's History of Printing Collection. Printing, especially twentieth-century developments of the craft, had interested Percy ever since he had become friendly with Francis Meynell at the time when Francis set up the Nonesuch Press. It was a subject in which he was increasingly dealing, in particular with the small private presses of the 1920s and 1930s.

Neither the lateness of the train nor the earliness of the hour put a damper on our welcome. "You're going to be staying at the Union League Club," Jim told us, "and the president of the club is giving a dinner party for you this evening. . . ." Mabel then chipped in to warn me that I'd be in a male stronghold, where women were admitted only on sufferance. "They make us use a special elevator and we're not allowed to step out of it except on the floors allocated to both sexes. So you'll be sleeping on the sixteenth — that's one of the mixed floors."

"Suppose I forget and get out on the wrong floor," I hazarded, secretly tempted to try it.

"You'll probably give some old man heart failure," said Jim. "Haven't you got men's clubs back home with the same ideas about admitting women?"

I had to admit that we had. Percy's club, the Bath, in St. James' made women guests enter through a side door as if they were being smuggled in. But I hadn't expected men to get away with such chauvinism in the States. As I had always been in sympathy with the Democrats and would have liked to see Adlai Stevenson become president, I was disconcerted to learn that for the next three days we were to be staying in one of the staunchest Republican strongholds of the Midwest.

The building where Jim and Mabel left us with a cheery "See you later" was sufficiently imposing. In the lobby I began to feel as out of place as if I had strayed alone through the portals of the Athenaeum Club in London. I said as much to Percy after we had been directed to a male-and-female elevator and whizzed nonstop to the sixteenth floor. Unbothered by his surroundings, especially as they were costing us nothing, he couldn't see why I was fussing.

We were staying at the Union League Club because Stanley Pargellis, the director of the Newberry Library, where Percy was to lecture, was an old friend of the club's president and had fixed up the hospitality for us. Pargellis was a big man, a larger-than-life character. His manner was as expansive as his girth, his handshake left one's fingers tingling. One's surname was jettisoned within minutes of an introduction (by no means

221

normal social usage then), backs were slapped, or an arm went around one's shoulders. Drinks were ordered in doubles. And that, we were soon to discover, was Stanley's problem.

As it turned out, I was taken care of on our first evening by Stanley Pargellis' attractive and charming wife, Betty, and Mrs. Mather, wife of the Union Club president, Percy having been carried off by Pargellis to a stag dinner at the Chicago Round Table, where he was to "sing for his supper" with an after-dinner speech. Thankfully, no such requirement was made of the visiting lecturer's wife.

I have little recollection of how the evening went. Undoubtedly, the ladies (there were two or three others) were agreeable, the hospitality generous, and politics not on the agenda. The menu, according to my journal, was lavish. "Too large and rich a meal for me," I recorded rue-fully. The tour was beginning to take its toll on us both. I had a nasty suspicion that I needed to see a doctor, but in view of the cost of medical treatment in the States, I knew I must wait until we got home.

"Good morning, it's eight o'clock, and the temperature is 10 degrees," chirped a room-service female voice giving us a call the next morning. Despite my doubtful state of health and the bitter cold, I enjoyed Chicago. There was a vitality and vigor about the city and in the people we met that was stimulating. Wherever one looked, a new building was going up to out-rival those around it. Marshall Fields was enormous, the largest store I had ever been in, a consumer's city of infinite choice. A pity that all I needed to buy was a pair of plastic overshoes to wear on the slushy sidewalks.

With Percy spending much of his time at the Newberry Library, I roamed the city on my own, taking a streetcar to the Art Institute to see an enchanting exhibition of miniature rooms, furnished to scale accord-ing to period, then going on to see the magnificent collection of French Impressionists, more of their work gathered together than I had ever seen in France. Another day, Betty Pargellis took me to the Museum of Science and Industry to have fun turning knobs and switches to set models in motion, while Percy was taken to lunch by a colleague at a restaurant in the city center. Afterwards, needing to visit the men's room, he found it was located on the top floor of the building. He was washing his hands when a man doing the same at the adjoining wash basin addressed him: "Say, you're a stranger here, aren't you?"

"Yes, I'm from England," Percy answered.

"Thought as much. Well, just come over to the window with me, and I'll show you something worth seeing."

222

Amused by the unexpected invitation, Percy went over to the window, where the man began pointing out the various landmarks to be seen in and around the city: the Wrigley Building; the Marshall Fields stores; the harbor where a couple of destroyers were moored on Lake Michigan; and many other sights and buildings of interest.

"So, friend," said the proud Chicagoan, bringing the aerial tour to an end with a flourish. "When you get back home, you'll be able to tell your folks you've seen the finest view from any can in America."

There was not time to visit more than a few Chicago booksellers, but we made a point of calling at Hamill & Barker's premises on Michigan Avenue, a fine long street that I unwisely tackled on foot and had my earlobes nipped by the icy wind that blows off the lake in wintertime. It was as cold if not colder than it had been in Bergen, and I hadn't thought to bring earmuffs.

Margery Barker and Doll Hamill, as dealers in antiquarian books, were an unusual partnership in a male-dominated trade. They specialized in English literature, made buying trips to Britain, and had not long since paid a visit to us in Takeley. They were members of the ABAA and Doll was already playing an active part in the work of the association and was in line for the presidency.

Not only had they been good customers of Elkin Mathews during the war years, they had been one of the several generous firms who sent us those never-to-be-forgotten food parcels full of the goodies impossible to buy in the UK. Since the war, they had continued to be among our best US customers. This satisfactory relationship would one day turn sour, for an unexplained reason that Percy was never able to fathom.

At some early stage in her life, Doll, perhaps a plain child, must have abandoned any ideas of femininity or glamour and settled for friendly relationships with the opposite sex and no more. A warm-hearted, sensible woman with a quick sense of humor, she was the front one of the partnership, and it was she who invited us back to her home in Hisdale County for the weekend after we left the Union League Club. It was then very much a rural neighborhood, and the rest and peace of the countryside were welcome. But Doll told us that already the developers were sniffing out likely housing sites.

Margery Barker, the senior partner, was a very different character from Doll, cool, clever, and wary of relationships, keeping in the background, where, we suspected, she took most of the decisions. They were knowledgeable and successful dealers, and it was a partnership that worked well, lasting many years until the older woman's death. In later years

223

Margery Barker was less and less to be seen by those who visited the premises. But by then we had, to our regret, lost contact with both women.

On our last evening in Chicago there was a dinner given by the city Book Chapter, and I found myself to my surprise sitting next to Kenneth Maggs of Maggs Brothers in London, the world of antiquarian books being a relatively small one. Like us, Kenneth had been doing the rounds and trying to keep the intake of food and alcohol within bounds.

"How d'ya like our Midwest voices?" the uninhibited wife of one of the booksellers shouted to me across the table towards the end of the evening, her own sounding like someone raking a gravel path. "Fine!" I said not altogether truthfully. But it was a jolly farewell party, more my style than the Union League Club, and anyway I had rather taken to the Midwest.

The weather had cleared when we took a flight back to New York. We had found that it was cheaper to fly than go by rail and pay for sleepers. "Our speed 300 mph," I recorded in my journal. "Some forty passengers aboard. We cruised at nineteen hundred feet. Aircraft vibrated strongly but not a bumpy flight. It took about three hours. . . ." At least we didn't have to suffer the claustrophobia of a roomette.

We were staying in Scarsdale with kind, ever hospitable Laurence for our last two days in the States, using his office in Rockefeller Center as our base in New York. Percy had some last-minute business calls to make; I was dashing around shopping for presents at Macy's and Altman (the latter I found not unlike Harrods), plus nylon shirts, nylon lingerie and tights, mostly unobtainable in England and in any case far cheaper in the States. As I hurried back and forth from Laurence's office, I discovered why the elevator attendant who was usually on duty during the daytime was always so glum when I bade him good morning and smiled and thanked him each time he operated the doors for my comings and goings. His response, "You're welcome," had become increasingly grudging until finally he turned on me and told me unsmilingly, "You've no need to thank me, lady. I'm just doing my job."

It was then I noticed that no one else ever thanked him. To have to respond so frequently to my unnecessary expression of gratitude had bored the poor man almost to tears. The words "thank you," I was learning, were not much used in New York.

Percy's last speaking engagement was at a dinner given us by the ABAA's New York chapter. Dick Wormser was host with his wife, Carola, tall and good looking, an antiquarian bookseller in her own right. Several

224

other American colleagues we had come to know through the league were also present. I would have enjoyed it more if a speech had not been required from me as well as from Percy. Worse still, I was expected to follow his polished, professional performance. As I explained at the outset, he was the speaker in the family; I was merely the talker. But this didn't get me off the hook. As always, there was a plentiful supply of "dutch courage," my savior on such occasions, as well as a memory dimmer, so that happily I seldom could recall much of what I had said.

We had been warned that we must attend the tax office in person before leaving the States in order to declare Percy's dollar earnings. Without the necessary permit we would not, we were told by Bill, be allowed to embark. Percy, always suspicious of bureaucracy, reacted to the prospect with gloomy forebodings, foreseeing many questions and much form-filling, with at the worst a delay, causing us to miss our passage the following day. Much to our relief, his fears turned out to be groundless. The interview was only a brief formality, the permit for us to leave the USA being issued with the minimum of fuss. The tax people couldn't have cared less about our politics, so long as we didn't owe them any money.

On a dull November morning Laurence, kind as ever, drove us to the dock to board the *Ile de France*. Again, after some hesitation, we had opted for a French boat, although we could have sailed on the *Queen Mary*, which was leaving at more or less the same time. We were both suffering from a hangover from the party the night before. When we went down to our cabin, a long way down it seemed, we looked around in dismay. It was little bigger than the boxlike roomette we had shared on the Chicago-Buffalo train and not anything like as well appointed. There was no porthole, and the temperature was tropical. It was the sort of accommodation that uncaring French employers might regard as okay for their servants.

We had booked tourist class in order that Percy could show a small profit on the trip. Taking me along had not come cheap, although I liked to think I had made some small contribution in providing wifely comfort and some necessary work as laundress along the way. The *Ile de France* had been cracked up to us as a luxury ship, the French answer to the *Queen Mary*. But luxury, it appeared, was not part of the deal for tourist class.

"I'm not going to be fobbed off with a miserable little box like this," Percy said determinedly. "You wait here and don't unpack anything, while I go along and talk to the purser."

He was back sooner than I had expected, looking a lot more cheerful.

225

"It's all right, we're moving. This ship is only half full, so we're being given a larger cabin one deck up. The purser is a pleasant young Frenchman. He asked me why we had chosen to travel on the *Ile* rather than the *Queen Mary*, so I told him we're francophiles. But I said that the main reason we chose his ship was because we knew the food would be better. After that he stood up, bowed, congratulated me on my French, and said he would at once give orders for us to be transferred to a better cabin. And we're invited to have a drink with him in the first-class bar this evening."

Our new cabin was certainly a considerable improvement. It was tastefully furnished, there was a porthole that opened (fresh air instead of recycled), and it was equipped with two wash basins, a shower, and a loo. It was, in fact, designed for three, but the third bed was moved out to give us more space.

Our evening drink with the young purser, who treated Percy with rather touching deference, became a regular date. In company with most Frenchmen, he had no wish to talk in any language other than his own if there was no need to do so. This suited Percy, who always enjoyed exercising his talents as a linguist in both French and German, and would have added Italian, given the opportunity to learn that delightful language. Apart from our sessions with the purser, he had little other opportunity for French conversation. Nearly all our fellow passengers were Americans, mostly young and eager with Paris as their Mecca, the Paris of Hemingway and Elliot Paul, which, I suspected, they would find no longer existed.

For much of the time we sailed in a grey blanket of fog, with the dismal hooting of the foghorn punctuating the empty hours. It was too damp to stay on deck; the rich food palled on our already jaded palettes, and so did the old movies showing in the cinema. To lower the book one was reading was an invitation to hear someone's life story or, even less entertaining, the grisly details of traumatic suffering from some major surgery. Here and there a bridge four sat brooding silently over their cards. A few fitness fanatics, wrapped in raincoats, would be seen each morning marching doggedly round the decks. As the ship ploughed on through the empty grey Atlantic, an uneasy feeling of being in limbo prevailed. Few, if any of us, were in the mood for shipboard jollity.

As always on a sea voyage, passengers coalesced into small groups that stayed together for want of better company. We became friendly with a young American artist who was coming to London to show his work in a gallery and through him with some art students on their way to study in Paris. A young British "Bobby" who had been to stay with war-time friends in New Jersey and on the strength of this brief visit was trying to make up his mind whether to emigrate to the States with his wife and baby became another shipboard friend with whom we, or rather I (Percy mostly preferred the company of a book) sat talking and speculating about passengers in other groups, as one gossips about the new neighbors down the road.

We could have done without the company of Albert, who, for some reason, joined our group. He was a little fellow, olive-skinned with sloe eyes that slid away when he talked to you. It was hard to guess his age; he had the creased look of someone who had been around for quite a time. He was travelling alone and leechlike was ready to attach himself to anyone prepared to listen to the hard-luck stories spewed out from wet, pink lips that smiled ingratiatingly when he got his victim cornered. Like a persistent fly, no sooner had some unfortunate passenger shaken him off than he would be buzzing around again, with more unbelievable tales of ill-treatment, persecution, and misfortune.

Before long, his victims — I was one of them — began comparing notes, finding that the stories varied according to his audience. Most of the time he carried around a guitar, which he would occasionally take up on deck when the weather briefly cleared and stand sadly strumming, humming a melancholy tune half under his breath. His accent was American, his appearance Latin. The good-humored young American who shared his cabin said he was a poor little mixed-up guy who was going to bum his way through France to Milan, playing his guitar along the way, and when he got there audition to join the orchestra at La Scala, where, he said, his uncle was one of the violinists.

"Well, that's his story, anyway," said his cabin mate.

The crossing took six days. On the evening of the fifth day, one of the art students who had been an unwilling listener to Albert's woeful tales happened on him standing alone on deck holding on to the rails with one hand and gripping his guitar in the other. Before the young man had time to speak, Albert, uttering a loud cry of despair, swung the guitar up into the air and hurled it into the sea.

Half expecting to see him jump in after it, the startled spectator ran forward to grab him. But this proved unnecessary. Crying to the heavens that he would never play again, Albert turned from the rails, rushed away, and disappeared below.

The news of this drama on deck soon spread among those of us who had received Albert's confidences. Two hours later he had not reappeared,

227

and no one remembered having seen him around. Nor had he put in an appearance in the dining saloon for the evening meal. His cabin mate went to look for him and returned to report that he was neither in the cabin nor taking a shower. It began to look as if he had, after all, made the fatal leap. Reproaching ourselves for not having been more sympathetic, we began a renewed search for him.

He was not on deck, nor was he in the cinema. None of the crew remembered seeing him. Then, in the last place we thought to look, we found him in the small, tucked-away chapel. He was on his knees at the altar rails, muttering prayers.

I didn't see him again, for the next morning passengers for the UK were required to vacate their cabins at 5:30 AM and be ready to be taken ashore in a tender. The company owning the *Ile de France* was not going to have her put in at Plymouth for the convenience of a dozen or so *anglais*. Back on British soil, the sleepy customs men were hardly bothering about us either, waving me through with my American booty of nylon goods, Christmas presents, and a bottle of bourbon.

"Special coach added to the London train for *Ile de France* passengers," I noted in my journal. "Shockingly old and decrepit but at least we were served a pretty good lunch." It was good to be home again; grand to be welcomed back by the children (none of my usual forebodings had been realized) and my beloved half-siamese cat. There was much catching up to be done, Christmas was not far off, and I was itching to get back to the book I had begun not long before we left.

"Now be sensible and don't put off going to see the doctor because of Christmas," said Percy.

Chapter 24

"I am in a small ward with four beds," I wrote to my mother from Bishop's Stortford hospital. "Dainty chintz curtains hang around each green-painted iron bedstead. With the curtains drawn back on either side, when my fellow patients sit up in bed, it's as if they were framed in little shrines.

"The wide windows are uncurtained. Wicker armchairs are grouped around the radiant gas fire, where those of us who are convalescent sit in dressing-gowns chatting and cozily toasting our toes.

"We are like a sisterhood, doing our best to be kind to each other. We listen to recitals of symptoms and operations with uneasy curiosity. We're all in awe of the brisk, competent ward sister who has a crocodile smile. At night a skinny black nurse comes on duty. She wears a red cardigan over her uniform. If I sit up and crane my head forward I can just see her seated beside the slow-burning stove in the larger adjoining ward. In the dimmed light when we are all supposed to be sleeping she looks like a presiding she-devil."

I was not an interesting case. Some minor gynecological surgery had dealt with my health problem; in a week I would be discharged just in time for Christmas. When the surgeon who had operated on me came to the ward the following day, he merely glanced at me from the doorway, remarked to the sister, "Ah yes, the lady novelist" (I had brought my portable typewriter with me) and not bothered to come to my bedside. We had not had to pay him — his fee had come from the National Health Service — so he was giving me no more of his valuable time. I was not, it seemed, going to die of cancer of the womb after all.

A couple of days after my operation a land girl (as she called herself) was brought into my ward with a broken leg. She was a large women of forty plus, unmarried, with the manner and voice of a master of fox hounds. She cursed her plight loudly (a five-bar-gate had fallen on her leg) but was surprisingly cheerful. Once her leg was set, she intended to

229

be back at work in no time, she told us. Meantime, she was going to catch up on some reading.

We watched her unpack her suitcase, taking from it first some farm journals and a book on cattle breeding. Then came a photograph in a silver frame, which she stood on her locker. A boyfriend, perhaps, we thought, although it seemed unlikely. Curiosity aroused, her fellow patients craned forward to peer at the photo. What we saw was a fine Herefordshire bull with a prize label hanging around his great, thick neck, his eyes gazing benignly into the camera. Aware of the ward's interest, she held up the portrait for us all to see. "Splendid fellow, isn't he?" she said proudly. "Had to bring him along to keep me company. Never go anywhere without him."

One morning in February I switched on the radio (we had not yet bought a television set) and heard the shock announcement of the death of the king. We had all been aware that he was a sick man, but as far as the general public was concerned, his death was unexpected. The monarchy stood high in public esteem, the king had won the people's affection and respect during the war years, and the whole country sorrowed for the death of a good man and a conscientious sovereign.

Shortly after our return from the States Percy had suffered the loss of a dear friend with the death of the musicologist Paul Hirsch. Paul was the kindest and most gentle of men and, despite his considerable scholarship, modest and unassuming. Many fellow countrymen who had fled Germany in less fortunate circumstances had reason to be grateful to Paul and his wife, Olga. We had come to know the family well during the war years and their home at 10 Adams Road had long been a welcoming port of call for us whenever we had reason to go to Cambridge. Nevertheless, Percy was surprised as well as touched to learn that it had been Paul's wish that he should be one of the two friends to give an address at his funeral. This took place in the Chapel of St. Giles' Cemetery.

"Rarely can it be said of a man that he had no enemies, but that one may truthfully say of Paul Hirsch . . . ," Percy said, speaking from his heart. "His mind was a sort of thematic catalogue of all the works of the great composers. . . ." Percy's address and that of the other old friend, Laurence Picken, were published by the Hirsch family for the mourners and for friends unable to attend the funeral under the title *Two Addresses Delivered at the Funeral of Paul Hirsch on 28th November, 1951*. Only a small number of copies of this eight-page tribute were printed. In recent years it has become something of a collector's item.

Later Percy had the melancholy task of helping Olga to dispose of what remained of Paul's library of fine books, the greater part of which had already been acquired by the Houghton Library at Harvard during Paul's lifetime. Strong character that she was, Olga bore her grief stoically, continuing to live at 10 Adams Road and busying herself directing the lives of her children and grandchildren and building up a collection of decorative endpapers, or as she preferred to call them, since many were from German books, *bunt papiers*. With her usual industry and thoroughness, she had enough specimens before long to publish an authoritative volume on the subject.

When I congratulated her on her book, which was a beautifully illustrated production, her deprecatory reply was typical: "Well, you see, Bar-ba-ra, life is so dull without Pauli, one has to do something."

It had been arranged between Percy and André that Jean-Marie, André's eldest son should come to us for three months after Easter to learn something of the rare book trade from the British point of view. André intended he should then return to Paris to work under his own direction in the Poursin antiquarian bookshop in Rue Montmartre — that, at least, was the plan.

"André was so keen on the idea I couldn't turn it down," Percy said to me apologetically, well aware of my lack of enthusiasm for giving up our spare room yet again to a member of Elkin Mathews' staff, if only a temporary one. "He's a pleasant young man," he added to cheer me up, "and he'll be out of your way in the office most of the time and probably off to London at the weekends."

It was true. We had received so much kindness and hospitality from the Poursins that it was impossible to refuse any request from André. And yes, Jean-Marie was indeed a pleasant young man, with a mop of dark curly hair and a pale sensitive face that would have been good looking had it not been pitted by acne. I had seen him once or twice at his parents' home in Paris and at their country house at Beauregard l'Eveque, where he had made me feel depressingly middle-age by insisting on always addressing me formally as "Madame."

What, I wondered rather desperately, was I going to give him to eat? He certainly was not going to get croissants for breakfast. As for lunch, could I really offer macaroni cheese or grilled spam? Then there was the question of female company. Was I going to be expected to rustle up local maidens for him — not that there were many around since the USAF's occupation of Stansted Airfield during the war and their continuing occupation of the Wethersfield base some twenty miles away. Or

231

could I count on him satisfying the physical urgings of a normal young man with weekend visits to London for French cuisine and female society?

A touch of French farce accompanied his arrival in London, where Percy and I were meeting him off the boat train at Victoria Station. Travelling on the same train was a troupe of dancers from the Middle East, whose tour of the UK had been well publicized. When the train drew in, it was a few minutes before we located Jean-Marie in the midst of a chattering bevy of dark-eyed, olive-skinned beauties. As a scramble of reporters and cameramen bore down on the girls, he evaded the press with aplomb and assured us that he had had a charming journey with *les houris*.

It was unlikely, I said, that he would find any in Takeley, thinking it was just as well to bring him down to earth. His English was already quite good, certainly much better than his father's, although some of the vocabulary of the Old Mill darts team, uttered in broad Essex, had to be translated by Laurie Deval. Hearing the comment "up in Annie's room" (the top section of the dart board), the puzzled Frenchman turned to Laurie for elucidation. "Mais qui est cette Annie?"

What Jean-Marie did find in Takeley during those two and a half months he lived with us was friendship. Percy felt he had done what was required by agreeing that André's son should come to stay and learn the business. He left it to Laurie to show the young Frenchman the ropes and generally take him under his wing. The two were much of an age and took to each other from the start; RAF slang was exchanged for Parisian argot. Away from the office there were sessions at the Green Man down the road, or evenings at the Devals who now lived down Takeley Street (a five-minute walk away from us) with their two small daughters. Percy and I saw little of Jean-Marie after office hours.

He turned out to be an easy, undemanding guest. His early discovery of a homesick French au pair in a nearby village (how he tracked her down I never knew) put to rest my fears of lustful eyes being turned on our nubile and very pretty fifteen-year-old daughter. In a novel by Colette she would have fallen in love with him; fortunately, she did no such thing.

As the weeks passed I got used to having him around as I had all the other lodgers who had come and gone during our married life; most of them had been oddballs, especially the rather mysterious Egyptian artist who had briefly lived with us in our house in Acacia Road in London and given me, as a parting present, the only piece of creative art of his that I ever saw, a bulbous grey pottery vase for which I had no great liking. As lodgers went, and mercifully all did go eventually, Jean-Marie was the easiest and least demanding of them all, accepting my decreasingly enterprising cuisine (macaroni cheese soon figured again on the menu) with apparent enjoyment.

While he worked dutifully enough in the office, it soon became clear that he had no intention of joining his father in the Rue Montmartre bookshop. Why then, I asked, was he spending the best part of three months learning how to catalogue rare books?

The question was answered with a smile and a shrug. It was "très agréable in Tackley" (the French never could pronounce it correctly as Take-lay), and we were all "très gentil." It had been his father's idea, not his. He had gone along with it because he had nothing better to do at the time. But as for working for his father, "Non, jamais! Ça serait impossible. . . ."

Poor André, he loved his children dearly, so much so that he was determined to arrange their lives for their own good. He was, as Jean-Marie once said ruefully, a good father but an autocrat, albeit a benevolent one. Rather than stay in Paris and have his life directed by his father, he would go to Brazil and work in his uncle's business. Which he did when his visit to us came to an end. Not that he ever settled in South America; like all Parisians he couldn't bear to be away from his native city for long. Nor did he ever become a bookseller, but that made no difference to his friendship with the Devals. Laurie and his wife Mary, were always welcome guests at Jean-Marie's Paris apartment whenever Laurie went to France on book-buying trips. Thanks to Jean-Marie, Laurie's French became fluent enough for doing business in Paris. This happy arrangement would last for many years, the friendship ending only with Laurie's premature death.

Shortly before Jean-Marie came to stay with us, Percy's name appeared on the Committee of Honor of a prestigious exhibition in Paris — "La Civilization du Livre" at the Galerie Royale, together with that of Georges Duhamel, André Maurois, and various other notable messieurs in the field of French culture. Not even one madame, I noted. Typical of the time.

It was as well that little was required of Percy but to lend his name, for he was on the point of being involved in yet another bibliographical venture in this country, which would take up much of his time for years to come. The French exhibition was intended to show, as the catalogue stated, "Les Richesses de la Libraire Française, des origines à nos Jours," its main and very French idea being to encapsulate the "esprit de l'homme" — the spirit of man. Was not the "religion" of the book the natural religion

233

of cultivated and sensitive people, the preamble to the catalogue suggested? Unlike the 1963 "Printing and the Mind of Man" exhibition in London, this allowed the selectors (Comité d'Action) a full rein to show almost any book they felt to be worthy of inclusion: science, history, politics, the arts, sports, or, as the catalogue put it, "un cheminement capricieux" — a capricious progression of thought.

Percy's help and advice was sought in tracking down exhibits that happened to be in the UK, some of which were in the British Museum. He had something of a problem explaining to the French that however much Frank Francis, the director of the BM, would have liked to accommodate the Academie Française, an act of parliament would be needed to allow him to lend a single book. To which the French replied that fortunately their national library did not suffer any such restriction. As usual, the British were out of step.

It was truly a magnificent exhibition but so diverse that one visit was not enough to appreciate all that was on display, although thanks to Percy's involvement we were able see it in advance of the actual opening. Rich, elaborate bindings combined with illustrated books by famous artists, including an early sixteenth-century copy of the *Fables of la Fontaine*, and so many other high spots of literature and the arts that one left, as so often after visiting such a prestigious, prideful national exhibition, unable to remember more than a fraction of what one had seen.

Busy as we both were just then, Percy, as the only Englishman on the Committee of Honor, felt bound to attend the official opening and wanted me with him. It was still much cheaper by sea than by air (and more to my taste), so we took the night ferry from Dover, arriving sleepless at our hotel (the rather crummy old Quai Voltaire) so early that there was no bedroom ready for us. Cross and tired, we demanded some place where we could at least doze until a room was available — and were shown into a smallish bathroom with one bath stool as a chair.

"All right," I said, "I'll sleep in the bath." With my overcoat spread on the bottom of the bath and Percy's coat over me, I curled up and slept, while he dozed on the bath stool. An hour or so later I was roused by a voice murmuring, "Ah, pauvre Madame!" as the hotel manager, who had come to tell us that our room was at last ready, gazed down in sympathy at my recumbent form in the empty bath. For Percy, who had been far less comfortable on the stool, no sympathy was forthcoming.

As of so many such occasions, especially on our whirlwind visits to France, the time gap has left little more than a memory of a melée of unknown faces, a clatter of exclamatory voices, continual handshaking accompanied by insincere murmurs of "enchanté," gabbled Parisian French, much of it incomprehensible, and my own stumbling efforts to contribute intelligently. Did Monsieur Maurois, whom I greatly admired, bow over my hand and tell me he was enchanted? Probably he did, but, alas, I've no recollection of being so lucky. And how does anyone ever manage to study the exhibits at such events?

Chapter 25

Ian Fleming could be a good friend to those whose friendship he valued, provided this did not involve much expenditure of time or energy. He could be casual to the point of rudeness, a not uncommon trait in old Etonians, but the friendships he formed lasted and were based on genuine and reciprocated affection.

It was thanks to Ian's efforts that Lord Kemsley was dissuaded from killing off the ailing *Book Handbook*, an austere little quarterly "for discriminating book-lovers" on the same lines as the pre-war *Book-Collector's Quarterly*, edited by Desmond Flower and A. J. A. Symons. Like other scholarly publications of its kind aimed at a small, inward-looking market, it never had much hope of a long life, and one wonders why his Lordship had been willing to give it his blessing in the first place.

Percy had contributed to the summer issue in 1951, with a pen portrait of the man who had bought the firm of Elkin Mathews in 1922, Dr. A. W. Evans. A scholar, bibliophile, and at the same time an astute businessman, Evans was someone for whom Percy had great respect and who became something of a role model for him as far as the running of a rare book business was concerned. The article was a "one-off," and at that time Percy certainly had no plans for a book of reminiscences about his pre-war days working with Evans and the other partners (a "rum lot," he called them) in Conduit Street and later in Grosvenor Street. Nor was the little quarterly able to pay more than peanuts for contributions.

All the same he was ready to do anything he could to help to save the only organ in Britain entirely devoted to book collecting. In this he had the strong support of John Hayward, critic, editor, and authority on English poetry, who shared a flat in Carlyle Mansions with T. S. Eliot.

Had Ian not been a tenant in the same building, renting a flat just above Hayward and Eliot, and on friendly terms with both, it is unlikely that Percy's influence would have been enough to make him take up the cause of keeping *Book Handbook* going. More than that — both Percy and John were urging that what it needed was a new look, a better image, and, naturally, a further injection of cash.

Given time, renamed *The Book Collector,* with John Hayward in the editorial chair, it could, they believed, be a viable proposition and a prestigious one that his Lordship would be proud to own. What was more, Ian, as owner of a very fine book collection, should be part of the editorial team.

The idea must have appealed to Ian's vanity. But he was glad to be of service to John, who was confined to a wheelchair with muscular dystrophy, and to talk Lord Kemsley into agreeing to give it a trial would be a feather in his cap. Fortunately, Ian was popular with both the Kemsleys and regularly dined and played bridge with them. When a restoration job was needed for the library at Dropmore, their impressive country house in Berkshire, Ian was called in to advise and promptly turned over the job to Percy.

Book Handbook had been published under the imprint of the Dropmore Press, a part of the Kemsley newspaper empire that had been set up to publish literary and prestigious books for the top end of the market. One of these would be the limited facsimile edition of the magnificent Holkham Bible, bound by Gray's in Cambridge on Percy's recommendation and published in 1954. Alas, the original is no longer at Holkham, the family having regretfully had to part with it in order to meet death duties.

When Lord Kemsley allowed himself to be persuaded by Ian to grant the quarterly a temporary reprieve, part of the deal was that the Dropmore Press should no longer be responsible for its publication. Instead, a new company, the Queen Anne Press, would be set up with a new editorial board — John Hayward, Percy, and Ian — and it would be reborn as *The Book Collector* under that imprint. Whether the three eminent journalists — Edward Shanks, Clarence Winchester, and Reginald Horrox — who comprised the previous editorial board were asked if they wished to continue, I have no idea. Since no financial awards went with the job, they would probably not have been over keen.

Number I, volume I, made its bow in spring 1952, a fatter, smarter version of its predecessor, with more illustrations. The price of a year's subscription was eleven shillings including postage in the UK. There were much the same specialist articles that had appeared in *Book Handbook.* One new feature that was to prove useful and popular was "Bibliographical Notes and Queries." This was in fact a resurrection of a defunct

237

little publication dear to Percy's heart, which he had for a time produced himself and reluctantly given up at the beginning of the war. He had even saved some of the 1939 queries, which came in very handy to fill a page or two of the first number. An article he had intended for *Book Handbook*, "Elkin Mathews in the Nineties," also appeared.

Ian never did write for *The Book Collector*. From the start he had no intention of taking on any editorial chores and was well content to leave the direction and style of the new quarterly to his fellow board members. He was, in any case, fully occupied just then. While John Hayward and Percy were putting their heads together over the first number, Ian was finalizing the typescript of *Casino Royale*, the novel he had written while on holiday at his Jamaican house and had brought back to England to sell to Jonathan Cape. It had been written, he told his friends, to take his mind off "the frightful prospect of having to get married."

This rueful comment from a trapped male who was at last having to give up his independence was characteristic but not to be taken too seriously. Anne Rothermere and Ian were well matched. It was no doubt sometimes a stormy marriage but never a boring one. Anne was a slim, attractive woman, already twice married. It was because her second husband was Lord Rothermere that Kemsley put his foot down when he learned that his foreign manager was openly having a well-established affair with the wife of a rival newspaper baron, telling Ian that he could not continue to countenance such an embarrassing situation. Either Ian must marry Anne and "regularize their position" or he must resign from his job. Ian had by then reached a time in his life (he was forty-four) when "settling down" with a woman he loved was by no means such a frightful prospect. Among Anne's qualities that had especially captivated him, according to his letters to her, was her "outrageousness." She was also intelligent, well read, and witty and, to Ian's delight, would soon bear him a son.

They were married in Jamaica with Noel Coward as best man, and when they returned to England as man and wife, Ian brought his completed novel with him.

Once *The Book Collector* was a going concern, it became established that the pre-publication quarterly meetings of the editorial board would be held in the Fleming apartment, when Anne would be hostess at the editorial lunch party. This was a cozy, convenient arrangement from Ian's point of view, allowing him to be kept in the picture without having to do any actual work. The venue was also convenient for John Hayward, who had taken on the editorial responsibilities and was carrying them out in the flat he shared with T. S. Eliot.

Like John, Percy was deeply committed to the venture, ready to do anything in his power to make it a success. This included writing articles and book reviews without payment, advertising the journal in Elkin Mathews catalogues, and collecting subscriptions from our customers, who were all urged to subscribe.

While John Hayward was prepared to bear the brunt of the editorial workload, some help was required, since getting about was difficult for him. This help was soon forthcoming from a young Cambridge graduate who had already done some well-regarded bibliographical research work and was recommended by Percy's old friend, Tim Mumby, the librarian at King's College.

"We'd better ask Philip Gaskell over for lunch," Percy said. "Tim Mumby says he's a clever young fellow, just the sort we want to help John. He thinks he'll enjoy the job and be able to put up with John and his ways."

When I learned that the young graduate we were to entertain had been researching eighteenth-century printing, was working on an important bibliography, and had one already in print, I expected a pale, bespectacled pedant, old for his years and unlikely to sparkle at the luncheon table.

Instead, I found myself entertaining a fresh-faced, amusing young man who told me that his hobby was gliding. After years of consorting with dedicated bibliophiles of all kinds, young, middle-aged, and ancient, I never failed to be surprised when I found personable young men (seldom young women) caught up in the curious pursuit of cancels and signatures, first issues, binding variants, and other bibliographical "points" of which, until I met Percy, I had been blissfully unaware, in company with everyone else I knew who enjoyed books but neither knew nor cared what edition they happened to be or how they were put together.

In the summer 1952 issue of *The Book Collector* Philip Gaskell's appointment as editor was announced. For a couple of years he used his talent for diplomacy as well as bibliography in working under John Hayward's tutelage (*The Book Collector* was ever John's baby) for a smallish honorarium. At the end of that time he resigned to take up the more prestigious and considerably more profitable post of dean of King's College, Cambridge. He was replaced by the assistant librarian of the House of Lords, Christopher Dobson, another agreeable young man, who stayed until the crisis came when Lord Kemsley's purse snapped closed. But that is jumping too far ahead.

To tempt the rare book trade to buy advertising space, the rates were made absurdly cheap; a whole page for one year cost only £8; a quarter page, £2 5s. While the response of the London dealers was reasonably good, those in the provinces, with the shining exception of Elkin Mathews and one or two other enlightened firms, were not interested. As for the American trade, only *The Amateur Book Collector*, published in Chicago, took a page. To our amusement their advertisement featured the one-time London barrow boy, Fred Bason, a self-publicist who liked to hold forth on book collecting in a series of diaries featured in a daily newspaper. It also offered, as a not-to-be-missed forthcoming attraction, an article on Swinburne's "Unpublished Erotic Verses to a Mistress."

Chapter 26

The letter with the bad news was completely unexpected. I had brought up the morning batch of mail to our bedroom as usual, where Percy was lying in bed waiting for it to be put into his hands. After some fifteen years of married life we were still content to sleep in a handsomely carved half-tester (a two-poster rather than four) that we had splashed out on at an auction when we first came to live in Essex.

Percy had never been an early riser. He saw no point in getting up and going downstairs to sort out his mail when he could have it brought to him in bed by his wife, who had to get up first anyway to see the children off to school (not the job of a man born in Queen Victoria's time) and feed her hens.

As I was usually in a rush, I seldom waited to hear if the mail contained anything of special interest. My own letters had, naturally, already been extracted. On that morning when he came downstairs for breakfast, the children having already left to catch the schoolbus, I could tell by his slow tread and the gravity of his expression that it was bad news.

He told me straight away: "Charles Stonehill is suing me for libel."

LIBEL! The word had frightening connotations for us both. It had happened before. In 1932 Percy had been sued for libel by a dishonest, small-time book dealer because of an article he had written in *The American Book Collector* in which he had rather rashly referred to a racket being carried on by the dealer in question. The fact that a few copies of the periodical had been sent to this country made a claim for libel possible, and a writ had been issued. It was a case Percy ought to have won, for the plaintiff was a crook and looked one. But Percy's too-clever counsel changed course in mid-trial in an attempt to win on a doubtful point of law, and Mr. Justice Avory ruled against us. The damages, though relatively small, plus the costs made Percy bankrupt.

This new threat had quite a different background. At an ABA committee meeting Percy had spoken against an application for membership from an international antiquarian book dealer. Charles Stonehill was a clever dealer and a rather engaging character whose methods of business Percy knew to be somewhat dubious. For this reason he spoke against the application and subsequently blackballed it when it was put to the vote, with the result that it failed to win sufficient support.

It was obvious that someone on the committee had told Stonehill who had blackballed him.

We went to see our solicitors in Bishop's Stortford that same day. We sat in the office of the senior partner, Mr. T——, grey-haired, nearing retirement, with a fatherly manner and some forty years of experience to give weight to his advice.

"You say you were in committee when you stated your objections to this bookseller becoming a member of your trade association? Then there is no doubt that the occasion was privileged. You were entitled to give your honest opinion without fear of adverse consequences."

"That is what I had assumed," Percy said. "Then Charles Stonehill has no case?"

"So it would seem," said Mr. T—— judicially. "On the face of it you have an unanswerable case. However, the plaintiff has clearly taken legal advice, and I think it would be wise for you to seek counsel's opinion. . . ."

"Suppose it's just a threat to scare you," I said as we drove home, "and he doesn't really intend to sue. And even if he does, why not tell him to go ahead — sue and be damned! It'll cost him a lot of money, and, as Mr. T—— says, he can't win."

Percy shook his head. He was still worried; the interview with our solicitor had only partly reassured him. "I don't know what Stonehill is up to," he said, "but I am sure Mr. T—— is right. We'd better take counsel's opinion."

The next step was to let the ABA committee know what had happened. A formal letter went to the secretary, and Percy had a talk off the record with Stanley Sawyer, the current president. Stanley, the senior partner of the old, established Bruton Street firm of Charles Sawyer and Sons, was a John Bull character, stocky, outspoken, obstinate, a man of principles and a loyal friend. A supporter of the league from the start, one of the few who had attended the Amsterdam conference, he had early on won André's approval and affection, as had his well-named attractive and sensible wife, Joy, whose well-spoken French made up for Stanley's lack. As Percy had expected, Stanley was furious to hear of the leak, swearing he would do everything possible to find out "who the bastard is and chuck him out of the ABA with ignominy. . . ."

Percy thought he knew who had leaked, but to name names without evidence was only going to lead to further trouble.

There was, predictably, shock and condemnation when the committee learned of the writ. Sympathy and support came by telephone and letter. One letter to Percy from Bob Gibbs, of Gibbs' bookshop, Manchester, an ABA committee member who had been absent from the meeting when Stonehill's application came up, threw some interesting light on the matter.

"I am certain that it has never been a personal matter so far as *you* are concerned," he wrote. "But do not lose sight of the fact that as far as other people are concerned it is a very *Personal Issue*. The Emperor of C. X. Rd. [a committee member with a Charing Cross Road bookshop] regards it as a definite vendetta against you and there is no need for me to tell you [to] what lengths his vindictiveness will carry him. I am sure of one thing . . . at the very slightest sign of any recoil which may involve him he'll rat. He is, I am certain, a coward at heart."

Gibbs was sure, too, that the likelihood of the identity of "the traitor" being disclosed if the case came to court would cause the action to be dropped "at the first sign of a fight." And he went on to say that he could not imagine any member of the committee being willing to brand himself in court "as the low down type he obviously is." He recalled that he had heard Percy on a previous occasion remark that although he felt he had to resist Stonehill's application for membership, he rather liked the man and was not motivated by any kind of malice.

I too thought that Stonehill's supporters would rat when it came to the crunch, but Percy, having once experienced a disastrous, long-drawn-out libel action, was not willing to take any chances, despite the fact that Stanley and another member of the committee were prepared to tackle Charles Stonehill and try to persuade him to drop the action.

When he came home after the consultation at Gerald Gardiner's chambers, Percy gave me a verbatim account of the interview.

"Would you say that the plaintiff is a rich man, Mr. Muir?" Gardiner had asked. A little surprised by the question, Percy had replied that he believed he was.

"In that case you will be wise to settle out of court," Gardiner said. "If the case goes to court, you will win it, I have no doubt, but when the costs go before the taxing master, you will find that you will still have to pay a proportion of those incurred and that will not be a small sum. As the plaintiff is, as you believe, a rich man, he will in all probability appeal, which will incur you in further costs. He even might take the case to the Lords. My advice to you, Mr. Muir, is to settle."

243

It was a bitter pill to swallow. Had the decision been left to me, I would have called what I suspected to be Stonehill's bluff. As Bob Gibbs had written, it was hard to believe that a member of the committee would have been prepared to go into the witness box and admit to having disclosed a confidential committee matter to an outsider. But having sought professional advice, Percy was not a man to disregard it. A form of words acceptable to the plaintiff was devised, Percy duly signed, and the case was dropped. From that time on we never saw or heard from Charles Stonehill again. He did not become a member of the ABA, and a few years later we learned of his death. Oddly enough, Barnett, the other man who had sued Percy for libel, also died within a couple of years of taking Percy to court. Clearly, it was a dangerous thing to do.

The ABA committee must have been relieved that there was to be no undesirable publicity, although there were those who, like me, had been itching for a showdown. The leak, which had undoubtedly been motivated by malice, effectively damned Stonehill in the eyes of most of the committee from then onwards.

"We're not letting Percy be out of pocket over this," Ian Grant, a fellow Scot and an old friend, said to me. For the ABA to pay Gardiner's fee of £50 was cheap at the price. One of those most distressed by the whole nasty business was Winnie Myers. Charles Stonehill was a Jew, and suspicion was bound to point at fellow Jews known to do business with him. Poor Winnie, who always did her best to be on good terms with everyone, had to face the knowledge that the so-called traitor was in all probability a fellow Jew.

Percy was well aware of her embarrassment when he wrote understandingly in answer to her letter of sympathy. By then he was worrying over a new problem that had arisen regarding the ABA's subscription to the league, which was considered too high by some, and he quickly pushed the Stonehill affair to the back of his mind, although he neither forgot nor forgave the traitor.

Since the successful London conference, there had been only some sporadic sniping at the league from the diehards who had opposed it in the first place. Now once again they were making themselves heard, grumbling at the size of the subscription and demanding that the ABA should put forward a resolution at the 1952 conference proposing that contributions from the member associations be reduced.

Percy strongly opposed this proposal, pointing out that the league's income of £700 a year was already far too small for all that it was expected to do. It was not even in a position to pay the out-of-pocket

244

expenses of its committee members when they travelled abroad to attend meetings. Nor could it afford to pay a full-time secretary.

As he explained in his letter to Winnie, bright ideas had been bandied about at previous conferences that would inevitably cost money. "It was no use saying that the league must cut its coat according to its cloth," he wrote. "If resolutions call for a certain type of garment, funds to buy it must be voted accordingly. . . . If, on the other hand, funds are to be cut, many of the resolutions will be voided because there is no money to carry them out. . . ." He was voicing the frustration of a man who has been planning for action and finds his so-called friends are attempting to tie his hands behind his back.

Once again he saw the ABA as a bunch of reactionaries (with several notable exceptions) preparing to throw a spanner into the league's youthful and vulnerable works. By writing to Winnie and spelling out the difficulties, he hoped to galvanize her, as immediate past president, into throwing her not inconsiderable weight to dissuading some of the malcontents from wrecking the Geneva conference.

"You see, Winnie dear," he wrote bitterly, "it is the paltriness of the whole thing that gets me down. It is as much as to say — 'you can spend your time and money, sweat and labor as you like. More fool you! We think what you have done is not worth what it has cost us, and we're going to show you in a very practical way by cutting your resources still further.' . . ."

He concluded his letter with the message that should the ABA's resolution be defeated, or better still not put forward, then he would feel it worth going on, continuing his efforts to shape the league into "the great power for good that it shows signs of becoming . . . then my time and efforts, such as they are, would always be at the league's disposal. But a truncated, enfeebled organization? No, I have no time for that."

In her letter to him she had asked if he would be willing to propose a toast to the league at the ABA's annual dinner, shortly to take place. It was an invitation he gladly accepted, especially "as no such toast has ever stood on our dinner agenda before."

The entry of Germany into the league had meant renewed contact with a number of the dealers Percy had bought from before the war. Throughout the 1930s he had made regular buying trips to Cologne, Frankfurt, Munich, and Berlin, mainly in search of collector's items in music. But he had bought books as well. With his ability to speak German fluently, he had the edge on most of his British colleagues, and such trips had been profitable and enjoyable.

"There's an interesting book auction in Marburg in July," wrote Helmuth Domizlaff. "Irma and I will be going, so why don't you join us there and then come back with us to Munich?" Percy had made only one business trip to Germany since the war, when he had gone by train through Holland and on to Hamburg to attend a book auction. He had bought well, finding little competition, but the devastation from the bombing of the city had been depressing, and he had not lingered. Now, seven years since the end of the war, he wanted to go south and combine the Marburg auction with another that was to follow shortly afterwards in Munich.

"If you can come with me, we'll take the car and make it a holiday as well," he said.

I was not going to say I couldn't, even though I was struggling to finish a book and had rashly taken on various other commitments. Novelists who live in villages are fair game to organizers of local events in need of a "name" to take part in an Any Questions team, be a judge in a beauty competition, hand out the prizes for this or that contest, and so on. As this can be regarded as PR appearances useful for promoting their books, it is thought unnecessary to offer a fee, especially as novelists come far down the line as a draw compared to show business people or television personalities and can seldom be regarded as glamorous.

I was a sucker for agreeing to such requests, especially when the date for my appearance was a nice long way ahead. In consequence I was apt to find to my fury and Percy's despair that I was committed to doing my duty at some worthy but tedious local event when he wanted me at his side at a far more interesting occasion in London, Paris, or Brussels.

"But why on earth did you ever agree to do it?" he would ask in bewilderment. "Why did it have to be you?"

I was never able to give a satisfactory answer to that question, except to point out that his diary, too, contained duty dates that I accepted as the necessary chores of being a chairman, committee or council member in the wider world beyond the Essex borders.

It was true we both needed a holiday; rewarding though it had been in many ways, the American tour had been anything but a holiday. I scanned my diary and found I could spare two weeks away from home without letting the locals down. As for my novel, taking the car meant I could put my typewriter on the back seat and keep the book going by tapping away in hotel bedrooms while Percy viewed sales or visited German bookshops. Not long before, I had agreed to write a monthly (soon to become weekly) column for a county newspaper. This was a useful addition to my income and posed no great problem over taking trips abroad. Banging out copy, mostly garnered along the route, from wherever we happened to stay, was a lot easier than gearing myself into creative writing with chambermaids clattering along corridors and looking in to see when the eccentric English frau was going to vacate the *Schlafzimmer* and go off to shop or see the sights like a normal tourist.

On that first post-war journey to Germany we took the ferry from Tilbury to Rotterdam. It was then run by an independent company, cheaper than the British Rail Harwich-Hook, comfortable and efficient and more convenient for anyone living in our part of Essex. Our route into Germany was along the banks of the Rhine to Cologne, where, for much of the way, the rail track and autobahn run side by side, at some points separated by only a few yards. It was a journey we had made several times before the war when we had travelled by rail, taking advantage of the subsidized "registered marks" with which the German government was then tempting foreign tourists. With one pound buying twenty marks instead of twelve, Germany was a cheap country for a holiday in the mid-thirties. Not that the supply of registered marks was unlimited; nor was one allowed to take them out of the country. That was strictly *verboten*, which didn't prevent us on one occasion from taking a chance and smuggling out (in my bra) some of our cheap marks to buy enough francs to pay for a long weekend in Paris.

The drive through the Rhineland to Cologne is beautiful and romantic much of the way (or at least it was) even on an autobahn. Glimpses of gothic castles perched on rocky heights atop the wooded hills flanking the wide winding river brought back memories of the stories of the brothers Grimm. Laden barges made unhurried progress. Now and then we passed a car ferry where a gap in the hills led to a little wine-growing town in a green valley. If war damage there had been, there was little sign of it along our route.

It was not until we reached the outskirts of Cologne that the effects of the war became very evident. There were some stark new blocks of apartments on the approaches to the town on bare, cleared sites, but very little redevelopment. When, some way from the city center, we stopped at traffic lights, a young man came to the car window. Would we like a guide, he asked in English. He could take us through the city, show us the Dom (the cathedral) and then guide us around the war damage. "Nein?" he shrugged philosophically. Then perhaps we could spare a few cigarettes? Percy gave him a handful, and, as the lights changed and we drove on, a shabby lad of twelve or so ran alongside our car, begging for *Groschen*. After giving him some small change, Percy commented rather sadly that it was the first time he had ever seen a German boy begging in the streets. Soon after we reached the open space opposite the famous Dom, where a large car park occupied what had once been several blocks of buildings. There our GB plates were a target for more touts and more would-be guides.

The great gothic cathedral with its elaborately wrought twin towers looked, at first sight, to have escaped the Allied bombing unscathed. But once inside we could see how much restoration had been done and how much more was needed. The work was being carried on steadily and had been for several years with teutonic thoroughness and skill — as we were to see happening in many parts of Germany. Later, when we visited Frankfurt, we were told that after a direct hit had destroyed the city's much loved Goethe *haus*, where the poet had once lived, volunteers had been there the next morning gathering up every piece of brick, timber, and stonework for storage, so that the house could be rebuilt just as it had been once the war was over.

Apart from the cathedral it was hard to recognize the city we had once known. Nearly all the shops in what had once been smart shopping streets were single-storied, patched up and roofed over where the upper floors had been destroyed. The shop windows made a brave enough showing of their wares — clothes, leather goods, jewelry, furniture, new books — but the antiquarian bookshops Percy had known had gone. Most of them had been owned by Jews.

We hadn't the heart to tour the city and look at more war damage. For my part I remembered with shame the satisfaction I had felt during the war years when I had watched the Flying Fortresses and Liberators taking off from the USAF base at Stansted on their bombing missions over Germany. Not just the Germans but also Europe was the loser from the Allies' policy of destroying historic cities — as the Germans had destroyed much of Coventry, Norwich, and other fine cities in their Baedecker raids.

Rather than spend a night in Cologne, we drove on to the pretty little village of Rolandswerth farther along the Rhine. There, sitting on the terrace of the wisteria-draped Hotel Gretendorf in the evening sunshine, we drank the local wine, watching little boys splashing in the shallows while the current carried canoeists in rubber dinghies downstream as it had carried us sixteen years ago, their double-bladed paddles needed only to keep a straight course, a lovely lazy way to travel. Then, when we camped overnight on a riverside site, it had been the "guns before butter" time, and I had kept my hands by my sides when young men in brown uniforms greeted us with "Heil Hitler" and the Nazi salute instead of "Guten tag" (good day), as had once been the custom.

Our meal that first evening of the trip, as recorded in my travel notebook, cost us seven marks and was excellent. The menu was a meaty soup (the Germans like soup at any time of the year) and calves' sweetbreads with peas and sautéed potatoes, followed by rhubarb tart with a big dollop of cream. In English money it worked out at around eleven shillings for the two of us, or roughly sixty pence.

There was plenty of evidence that the rebuilding of Germany was going on apace as we drove along the autobahn to Marburg the next day. Every few miles we saw depots stacked with great piles of building blocks. Trucks were pulling in to load up; others, often coupled together, were grinding along in the slow lane. Private motorists tore past at speeds that made my hair stand on end, while peasants just a few yards from the autobahn were cultivating their strips of land as they had done for generations, with oxen yoked to the plough. Slow, patient beasts with great, superfluous horns. Only once did I see a tractor in the fields.

As we neared Marburg, the occupying powers, American, French, and British were much in evidence. "Smart modern American Barracks in Gliesen," I noted in my journal. "A few small houses being built, presumably for the Germans. Little Christmas trees are tied to the rafters to keep evil spirits out before the roofs go on. Saw an enormous tank, labelled Panzer Corps, half into a garden amidst the ruins of the garden wall as we drove into Marburg. Bored young soldier guarding it. Someone had blundered. . . ."

Percy had known the auctioneer of the book auction we were attending before the war. In Germany, unlike in England, several of the bigger dealers in rare and secondhand books ran auctions. For dealers from abroad attending the sale, it was the agreeable custom for the auctioneer to offer hospitality.

"Herr M—— wants us to come to them for a meal this evening," Percy said, after reading a letter that had been left for him at our hotel. "I think we should accept. He was very kind and helpful to me before the war, when I attended his auctions. And he says he hopes we might be able to arrange for his eldest son to come to England on a visit to improve his English." On this and later trips to Germany the dealers with whom we were on friendly terms were liberal-minded and, as they assured us, had been opposed to Hitler all along, so far as it was possible. Many, like the Domizlaffs, had helped and hidden Jewish friends. Not so Herr M——.

Percy had been told that he had held a party ticket but had never been an active member of the party. Too old for military service, he had kept his head down and his business ticking over as had the majority of his generation in his position.

He turned out to be a friendly old man, very much the kind German "papa," presiding paternally over his family from whom he clearly expected respect and obedience. His wife was equally kind, welcoming us smilingly into the family circle, filling our plates generously as we sat round the family dining table in their comfortable bourgeois home. The talk was mainly shop — of prices, colleagues, and the problems of the rare book trade. There were subjects it was best to avoid. Tact was required on both sides.

The two sons said little, leaving the conversation mostly to their elders. It could not have been easy, I thought, for German teenagers, brought up as Hitler *Jugend* to accept the presence of occupying forces in their town. On the other hand, when one remarked to me somewhat resentfully that the Americans had taken over the town's tennis courts, so German boys couldn't use them, I failed to feel much sympathy.

I was glad when it was time to leave. Kind and friendly though our host and hostess were — to us, at least — the question stayed at the back of my mind: How could it be that they had accepted, if not actively supported, the repugnant doctrines of Hitler and his fellow Nazis, who denied all rights of and treated with bestial inhumanity Jews, Gypsies, and all those they labelled as *unter Mensch?* After seven years it was still too soon to put such a question. Had I asked it, I doubt if the answer would have satisfied me.

Very conveniently for us the auction took place at our hotel. One glance at the books laid out was enough to tell me that I was right out of my depth. With most of the day at my disposal while Percy first viewed and then attended the sale, I pondered whether to explore the town on my own or justify having lugged my typewriter up to our bedroom, and set to work on my book. Duty won, at least for the morning. But writing in unfamiliar surroundings was always hard. Without domestic demands, the interruption of the telephone, or a tradesman's knock, I should have settled down, dutifully tapping away the whole, empty morning. Instead, I wasted my time studying the local guidebooks and writing postcards to family and friends. Some work got done, but by no means the task I had set myself.

The Domizlaffs had turned up that morning. I had not met Irma before, and I knew at once that we would get on. She was a warm-hearted, practical woman, with a firm, tanned face that needed no make-up, smiling eyes, and short, crisp grey hair, softened by a curly half-fringe. She had been a dancing teacher when Helmuth married her. To see them waltz together, as we would do in Munich and Vienna, was a joy. They seemed essentially right for each other. Irma, devoted, sensible, taking charge of the home, was just the wife a gentle, artistic man like Helmuth needed.

When I found she had no English, I was determined we should communicate. I had picked up a few scraps of German and struggled to make myself understood with a dictionary and German phrase-book, the kind catering for angry or distraught tourists in perpetual trouble ("I do not like this room . . . send for the Manager!" "I am ill. Fetch a doctor. . . ."), not much of a help in getting a friendly conversation going. Pantomime was better and more fun. Irma was quick at getting the gist of my meaning and would laugh and offer me the German words I needed without uttering a word of English.

"You are learning," Helmuth would say when he and Percy rejoined us. It was true. I was making some progress — as Irma intended. Listening to Percy talking German so fluently, I longed to do the same. Alas, I was no linguist.

In the afternoon while the Domizlaffs and Percy were at the auction sale, I took a look at Marburg, an old Hessian town on the banks of the river Lahn. A gothic castle stands rather gloomily atop the hill dominating the town; a greyish influence of Lutherism pervades the older part. There was little sign of war damage. The military presence couldn't be missed with bored off-duty soldiery strolling around the streets. Presumably, only the officers monopolized the tennis courts. It was not the sort of place to attract foreign tourists. Not that many were coming to Germany then. No touts or would-be guides approached me as I wandered through the streets peering into cool, empty churches. One, the thirteenth-century *Elisabethen-Kirche*, commemorated in early graceful gothic style Elizabeth of Hungary, who, said my guidebook "died worn out with good works at the age of twenty four."

From Marburg it was an easy journey along the autobahn to Frankfurt. Herr Schumann's bookshop, visited by Percy before the war, was still there, open for business. First, before getting down to work there had to be a protracted exchange of pleasantries. We were then invited to sit down at a table. A card index was brought by an assistant, and Percy began to pick his way through it; the books he wished to see were promptly brought for his inspection. If customers wished to browse, they were allowed to do so, but the serious buyer was expected to sit and be waited upon.

Methodical the system might be, but to me it seemed somewhat soul-less. If one didn't browse along the shelves, where was the excitement? Where the hope of finding a bargain? Admittedly a slim hope, as far as I was concerned, since I was highly unlikely to find any English books. It was more interesting to take a look at Frankfurt. There was still war damage to be seen but nothing like the devastation we had seen in Cologne. The town looked busy and far more prosperous, the shops well stocked, the public gardens well kept and bright with spring flowers.

From Frankfurt we took a cross-country route to Munich through the lush, peaceful valley of the river Neckar, stopping for the night in the ancient university town of Heidelberg. In the evening light the castle built of the local pinkish stone looked like a musical comedy backdrop. The medieval streets of the old town, where stone archways led into shadowed courtyards, brought to mind the gay, lilting lyrics of *The Student Prince*, but instead of duel-scarred, wine-drinking German students, the streets were full of beer-drinking GIs. Outside shops supplying food and drink, enterprising shopkeepers had installed vending machines to cater for the needs of hungry young soldiers after shop hours. One, to my surprise, sold nylon stockings — to soften the hearts of local maidens, perhaps? Was there one vending condoms, too, I wondered. Our route into Munich took us along the Bavarian Romantische Strasse (Romantic Street), where painted timber-framed houses, some depicting pastoral scenes, line the streets of places with names like Dinkelsbuhl. Steeply pitched thatched roofs, their deep eaves like over-hung brows, gave shade to passers-by from the sun's heat, throwing shadows half across the road. The Goldene Rose Gasthaus, where we had once spent a night, was still there. A sweetish odor of cow dung from middens verging the road (the bigger the midden, the richer the farmer), with brown hens picking about on them, took me back nostalgically to our 1930s holidays. For once all seemed as it had been in those halcyon pre-war days.

The Domizlaffs had booked us into a small, newly built guest house close to their own apartment that overlooked the Englische Gartens, the city's delightful and extensive park. "We are walking there every day," they told us, anglophiles both of them. Helmuth ran a successful busi-ness in rare books from home, and Irma in her quiet way took charge of everything else.

We had come to Munich for Percy to attend another book auction at the well-known fine art auctioneers, Karl and Faber, but much of our time was spent at the Domizlaffs'. While Percy and Helmuth worked together, I was taken by Irma on a sightseeing tour of the city in her Volkswagen. It was a sad pilgrimage through streets of empty, boarded-up buildings, baroque houses pockmarked by bomb fragments, gaps where once some fine civic monument, church, or theater had stood. From time to time Irma would gesture to what had once been part of the city's heritage, with a sigh and a murmur of "Alles kaput, alles kaput . . ." I thought of Coventry, of the city of London, of the Baedeker raids and sighed in sympathy and for the destructiveness of man. But when I walked about the city on my own, I could see how much restoration work had already taken place. It was like someone smashed in a road accident being put together in hospital — a new arm or leg, a reconstructed nose. . . . True, he would not look quite as he had before, but at least he was on his feet again and no longer a wreck. In the years to come we would visit Munich many times and on each visit see that more progress had been made, until the scars were all healed, and only the old and some of the middle-aged remembered what it had looked like in the early post-war years.

The trip paid off. Of the lots he wanted, Percy bought well, with little competition against him. It was a good time to buy, before the mark began racing ahead.

We took a different route on the way home, passing through the Dutch town of Arnhem, largely rebuilt. At the hotel where we stayed over-night the friendly, talkative proprietor told us, as no doubt he told many foreign guests, of how it had been during the British air drop in 1944, which had so nearly succeeded in shortening the duration of the war.

"There were dead Germans lying everywhere in the streets, grenades clutched in their hands . . . ," he recalled with satisfaction. "I watched the British parachutists dropping from the sky," his son chipped in. "It was tremendously exciting, but then I was sent into the air-raid shelter and not allowed to come out for a whole week. . . ."

253

Chapter 27

It felt strange to arrive in Geneva and not be greeted by William Kundig. Instead, it was Nicholas Rauch, president of the Swiss association, who had attended the London conference, who welcomed us to the league's fifth annual meeting. William had died from a heart attack while in the United States earlier in the year.

For my part I missed William. I felt sad that he was not there to play host to the first conference to be held in his country. I had liked him and enjoyed his company despite the bombast and showmanship that had put Percy off. If his warmth and friendliness towards me was calculated, as Percy maintained, I had found it agreeable, never being averse to male attentiveness so long as it came from someone interesting or entertaining, and William had qualified on both counts. Although Percy never really took to him, they were able to work together in amity, appreciating each other's qualities and sharing a similar sense of humor.

Poor Juliette, her long face pale and sad, put in an appearance at one or two of the functions during the four days of the conference. She was left a rich widow, but, although William had often treated her unkindly, her life must have been dull and flat without him.

The Swiss had chosen to hold the conference at the end of July, which meant that Percy and I had hardly got our breath back after our German trip before we were off again, although this time for only six days. It was to be Percy's last conference as president. He had done his best to persuade André to step into his shoes, as the obvious and best possible successor, but André had insisted that Georges Blaizot was the man for the job (it was time to have a French president) and had undertaken to persuade him to stand. Failing André, Percy was happy to hand over to the quiet, courteous Georges, a man much more to his taste than Kundig had been.

The weather was brilliant. We had arrived on the Saturday evening and booked into the Hotel du Rhone, where the conference was being held and most of the executive were staying. It was too big and too grand for my taste; flunkeys — and there were plenty — unnerve me. The conference was to open on the Monday morning, preceded by a "Vin d'honneur" to which our hosts had cordially invited "Les Dames" as well. This being Switzerland, where women still did not have the vote, the invitation assumed that the delegates would all be "les Messieurs," which they were not.

We awoke on the Sunday morning to a picture postcard scene. The hotel stood where the fast-flowing waters of the Rhone spill down into the great, wide-spreading lake of Geneva, so that the cool shush-shush of rushing water greeted arrivals and departures and could be heard in the bedroom if one opened the windows. White sails dotted the lake; houses along the shore looked like cut-outs against an azure sky. Percy, as usual, had to chair a pre-conference committee meeting. I was free. The morning was mine to spend as I fancied.

Later, when the rest of the delegates arrived, there would be the greetings and embraces, the babel of voices in different tongues, the cigarette smoke (we were all smokers in those days), the heat, the drinking, and the long-drawn-out meals. But first I would go out walking alone.

"Don't be late, then," said Percy. "We'll all be lunching here after the committee."

I promised not to be and set off in my sandals and cotton dress, barelegged (I could change on my return for the smart luncheon party) with a few Swiss francs in my pocket — just in case. I had walked along the lakeside on previous visits. For a change I turned inland, thinking I would have a look at the part of the city away from the smart shops and hotels, where the not-so-smart people lived. For a young (well, youngish) foreign woman to walk alone in downtown Geneva on a Sunday morning could hardly be called risky. I didn't expect to be pursued by lustful young males, as I might have been in Italy, as I walked along tree-lined streets of neat houses, passing an occasional school or grey parish church, with the cars of the devout parked nearby. It was all very quiet, tidy, and rather boring.

I had strolled along aimlessly for nearly an hour, expecting before long to leave the streets behind for green fields and hills. But the streets went on, the temperature climbed, the heat from the footpath began to burn through my sandals. I looked at my watch. It was time to turn back. Common sense told me I had better take an autobus to the town center. I had seen stop signs, but not one autobus had passed me going either way. A taxi then? But where to find one? It looked as if I would

255

have to walk. In the midday heat the prospect was daunting. The street map I had thrust into my pocket was not intended for foolish foreigners who stray from the main streets, and I had diverted more than once, as the fancy took me.

The man washing his car outside a modest semi in a side street was the only soul in sight. I summoned up my French and approached him.

"Pardon, monsieur . . ." Was it possible, I asked, to take an autobus to the city center, or perhaps hire a taxicab?

He straightened up and turned, car sponge in hand, to survey me. He was a well-built man of average height, forty or so, fair-haired with blue eyes that matched his blue overalls. Good looking in a rugged way, with something vaguely nautical about his appearance.

"Vous êtes anglaise, Madame?" he inquired. As usual, my accent had given me away. I admitted it and explained I had walked too far and was hoping either to catch an autobus or find a public telephone so that I could call up a taxi.

He laughed. "Mais, il n'y a besoin, Madame," he said. There was no need. His car was at my disposal. In any case, there were no autobuses on Sundays from that district, and to find a taxi would take time. It was certainly much too warm for me to walk, and it would be a pleasure for him to drive me back to my hotel.

I was born incautious. I thanked him and accepted gratefully, telling myself that to refuse such a well-meant offer would be ungracious. It looked a rather battered old car, but as he dusted down the passenger seat for me, he assured me it was road worthy. We had driven for five minutes or so, when he drew into the curb outside a corner café-bar.

Perhaps I would like a glass of wine? On such a warm morning it would be refreshing, n'est-ce pas? And he himself was thirsty after working on his car.

The Swiss, I told myself, were a sober and trustworthy people, and this one looked a nice man. So, pourquoi pas?

As we sat over our glasses of cool white wine, he told me that he had served in the Swiss Navy during the war. Until then I had not even known the Swiss possessed a navy, but I hid my surprise. Before that he had, he said, worked for two years as a chauffeur in London. There was no reason to disbelieve him, except that I had found his English rather worse than my French when I had tried conversing in franglais. So we stuck to French. He asked me what had brought me to Geneva, and I told him of the coming conference. He said he had read about it in the newspaper. I felt his blue eyes studying me and wondered if he found it hard to believe that a delegate's wife would be wandering alone away from the center of the town on a Sunday morning.

We finished our wine. I said I was anxious not to be late and felt I should be getting back. As he ushered me to his car, I told him where I was staying, wishing it didn't sound so grand. "Oui," he said. "Je le connais — " and he added with a smile: "C'est un hôtel de luxe." As we headed for the city center I debated in my mind whether I should invite him to come in for a drink. In his overalls he looked a working man. Might one of the flunkeys try to turn him away? Percy should be grateful to have me brought safely back to base. But there might well be raised eyebrows from his fellow committee members — and their wives. All the same. . . ."

We were in sight of the Hotel du Rhone, and I was still wondering what to do, when he drew into the curb and stopped. "I am going to bid you goodbye here, Madame," he said. "It is better that I do not drive you to the door of your hotel. My car is old and I am not very smart in my overalls, and perhaps your friends will be on the terrace waiting for you."

He got out, opened the door for me, and held out his hand. "It has been a pleasure for me to have been of service to you, Madame," he said as I put my hand in his. I felt the warm pressure of his grip, then with a smile and a little bow he got back into the car and drove away.

The committee meeting was over; Percy and André and the other members with a couple of the wives were on the terrace drinking wine when I joined them. Someone offered to get me a glass.

"Thanks," I said, "but I won't have any more just now. I've been drinking with a Swiss sailor." They all laughed, and no one believed me. I was incorrigible, they said.

It was a successful conference. The ABA, under the chairmanship of Stanley Sawyer, had had second thoughts on pressing for a reduction of the subscription, and unanimity prevailed on all important decisions. The entry of Germany into the league, with its large membership, meant that a supplement to the directory was needed. Once again the time-consuming and unpaid job of sorting and editing the entries fell to Percy and André. For the league, this meant further income from advertising revenue as well as a boost for the directory's sales in Germany. This was the good news. The disappointing news was that the other important project, the dictionary of terms taken on by Hertzberger in Copenhagen, had still to be completed.

The German delegation was led this time by Ernst Hauswedell, who ran an international book and fine arts auction business in Hamburg. Like Helmuth he spoke excellent English. He was a charming, highly civilized man, with an imperturbable manner that never faltered, a characteristic of successful auctioneers.

He was known to have a weakness for pretty women and had come to the conference with his very pretty new wife, Waldtraut, who had been someone else's wife not long before. According to a story going the rounds, a member of her family had come to one of Ernst's auctions and jumping up in the middle of the sale had pointed his finger at Ernst, shouting the accusation: "Adulterer!" Without turning a hair, so the story went, Ernst had calmly continued to take bids for the lot he was selling.

Already there were rumblings of disagreement in the ranks of the German dealers over the alleged domination of the trade by the larger firms, many of whom also ran auctions. Unlike in Britain there was not the clear distinction in Germany between auction houses and antiquarian booksellers. Eventually, the quarrel reached the point when, failing agreement between the two sides (the Verband, to which the auction houses belonged, and the Vereinigung, representing mainly the smaller dealers), Germany temporarily had no representation in the league. Invited by both sides to act as honest broker, Percy would make a trip to Germany to try to achieve a compromise, "an almost impossible task," he declared. But some good did come of his efforts, and the problem of representation in the league was eventually solved.

The Swiss had arranged a couple of treats for us; we were taken for a cruise on the lake, with luncheon aboard, on the first afternoon, disembarking for a stroll in the Jardin Anglais, regarded by the British as a charming, unspoken compliment. Later in the week there was a visit to the private library of Martin Bodmer, a Swiss collector whose name was known to the rare book trade worldwide. This was a very different affair from the never-to-be-forgotten Foyle outing. Everyone behaved impeccably, gazing respectfully with polite murmurs of admiration at the fabulous collection of fine volumes and rarities displayed for our benefit. Not a few of these had no doubt been acquired from some of those present. Promptly at six o'clock the party ended, and we were returned sober and suitably impressed to our respective hotels.

The Swiss ladies' committee opted for safety, as we had in London, and the special event for *les dames* was tea on the terrace of one of the smart department stores. Very sensibly this time there was no press photo call. With the program curtailed to four days we were all less exhausted and in better shape than at previous conferences for the grand finale — the traditional farewell dinner and dance.

At the final session of the assembly Percy had kept to his declared resolve and duly stepped down from the office of president. He had then unanimously been voted President of Honor — not altogether to his surprise.

It was a position he was quite willing to accept; he was not yet ready to retire to the sidelines, and it allowed him to continue to work with the committee and use his influence in shaping the league's future. A time would come when he would feel that his counsel was no longer wanted by the younger members, but that was some years away. It was on his proposal that André, a vice president from the formation, was also voted a President of Honor.

Einar Grónolt Pedersen, another of the old guard who had served his term of office, was persuaded to stay on for another three years without too much difficulty — to everyone's satisfaction — but Menno was not to be persuaded to do the same. Behind the scenes the question of what to do about Menno had been exercising the minds of the rest of the committee. As the man who had thought up the idea of the league, he could hardly be allowed to retire without some sort of official recognition or accolade.

"Why not invent a new office and nominate him Father of the league?" suggested someone. This was hailed as a splendid solution; the title should, it was agreed, confer ex-officio status, which would please Menno (if not everyone else), and it would be non-perpetuating. Duly proposed by Georges Blaizot at the final session of the assembly, it was agreed by acclaim. The vacancy caused by Menno's retirement from the committee was then filled by the election of the past president of the Italian association, Dr. Aeschlimann, a quiet scholarly man who gave the impression of being somewhat remote from events but was well liked and already a familiar face at conferences, with his equally quiet intellectual wife, who composed music, but of what kind I never discovered.

While everyone was congratulating Blaizot on his unanimous election as president, poor Ingelese was in tears, sobbing that we were all trying to kill her husband. It was true that as a diabetic Georges' health was not good, yet ironically it was Ingelese who would die in a very few years, tragically young, while Georges lived until 1976.

With Percy now an ex-officio member of the executive, Stanley Sawyer was voted on to the committee in his place and quickly became known as "John Bull," a nickname he accepted in good part, even signing himself "John Bull" on my menu card at the farewell dinner. Sturdy and stubborn, refusing to speak any language save his own, he admittedly did conform to the continental idea of a typical Briton. But at the same time

he was a man to inspire affection, being completely unpompous and possessed of a strong sense of humor. In common with Dudley Massey,
another hopeless linguist, he seldom travelled abroad without Joy, his
French-speaking wife, who was much admired by André.

An innovation at the Geneva conference was the book exhibition and
sale (including stamps) organized by the Syndicat Suisse in Nicholas
Rauch's auction room during the conference week. The businesslike Swiss
had thought it only sensible to offer their guests (two hundred delegates
from the thirteen countries) the opportunity to buy a few books from
Syndicat members based in other parts of the country as well as from
those in Geneva.

Nicholas Rauch had by this time taken over Kundig's business. He
was a very different character from William, with a quiet pleasant manner and none of William's showmanship. He had an attractive, vivacious
wife, who, like most of the educated Swiss we met, spoke good English.
As host and hostess, both were indefatigable in making the four days a
success. Alas, before very long we would hear that Lucy Rauch had died
of cancer. Nicholas would die of the same disease not so long after.

Our hosts kept us so well lubricated at the farewell dinner, held at the
Restaurant du Parc des Eaux Vives, that by the following morning my
memory of the party was patchy. As always there had been a lot of
speeches, including Georges Blaizot's — with an uncalled-for contribution by an intrusive mouse.

It was a shame about the mouse, for Georges had written pages of an
elegant speech with many a well-turned phrase. Having put on his spectacles, he was proceeding to read it to us when the mouse appeared. The
room in which the dinner was held was lit by strip lighting concealed
under a border of decorative glass running all the way round the ceiling.
The mouse, which had somehow found its way into the space between
the glass and the ceiling, apparently decided it would like to join the
party. Sharply silhouetted by the lighting, it scampered back and forth
above Georges head, occasionally pausing to peer down at the festive
scene below. With his eyes on the pages of his speech, Georges read on,
happily unaware that the attention of his audience was being diverted
elsewhere.

"Une souris! Regardez!" A half-suppressed titter or two caused Georges
to raise his head once, inquiringly. But there were more pages to read,
and he pressed on. By then eyes that had been politely concentrated on
Georges were gazing upwards at the ceiling. There was discreet pointing, nudges. "Ah, mais la pauvre petite," whispered soft-hearted ladies.

260

Winnie Myers, Stanley Sawyer and Charles Howes, part of the British delegation at the 1952 ILAB Geneva conference.

Percy Muir and André Poursin at the 1952 ILAB Geneva conference.

"Oh, the poor little thing! How on earth could it have got up there? The lighting must be singeing its whiskers . . . the management should be told. . . ."

Perhaps it was only rodent curiosity; having stolen poor Georges' thunder, the mouse disappeared like a conjuring trick as suddenly as it had appeared, just before Georges brought his speech to an end.

In his report on the Geneva conference Georges paid a generous tribute to Percy's chairmanship. "Thirty questions were on the agenda; all of them were discussed and resolved. . . . The accomplishment of such a task in such a short time was due to the conduct of the discussions. Tribute for this must first be rendered to the tact and resolution of the Chair. . . ."

There had been throughout, Georges wrote, "an excellent spirit of amity and cooperation. The league had now become a 'fraternité'. . . ."

This had always been Percy's and André's aim. Realists both of them, they knew that such a happy state of affairs could not be taken for granted. Other countries would soon be knocking at the door and would perhaps bring with them fresh problems. Meanwhile, Percy felt he could go home well content.

While Percy, relieved of the burden of the presidency, stayed in Takeley cataloguing the stock he had bought in Germany (Geneva had proved too expensive for stock buying), I was slumming it with the children in West Mersea in a dilapidated caravan, or trailer. Percy had bought the van earlier that year — an impulse buy that we all came to regret. As we should have known, we were not the sort of family to make a success of caravan holidays.

He had spotted it standing forlornly in a field as we returned one day from visiting my mother. It bore a notice "For Sale," which had probably been there for months, for it had long been abandoned by its former occupants.

"Shall we buy it and keep it on a site by the sea at Mersea?" he asked the children, who chorused "Yes" with enthusiasm. The farmer said the price was £60 and must have been surprised and pleased when Percy paid on the spot.

The West Mersea site had not yet been developed and had no amenities bar a stand-pipe for water and some primitive toilets. The sea was within reach, if we were prepared to walk across several hundred yards of sticky black mud. And the site was at the opposite end of the island from my mother's house — perhaps just as well.

After the dolce vita of the Hotel du Rhone, a week in a cramped van with a leaking roof was certainly coming down to earth. Mersea Island was not a smart resort; one wore old clothes, jerseys, and worn-out tennis shoes, and no one bothered. But the place had the curious appeal that islands exercise on those in search of a different way of life, even when easily accessible, as East and West Mersea are with their causeway to the mainland, impassible only during high spring tides.

There were sailing dinghies for hire from boat yards, where fishing nets lay drying in the sun. I could take the children sailing along the creeks; artichokes grew wild on the sandy banks along the coast road with its picturesque mix of nineteenth- and twentieth-century houses overlooking the estuary, unplanned by the dreaded post-war developer. After washing the black mud from our feet, we could go along to tea in my mother's tidy little weather-boarded house, the top windows giving a wide, refreshing view of the Blackwater and the sailing boats bobbing on their moorings. Several of my father's novels had been written in the solitude of an old houseboat ending its life in a mud berth near one of the little tarred oyster huts. It had made a snug enough study for a man who loved the sea.

Chapter 28

Another title was added to Percy's growing list of publications in 1952. During 1948 and 1949 he had persuaded the ABA to sponsor a series of lectures on book collecting by various experts in the field. They were primarily intended for the so-called "Bibliomites," the aspiring young post-war recruits to the rare book trade, the main aim being to introduce them to "certain accepted theories and practices in the trade." But there was no bar to anyone else attending, and, since a second aim was to show the large degree of empathy between dealer and collector, the lectures attracted a number of the latter as well.

The series was a success. When it ended, there was an immediate demand for the lectures to be published. It was thanks to Desmond Flower, one-time co-editor of *The Book-Collector's Quarterly* who had since become managing director of Cassells, that *Talks on Book-Collecting* did finally appear as a handsome, illustrated hardback, with Percy as its editor.

The lectures had been held at the National Book League, and Percy had introduced the series with a general survey of "The Nature and Scope of Book Collecting," the heading of the first of the seven articles to be printed. To say it was a masterly summary would not be an over-statement. There had been other contributions to the series, but as informal talks these did not lend themselves to publication. In his preface to the book, Percy was dismissive of "frivolous amateurs" in bibliography, whom he labelled "flibberti-gibbet point-mongers." These were, I was given to understand, the would-be-clever Johnny-come-latelys who deserved reproof for making life harder for sensible rare book dealers and should on no account be taken seriously by eager young Bibliomites.

The other contributors, all good friends of Percy's, were well-known experts and bibliophiles in their various fields. There was E. P. Goldschmidt with "The Period Before Printing," Simon Nowell-Smith (librarian of the London Library and a keen collector) with "The Language of Book Collecting," John Carter with "Fashions in Book-Collecting," Howard

Nixon, of the British Museum with "Binding and Binders," Ifan Kyrle Fletcher with "Theater for the Collector," and "Milestones of Civilization" by Dr. Weil, from whom Percy had in the past bought many books for Ian Fleming's collection.

It was a well-presented book, of which all concerned could feel proud, and deserved to have been kept in print which, alas, it was not. As a textbook for newcomers to the trade it was an invaluable aid, as it was for the tyro collector. The advice and information given is as valid today as it was in 1952.

Winter was a time when we could settle down to writing with fewer distractions. Percy was working on a history of English children's books, a subject dear to his heart. At the same time, he was reviewing new publications for *The Book Collector* and carrying on with his reminiscences.

He had long since given up using a typewriter, preferring to write by hand with a fountain pen. The manuscript would then be handed over to Reg Read for typing. There would be few corrections, and the writing would be completely legible. The original copy was almost never junked but was stashed away with the carbon copy of the typescript.

I envied Percy his big desk in the office where he did all his personal writing as well as the cataloguing for the firm. Layers of business detritus would accumulate on this desk, but no one was ever allowed to tidy it up.

For me, at that time, there was no alternative to my little davenport in the sitting room, the lid of which would be propped up to accommodate my portable Remington, my typescript having to be crammed inside when I was not working. I was hard at work that winter on a book that was a new departure for me, a fictionalized local story. A small village school not far from where we lived had been closed by the county council on the grounds that it was too small to be viable. There was nothing new in that; it was happening to many rural schools throughout the country. But this time the villagers decided to fight the decision and carry on the school themselves with volunteer teachers.

For a year they kept going with almost a hundred percent support from the community, and for a year a schoolbus waited in the village in vain each schoolday to bus the children to the neighborhood school some four miles away. After the statutory waiting time, the bus would depart and make the scheduled journey empty, to the irritation of the rate-payers. The story was soon taken up by the press, the rejected schoolbus and its driver becoming a target for local press photographers.

Although the villagers lost the battle in the end, I thought it a story worth telling. Listening to the different accounts of this small rural rebellion when I paid a visit to the village, a book began taking shape in my mind. The people involved had been willing to talk, still smarting from their clash with bureaucracy, but not to be named or quoted. For that reason I wrote the story as a novel, with a cast of fictional characters; it was, nevertheless, a true story and a thoroughly satisfying book to write.

The year 1953 — Coronation Year, as the press never let us forget — began inauspiciously with a particularly nasty influenza epidemic. "Forty children away sick from Takeley school," I noted in my diary after one of my official visits in my capacity as a school manager. This was nearly half the school roll. Soon afterwards the virus struck in my own home, laying low first Helen and David and then me, ignoring Percy as usual. Throughout our married life he was remarkably immune to infections and more than once was the only member of the family up and about when some virus was around. This meant he found himself having to do a stint in the kitchen, a situation he did not enjoy.

"I'm going to put you all on a course with a new pill," said our doctor, when, after a brief recovery we all had to return to bed with even higher temperatures, "and we'll see what happens." The pill was M and B, named after the pharmaceutical firm May and Baker, which had developed it. At that time it was looked upon as something of a miracle cure. We obediently swallowed the prescribed course of large, yellow pills, suffered no side effects, and were, indeed, quickly cured.

More disastrous than the flu epidemic was the freak storm that struck the east coast on the last day of January. On that evening, when I went to the field where I kept my hens to shut them up for the night, I found the heavy wooden ark that housed them overturned and the frightened hens scattered in all directions. The force of the wind had been such that it had lifted the ark from the ground, carried it several feet and thrown it on to its side. That same night the combination of an exceptionally high tide with a gale force northwesterly brought death and destruction to the East Anglian coast, causing the worst flooding of the century. The coast of Holland, too, suffered badly.

In mid-January my diary records that Percy and I delivered our son to his boarding school in a more cheerful mood than was usually the case. For the first time, at the age of eleven and a half, he was proudly going back wearing long trousers. On the way home we stopped to visit the poet and literary editor "John Gawsworth," finding him, as usual in his local pub just across the way from his cottage in Stebbing — all too near for his own good. A likeable eccentric and literary odd-job man, he had edited several limited editions of selections from twentieth-century writers and poets. Why he had adopted the rather dreary pseudonym of Gawsworth in place of his own much more interesting name of Terence Fytton Armstrong we never knew. His poetry had not enjoyed a wide circulation; much of it had been published in small or limited editions, some of them self-financed. On the other hand, his editorial jobs had brought him into contact with most of the well-known literary figures of his time, many of whom had become personal friends, for he was an endearing character, drunk or sober, with a talent for friendship.

By this time he was financing his drinking problem by selling off books from his library, together with personal correspondence from collected authors and poets that Percy was very happy to buy from him; it was a well to which we would return a number of times. I think it was on that occasion, that John (or Terence) informed us that he had ennobled us both. He had made Percy, he said, an earl in his hereditary island kingdom, where he solemnly assured us he reigned by right of inheritance. Where this mysterious island was situated we never discovered, but we were not his only friends to be so honored.

My diary also recorded a January meeting in the village to discuss the celebrations for the coronation of Queen Elizabeth II. Up and down the country in towns and villages and on housing estates little groups of loyal subjects were doing the same thing. Coronation mugs had to be ordered for the village children, and, to level things up, pensioners would be given a coronation party. The royal event clearly called for fireworks, and, as all this had to be paid for, most places began planning the usual money-raisers — bazaars, dances and the inevitable summer fête.

In Takeley our program would include all these events plus the provision of commemorative roadside seats for the old age pensioners trudging up the hill to the Post Office to collect their pensions. It was a nice idea, but our smart teak seats, it would transpire, would be mainly used and appreciated by the "roadies" (bums) pushing old prams full of their worldly goods, as they made their way to the casual ward in Braintree, than by our pensioners, who sniffed at resting on seats used by "all those dirty old men."

It was inevitable, so my family said, that I should be landed with the job of Honorary Secretary of the Coronation Committee. In that capacity I was determined that the village should have a commemorative Coronation Bus Shelter, my male fellow parish councillors having previously vetoed the idea on the grounds that people waiting for a bus could well provide themselves with raincoats or umbrellas as they had always done. There was no need to cosset them at public expense, they maintained. "We didn't have a bus when I were a lad," ran the argument. "Had to walk two miles to school an' all. . . ."

I did get our Coronation shelter, but I had not foreseen that it would provide local vandals with a splendid surface for increasingly obscene graffiti, nor that it would be knocked over by a lorry and soon after being re-erected be blown apart by a gas explosion.

From spring to autumn we had a series of house guests. Jacques, André's younger son, was the first to arrive. He was "un pauvre garçon," said his father. His military service had been spent unpleasantly in Indo-China, from where the French had been forced to withdraw after heavy fighting, and where he had caught TB.

He was supposedly staying with us in order to learn English. Cured of his TB, he still had little energy or desire to speak any language save his own. Small and dark-eyed like his mother, he was a smiling, amiable young man prepared to accept philosophically his father's wish that he spend a month in a boring English village in the wake of his sister and older brother. To show he was willing he spent his first morning in Takeley struggling to read an English novel with the aid of an English-French dictionary. Concluding that it was a hopeless and tedious task, he soon gave up and made no further attempt to master the language for the duration of his stay, replying in French or with a polite "pardon" to any remark addressed to him in English.

It was an excellent chance for me to learn French, for he liked nothing better than to sit talking after the evening meal, recounting his experiences as a soldier. He had many a tale to tell of the French resistance during the war and of his soldiering in Cambodia, and pretty horrifying some of them were. I found it strange and disturbing to hear a quiet, pleasant young man speaking of torture as sometimes an acceptable means to an end. We would argue at length over ethics in times of war, an exercise punctuated by my frequent searches for the right word in my own English-French dictionary. Long before this, Percy would have returned to his book or to a radio concert in the sitting room.

Jacques had brought with him a pack of Tarot cards, and he, Helen, and I would sometimes play in the evenings. She had just passed her sixteenth birthday, was very pretty, and spoke French well. Jacques was agreeable to taking her to one of our village dances, and once again I wondered . . . but he had already given his heart to a girl in Paris, and no romance developed.

"He'll have to speak English if I take him up to London," said Percy, feeling he owed a duty to André to encourage the young man to learn. So Jacques was taken to London and left to get along on his own.

"Well, and how did you get on?" Percy asked when they met at the end of the day. "Fine," replied Jacques in French as usual (he understood more English than he let on). "I ran into a girl I'd known in Paris almost at once, and we spent the time together. She knew London well, so we had no problems. It was very agreeable."

While I did my best to fulfill my obligations as a hostess, carry out my duties as honorary secretary, to our coronation committee, and squeeze in some writing time on my village rebellion book as well, Percy was putting together a "Catalogue to Celebrate the Coronation of Her Gracious Majesty Queen Elizabeth II" — Catalogue Number 133. Most of the rare and secondhand book trade was doing the same, but we did scoop the field with one item. This was a manuscript book containing one of the earliest known versions of the national anthem, c. 1745. It included a fourth verse, long since dropped. It was offered at what now seems the ludicrously low price of £25 and was quickly snapped up by a private American collector.

There were many other items appropriate to the royal event, mostly documents relating to past royal personages and events, including an eye-witness account, in a holograph MS by the Garter-King-at-Arms, of Charles II's procession to London on his restoration, in 1660. This too was quickly sold when the catalogue went out in June.

Two minor but amusing items for ephemera collectors were a couple of eighteenth-century trade cards, advertising such unlikely trades as "Suppliers of Asses Milk" and "Original Portable Soup-Makers to H.M.'s Royal Navy."

Such out-of-the-way trifles usually came to us through private buying or from one or two of the faithful "runners" who regularly turned up in Takeley with offerings, knowing that they would be given a fair deal. Others came from our continental buying. Because of the renewed activities of the ring, Percy had given up attending regional book auctions. Many of the former ringers, including some ABA members, were once again operating blatantly at most of the important auctions. This resurgence of illegal activity would before long bring about a fresh anti-knock-out campaign, in which Laurie Deval, as well as Percy, would play no small part.

Jacques departed at the end of his month's stay to work in the family buckle-manufacturing business and was immediately replaced by his sister, Anne-Marie, on her second visit to us. She was by this time a very pretty, confident little teenager. She had, said her father, rather anxiously, as he entrusted her to our care, "the body of a woman with the mind of a child." This was hardly fair, for she was an intelligent girl and a better linguist than either of her brothers, but I noted André's warning. Within two years we would attend her wedding in Paris.

We had already been to the wedding of another French bookseller's daughter. Never having been a guest at a foreign wedding before, I was unprepared for the festivities that followed high mass and the marriage service (the happy couple had to endure a lengthy homily on their knees before the priest) and for the plate to be passed round for contributions to a selected charity. Naturally, I had brought no money and only just had time to nudge Percy for a franc note before the plate reached me. The richness of the wedding feast was less of a surprise, but I hadn't expected that the subsequent party, which began with sedate ballroom dancing and went on long into the night, would end with the old-fashioned party game of "kiss in the ring."

There was a league committee meeting in London in May. Stanley Sawyer, as ABA president and ILAB vice president, pushed out the boat with a dinner at the Savoy for the committee members and their wives. We brought Anne-Marie with us when we came up for the dinner and returned her to her parents *virgo intacta,* to the best of my knowledge.

Before we left for another buying trip in Germany, planning permission came through at last for our house extension and central heating. We had had to join the usual queue for our plans to be passed by the local authority, but we had no special problems in obtaining the necessary permit. With the extension came a welcome improvement grant. The young architect we employed for the job would blend in the alterations so well that the picturesque Tudor character of our house appeared unchanged. We had committed no sacrilege; we had merely made ourselves a lot more comfortable.

Most of our second German buying trip was spent in Munich, although this time we stayed in a village a short train journey from the city in the home of a family doctor whose wife shared with her sister the ownership of an antiquarian bookshop, an old established business they had inherited from their father, in the university area of the city. There Percy could always find stock to his liking, especially children's books. The doctor and his lively, energetic bookseller wife, Lotte, were kindness itself to us, insisting that we should stay in their comfortable modern house in the little village of Vierkirchen, where the doctor had his practice.

Our links of friendship with the whole family would strengthen through the years as first their elder daughter and then the younger came to stay with us, both as diligent at learning English as Jacques had been reluctant.

While we were staying in Vierkirchen, Percy commuted daily to Munich on the electrified railway, a minute's walk from the doctor's house. Mostly I preferred to stay in the village. I had brought my typewriter, but I enjoyed accompanying the good doctor on his morning round of visits. It was flat, farming country; dark patches of pine forest alternated with cornfields and pastureland. The timbered farmhouses were big and deep-eaved with always a steaming midden heap nearby. The woods still harbored a few deer; there were plenty of edible fungi to be picked in the fields. It was still a slow-paced traditional way of life, but villages that had not so long ago been no more than a few peasant cottages and a farmhouse clustered around the church were beginning to grow, as more and more neat brick houses were built to cater for the flood of refugees from the Soviet-controlled East Germany.

"It is so difficult," sighed our German friends. "Of course they must come to the West, and we must all help them. They need homes and work, naturally. Many have fled with nothing. But there are so many of them. . . ." The doctor himself was employing an East German girl with a family to support as a general maid servant. The Berlin wall had not yet been built, and those who could flee from the communists were leaving in a steady stream. It was a hemorrhage of the skilled and able, which was, inevitably, going to be stopped before long.

Delightful as it was to stay in the country with our kind doctor friend, a companionable man who enjoyed having company while his bookseller wife was in her shop in Munich, I could never quite overcome the revulsion of knowing that we were in Kreis Dachau, within a few miles of the site of the infamous concentration camp of that name.

The doctor found it hard to understand our reluctance to drive with him to the picturesque Bavarian town of Dachau, his nearest shopping center, serving a scattering of surrounding villages, including his own.

"But it's a pretty little town," he said rather sadly when I felt unable to accept the picture postcards of the place he had kindly bought for me to send home. As we knew, throughout the war he had been far away from the neighborhood, serving as a doctor on the Russian front.

"No one knew what was going on," he murmured as he put the rejected cards away.

No one? It was hard to believe.

On one occasion Percy and I did find ourselves driving past what had

271

been the concentration camp. We had been told that German students from Munich had walked barefoot to the site to show their shame at what had happened. But on that day there was not a soul in sight, just an empty, derelict, desolate area surrounded by high wire fencing. We did not stop. To see the wire fencing as we drove by was enough to give us both a shivering sense of horror.

Percy had timed our return so that we were in good time for the run-up to the coronation. The preparations in the village were all in hand; the children were to have their party and their pottery mugs imprinted with Her Majesty's crowned head. These would no doubt end up in the bathroom as tooth mugs if they weren't broken first. And our local pensioners (few of whom had TV sets) were to be given the opportunity to watch the coronation on a large-screen television set at the village hall, with transport for the not so mobile.

My eldest sister arrived on a three-month home leave from her overseas civil service post in Malaya. As a head of a department, she had been allocated a couple of tickets for one of the stands on the coronation route. A kind and generous aunt, she proposed taking her niece with her. This, as they were to find, was going to be as much of an ordeal as a pleasure. The ceremony was due to start at 11 AM, but the instructions with the tickets stated it was necessary to take one's seat not later than 8 AM. After that time access could not be guaranteed. To bring food and drink was advisable. There would be a number of portable loos, courtesy the Duke of Norfolk, who was in charge of the arrangements, but access to these was not guaranteed either. And nothing could be done about the weather, except pray for a fine day.

It was a shame that the coronation should have coincided with one of the coldest Junes of the century. On the morning of the great day the temperature at 4:30 AM, the time at which my sister and Helen needed to leave home in order to reach their stand before the deadline, was not much above freezing point. June or not, it was a day for overcoats. Not that they or many other loyal spectators had thought of wearing one.

Despite the weather, it was splendid pageantry. The monarchy was at the peak of its popularity, the British delighted with their young queen, willing to shiver for hours in the cold and at times the rain to see her go by. Sightseers massed along the route in enormous numbers, many having camped at vantage points all night. For those unable to make the journey to London, there was the nonstop coverage by BBC TV and radio. Friends and families gathered together for coronation "telly-parties," the more sophisticated with champagne to toast the new reign. My party was with the Takeley old age pensioners at the village hall (sandwiches and cups of tea), Percy's at the Devals.

"Well, was it worth going up?" I asked Helen when she and her aunt arrived home late in the afternoon, weary and chilled.

"Oh yes! It was freezing cold and we were sitting there for ages, but yes, of course it was worth it!" said my daughter, and my poor sister, still trying to adjust to the rigors of an English summer after the tropical heat of Malaya, nodded in loyal agreement.

At the end of the week we saw the whole show over again in "glorious technicolor" in the warmth and comfort of our local cinema.

Chapter 29

It was not long before there was another guest in our spare room, a young German, the son of the Marburg auctioneer. He was a serious young man who was diligent at improving his knowledge of English. It had been arranged that he should come to us on an exchange visit. Helen, who had recently added German to her school studies, would go to stay in his family in her summer holidays.

Percy had been keen to promote such exchanges between league members, believing it was one of the best ways of breaking down national barriers and prejudices among the next generation. The subject had been on the agenda at ILAB conferences, with proposals that the league should act as an agency to arrange such exchanges. That it was a good idea was warmly agreed, but we were in the very small minority to put it into practice with our daughter, a willing traveller to other lands, and our son, whom we would send off on his own for a seaside holiday with a French family in Brittany in 1954. Soon many schools in both the public and private sectors would take up the idea and make the necessary arrangements, although during the 1950s, exchange visits would mostly be with French rather than German families.

Our young German guest was a well-brought-up young man and very correct in his behavior. He had, perforce, been a member of the Hitler *Jugend*. As a boy in his teens during the occupation, he had not learned to love the British, and, although I did my best to make him feel at home, I doubt if the visit did much to improve his image of us as a nation, for although the young people I introduced him to were pleasant enough to him, they were not noticeably friendly. I doubt, too, if our own easy-going lifestyle was as much to his taste as it was to some of our other exchange visitors. I felt sorry for him, he was such an earnest young man. But at least he learned something of the running of a British antiquarian bookshop (he would be going into his father's business) and improved his knowledge of English. While I marginally improved my German.

After the departure of our young German guest, I took a break from writing, joined a local tennis club, and took in a couple more guests, my young nephew and niece once again. I was fond of them and enjoyed having them to stay, although admittedly two boys will always get up to more mischief than one. Helen, having by then gone to Germany on her exchange visit, the set-up was rather as in the *Just William* books, with Brenda in the roll of Violet, the disregarded, lisping little sister who tags along after the two boys. That they once subjected her to electric shock treatment by persuading her to put her finger into an electric light socket (to see what happened), I did not know until many years later. By good luck she lived to tell the story but never forgot the 240-volt shock that sent her flying across the garage floor.

My novel about the so-called rebel school (*Rebellion on the Green*) had been dispatched to the publishers, and I was letting the plot for my next book work in my mind before putting it down on paper. My job with the village coronation committee was finished, the bus shelter erected, the commemorative garden seats in place. With all this satisfactorily accomplished, I felt virtuous and free to enjoy the last weeks of summer with the children.

It was the turn of the Italians to host the league conference in 1953. I had hoped the venue would be Florence, but they chose Milan and had made the date the end of September.

"André wants us to spend the night at their country house on the way and then drive on to Milan with them," Percy said. "It will mean crossing into Italy over the Mont Cenis pass. André says he knows the route, and there shouldn't be any problem at that time of the year. We'll come back on our own along the Italian Riviera."

My sister would still be on leave, so we invited her to come with us. Like us, she had never been to Italy and was delighted to be included. With the conference taking place at a later time of the year than usual and with a greater distance to travel, there would be a smaller British delegation than in Geneva, and it would be led by Charles Howes, a dealer from Hastings who had followed Stanley Sawyer as president.

Percy knew Charlie as a colleague and fellow member of the ABA committee. He was a provincial bookseller of the old sort, self-taught, rough-hewn, and not reluctant to join the boys in the ring if the occasion demanded it. Nevertheless, Percy liked him, and they got along well as ABA colleagues. Neither of us had met Mrs. Howes, and Charlie did not bring her to Milan. Had he done so, we might have made different plans for attending the Austrian conference the following year.

The sun was shining when we left Beauregard on a late September morning and headed southwest, with the Poursins leading the way in their Citroën. There was a long mountainous journey ahead, and secretly I quailed at the prospect, although André had assured us that it was a good road over the French Graians, a range with peaks of more than eleven thousand feet. Our pre-war MG was a great improvement on the late unlamented Lancia; all the same, she was already middle-aged and not to be taken for granted.

By the time we came to Lyons, it was raining hard. André was, as usual, determined not to miss the opportunity of calling on an antiquarian book dealer in the city, so we drove through the busy, congested town center to find his shop. The man was *raisonable*, bargains could sometimes be found, said André. No matter that we were aiming to reach Turin before nightfall, we must pay the shop a visit.

By then it was far too wet to wander around Lyons while the formalities of introducing André's *bon colleague anglais* took place and some buying could be usefully done. Instead, Edith, my sister, and I stayed in the car, Edith patient as usual, my sister and I bored and fidgety, watching the rain bucket down and the minutes tick away — until the men reappeared with a purchase or two and having obviously been offered suitable refreshment. It was time, declared André, to study the Michelin and find a restaurant for lunch.

On our way again, nearly two hours later, the rain was still pouring down. We were heading for Mondane, a long ascent on the Trans-Alpine highway with flood water pouring off the road surface. Instead of the spectacular views we had been promised, a grey curtain of rain hid the peaks and glaciers as the MG's windscreen wipers worked at top speed to do their job. We were lucky to be on a relatively level stretch when we rounded a bend and found ourselves in a pond of volcanic mud where a torrent from a mountain stream had flooded down to wash part of the road away.

Both cars came to a halt. There was nothing for it but for everyone to get out and push. No one had thought of putting wellies in the car; it wasn't that sort of trip. Stripping off shoes and stockings (not on any account to be sacrificed), Edith, my sister, and I stepped down into two feet of warm grey sludge, and, with some concerted shoving from us all, the car wheels found their grip and we were through. By then all hope of reaching Turin that evening had to be abandoned.

A large, empty, and partially destroyed hotel (a war-time casualty) with skeleton staff provided us with shelter for that night. They had been unprepared for guests, but being French, they served us a respectable meal. We still had some three thousand feet to climb when we set off the next morning, and it was still raining. The cars' mud baths had made them splutter. When we were less than three kilometers from the wide saddle of the Mont Cenis pass, the MG, which had been gamely struggling not to be beaten by a Frenchie, burst a lung, or rather her water jacket.

"Mon Dieu! Quel est arrivé maintenant?" cried André, hurrying to the rescue, as usual convinced that only he was capable of handling the situation, whatever it was. Unwilling to be proved incompetent, Percy had a guess at the trouble and thought there might be a spare jacket in the emergency kit. Mercifully, there was.

Under my upheld umbrella and with André freely giving instructions, the replacement was effected, and we made it into Italy. But there could be no making up for lost time on the descent from the pass and through a primitive customs post ("loo a hole in the ground with a foothold on either side," I noted) into the valley. "Peasants herding sheep, cattle and goats walked or cycled along the crown of the road, holding black umbrellas over their heads, whether riding or walking. The girls wore black cardigans over cotton dresses and paid little attention to the traffic as if the road belonged to them," my journal continued. No doubt they considered that it did.

Milan was steamy hot. We were booked at a newly built hotel with air conditioning, then a novelty. But like many other innovations in early postwar Italy, it could not be relied upon to work. There was a row of buttons by our bedside to be pressed for desired services. They would bring a chirruping reply of "pronto," but the service seldom lived up to the word.

Lacking the charm of Venice and the grandeur of Rome, Milan could score with the da Vinci *Last Supper,* rescued after a raid in 1944 that had largely destroyed the chapel that had contained it. Now visitors to Milan were once again able to visit it and marvel. They could be impressed by the Piazza Duomo with its medieval palaces and great gothic cathedral and stroll pleasurably through the smart galleria that leads off the palazzo, where everyone seems to meet and we found ourselves constantly bumping into other delegates.

The Italians were naturally not going to be outdone by the previous host countries either in hospitality or in the treasures they showed us. Aside from the four general assembly sessions, they were determined that we should see as much of their cultural heritage as could be squeezed into five days. It was a rich diet.

Delegates of the 1953 ILAB Milan conference examining a rare manuscript.

As usual, a tour of the city had been arranged for the ladies while the delegates were attending the first general session. This rather surprised us by including a visit to the extensive cemetery, where we were taken to see the tombs of the rich Milanese merchants whose families had vied with each other in honoring their dead with enormous ornate mausoleums, each more hideous than the next. The cemetery did contain some fine sculptures, but it was the memory of those monumental monstrosities, of which our guide seemed oddly proud, that remained with me rather than the classical beauty of the sculptures.

My Milan journal recorded that our guide for the tour of the cathedral was "a funny little man in a wide-brimmed hat who made too many well-used jokes in bad English, repeating them in bad French to make sure none of his flock missed the point." Apart from the awe-inspiring size of the cathedral, the memory that stayed with me was of the tiny figure of the Virgin Mary (brass, I think) on the great main door, which women wishing to conceive came to touch in the hope that the Virgin would grant their wish. Over the centuries the touch of thousands of hands and lips had worn down the surface and features of the little icon so that only the shape remained.

Milan had suffered much war damage, and there was a great deal of rebuilding in progress. It was while we were in an old courtyard being shown yet one more medieval church that my guardian angel came once again to my rescue. As my sister and I stood with our group looking up at an inscription over the doorway, there was the staccato sound of small stones hitting the ground near me. Instinctively I stepped back; almost immediately a large chunk of masonry weighing at least half a ton broke away from above the doorway and crashed to the ground at my feet.

My sister, who had seen the masonry beginning to come away, had tried to cry "Look out!" but horror had strangled her cry of warning in her throat to a barely audible squeak. Had the chunk hit me, it would have certainly split my skull. After that escape from death, I walked warily, like Agag, for the rest of our stay in Milan.

Percy, always obsessively punctual, found it hard to adjust to the Italians' habitual unpunctuality. Invariably we arrived before our hosts, who never appeared the slightest embarrassed at not being there to greet us. The French knew better, declaring that while in France it was normal to arrive half an hour late for a party, in Italy there was no point in turning up earlier than an hour after the stated time. With a few notable exceptions, we found the Italians agreeable but casual. For me almost the best part of being in Italy was listening to Italians talking (or sometimes singing) their beautiful language. Admittedly, they are a noisy people, their passions quick to bubble to the surface in a torrent of words. But even *fortissimo* Italian never grated on the ear, at least for me.

Nor could I be cross with the hairdresser who paid no attention to my wishes while setting my hair for the farewell dinner, when he sang snatches of opera not quite beneath his breath while he worked.

The general assembly sessions took place in an impressive salon in the Museum of Natural Sciences, where the members of the committee sat on tall chairs against a background of carved oak panelling, resting their papers on an elaborate, curved, marble-topped buffet with an enormous oil canvas of some homeric scene as a backdrop.

The Milan conference saw the publication and distribution of *A Compendium of Usages and Customs of the Trade*. This useful volume defined the customary practices of the rare book trade (as William Kundig had once proposed) for use in disputes, litigation, or legal difficulties. The delegates were, for the first time, also issued with Cards of Welcome for use when travelling, an idea proposed and carried out by the French. These were to show that the holder had paid his or her subscription to the league and could be trusted as a reputable dealer who, in the event of litigation, would submit to the arbitration of the league.

Percy and Stanley Sawyer had been working together to establish the right of booksellers to return books insufficiently described in auction catalogues that later turned out to be unsatisfactory, a source of dispute and ill-feeling for many years between the rare book trade and the auction houses. With the league's muscle behind them, they had achieved their objective, the "right of return" having been accepted in twelve out of the thirteen member countries. On hearing that "evasive action" from one American auction house was the reason for a less than a hundred percent response, "unanimous disapproval" was expressed by the assembly. Presumably, this general condemnation later had the desired effect.

As always, the league was in need of more cash to carry on with its agreed work. The solution thrashed out at length between the presidents and the committee was a voluntary increase to be paid by eight of the member countries. This excluded the UK (the ABA thought they were already paying too much) and the Scandinavian countries, with their small membership. The rest agreed to a small percentage increase ranging from ten to twenty-five percent.

"A happy solution to our financial problems," said Georges Blaizot, with relief. Once again the tactics initiated by Percy of getting the hard bargaining done behind the scenes at meetings of the presidents had paid off.

Freed from the obligations of president, Percy still felt in duty bound to attend committee meetings as well as general assembly sessions. But in Milan there was at last time for him to visit a few bookshops as well, in the hope of paying some of the expenses of the trip. This turned out to be less rewarding than he had hoped, for he soon found that to buy and have the books sent back to England involved arrangements of such Byzantine complexity that he lost patience. Bargaining had always been distasteful to him, and aiding and abetting dealers to dodge tax and export regulations was even more so.

This being Italy, the venue for the farewell dinner could hardly have been more romantic. Coaches were hired to drive us all to Lake Como, where we dined in the ballroom of the Grand Hotel Villa de'Este, the honeymoon choice of many a British bride and bridegroom in pre-war days. After the dinner and not-to-be-avoided speeches, we danced until two in the morning on the cool mosaic floor, ending the evening with Ingelese Blaizot singing French love songs and Percy responding with English ones.

After seeing my sister off on her flight back to England, her leave being nearly over, Percy and I set off on a leisurely return journey along the Italian Riviera. Less taxing than our route into Italy, the miles and miles of *plage*, edged with the ubiquitous red cannas and frowned down on by granite cliffs, soon became boring. Here and there the road ducked into a narrow tunnel only to emerge to more plage and cannas. But Alassio, with its palm trees, its pink-washed, green-shuttered villas picturesquely perched above the sea, carnations growing wild along the roadside, looked as if it was posing for a holiday brochure. In contrast, the frontier at Ventimiglia was sadly depressing. Gaps, derelict houses, buildings pock-marked by shells told their story of the years of war and neglect. Little seemed to have been done since.

Then we were back in France, where the peasant farmers were drying out the harvest, spreading hand-threshed corn over their flag-stoned yards before sweeping it into heaps of golden grain. We made use of the air car-ferry from Dinard to Lympne — quicker and no more expensive than the Calais-Dover crossing, some years away from roll-on, roll-off.

While we were in Milan the news of Percy's mother's death had caught up with us after the funeral had already taken place. She had died when we were on our way to Italy, and Percy's brother had not been able to get in touch with us until we arrived in Milan.

"We had said goodbye to her," Percy said without emotion after he read the telegram. Shortly before we left we had gone to see her in the

281

residential home where she had been for some weeks. The senility that had been creeping upon her slowly for a couple of years had by then destroyed what was left of her once strong and independent personality. When she talked, it was as if she was back in the early days of her marriage. Perhaps she had recognized Percy? Perhaps she had not been unhappy lying there quietly lost in her memories. We couldn't be sure. It had been strange to hear her talk of Percy's father as if he was still with her. Saddened though I was by my mother-in-law's passing and for her eldest son's absence from the funeral, I could feel no grief, for the last months of her life had had no meaning. There remained the melancholy task of sorting out her effects and a lifetime's accumulation of family letters and photographs. What did one do with them? Would future generations really want to gaze at stiffly posed studio portraits of late-Victorian ancestors? It seemed unlikely. All the same, they were stored away with the rest of our family clutter. To hoard comes all too naturally to dealers in books and ephemera.

Chapter 30

Nothing sets an antiquarian bookseller's adrenalin flowing more than the prospect of acquiring an important private library. Several had come our way during the years following our move from London to Essex. There had been A. J. A. Symons' (a second bite of the cherry), the extensive Sir Wilfred and Alice Meynell library, many books from the R. W. Chapman collection, and from Buxton Forman and Holbook Jackson, to name a few that Percy had handled with pleasure and profit. Probably the most exciting collection of all was that of Ian Fleming, which Percy sold complete on behalf of Anne Fleming, Ian's widow, after Ian's death in 1964. But that's another story.

Mostly, libraries came to Elkin Mathews through personal friendship, which was how it was that Percy came to deal with the late Sir William Rothenstein's library, his original portrait drawings, and his collection of works by contemporary artists.

In the late 1920s Percy had rented a cottage in the northwest Essex village of Great Bardfield. It was old and picturesque enough to catch the eye of a townsman and, typically for the time, had few amenities. His first wife, used to the conveniences of urban life, failed to share his enthusiasm for picnicking weekends with evenings lit by oil lamps and meals cooked on an old kitchen range. Finally, she struck and stayed in London.

It was during this time that Percy came to know the nucleus of what was to become "the Bardfield Group" of artists. Edward Bawden was living a hundred yards or so along the road from Percy's cottage, and John Aldridge was almost opposite. Writers as well as artists were drawn to the area. It was not too far from London, and rents were low. Even so, after the breakup of Percy's marriage, a second home was a luxury he could no longer afford, and for a time, during the war years, most of his Bardfield friendships lapsed, although he made a point of visiting A. J. A. Symons at Finchingfield until A. J.'s death in 1941.

It was towards the end of the 1940s that I came to know Charlotte Bawden through our mutual interest in the Women's Institutes. Charlotte introduced me to Duffy Rothenstein, a portrait painter who specialized in painting children. Duffy was then married to the artist Michael Rothenstein, and they had not long before come to live in Great Bardfield with their two children. I wanted a portrait in oils of my daughter, and Duffy, with her pre-Raphaelite looks, could charm any child into sitting for her.

Helen was no exception; the portrait I commissioned was a success, and a friendship was formed. Thus, we began visiting Bardfield again; Percy renewed his pre-war friendship with Bawden and John Aldridge and came to know Michael, who was the younger son of Sir William Rothenstein, and some of the other artists who were beginning to form a small colony in the village, attracted by the fact that it had character yet was still unspoiled.

Sir William Rothenstein had died in 1945. He had been a man of dynamic personality, a talented artist who had painted the portraits of most of the notable men of his time. The estate was large and complicated, and it was not until 1953 that Michael and his elder brother, John, then director of the Tate Gallery, asked Percy if he would handle the books, papers, and drawings on behalf of the family, beginning first with the sale of Sir William's personal library.

The books were just the kind that Percy enjoyed cataloguing. It meant a great deal of work, for there were more than seven hundred separate items, including the chef d'oeuvre — Sir William's own heavily corrected proof copy of his autobiography, *Men and Memories*, two volumes in an elaborate blue morocco binding. There was also a holograph Beardsley MS of his poem *The Three Musicians* and some Beardsley letters. The library was strong in contemporary authors who had sat for Sir William and more often than not presented him with a signed copy of their current work, as had George Meredith, George Moore, Bernard Shaw, and Siegfried Sassoon. John Gawsworth, never one to do things by halves, had presented two volumes of his privately published poems.

Apart from literary items, the library ranged widely, including Asian and Oriental art. Percy issued the catalogue in September 1954 with Max Beerbohm's funeral tribute to his old friend Will Rothenstein as a foreword. Orders poured in, mainly from private and institutional buyers in the United States. Within a very short time more than ninety percent was sold. But this was by no means the end of it; a catalogue of Sir William's original portrait drawings was to come, together with the work of artists he had added to his collection. Then there were the lithographs, in the hundreds. Selections of these would appear in our catalogues for years to come.

In February 1954 Percy received an intriguing letter from Belgium. Some while before, when he was on a combined buying trip and committee meeting in Brussels, he had, as he put it, sown some seeds. Although since then there had been no signs of germination, he had not quite given up hope. From the days when he had first begun to buy books in Brussels the possibility of finding some relics of Emily or Charlotte Brontë had always been at the back of his mind. There was one bookseller in particular, a middle-aged, rather formal man with a schoolmasterly manner, with whom he had always got on well and who he felt was the most likely to come up trumps.

"It is strange," he would remark to this gentleman, "that one never hears of anything connected with the Brontë sisters turning up here in Brussels, despite the time they spent at the Heger establishment."

Monsieur van der Perre would agree it was rather surprising, and he would add with a smile that he had not forgotten Monsieur Muir's interest in the sisters.

His letter was brief. If Percy was still interested in Brontë relics, he wrote, there would be something to show him next time he was in Brussels. That was all. The letter gave no details.

This was maddeningly vague. Percy at once put in a call to Brussels. The "relics," said Monsieur van der Perre, were exercise books, but he did not enlarge on the contents. They would be put aside until next time Monsieur was in Brussels.

The following day Percy was on his way to Belgium. He was far too impatient to wait. Besides, as he said later, dealers had been known to change their minds, or be tempted by an unexpected cash offer. To his exasperation, when he arrived at the shop the next morning, he was told that Monsieur was at an auction sale and would not be back until the late afternoon.

Percy had not said that he would be arriving that day, so it was not possible even to see the Brontë material and satisfy his curiosity. There was nothing for it but to mooch around the city, visit a few colleagues, and pretend he was in Brussels for quite another reason than the true one.

When he eventually returned to the shop, the proprietor was still absent. "Perhaps Monsieur would like to look at some books while he is waiting?" suggested the good-looking, smartly dressed assistant brightly.

As he later discovered, she was rather more than an assistant. Monsieur van der Perre's stock was mainly prints and architectural books, as Percy well knew. Concealing his impatience, he pretended to look along shelves that were of no interest to him. It was the Brontës or nothing.

"I was tired from my day-long wanderings. All I wanted was to clinch the Brontë deal, if it was possible, return to my hotel, and go to bed," he told me later.

Presently Monsieur van der Perre arrived. He, too, was tired; he had had a long day at the auction sale. He greeted Percy courteously but rather wearily. "I am glad to see you, my friend," he said. "But let us not discuss business tonight. "Let us instead relax with a whiskey-soda . . ."

"I won't be more than a couple of days at the most," Percy had said to me when I saw him off to Brussels. That was the last I heard until four days later a telegram arrived. The message was: "Returning home today," with the time of the train I was to meet at Stortford station.

When Percy's train drew in, I was on the platform, eagerly scanning the alighting passengers. There he was, waving and smiling broadly.

"Ah, it's good to be home. All well?"

"Of course, but what were the 'relics'? Have you got them?" I was bursting to know the outcome.

"Something far more exciting than I had ever expected," he said, smiling contentedly. "I'll show you when we get home."

Once we were home, he took from his briefcase two plain school exercise books, the covers a little faded, the corners a little dog-eared. In one was an essay in French in Charlotte Brontë's writing, *un devoir* for Monsieur Heger. The subject Napoleon. The other was by Emily, a strange, philosophical allegory that she had titled "The Palace of Death." A polished version of Charlotte's essay had been published in Mrs. Gaskell's life of Charlotte. Emily's had never before come to light. Apart from a minor correction or two by Monsieur Heger, it was just as she had written it in her clear, sloping hand. The books had come from a descendent of the Heger family (Monsieur van der Perre was cagey as to which one), their provenance was impeccable, the price not unreasonable.

I held the exercise books in my hands, first one and then the other, trying to picture the two young women sitting at a table in their teacher's house working on their *devoir,* dipping their steel-nibbed pens into an inkwell, in both their minds the hope of one day having a school of their own. And that had been one hundred and eleven years ago. It was an odd, almost uncanny feeling.

The destination for this remarkable Brontë material could be no other than Haworth, the birthplace of the Brontë sisters, although the Brontë Society was not in a position to pay the sort of price it would have made in the United States. However, a price was agreed, and Elkin Mathews made a reasonable profit on the deal. Not long after this acquisition was put on show at the Brontë Museum, Margaret Lane gave a radio talk on Emily's essay. This appeared in the BBC's publication, *The Listener.* The essay was, she wrote, "as sombre a piece . . . as can ever have come out of a boarding school for young ladies. . . ." Brontë enthusiasts can read it both in the original French and in a translation in *The Transactions of the Brontë Society* for 1953-54.

In July 1953 Percy signed a contract with Chatto & Windus for the publication of the reminiscences he had been writing for *The Book Collector*. The work was not named, probably because he had not then hit on the clever title of *Minding My Own Business*. It was a fairly standard agreement for that time — 12½ percent on the first 3,000 copies sold and 15 percent thereafter with an advance of £250. These were the same royalties that I was currently getting from Hurst and Blackett, and as I took it for granted that Percy ought to be worth more to a publisher than someone like me, I urged him to go to a good literary agent. This he refused to do, either for his reminiscences or his bibliographies, preferring the direct contact with his publishers, which always remained cordial. As far as his own writings were concerned, he was the least commercially minded of men. Chatto was clearly being cautious and did not expect to find itself with a bestseller on its hands. Nor, in fact, did the firm ever reprint the book, successful though it proved to be.

As it turned out, publication was postponed (Chatto's lawyers fussed over sections that referred to people still alive), and it was *English Children's Books* that appeared in April 1954. This was Percy's ninth book and by far the most handsome. Batsford had published it as a quarto with numerous illustrations. It had a charming Kate Greenaway jacket from an illustration in *The Girl's Own Paper* (1886) and some attractive color plates.

The book was fittingly dedicated to the man who, in 1949, had bought the major part of the famous Bussell Collection, which had formed the basis of the National Book League's Children's Book Collection in 1947. This was Edgar Oppenheimer, the American owner of a world-famous collection of children's books. He and Percy had met in 1951 in New York, where Percy had been invited to see the Oppenheimer Collection. It had been a fruitful meeting and subsequently brought Percy much help and advice when he got down to the job of covering three centuries of children's books. One of the most time-consuming tasks of compiling such a book was in hunting down the desired illustrations — more than one hundred of them in this case. Mr. Oppenheimer had helped there, too, as had Dr. D'Alte Welsh, another good friend and customer.

Batsford had intended the print run to be 3,500 copies. Percy had settled for a royalty of 10 percent, rising to 15 percent for copies sold over that figure (which Batsford, in any case, did not expect to exceed), but, in the event, as an American publisher took 1,000 copies they ran off 4,000 and had to pay up another £50 on top of the agreed advance of £250. The published price was 42s., reflecting that the number of illustrations made it an expensive book to produce.

Despite the price, it got off to an excellent start, with more than 2,000 copies sold before publication. The reviews were uniformly good, with only a minimum of the nitpicking that few reviewers can resist. The blurb truthfully called the book both "scholarly and entertaining." Percy was happy with its appearance and general presentation but chagrinned to find that despite all his care, some minor errors had crept into the text. These, as they were pointed out by correspondents, were instantly corrected in his master copy and would be in the second impression. A third impression would appear in 1979 and a fourth in 1985.

In a letter to Sam Carr, Batsford's managing director, Percy wrote: "The book was as good as I could make it and I am glad you find it excellent. I for my part feel that its kind reception is due to no small degree to the beautiful turn-out you have given it. . . ."

The association between author and publisher had been a harmonious one from the beginning ("I consider I have been treated most handsomely and considerately," Percy wrote in the same letter) and would continue over the years with the amended second impression of *English Children's Books* appearing in 1969. His second Batsford title, *Victorian Illustrated Books*, would be published in 1971. For a time, during the 1960s, Percy acted as general editor for a Batsford series of collector's books, but this eventually ran into the ground due to the difficulty of finding willing and able authors to write such books.

A few years after the publication of *English Children's Books*, Percy learned with surprise and some gratification that it had become required reading for students doing a course on librarianship, when one of the staff at our local public library greeted him respectfully by name.

"Oh, so you know me," Percy said. "Yes, of course, I do, Mr. Muir," replied the young lady. "I had to read your book for my course."

The February trip to Brussels was not the only continental treasure hunt that year. An unexpected summer expedition to the Midi with Dave Randall, the head of Scribner's Rare Book Department in New York, turned out to be one of those once-in-a-lifetime antiquarian bookseller's dreams come true.

Dave tells his version of the story in his autobiography, *Dukedom Large Enough*. It began when an attractive young French girl walked into Scribner's rare book store and showed Dave some books she had brought with her from France and hoped to sell. They came, she said, from the family library housed in a chateau in the Midi. Among a number of desirable volumes, including presentation copies of works by important nineteenth-century writers, were several by Walter Savage Landor, annotated in his own hand. These turned out to be the author's personal copies, and Mademoiselle disclosed that they were in the library as a result of Landor's love affair with a member of her family.

With a deal satisfactorily concluded, Dave began looking into the possibility of more from the same source. After some correspondence and research, he learned that books from the library had been put into auction from time to time, suggesting that the best items would probably have gone. After that, what with the chateau containing the library being right off the map and Dave having plenty of work in hand just then, his enthusiasm cooled. Nevertheless, the thought of sometime making the trip to see what might still be there remained at the back of his mind — until some months later he was reminded of it when he needed to make a business trip to Paris.

"Dave Randall has been on the phone," Percy said, coming over to the house from the office one fine summer morning. "There's a library in the Midi he's interested in. As he hardly speaks a word of French, he's not keen on going on his own, and he wants me to go with him. He thinks there might be enough there to make it worthwhile for us both. Scribner's will foot the bill, so I've said I'll go with him. The plan is for him to stay here overnight so that we can set off together for Dover the next morning." A few days later, Dave arrived on a morning train. He was a big, broad-shouldered man with a good-humored, easy manner, shrewd brown eyes, and a remarkable capacity for holding his liquor. He and Percy were old friends since before the war and had concluded many satisfactory deals together. He was straightforward and good company. I, too, liked him.

He settled down comfortably in our sitting room as soon as he arrived — dry martini in hand (his usual tipple) and was soon unloading his latest stories of the book world, for he loved talking and was a practiced raconteur. I suspected he had spent most of the journey from London to Bishop's Stortford in the refreshment car, but if so it had no effect on the flow of anecdotes. It was only when he began to tell us the story of a book-buying trip that he had recounted only ten minutes earlier, repeating it word for word, that I decided my suspicions were correct. Not that it mattered; it was a good enough story to bear repeating. The trip ahead was to prove a sterner test of his drinking capacity.

The two men left for Paris the next morning and from there took an overnight train to the nearest town to their destination, where they were met by the Countess, the owner of the library and the mother of the pretty girl who had sold the Landors and other books to Scribner's and was then living in Paris with her husband, the Irish-American writer, Donn Byrne.

The Countess, an attractive woman of considerable charm — as I was left in no doubt of later — then drove them to the chateau, miles from anywhere, full of history, and in serious need of repair.

"A charming weekend followed," wrote Dave, recalling the visit several years later. The downside was that there were no books of the kind he had envisaged. The library was large, cluttered, and ill-lit. Someone with a practiced eye had clearly been through it already. No real rarities remained.

The Countess told her guests that they were welcome to look where they liked — in the closets and cupboards and in the many upstairs rooms. Thanks to its isolated position, the chateau had escaped the ravages of the wars but not of time. There was a muniment room full of family documents, but these, said the Countess, were not for sale.

Percy, poking around in one of the cupboards, did find one valuable book of particular interest to Dave. This was a first edition of Thoreau's *A Week on the Concord and Merrimack Rivers*, a presentation copy to Landor of the author's first book. Dave's chagrin at not having discovered it himself was offset by the knowledge that this lucky find alone made the trip worthwhile. Determined not to be outdone by Percy, he doggedly continued to search.

"The evening before our departure I went prying around the plentiful old closets . . . partly to see if something hadn't been overlooked and partly to prove to Muir that, by golly, I was as good a needle-in-the-haystack hunter as he was. . . ."

This time Dave came up trumps. On top of a large pile of books and documents was a manuscript in French that made him pause and study the title page. Although he did not at once realize it, what he was looking at were the memoirs of a king of England — James II — written in the king's own hand when he was Duke of York. With the manuscript was a certificate of authentication signed by five officials.

With mounting excitement, Dave took the manuscript to his room to study and was soon convinced that it was authentic. The question then was would the Countess be willing to part with it? And even then would the French government be willing to grant an export license, since it could be classed as a national treasure?

The following morning he and Percy put their heads together. Percy was able to translate the preface, which explained how the manuscript came to be in the possession of the Countess's family. It had been entrusted to Cardinal de Bouillion by the king with the instructions that it was to be shown to no one during his lifetime. The cardinal had fulfilled his duty and faithfully guarded it in his own library unseen by anyone for the remainder of his life. After his death the library had passed into the keeping of his nephew, an ancestor of the Countess; there it had remained undiscovered until Dave had pulled it out of the closet.

He was due to leave that same day and felt he should try his luck with the Countess before his departure. Percy's advice was not to rush it, better to wait for the right moment before broaching the matter, especially as the Countess had already demurred over selling the Thoreau book, also a family treasure, although she had given way in the end. "The problem was solved in the simplest way," Dave wrote. "I returned to London and left Muir to attend to the details."

Percy had asked Dave to ring me as soon as he got back. I had heard nothing since they left and was waiting eagerly for news.

"Well, how did you get on, and where's Percy?" I wanted to know.

"Had to leave him behind," Dave said with a chuckle. "He's staying on at the castle with this Countess we've been to see. Oh boy, has she taken a fancy to him! Sure, we found a thing or two. Could be big, but Percy'll tell you about it when he gets home — if she'll let him go."

In his own account of the purchase of the James II memoirs, written to a friend, Percy described his last evening at the chateau.

Earlier the Countess had driven him forty miles to have drinks with some friends of hers. On their return she cooked them a meal, her only servant being a dimwitted old man.

"After a late supper the Countess invited me to see the view from the battlements by moonlight," Percy wrote. "We climbed a spiral staircase in one of the towers and as we emerged into a kind of loft I saw that the floor was covered with an amazing variety of receptacles — buckets, baths, chamberpots, even a bed-pan or two. My hostess explained that this was a precaution against a repetition of her experience during the previous year's rainy season when water had streamed through the roof and brought ceilings down.

"As we came up onto the roof she pointed out that all the lead was porous and needed replacing. She had had an estimate for renewing it, but the required sum was entirely beyond her means.

"'And you had hoped perhaps,' I suggested, 'that Landor's books might provide for the possibility of having the work done?'

"'Yes, but you have removed that foolish idea from my head. I am sure your valuation is an honest and accurate one. But the sum you offer would go nowhere. Perhaps though you will still find something, somewhere that will keep a roof over my head.'

"'We have,' I said, and at three o'clock in the morning on that moonlit roof I told her what we had found. I was not surprised to learn that she had no idea of the nature of the document. She wanted to see it at once so we went down to examine it. She was quite indefatigable and would have sat up all night poring over it. . . ." Finally Percy persuaded her to retire to bed, taking it with her, and he was able to sleep for a few hours.

Torn between reluctance to part with such an important family heirloom and her worries about the roof repairs, the Countess decided to leave her daughter to make the final decision, for after all, she said, it was part of her inheritance.

"But without the repairs your chateau will soon not be worth inheriting," Percy reminded her.

She acknowledged that he was right. "You will meet my daughter in Paris on your return to France," she said. "I am sure she will see the point of your argument. But if she says I am not to sell, I shall be glad."

Percy left later that day without any decision having been made. There was one other condition: Should the deal be agreed, a complete facsimile of the document must be made and enclosed in a copy of the original eighteenth-century binding, both to be given to the Countess at the buyer's expense.

Not long after Percy's return home, he and Dave learned that the daughter had agreed to the sale. (Permission was also eventually obtained from the French government.) Dave was then back in New York, so it was Percy who travelled again to the chateau, this time on his own, to complete the purchase arrangements. Whether he would have liked to linger there awhile (as Dave made out), I never knew. But he did do

André a good turn by giving him an introduction to the Countess, to the benefit of them both.

By the time the manuscript reached New York, Dave was on the point of leaving his job at Scribner's to become librarian of the Lilly Collection at Indiana University. As he recorded in his autobiography: "It became my first major addition to the Collection and was published by the Indiana Press in 1962. Subsequently it was published in London by Chatto & Windus."

Understandably, Dave does not mention his farewell lunch with Percy and the Countess, nor his journey on the train back to Paris. Before he left, she had taken them both to a favorite restaurant of hers, where Dave had insisted on trying the locally produced marr, a potent form of brandy made from the skins of the grapes. Both Percy and the Countess warned him it was a lethal drink, but Dave was not a man to forego a challenge. After plenty of wine topped by a couple of glasses of marr, it became something of a problem to get him aboard his train, as he repeatedly declared his devotion to the Countess, with many attempts to embrace her. Somehow the two of them managed to bundle him into his seat while he was bewailing having to leave "lucky old Muir" to stay another night in the chateau.

Before the train left, Percy thought it would be as well to give the guard a tip to keep an eye on Dave and enough money to pay for anything he might want on the journey, also to cover the price of his ticket should he lose it, which seemed probable. As the train pulled out, the last they saw of Dave was a grinning face at the window and a drunkenly waving arm.

Some while later Dave recounted what had happened on the journey. He had slept like a babe, he said, most of the way to Paris. Eventually, he had been awakened by the guard, who handed him coffee and sandwiches and thrust a bundle of francs into his hand.

"That was great, but then I couldn't find my goddamn ticket. Went through all my pockets, and it wasn't there. When I told my problem to a guy in my compartment who spoke English, he asked if I was in the habit of commuting to work by train when I was back home. I said he was dead right, that I worked in New York and took the commuter train every morning. 'Well then,' he said, 'where do you put your ticket?' And by golly, there it was, stuck in the band of my goddamn hat."

Chapter 31

Winston Churchill's illness in 1953 had been played down by the Conservative party. The public was not told that he had, in fact, suffered a severe stroke. It was stated only that he was not well and was in need of a rest. At the same time, his deputy, Anthony Eden, was ill with gall bladder trouble and in no condition to take over. It was clearly not a good time for Churchill to retire, nor was he ready to do so, but, inevitably, the news of the nature of his illness leaked out. Although he had apparently recovered well enough to deliver a major speech at the Conservative party conference following the summer recess, few people believed he could continue much longer.

Anthony Eden, waiting in the wings to take over, was a popular figure with the public before his career was destroyed by the Suez fiasco. During 1954 the *Daily Mirror* decided it was time he was given his chance and began a strident campaign calling for Churchill's retirement. While we deplored the tone of the attack, many people, Percy and I included, tremendous admirers of Churchill though we were, believed the message was right. All the same, when a year later Churchill did go, our sense of loss was strong. We felt it was the end of an era, and the press uniformly treated it as such. Always excepting the communist papers and journals, our British-born Press Lords were loyal in their support of the monarchy and, in general, reasonably restrained in their comments on "the establishment."

To most of us the future looked reasonably bright, apart from unease about The Bomb, mostly pushed to the back of our minds like the inevitability of death. Restrictions had eased, food rationing ended, houses were going up all over the place, including in Takeley. Unemployment was not the problem it was to become. National Service gathered in the lads who would otherwise have been hanging around street corners and kept them, as we believed, out of mischief. They had grown up to accept conscription as they accepted having to go to school. One option to serving in the armed forces was to work down the mines as a "Bevin Boy" (taking the name from Ernest Bevin, the Labour foreign secretary, whose idea it was), an alternative that proved neither popular nor successful.

The years 1953 and 1954 had seen stable prices, reduced taxation, and a balance of payments surplus. New cars had become easier to buy. One way of jumping the queue, which is what we eventually did, was to opt for a trade van, thus saving purchase tax, trade vehicles being for some reason exempt. Our van was a sturdy grey workhorse, a Standard 1500, just the job for carrying cartons of books, or for kipping down for the night on holiday journeys. It was the first brand-new car we had ever owned and was trouble free for all of the three years we ran it.

Internationally, the picture was less rosy. The buildup of nuclear weapons motivated some to parade their consciences in marches and demonstrations, their ranks swelled by the activists of the "far left," insidiously fomenting trouble.

The Iron Curtain had come down to cut off much of Europe from the West, traitors were being unmasked in the United States, there was a guerilla war being waged in Malaya. Hapless victims of the Nazi regime, washed up in Germany and Austria by the tides of war and left stranded and stateless, were still rotting in displaced persons' camps, waiting to find a country that would accept them. To visit one of those camps, as I did later, was a heartbreaking experience.

Austria, where some of the camps were sited, was still under the Four Power Military Control Commission, with the country divided into four zones — American, British, French, and Soviet. In Vienna, where the 1954 ILBA conference was to be held, the four powers alternated in controlling the city on a monthly basis.

"We'll have to drive through the Soviet zone to get to Vienna," Percy said, when we discussed our plan to combine attending the conference with a family holiday. Helen, who was working for her A levels in German would clearly benefit from coming with us, and David had been invited to stay at the home of Christian Nebehay, the president of the Austrian association, whose son, Nicky, was David's age.

Percy's experiences in Russia during his abortive buying trip in 1928 had given him an almost paranoid aversion to having any dealings with Russians. Determined as he was not to miss going to a city he loved, he viewed the prospect of entering territory under Soviet control with considerable misgivings.

"Don't worry, you won't have any problems," Nebehay had told him confidently. "All you'll need is a permit to enter the zone, and the Russians are quite happy to issue these to our delegates." Not entirely reassured, we went ahead with our plans. There was to be no tearing along the autobahn; instead we would spend a leisurely week en route, revisiting the places where we had stayed on walking holidays before the war without the responsibilities of parenthood but troubled by consciousness of the increasing Nazi menace.

What we had not planned for in 1954 was that we were going to be a somewhat ill-assorted party of six, instead of a family of four.

"Charlie Howes wants to join us," Percy told me, returning home after an ABA committee meeting a month before our departure. "He says he'd like to take his car and bring his wife. He didn't enjoy being on his own in Milan, and she says she'll come with him this time and they'll make it a bit of a holiday. But she doesn't drive, and as he doesn't fancy doing all the driving himself he's asked me if they can join up with us. The idea is for me to drive their Wolsey some of the time while you drive the children in the Standard. I think he's a bit doubtful about finding his way. He's no linguist — says he can't speak a word of French or German. So I felt I could hardly refuse. He's a decent old chap, and we've always got along in committee."

I couldn't remember ever having met Mrs. Howes, nor could Percy, but I agreed that he could hardly have refused Howes' suggestion, and if he was ready to act as relief driver cum interpreter, I would be willing to do my share of the driving. As for Charlie's wife, I assumed she would fit in and we'd all travel happily together to Vienna and back.

It was arranged that the Howeses would travel separately to Calais from their home in Hastings, and we would meet them at the port. Meanwhile, Percy pored over maps and planned a scenic route into Austria, paying some heed to gastronomic pleasures on the way, especially in France.

A month later, complete with our entry permits for the Russian zone, we flew (in an airplane that carried cars) from Lympne to Dinard and kept our rendezvous with the Howeses in Calais. And there they were waiting for us, an elderly, soberly dressed couple standing beside their elderly Wolsey, unmistakably British among the hurrying, jabbering continentals. He was stocky, she was dumpy, with the no-nonsense manner of someone determined not to be cheated or put upon.

As soon as we had exchanged greetings, Mrs. Howes pointed to her feet, which were clad in brown leather children's sandals.

"I'm wearing me Start-rites," she said in the self-congratulatory tone of one who does the sensible thing. "I thought we'd be doing some walking so I made up me mind I'd be comfortable." They'd brought plenty of provisions, she assured us, and she felt they had taken all the right precautions for a hazardous journey in unknown territory. They had had a calm crossing, Charlie was in a jovial mood, his "misses" (as he invariably called her) ready to put up with the expected discomforts of "abroad" and the foreignness of foreigners. Helen was invited to travel with them in the Wolsey, and Charlie was game to do the first day's driving through northern France. Nor was he averse to having a pretty young girl aboard as interpreter (her French was by then fluent) if needed.

We started off for Laon, the first leg of the journey, with a full reservoir of goodwill, which would drain away fairly quickly before we reached Vienna. Our Michelin guide told us that Laon was a city with a long military history, ramparts, a citadel, and a fine romanesque cathedral. What we found was a bright, new, modern town with a big, brand-new hotel, where we stayed the night. The bedrooms had bathrooms en suite, rare indeed in provincial France in the 1950s, and the plumbing could not be faulted, even by Mrs. Howes. Some buildings in the old city still stood clustered around the cathedral, standing on higher ground, miraculously having survived the bombing and fighting. The town center, which had been almost totally flattened, had been replaced completely with modern shops, banks, and offices, and only here and there was a ghostly glimpse of the past.

André had insisted on driving out from Paris to be our host on our first evening in France. As usual, there was no gainsaying his choice of what we were to eat. "It was tête de veau, mouton garni with pommes croquettes for all of us," I recorded in my diary. "The Howeses ate in silent doubt; the rest of us with enthusiasm." André already knew Charlie from the Milan conference and accepted him as *un bon collègue anglais*. . . . He did his best with Charlie's wife, who regarded him dubiously from the start. Frenchmen, she knew very well, were not to be trusted.

"Votre ami 'Owes," commented André to Percy as he got into his Citroën to drive back to Paris, "il est un brave type. Mais Madame 'Owes —" with a Gallic shake of the head, "ah mon Dieu! . . ."

That the Muir family and the Howeses were ill-matched for travelling together was soon all too apparent. For us, local cheese, garlic sausage, or pâté with a yard of crusty bread and a bottle of *vin du pays* was fine for our roadside picnics. But Charlie and his misses (we never did learn her first name) looked askance at such homely French fare, preferring to fish out cans of pallid luncheon meat from the stock of provisions they had brought with them. Nor was any meal complete without the ritual of a "brew-up" of strong tea, for which they had everything necessary bar fresh milk. It was Helen's job to buy this in the little towns where we stopped en route. She was also seconded to the Howeses as interpreter and soon discovered the cause of Mrs. Howes' increasing discontent: Charlie was in charge of the money supply.

It was he who had drawn their foreign currency and travellers' checks. When she wanted spending money to do a bit of shopping, he rationed her, she complained bitterly to Helen, to the equivalent of five shillings a day. We suspected that at home Charlie had to do what he was told. Now he held the purse strings and was getting his own back. "Can't help it. You'll have to make do. That's all I can spare you," he would say, "or I'll run out of foreign money." And she would stump off in her Start-rites in disgust, sniffing critically at the mouth-watering displays of food on the market stalls as she tried to eke out her few francs, while Helen did the interpreting.

We spent our second night in Toul, another largely rebuilt town, our hotel modern and clean, very different from the dusty, drab provincial hotels of pre-war days. Percy had chosen Toul because the town had a restaurant recommended by our Michelin guide. This meant little to the Howeses, Mrs. Howes having already declared more than once that she didn't like food that was "messed about."

They came along to the recommended restaurant, nevertheless, Percy believing that his role as guide, interpreter, and relief driver ought to include introducing Charlie and his wife to the delights of high-quality French cuisine. Why he tried so hard (with little success) to educate their taste buds I never understood, or why he persisted for so long.

To us, after the driving was done, the car parked, our suitcases unpacked, the evening meal was the culminating event of the day. The anticipation of the sort of food we seldom encountered at home was part of the fun. First, the stroll round the town, then the apéritif at the bar with an anticipatory study of the menu and the wine list; finally, happy and relaxed, we would settle down to enjoy the dinner itself.

For the Howeses, who didn't go in for apéritifs (Mrs. Howes stuck to mineral water, Charlie to lager), the whole business was hazardous. The wrong choice of a dish could mean good money wasted, waking up hungry in the night, if not worse. When the waiter brought the menu, a long debate ensued. Percy would patiently translate the delicious *specialités de la maison* into prosaic English. Doubts would at once be raised. The ingredients were unfamiliar, disliked, or thought too rich for elderly stomachs. The waiter would hover, give up, and fail to reappear when

298

wanted. Or worse still, would announce that the dish deemed to be safe was "off." So back to square one.

This pattern for our evening meals continued through Lorraine and Alsace and into Germany until we came to Munich, where we spent a couple of nights, Percy astonishing his family with his patience, still doing his best to educate the Howeses' all too British tastebuds.

It was not until our second night in Munich that he gave up. The Muir family had been invited out for the evening by the Domizlaffs. Left on their own, the Howeses had spotted a modest little restaurant advertising "English Spoken" and decided to try their luck. The next morning when we met at breakfast, the Howeses were looking pleased with themselves.

"Well, how did you get on last night?" Percy asked. "Did you find the restaurant I recommended?" "Oh, we didn't go there," said Charlie. "We strolled along for a bit, then we found a nice little place where they spoke English and did us proud: 'am an' eggs and a pot o' tea. Best meal we've 'ad since we left 'ome."

"That's right," chimed in his wife. "Much the best!"

After Munich there were a few more days of driving south through the beautiful region where Hitler had once had his mountain eyrie, now guarded by American soldiers. Misty views of mountain ranges, dark pine forests, and lakeside villages still undiscovered by packet-tour coaches — this was the Austria where in the mid-thirties Percy and I had walked and I had bathed naked in the cool lake waters without a tourist in sight. As then, there were rooms to be found in a clean, simple *Gasthaus*, where the price for bed and breakfast and an evening meal of fresh fish from the lake had risen surprisingly little. Had we wished, we could have stayed a week in the village of Mondsee for as little as £4 a head for part-board.

Before approaching the dreaded Soviet zone we checked and re-checked our passports, *carnets,* and luggage (might some of the books we had brought with us be thought subversive?) and were steeling ourselves for a grilling by grim-faced communist border guards or even intelligence officers. I was going to refuse to be body-searched and ready to defend my virtue, and Helen's, if it came to that. In fact, she was already two inches taller than I was and well able to defend herself. I didn't worry much about Mrs. Howes, for I doubted that she was in much danger.

In the event, our reception at the zone border proved a total anticlimax. "Two glum looking Soviet guards did no more than give a cursory glance into the cars when we were stopped," I recorded in my journal. "They didn't even bother to scan our passports when Percy proffered them, merely waved us through. But we noticed that the American border guards were stopping every car leaving their sector just across the Danube. . . ."

We had booked rooms in Vienna at the famous Sacher Hotel, where the Poursins and several other delegates were also staying, but somewhat to our relief not the Howeses. It had long been rated the best hotel in Vienna (fortunately, the exchange rate was then in our favor) and was redolent of past grandeur — haunted, I kept feeling, by the shades of archdukes and dashing hussars with waxed moustachios and lovely, gay lady friends. The hall porters were fatherly, the atmosphere not unlike that of gentlemen's clubs in London's St. James' Street, except that ladies were welcomed. At most times of the day elderly gentlemen were to be seen wearing bow ties, sitting in what was no doubt their usual armchair, drinking coffee with pince-nez poised over newspapers supplied by the management.

"Our bedroom is enormous," I wrote in my journal. "There are two big grandfatherly wardrobes, a chaise-longue and a round mahogany table covered with a lace cloth. Two tall mirrors face each other on either side of the room, so we can see ourselves back and front. There's a writing desk stocked with Hotel Sacher writing paper and a rather forbidding oil painting almost black with age takes up most of the wall space opposite the king-size double bed. Could it be that the Emperor Franz Josef will be gazing down at us when we're in bed?"

The bathroom en suite was almost as imposing, the bath a six-foot enamel tub on claw feet with large brass taps. I was revelling in all this old-time luxury as I unpacked, when I found to my dismay that somewhere along the way I had lost the top part of the dress I had planned to wear at the farewell dinner; at which of our several hotels it might still be, I had no idea. Had Mrs. Howes secretly impounded it as she had on one occasion impounded a trophy David had dropped and kept it hidden while we all searched for it, "to teach him not to be careless"? An unworthy thought. All the same, I was not going to let her hear that I had left it somewhere.

Awaiting us in the bedroom was a posy of flowers and a dainty greeting card. The Austrian inscription had been translated very charmingly into English for the benefit of the English-speaking ladies.

It read: "As a sign of respect and adoration greeting cards were used to welcome ladies in former times. Resuming this old custom may we wish you, Madam, cheerful and happy days in Vienna."

300

Compared with the French and British and German associations, the Vereinigung der Antiquare Österreichs (now the Verband der Antiquare Österreichs) was small; that they were willing to host the conference at a time when their country was still not free of military control was largely due to their indefatigable president, Christian Nebehay. Christian, whom Percy had known before the war, had an elegant gallery just off the Kärtnerstrasse and was more of a dealer in pictures and prints than in books. His brother, a quiet and rather retiring character, had a bookshop in the Ringstrasse where Percy could usually find things to buy.

Christian was a delightful companion — tall, good looking, and witty, with more than his share of Viennese charm. Since he and Percy had met again through the league, their friendship had ripened. A proud man, there were times when Percy's good offices were needed to assuage wounded *amour-propre* during an occasional clash in his dealings with some members of the league committee.

After Percy and André gave up their task of preparing the directory and the first supplement to it (which was completed in time for the 1955 conference in New York), it was Christian Nebehay and his fellow Austrian, Fred Frauendorfer from Zurich, who took over the responsibility for keeping it up to date.

All the league conferences had their own characteristic flavor; Vienna's was bittersweet. There were the Russians, an ever-threatening presence, like a sinister black spider lurking in a dark corner. They had taken over the once fashionable Hotel Bristol and, according to the Viennese, turned it into a slum. Typically, our Viennese friends joked wryly about the Russians or shrugged their shoulders and said nonchalantly that they hardly noticed them. It was true that we saw no Russian soldiers in the streets during our stay. But the women, said our Austrian friends contemptuously, were easily recognizable by their dreary, ill-fitting clothes.

The day after our arrival, Professor Otto Deutsch came to the Sacher to drink coffee with Percy. Of Jewish birth, he had fled to England before the war and settled in Cambridge. Through the Hirschs Percy had come to know him well and had done some translating for him. It was in Cambridge that Deutsch had completed his magnum opus, the complete catalogue of the works of Schubert, a composer with whom his name is now permanently linked. After the war, despite the pleadings of his friends, he had insisted that he must return to Vienna. Yes, he had not been unhappy in Cambridge, he agreed. "Then dear Otto, why not stay?" Otto had smiled and shaken his head. "No, I must return to live in Wien. In England it is mutton, mutton, mutton, and never a weiner schnitzel."

A spare, grey-haired, professorial figure, formally dressed, he was looking spruce and well when he turned up at the Sacher.

"It's good to see you, Otto," said Percy. "I hope you are now happily settled in Vienna?"

"Yes, I am very happy, my dear Percy," Otto replied. "Really, I have only one complaint, just a small one. I don't much care for my address."

Percy had forgotten the address. With a smile and a shrug Otto reminded him. It was Stalin Platz.

We had arrived with two days in hand for book buying before the opening of the conference, but we were not the only ones. Bumping into other early birds, hurrying around to pick up the bargains before everyone else arrived was part of the game. Percy had been eagerly looking forward to this first post-war visit to the antiquarian bookshops he remembered from the 1930s. Many were still there. It seemed as if little had changed as the owners came forward to greet him in the formal, old-fashioned way: "Herr Muir! Ich habe die Ehre!" (I have the honor) and a bow as they shook his hand and recalled the books he had bought on his last visit, as if it had been only a few weeks before. If I was with him, the greeting for *die gnädige Frau* would be "Ich Kuss die Hand," and my hand would be raised towards lips that seldom actually touched it.

While Percy sought and sometimes found the sort of books he was looking for — elegant bindings; dainty, delicately tooled little volumes with moirée silk, gilt-bordered endpapers, no doubt once a gift to some pretty lady; miniature books finely engraved; colored costume plates; and other such pleasing trifles (many would go to Altman's in New York or to Kitty Gregory's shop) — Helen and I wandered off to explore Vienna.

As if under a spell, for Vienna's special magic had captivated us as it had Percy on his first visit, we walked and walked. The music of Strauss and Lehár spilled out from cafés and restaurants. In the square beside the cathedral of Saint Stephen, with its slim tower rising more than four hundred feet, fiacres looking like museum pieces waited to be hired, patient grey nags standing quietly between the shafts. We climbed up the many steps through the formal gardens leading to the Belvedere Palace and looked down from the terrace at the wide view of the city; we lingered in the spacious elegance of the Hofburg, from where the Hapsburg dynasty had once ruled its empire. In the old part of Vienna, where the streets were narrow and winding, we wondered at the proliferation of stationer's shops and were thankful to discover two laundrettes (novelties at home), for we had been ten days on the road. Although the Austrian

302

schilling was cheap for us, laundry charges at the Sacher Hotel were not.

The clothes in the windows of the smart shops in the Kärtnerstrasse (equivalent to London's Bond Street) were far more stylish than any we had seen in Germany, the souvenirs more tasteful. But shopping was not always easy, for there was that little word *leider,* with which we were to become all too familiar. It would usually be accompanied by a charming but regretful smile and a spreading out of the hands. No people are better at telling you nicely that they haven't got what you want and have no idea when they can supply it than the Viennese, the rough translation for *leider* being "Sorry, love, you're out of luck."

The Russians were due to hand over control of the city to the United States the same day that the conference was to open with an evening reception. The news that the military formalities would be taking place that morning spread among the guests, and a number of us went along to the Hofburg to watch the proceedings.

The day was fine, the Hammer and Sickle flag streamed out in the breeze from the flagpole in the center of the courtyard. Detachments of the four war-time allies paraded to martial music. The British and French, on this occasion, were playing a minor role, leaving center stage to the main performers.

The Soviet soldiers in their grey uniforms, youthful faces expression-less, came first, marching with faultless precision to line up in front of the flagpole. The American troops then followed, to halt and face them. Commands rang out; the two ranks of soldiers, standing rigidly to atten-tion, stared blankly at their opposite numbers as their commanding officers stepped forward and saluted each other. A moment's silence, then the band struck up, and, as all eyes and spectators' cameras focused on the flagpole, down came the Hammer and Sickle and up went the Stars and Stripes.

Up it went to the top. But then instead of streaming out in the breeze as the Soviet flag had done a couple of minutes before, it hung limp as a damp rag. Beside me an American girl lowered her camera and cried out in disgust: "Now can you beat that? Just look at it!" All around, other poised cameras were lowered. One could see what had happened; the top edge of the flag had been left unhitched to the pulley.

No doubt it was lowered and fixed and hoisted again correctly, but we didn't wait to see. The moment had passed. The square emptied, the ceremony was over — until next time. It would not be very long before Percy and I would be back in Austria on the day that the four-power occupation ended. We would hear the official announcement on the radio in company with an Austrian friend at a Gasthaus in the beautiful city of Salzburg, and we would drink with him to the health of an independent Austria.

"In general the Viennese are gay, pleasure-loving and genial," wrote the author of the article on Vienna in the 1911 *Encyclopedia Britanica.* In 1954, despite Hitler's invasion of their country, the war and its after-math, the description still fitted. True to form, the program they had arranged for their guests was lighthearted, with the minimum of formal-ity. On the morning after the official opening, they took us in coaches to the Vienna Woods and then on to the delightful palace of Schönbrunn, with an al fresco lunch in the gardens.

In Milan the Italians had shown us the mausoleums of dead Milanese; the Viennese gave us glimpses of the lavish and enjoyable lifestyles of their long-departed grandees. After we had admired the elegant state rooms in the palace, we were led to the stables to see how grandly or sportingly the nobility had travelled to their public and private engage-ments in their gilded coaches, their stylish carriages, their dashing equipages — it was a fascinating collection of horse-drawn conveyances. One could almost hear the trumpets of the postillions, the rattle of wheels on the cobbles, the clip-clop of well-groomed horses.

Nusdorf, on the outskirts of Vienna, is where the Viennese like to spend an evening sitting out of doors, drinking the wine produced by small local vintners, who then sell it in their own wine bars. When the new season's vintage is ready, a green bush is hung outside their pre-mises, and the customers come to sit in the garden drinking, listening to music, and eating the sandwiches they bring with them as essential "blot-ting paper." For *heuriger* wine is young and like the young can surprise one.

We were all driven out to Nusdorf on the second evening of the confer-ence for a traditional heuriger party, which was when many of the guests came to grief.

"Be careful!" Christian Nebehay warned everybody. "Remember, it is important to eat as well as drink. You have tickets for *drei viertels* of wine (about three generous glasses full), any more it is your own respon-sibility."

The evening was warm; we sat on benches at wooden tables in a rus-tic garden with the sandwich pack of bread and cheese and sausage given us by our hosts to accompany our "drei viertels" of cool refreshing wine that slipped down so pleasantly, so easily. Surely it was harmless enough?

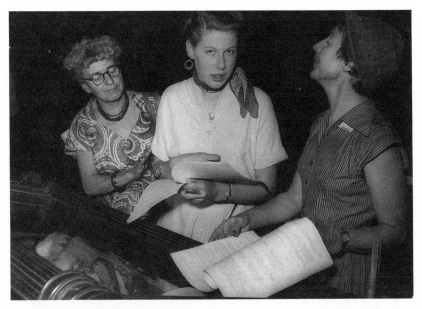

Frau Domizlaff, Helen Muir and Frau Dr. Karl examining a manuscript in a Vienna library during the 1954 ILAB Vienna conference.

Delegates of the 1954 ILAB Vienna conference at a heuriger party in Nusdorf.

Soon the party grew lively — and livelier. I was not the first casualty — when it hit me, I had drunk only two viertels — nor was I by any means the last. How the party ended, or when, I've no recollection. But in the morning pale-faced delegates were skipping breakfast and responding wanly to inquiries as to how they were feeling by Austrian friends, tactfully hiding their smiles. After all, they did warn us.

The state opera house, which was adjacent to the Sacher, was in the process of being rebuilt while we were in Vienna. We were reminded of this around six every morning, when the hammerings and bangings began. On our next visit to Vienna we would proudly be shown round the finished building.

An evening at the opera, or an operetta, had to be part of a conference in music-loving Vienna. Since we couldn't be taken to Mozart at the opera house, there was, by a happy chance (or could Christian have fixed it?) a performance of Johann Strauss' ever-popular *Die Fledermaus* at one of the theaters, for which the Austrian association had taken tickets for all the delegates and "their ladies."

It was a delightful performance, even if the drinking scene with the drunken jailer (who took the opportunity to include his cosmopolitan audience in his jokes) did remind us of our over indulgence the night before, which some might have preferred to forget. The night at the opera was very much in keeping with the lighthearted mood of the conference week.

Earlier during our stay we had taken a tram car (a "No Smoking" sign in four languages was another reminder of the military occupation) to the Prater, Vienna's permanent fairground, urged by my son, who was clamoring to ride on the huge joy wheel, the Reisenrad, which had been designed, we discovered, by an Englishman. By then it had been made internationally famous by the performance of Orson Welles in *The Third Man*. It was early afternoon when we got to the Prater to find the fairground almost deserted. There was the wheel, dauntingly big, gyrating high above our heads, its little wooden compartments mostly empty of passengers, swinging up to a height that had David thinking again. Like me, he had a poor head for heights.

"Of course, it's absolutely safe," I insisted, gritting my teeth as Helen and I clambered up into our seats. When the wheel swung us slowly upwards, the people on the ground below became tiny dwarfs and the panorama of Vienna spread out like a great map below us. Helen, untroubled by heights like her father, walked out on to the little platform as the two men had done in the film, but I stayed in my seat, the remembrance of the Orson Welles scene bringing a frisson of fear as the wheel swung us to the top of its orbit and then slowly brought us down again to earth. My son, who, had chickened out of a trip on the joy wheel, had been squandering his schillings on the Viennese sideshows, so much more entertaining in their novelty than the home variety.

"When I have a problem, I ask myself what would Percy have done," wrote Georges Blaizot in a letter to Percy not long after he had been voted president. The two men usually saw eye to eye on league business, but Blaizot was never above taking advice from his two Presidents of Honor, both of whom regularly attended the committee meetings. This happy situation would continue through Stanley Sawyer's presidency; thereafter, the influence of the founding fathers would increasingly lessen.

The Vienna conference saw the end of the league's responsibility for the Confidential List, or so-called Black List, which Kundig had used so effectively to make the Argentines, among others, pay up. There had been much debate about this list, which had brought protests from those who considered they had been unfairly labelled as defaulters. In future it was to be left to the presidents of the member associations to send confidential lists to other presidents, as well as to the league for information only. Both Percy and André had been in favor of this approach, so as to safeguard the league from the threat of legal action.

In Milan the league had been given the difficult task of compiling a report on import and export conditions operating in the thirteen member countries. These varied greatly (Italy was one of the worst sufferers) and had been making life unnecessarily difficult for dealers who did international business, especially since the war. The task had been completed, Georges Blaizot told the delegates. The report could be described as "a tool that would be used to influence the governments or administrations of each country." In other words, the trade now had the facts and figures needed to support a strong lobby against the stranglehold of bureaucracy. For a start, the report could be sent to the various national government departments as indicated by each president.

Together with the directory and the dictionary of terms (to be published later that year, Hertzberger promised), the report, printed in French and English, was one of the league's most useful publications, producing an immediate demand for more than one thousand copies.

Doll Hamill, of Hamill & Barker in Chicago, who had followed Dick Wormser as ABAA president (Dick had replaced Laurence Gomme on the league committee), had brought with her an invitation for the 1955 conference to be held in New York in October. When this was discussed

307

among the presidents, the committee was somewhat embarrassed by complaints about the distance and expense of attending. The cost of air travel would be prohibitive for many, it was said. "Very few are going to want to spend the money on the fare or spare the time," some delegates protested. And the Scandinavians pointed out that October was too late in the year for them, in any case.

To accept would mean a very limited number of delegates from Europe. On the other hand, as Percy argued in committee, how could they turn down the American invitation? After all, American delegates had been regularly attending conferences in Europe. He would certainly go to New York, he said.

In the end, after much discussion, Doll Hamill's invitation was accepted on a proposal from the president of the French association, Monsieur Chretien, and, as reported later, "greeted by applause," Blaizot having used his influence to persuade the objectors to keep quiet.

The old thorny problem of rule 7, which had had the effect of excluding the unfortunate Hans Goetz from membership because of the Danes' dogged refusal to accept him, came up once again, as it had done at every meeting since Copenhagen. The committee was heartily sick of the problem, and, in an attempt to keep it off the agenda (where it invariably caused heat) in future, they suggested a revision of the rules to free the league from having to intervene in the internal affairs of associations. As Goetz' membership of the ABA long pre-dated the formation of the league, successive presidents had continued to maintain that rule 7, which denied membership of the league to any dealer not acceptable to his or her own association, should not be retrospective. This was a point of view the Danes were unwilling to accept.

In New York the committee would be asked to draw up a new set of rules in the light of experience. It is agreeable to record that when Percy wrote Hans Goetz' obituary many years later, he was able to record that Goetz was finally granted membership of the Danish association.

Frantic telephoning to hotels we had stayed at en route had not brought me the top half of my farewell dinner dress. Each day when I asked the kindly hall porter if there was a parcel for me, he shook his head and replied with a sympathetic "Leider." On the last morning it was still "Leider."

"Oh dear," I cried in despair, "Now I've nothing to wear for tonight's party," for by then I had already told him of my problem.

"But gnädige Frau," he replied, smiling in his fatherly way, "you must not be unhappy. Why not wear that smart costume you wore for the reception last Sunday? You looked very nice in it, and it will be quite suitable for your party tonight."

Had he really remembered what I, among all the other ladies, had worn that evening? True or not, only a porter at the Sacher would have offered comfort so charmingly.

I took his advice, forgot about the top that had gone missing (I retrieved it on the way home), and enjoyed a particularly delightful farewell dinner, followed by a dance with much Viennese waltzing that lasted well into the next morning. For our seventeen-year-old daughter, led onto the floor by the debonair Austrian president for the first dance, it was an especially memorable evening. Our stay in Austria had done wonders for her German.

We had seen little of the Howeses during the conference but were committed to escorting them safely back to England. When I suggested to Percy that it might be a happy solution for all concerned if they went back on their own with a route he could provide for them, he wouldn't consider it.

"I can't ditch them now. I promised we'd travel together both ways. Charlie will be relying on me to get them safely home." Of course, Charlie Howes was not the problem. He had a nice, quirky sense of humor, and Helen, who had travelled much of the way in the Wolsey, got on with him well, swapping Shakespearian quotations, in which he was well able to hold his own.

Whether his wife, stumping about in her Start-rites, enjoyed the holiday, it was hard to tell. Fish never do look happy out of water. But she had opted to come, perhaps to keep an eye on Charlie, and maybe he would have been lonely in Vienna on his own.

So we set off for England, in tandem once again, all of us tired and somewhat short-tempered after too many late nights and too much food. We took a shorter route back, called at few bookshops, and this time Percy allowed the Howeses to pick their way through the menus unguided at our overnight stops through Germany and France.

In Munich, where we stayed overnight, my aptitude for adventure led me into one more when I set off alone in the car to join the rest of the family at the Domizlaffs and was caught in a violent thunderstorm. It was already dark and as lightning flashed and the rain beat down obscuring the direction signs, I was soon driving along deserted streets, hopelessly lost.

The sight of two figures standing silhouetted against the light in the open doorway of a smart-looking residence encouraged me to pull up

309

and climb the flight of stone steps to ask for directions. Whereupon one of the figures, a large, heavily built man with a genial manner, replied in English and invited me to come in out of the rain.

"You are from England? I am glad to meet you," he said, cordially extending a hamlike hand. "I know London well. I have fought in your Albert Hall . . . ," he continued as he ushered me indoors.

Fought? From his appearance I guessed (correctly) that he must be a boxer and, from his style of living, a successful one. I have never thought much of boxing as a sport, but this large, friendly individual could not have been more helpful, insisting on telephoning the Domizlaffs to assure them that I was safe and refusing to let me go on my way with directions he had given me for reaching my destination, until the storm had abated.

My rescuer, as I later learned from Helmuth Domizlaff, was Max Schmelling, former heavyweight champion of Germany and one of the country's most popular sporting heroes.

Mrs. Howes was still wearing her Start-rite sandals when we came at last to Calais. She was, she said, looking forward to a good English meal when they reached Dover. We were all parting amicably; tempers had mostly been kept in check during the return journey. We shook hands all round; there were no embraces or plans for future reunions. It had been an interesting experience, Mrs. Howes granted after she had thanked Percy, but she didn't mind saying she'd be glad to be back in Hastings.

Charlie said he wouldn't be sorry either, but he thanked Percy warmly for all he had done to make the two-way trip enjoyable.

"I know we'd never 'ave managed it without you, Percy. And it's been a real education for us both!"

"But aren't we lucky to be British, Mr. Muir?" added Mrs. Howes.

Chapter 32

The autumn and winter of 1954 were relatively uneventful for us. Percy was working on a catalogue of the Rothenstein collection to follow the memorial catalogue of Sir William's library. He also had his many new purchases during the trip to Vienna to catalogue. Cataloguing new purchases was never postponed for long and was a job he always enjoyed. Apart from this necessary Elkin Mathews work he was carrying on with his contributions to *The Book Collector*, now jogging along pretty well, or so the editorial board believed with misplaced optimism.

That contributors were paid not in cash but with offprints of their contributions did not bother him, for writing these reminiscences was a pleasure not a chore. He had just begun a new series under the heading "Bibliomanes," the first of whom was A. J. A. Symons. Hugh Walpole was to follow. In any case, although *The Book Collector* could not afford to pay, there was the prospect of the series proving profitable, for Chatto & Windus were showing interest in publishing it as a sequel to *Minding My Own Business*.

I had my thirteenth novel to finish, and my diary was, as usual, dotted with dates for village events and committee meetings. Through the war years I had trained my family to accept, albeit resignedly, fairly frequent adjustments to the time of the evening meal so as to fit in with whatever meeting or charitable function I felt impelled to attend. That I did feel so impelled often mystified them, especially Percy (sometimes it puzzled me, too), who could appreciate that it was right that I should support a Liberal party fund raiser, but why on earth the British Legion Christmas party? Why, indeed? Absurdly, I would feel guilty, as a parish councillor, if I failed to appear at such worthy village events.

An unexpected bonus for me that winter was the serialization in "Woman's Hour" of my novel *Neighbourly Relations*. The effect on the book's sales was not remarkable, and the payment was well under a hundred pounds, but the boost to my morale was considerable. Perversely, I did not enjoy listening to the broadcasts even though I could not fault the very professional adaptation by Honor Wyatt, in which I had not been consulted. Somehow the characters in the story were no longer the people I had lived with during some eight or nine months. It was not my book any more. But the serialization did boost the sales of my previous novel, which was still in print.

Percy had tried his hand at writing fiction once or twice but had never completed either a novel or a short story for publication. Although he said he had no talent for fiction, I suspect the medium had always attracted him.

"Have a look at this," he said to me one day a few weeks before Christmas. "Then tell me if you like it."

He handed me a typescript and went away. It was entitled "Just in Time," a short story told in the first person, subtitled "A Nightmare;" the plot concerned a bad attack of bibliomania. I read it at one sitting and told him, truthfully, that I thought it was jolly good. Although it was hardly a Christmassy tale, he had 250 copies printed and we sent them off to friends and customers on our mailing list, with our best wishes for Christmas 1954. The small residue that remained were given from time to time to friends who came to Takeley and were always signed by Percy. They would, after his death, occasionally appear in dealer's catalogues at a price that would have greatly amused him. Among those who wrote to say they had enjoyed the story was Siegfried Sassoon.

"I never thanked you for your Christmas story," he wrote from Heytesbury House, "which was a vintage. I could do with some more. But I look forward to your bookselling memoirs, of which I read the Symons chapter when staying with [John] Sparrow. I am sending the copies [typescripts of poems that Percy was selling for him] . . . which you need. I would prefer to present them as I don't want money for my heart's blood. . . . The Buffalo man, whose letter I enclose, will get nothing from me in MS. Until I took to poetry notebooks, about 20 years ago, I carefully destroyed all first drafts and have never been a copiously revising writer in verse or prose. . . ."

With this letter Sassoon sent Percy a letter he had received from the curator of the University of Buffalo Poetry Collection, Gene Magner, offering to buy some of Sassoon's manuscripts and saying how much they would like to acquire "a packet of worksheets of any of your poems. . . ."

Percy was to tell Buffalo that Sassoon was "unable to give away any of my poetry notebooks (which I value and which contain quantities of unpublished stuff which I'm not sure of). . . ."

Heytesbury. 15-2-55.

Dear Percy. I never thanked you for your Xmas story, which was
a vintage treat – I could do with some more. But look forward to your
bookselling memories, of which I read the Symons chapter in that magazine.
when staying with Sparrow. / I am sending the copies of the T. which
you need. I would prefer to present them, as I don't want money
for my heart's blood – though G.K. let J. G. W. have 20, at his urgent
request, so did get £21 toward the costs. (These copies are from £2
extra ones.)   The Buffalo man whose letter I enclose will get
nothing from me in M.S. Until I took to poetry notebooks, about 20
years ago, I carefully destroyed all first drafts — & have never been
a copiously revising writer – in verse or prose. The poems I write
now are usually done in pencil & then inked in, with very few
alterations. All this about 80 drafts, all kept, seems to me
typical of the self-conscious way poets behave, especially in U.S.A.
The book issued by Buffalo – Lockwood a few years ago, with
analyses of S. Spender's revisions & others was enough to make
a cat laugh. They will never find out how real inspiration
happens. How people improve their productions is interesting,
of course, And, as a general rule, I believe masterpieces are
improved by cutting something out rather than by additions &
~~restore~~ minor alterations — / Though in some cases one or two
words altered makes all the difference to a lyric – like
Landor's Rose Aylmer – which began "Sweet Aylmer"!)
So will you very politely transmit my apologies for being unable
to give away any of my poetry notebooks, which I value, &
which contain quantities of unpublished stuff which I'm not
sure of.) Texas over again! /
I read your letter about the T. with much interest & sympathy.
Your attitude is sensible. This next world they talk about, if
there, must be something quite different to this, surely, (though
Laurie Whistler – here recently, & an Anglican – said he
doesn't see why it should be different to this one!)

A letter from Siegfried Sassoon to Percy Muir.

T.E.L. (in a letter I was reading just now) says (to Granville-Barker) 'at bottom we are carnal: our appetites & tastes & hopes & ideals are beast-qualities, coloured or shaped somewhat fancifully, but material always, things you can cut with a knife'. No doubt it seemed so more than usual to T.E. in a Tank Corps Hut. But life is physical. The other side of the question, we know, is that religious experience & confirmation are outside of thought — something which just happens to people — which is what I have longed for, with occasional insubstantial intimations which was just enough (split-second experiencings suggesting some message from outside oneself) to make one hope.

Your philosophy is a wise wise one. Get on with the job of being alive, & be as decent to others as can be managed. The whole business is too extraordinary for words — & if there is'nt a creative purpose behind it — well, as Hodgson says somewhere, 'a greenfinch in a hedge takes a lot of explaining'.

By the way, Geoffrey has passed on to me an 1819 song to David with an 8 line poem about Smart in it by R.H— No indication who it belonged to. (Came from Arthur Rogers. £5.) Of interest (though not a good piece of verse) owing to the song of honour being so influenced by Smart.

Yours, S.

Have provided a 'worksheet'
for you.

Conclusion of the letter from Siegfried Sassoon to Percy Muir.

May we have some of your manuscripts? You will realize,
I know, that we are interested in the original worksheets--all the
papers used toward the making of a particular poem. We have files
which contain over eighty versions of a single poem. Some poets will
put a poem through fifteen stages, some two, and of course many do
their several rewritings by crossing out and adding until all of a
page's available space is thoroughly used. I say this that you may
be assured that manuscript-poetry in any physical condition is of
the greatest interest to us.

A packet of worksheets for any of your poems would open
your file with a fine vitality, and I am certain that a study of
them before they achieved final form would be more than rewarding.

As a last note--whenever it is possible for you to be in
Buffalo, please visit us.

Sincerely,

Gene Magner

Gene Magner, Curator
Poetry Collection

*A verse written by Siegfried Sassoon on a letter from Gene Magner,
Curator of the Poetry Collection at Buffalo University.*

At the bottom of the Gene Magner letter he had scrawled a verse
headed "Heytesbury House Hymn," beginning "We'll run no Muir a-
rollicking in Buffalo, N.Y. . . ." This letter is one of many Sassoon wrote
to Percy over a period of some thirty years. It is longer than most and
has some philosophical musings: "Get on with the job of being alive and
be as decent to others as can be managed . . . the whole business is too
extraordinary for words — and if there isn't a creative purpose behind it
— well, as Hodgson says somewhere `a greenfinch in a hedge takes a lot
of explaining.'"
In May 1955 Percy and I were off to Germany again, on our own this
time, driving via Ostend to Munich. Percy had arranged to spend a couple
of days with André in Cologne. There was some final work to be done
on the supplement to the league directory, and André proposed taking
Percy along with him to a factory where he wanted to buy machinery

for his buckle-making works, antiquarian books being only a part (though an important one) of his business interests. In my diary I noted that he returned from his factory visit delighted with the neatness and ingenuity of the German products. Better, he admitted ruefully, than any he could buy in France.

I was happy to be left on my own all day to potter around as I chose, exploring what remained of Cologne, seeing new buildings rising and noting the changes since our last visit. As always my writer's notebook was in my pocket.

"In the cathedral men in red robes pad silently about proffering collecting boxes," I wrote. "Outside, the whole structure remains in a frame of scaffolding. Ruins still everywhere, little temporary homes are dotted about on cleared bomb sites. One hovel has a tiny garden in front, bright with spring flowers. Another has been incongruously smartened with sheets of black glass, like a beggar donning cast-off finery. Was told that prostitutes live in the basements under the ruins, emerging at night like cats on the prowl. Had cafeteria lunch in Woolworth Haus. Customers around me eating great platefuls of bean soup, twenty-five pfennigs a portion [about eight pence]; Woolworth's windows dressed with Mutzie Tag [Mother's Day] displays offering Cologne's mums diaphanous nylon nighties, amongst other supposedly appropriate gifts. Hard to imagine the stout local hausfrauen wearing them. . . ."

On the morning we left for Munich I noted that newspaper headings announced "Germany Joins NATO." Apart from a few flags flying around the railway station, the news seemed to arouse little public interest.

"Veni, vidi, vecci, Herr Muir," said Dr. Karl from the rostrum as Percy walked into Karl and Faber, the fine art auctioneer's salesroom, the next morning later than he had intended, glanced at the volume being held up by a porter, made a bid, and saw the hammer come down in his favor. Continental auctions were more to his taste than the big London book auctions; there was little competition from British colleagues, and in general he preferred the company and enjoyed the warm welcome and hospitality invariably accorded to foreign dealers.

While Percy bought books, I wandered around in the shops looking for copy for the column I was writing for an Essex weekly newspaper, being pursued by shop assistants eager "to help" me. My attempts to shake them off by pretending that I didn't speak the language only had the effect of sending them hurrying off to bring an interpreter. This would usually be a somewhat intimidating female who, having tried out her correct English to no effect, soon made it clear that foreign shoppers with no serious intention of spending money were not wanted in that store, and suspicious glances would follow me as I made for the exit.

In July the blow fell without warning. The summer issue of *The Book Collector* had gone out as usual; the autumn issue was already planned, to include, among other attractions, an account of how Donald and Mary Hyde jointly built up the Hyde Collection. Then out of a blue sky came the news, in the form of a cyclostyled document addressed to each of the editorial board, announcing that the Queen Anne Press would be closed down and *The Book Collector* would therefore cease publication. There would be no further issues, and the outstanding balance of the subscriptions would be returned.

"You will probably have heard that *The Book Collector* is to be closed down," Percy wrote disgustedly to Ian Parson at Chatto & Windus. "The method of doing this has some features which are quite astonishing and of which I totally disapprove."

Kemsley's decision had, in fact, been taken without prior consultation with his editorial board, and Percy and John Hayward were still in a state of shock. From their point of view, the journal had established itself very successfully during the three years of its life; subscriptions were increasing, advertising revenue was up. It had some excellent contributors. It was, in their eyes, a publication that Lord Kemsley should be proud to support. That it was not making him any money seemed to them irrelevant. He was a rich man, the year before he had financed the publication of a facsimile of the Holkham Bible, a very prestigious and expensive undertaking. If *The Book Collector* could not be regarded quite as the jewel in the Kemsley empire's crown, it was certainly well worth preserving.

His Lordship saw it differently. He had given the journal three years to establish itself, and that was enough. He was no longer interested and was not willing to lose any more money. It was all very disappointing. Although John Hayward had regarded *The Book Collector* as his baby from the beginning, Percy had played a considerable part in helping to establish it on a sound basis. He felt it was irreplaceable and was deeply distressed that it was to be killed off without anyone being given a chance to plead for a reprieve. Had he been able to afford it, he would have been very willing to guarantee its future himself. But we had not and were unlikely to find that sort of money.

Was there anything that could still be done? For Ian the descent of the Kemsley axe was no great blow. He had enjoyed being one of the editorial board, but he had too many other interests to take this particular one seriously. Nevertheless, he recognized how strongly Percy and John felt, and because of his affection for them both he was willing to help to the extent of offering to take the journal off Kemsley's hands — if the price was not too high.

"You can have it for £50," Lord Kemsley told him, glad to be shot of a loss maker.

"Done," said Ian. And (so the story goes) he put a check in the post the same day. It was a typically generous gesture made for the benefit of two good friends. Equally typical, having made the gesture, he had no intention of allowing himself to be involved in what must follow. Financial guarantors had to be found, also a printer and a distributor. This, he made clear, was up to his co-directors.

The guarantors were found by Percy, both in the UK and in the US. Ian had already volunteered; Robert Taylor, an American collector with many friends on both sides of the Atlantic, was another; so was Major Abbey, owner of a famous collection of color-plate books. And there were others.

"With this generous co-operation future publication is assured for a minimum period of two years," Percy wrote a month after Ian's take-over. He foresaw that the guarantors would be called upon from time to time to stump up to cover an anticipated deficit, and this must not be counted on to continue indefinitely. Meanwhile, the editorial board, strengthened by the addition of John Carter, and with Christopher Hobson remaining as editor, would make it their aim to see that *The Book Collector* became self-supporting by the end of the two-year period. So wrote Percy in a report on the position that August. A private company would be formed to take over responsibility for publication and the shareholdings divided among the board members.

This was all going to mean some belt tightening, a rise in the price of the subscription to thirty shillings (post free), and a rise in the advertising rates. In August no printer had been found, but before very long James Shand, of the Shenval Press, would come riding to the rescue like a white knight to take over not only the printing but also the distribution of the journal from Shenval's offices in Frith Street. This was the best possible news for the board; the Shenval Press under James Shand's direction had a reputation for fine printing second to none. "In short," wrote John Hayward in the Winter issue of 1955, "*The Book Collector* could not be in better nor more willing hands."

Percy had known James for some years and had been a contributor to *Alphabet and Image*, that wonderfully lively but short-lived magazine devised by James to show the best of modern typography in the early post-war years. It was a happy coincidence that the Shands (James had recently remarried) were about to become neighbors of ours in Essex, having bought Kingsley Martin's cottage at Little Easton near Great Dunmow. The shared interest in *The Book Collector* would serve to strengthen the friendship between the two men that was to last until James' untimely death, while his delightful wife, Lucilla, became an equally dear friend of mine, as well as Percy, and remains so to this day.

The autumn issue went off to the subscribers somewhat late, but at least no subscriptions had to be returned, and by the winter all was running smoothly under the new regime. Problems would inevitably arise, as John Hayward increasingly came to believe that editorial decisions were his alone, eventually bringing about John Carter's resignation. Ian's interest dwindled, although he and Anne continued to play host and hostess to the quarterly editorial luncheons if they were at home. But as Ian wrote in a rather exasperated letter to Percy, "to offer suggestions to John is a waste of breath." Nor did he ever write even a book review for *The Book Collector*, although he contributed to other periodicals at that time. Percy, on the other hand, remained involved for the rest of his life, reviewing books regularly as well as contributing bibliographical articles from time to time. He it would be who, in 1965, would sorrowfully write Ian's obituary.

"It must be said," he wrote, "that from Ian's point of view *The Book Collector* became more and more a pleasant toy to dine out on and to astonish people with the fact that the creator of James Bond was at the head of the board of an erudite publication of this kind.

"Similarly he delighted in throwing off references to his collection of `milestone' books. . . . Despite the fact that the first item under `Recreations' in his *Who's Who* entry is `First Editions,' he made no further addition to his collection and came to regard it more as an inflation hedge."

It was not Percy's way to regard his friends through rose-tinted spectacles. His friendships were on a "with all faults" basis. His with Ian lasted some thirty-six years with few gaps of more than a month or so. Ian had known Percy before I did, and after we were married the two men continued to meet for lunch, or sometimes for a game of bridge at White's as they had done before. On occasions when Ian took to his bed with flu or some other complaint, which he did quite often in the mid-1930s (through eating infected caviar in Russia, he had a problem with a tapeworm, which he called his Loch Ness Monster), we would be invited to his bachelor flat to help relieve the boredom. I would then be offered the run of his collection of erotica to keep me quiet while he and Percy chatted. This was while we were living in London. As Percy's wife I was accepted, perhaps even liked (I could never be sure), and was treated civilly when, after we had moved, he would come to visit us in Essex. But, though I read his first novel, *Casino Royale*, I am sure he never read any novel of mine.

Percy summed up his friendship with Ian in the final paragraph of his *Book Collector* "Personal Memoir": "He could be, as I often told him, the most exasperating, pig-headed creature in existence. He called me a short-sighted, small-minded puritan. Our long friendship was strong and deep enough to withstand the worst we could say of each other and it would be hard to say better of it than that."

We were both looking forward to our second visit to the United States. Percy, who loved plotting itineraries, had decided we should go by sea first to Canada to visit one or two of the universities whose librarians regularly bought from our catalogues. At least one of these wanted him to give a talk, which would be a useful contribution to the cost of the trip. We planned to sail a couple of weeks before the opening of the conference in New York on October 9th. The supplement to the directory was at last finished, and Percy would be presenting it to the general assembly. Much to his disappointment André had decided not to attend — it would be the first league conference he had missed — and there would be, as predicted, a rather smaller ABA delegation than usual. As vice president of ILAB, Stanley Sawyer would definitely be going.

Bureaucracy had long been a dirty word for Percy. During the war he had fought many a paper battle with the Board of Trade on behalf of the ABA, and neither of us had forgotten the inquisition we had undergone at the American Embassy when applying for our visas in 1951. When around midsummer he received the form circulated to all booksellers who might be intending to go to New York for the conference, he decided it was high time to make a personal protest.

"Antiquarian booksellers proposing to attend . . . may now be assumed to be wrestling with the fearsome document that must be completed before an interview . . . by the American authorities to decide on the granting of a visum," he wrote in a formal letter to the ABAA. "Forty-eight questions have to be answered and many have sub-sections, in one instance entailing eleven supplementary answers. . . . Full details [are demanded] of the applicant's domicile since the age of 14. Another question asks what is his 'ethnic classification'? Most of the answers must be given for one's wife also, whether she be travelling or not."

He went on to point out that as well as filling in the application form, personal attendance was required at the US Foreign Office service, which would include cross-examination on one's opinions and habits and the taking of prints of all the fingers of both hands.

"Our affection and admiration for our American friends is unexampled," he wrote, to show there was no ill-feeling in his protest. "There is probably no sphere in which Anglo-American friendships are more firmly cemented than in bibliophily. This fact emphasizes the more strongly the grimness of this reminder of the official view that cousins are indeed distant relations."

In fact, it was not only the British who had to wrestle with the document, it applied to all the other European delegates — communists perhaps hiding in bibliophile clothing? (Some years later a bookselling couple, the Krogers, were arrested and convicted as communist spies!)

Poor Doll Hamill! Percy's righteous anger at the US State Department's mistrust of all foreigners wishing to visit the United States was just one more headache among the many making life tough for her as ABAA president with a conference to host. She must have known perfectly well that even if the ABAA supported Percy's protest, it wouldn't have the slightest effect. If a group of Europeans disliked having to answer questions designed to keep out undesirable foreigners, so what? No State Department, American or otherwise, was going to be persuaded that a bunch of antiquarian booksellers were special. After all, in their view, most of the trouble in the world had been caused by people writing and distributing books. One had only to think of Karl Marx . . .

Doll wrote back apologetically, agreeing that it was all very tiresome, but there was nothing she could do about it. That was the way things were just then, with the cold war looking, to some people, as though it might hot up at any moment.

We, at least, were spared another visit to Grosvenor Square and the inquisitors. It was sufficient that we had already had our fingerprints taken in 1951. Our "visum" (a word that no one else used for the plural of visa) came through, and, as far as I know, none of the other delegates was turned down as "undesirable."

I was busy with my domestic preparations for a three-week absence from home and with getting ahead with my journalistic commitments when I learned that my thirteenth novel was to be published in September, ten days before we were due to leave. And the publication date would be the 13th of the month.

321

"Why the 13th?" I asked Geoffrey Halliday, Hutchinson's Hurst and Blackett manager, with whom I was on excellent terms.

"Oh, I'd forgotten it was your thirteenth book," he said. "No, the date wasn't deliberately chosen. It just happened that our autumn list was scheduled for mid-September. Anyway, don't worry. No reason why it should be unlucky. Your advance sales are very satisfactory. That "Woman's Hour" serialization of your last book has certainly helped."

I thought it over, told myself I was not superstitious (which was not true). If I was stuck with the 13th, I would turn the date to my advantage, give a launch party on publication day, invite thirteen guests, and get some publicity by notifying the local press of my challenge to superstition, which ought to be worth a paragraph or two. I had never had a launch party for any of my books (Hutchinson wouldn't have rated me as worth the expense), and this seemed as good a time as any to give one.

My family, bless them, were cooperative. Not that Percy had any faith in PR gimmicks and would certainly not have contemplated Elkin Mathews celebrating with wine and canapes the publication of one of his own books. But then these were always well heralded in his catalogues, whereas my own literary efforts were most unlikely to be bought by our customers to add to their collections of modern first editions — as I was well aware.

Everyone I invited accepted — without apparent qualms — bookish neighbors, including a couple of publishers, a fellow writer or two, the editor of the Essex newspaper for which I was writing my column. We were not, in fact, thirteen, because I had excluded the family from the count, but if my guests had had any doubts about accepting, there was enough drink to wash such fears away. Percy, always a good host, saw that glasses were kept filled, and everyone drank to the book's success and to our forthcoming visit to the United States.

The evening went so well that by the time the last guest had departed with a signed copy I no longer cared whether it brought me publicity or not. It had been a very good party.

The autumn term was Helen's last at Bishop's Stortford High School. With her A levels behind her (she had achieved scholarship level in the three she had taken), she was enjoying the privilege of opting out of boring routine work and the status of her own reserved seat in the school library, where she could swot in peace and quiet for her Oxford University entrance exam. The competition for a place in one of the five Oxford women's colleges was tough. The time when men's colleges would become co-ed was far off.

The week after the party I dashed up to London to do the last interview in a series I was writing for *Home and Country*, the Women's Institutes magazine. It was close to our departure date, and I was congratulating myself that I had time to squeeze in the final article of the series.

The interview was with Dame Frances Farrer, general secretary of the Women's Institutes, a kindly but rather awe-inspiring lady who had become something of a legend in the WI, having held the office for more than a quarter of a century. I left home that morning with a slight feeling of unease. Helen had complained of stomach ache and of not feeling well and had stayed home from school, but Percy was working in the office, so she was not left on her own. There seemed no reason to cancel my appointment.

The message from Percy came when I was with the Dame in her office. It was to say that I must return home at once. The doctor had been to see Helen and had diagnosed acute appendicitis. He was returning that evening to examine her and required that I should be there. He thought it probable that she would need to be operated on that night.

My heart lurched. Why had I ever given that wretched party? But that was absurd, how could it have had anything to do with this sudden, frightening illness? Trying not to panic, I made my apologies, caught the next train home, and was there when the doctor arrived to make his examination.

"But I can't go into hospital now, I'm just about to sit for the Oxford entrance," protested Helen, frustration surmounting pain as the doctor told her that prompt surgery was essential. To which he replied that if her appendix ruptured, as was more than probable without surgery, she might well be in hospital for a month with drainage tubes in her tummy, always supposing she survived. "So you'd better be a sensible girl and not argue about it," said our Scottish doctor crisply, "and we'll get you into hospital this evening." After that there was no further argument.

"I've cancelled our sailing," Percy said, when I returned from accompanying Helen to the hospital. "I know *you* won't go now, and I'm not going without you. I'll let Doll and the committee know tomorrow."

He had made up his mind. The letters and telephone calls that came over the next few days begging him to change it had no effect. I said he should at least fly to New York for the five days of the conference, but he was adamant that he was not going. Nor did he appear as disappointed as I had expected. Was he, perhaps, in his heart relieved to be spared the strain of long-distance travelling, plus the inevitable in-fighting that most conferences engender, not to mention generous but unrelenting hospitality?

I, too, found myself accepting the cancellation of our trip philosophically, disappointing though it was. "Well, if you *will* challenge fate," said various less-than-kind friends with "I told you so" grins. At that, the irrational feeling of guilt that I had been suppressing would surface from my subconscious. Could it really have been my fault? "But that's ridiculous!" said my common-sense self.

The appendectomy was straightforward ("Just in time," said the surgeon). Helen made a good recovery and was soon sitting up in bed with the suitcase of books she had insisted on taking with her piled up on her locker and overflowing on to her bed, while the nurses tutted. Soon she was home again, convalescing in the garden in an Indian summer, surrounded by her books with still some time in hand before her exams. By an odd coincidence she was almost the same age as I had been when I had an appendectomy.

As for the debut of my novel, there had been a paragraph or two in the local press, and my editor, on learning that Helen had been struck down shortly after the launch party, thought the conjunction of her illness and a 13th-of-the-month party worth a further comment on the tricks Fate plays with those who think they can flout superstition. I felt I hardly deserved the good news that sales were up on my previous book and the magazine *Home and Country* wanted to buy the serial rights.

We were not the only last-minute dropouts. Georges Blaizot, who was to have presided in New York, was taken ill in September. This meant that Stanley Sawyer must take his place.

"This is a burden," Percy wrote worriedly to Laurence Gomme, "for which poor Stanley is totally unprepared. I have no doubt he will acquit himself admirably on the circumstances, but I fear there may be unexpected trouble awaiting him. . . ."

The trouble Percy feared was likely to come from Menno Hertzberger getting up "to his usual Machiavellian tricks." Stanley and Menno had never hit it off, and Percy thought it possible Menno might form a small group to oppose Stanley's election as the next president. It was bad enough, wrote Percy, for Stanley to find himself unexpectedly chairing the conference; opposition to his candidature could cause considerable embarrassment. "His defeat is unthinkable . . . but if there were a sizeable opposition . . . a terrible split might develop in the league." To avert this, Percy asked Laurence to alert Stanley's many supporters.

It was at this point that the pressure on Percy to fly to New York was considerable. Doll Hamill, too, had been relying on his help and experience and wrote begging him to change his mind. By the end of

September the news had circulated that we would not be attending the conference. Letters poured in with expressions of sympathy and, in some cases, barely concealed exasperation for Percy's decision not to be there. I had no intention of doing other than stay with Helen and be at home when she sat for her university entrance exams, but there was still time for Percy to book a return flight to New York.

"Don't you think you really should go?" I asked him. "I hate to think you're missing it because of me."

He shook his head. "No, I'm not going without you, and I know you can't leave Helen now. Stanley will read my report on the supplement. They'll have to manage without me." The supplement on which Percy had spent hours of unpaid work concluded with the editors' Final Advice to their successors: "Never undertake another supplement!" they warned. "Prepare a new edition; that is easier and more profitable."

In many ways it was sad that we should not attend this first American league conference and thus miss meeting some of the friends we had made on our previous visit to the States. Percy had already written a preview of the New York conference program for the ABA's newsletter. The Carnegie Foundation was giving a reception, the Grolier Club had arranged a special exhibition, there was to be a cruise round Manhattan Island, a visit to the Radio City Music Hall, and a day-long trip to Yale. It all sounded delightful. It was a shame we wouldn't be taking part, but I had given up feeling guilty. Helen was better off without her unpredictable appendix. It was just a bit of bad timing.

I put away the dresses I had planned to take and then reflected that they might well come in handy next autumn, if the fashions had not changed too much. For Stanley had gone to New York with an invitation from the ABA for the 1956 conference to be held in London, and, God willing, we would certainly be taking part. The wheel had nearly turned full circle.

Shortly before he left for New York, Stanley wrote to Percy about some league business on the New York conference agenda. In his letter he referred to an ABA committee meeting that Percy had not attended.

"Another interesting item which should amuse you," he wrote, "is that the ABA will vote *against* alternative year conferences. They prefer one every year." And his letter ended: "I can almost hear you laughing!"

By all accounts the New York conference was a great success. *The Book Collector* reported that "The United States, under the ABAA's president, Miss Frances Hamill, excelled even their national reputation for hospitality." The writer noted with satisfaction the election of Stanley Sawyer as the new president of the league.

Percy's fears of a possible split amongst the delegates over a candidate for president had proved groundless. Thanks to some diplomatic work behind the scenes it was Menno Hertzberger who had proposed Stanley. There had been no other candidate and Stanley had been unanimously elected.

The British had gone to New York with an invitation for the 1956 conference to be held in London. Hertzberger had also brought an invitation from the Dutch, but it was the ABA's that was accepted. In 1957 the conference would be held in Munich.

The announcement that the long-awaited dictionary of terms was about to be published was hailed as the high-spot of the business. It was badly needed and, as with the directory, it would also bring in funds from sales to the book trade. It was sad that neither of the editors of the first supplement to the directory were there to present it to the assembly. Percy and André were passing on the burden, with some relief, to the new editors, Christian Nebehay and Frederick Frauendorfer.

That the league should mount an international book exhibition had been discussed at previous meetings. Now there was an offer from the president of the French association to organize one in Paris. However, there was still the problem of how to pay for it so, once again, it was left to the committee to see what could be done. Another suggestion, proposed by the German association, was an exchange scheme for the employers of trainee booksellers. In theory an admirable idea, but, as Stanley pointed out, not so easy to put into practice due to varying regulations over work permits. In fact, there had already been several such arrangements made unofficially.

Although the problem of book auction rings was not raised at the New York conference, Doll Hamill and Dick Wormser (who had been elected to the league committee) had both tackled Percy about the ABA's ambivalent attitude to members of their association who took part in rings. It was the knowledge that they would be likely to bring up the subject at the next conference in London that spurred on Percy's determination to force the ABA to take a public stand on the issue.

One morning towards the end of 1955 I heard shouts of joy from Helen. She had been rushing to the door to meet the postman every day for a week. That morning the letter from Oxford had at last arrived to tell her that she had won a place at Lady Margaret Hall College to read modern languages. David still had another year of school ahead, but college had no appeal for him, he wanted to be involved in farming. However, after a few years of farming and selling agricultural machinery, followed by a year savoring the bright lights of London while working in a store, he settled for a career as a craft bookbinder and restorer, much to his father's satisfaction. From restoring fine books to following in his father's footsteps and selling and buying them was, perhaps, a logical progression.

For Percy and I there were many challenges ahead. Although Percy would play a part in the affairs of the ILAB for some years to come, by 1960 he felt, rightly or wrongly, that his role as an "elder statesman" was appreciated less and less by the newcomers to the league committee. He was proud of his part in the formation of the ILAB and did not lose touch with the friends he had made during those early, exciting years; but there were other things to do. The most important of these was his chairmanship of the Impact Committee for the "Printing and the Mind of Man" exhibition, and the subsequent publication of the book with the same name in collaboration with John Carter.

Both of us continued to be very busy. Looking back it's a wonder how we fitted it all in — writing, committee work, travelling, family, friends — but somehow we did, and we would not have wished it any other way.

A Postscript

In the autumn of 1955, when the sale catalogues went out for the auction of the contents of Lowther Castle, the family seat in Cumberland of the Earl of Lonsdale, to the big operators in the antiques and antiquarian book market, it looked like the best carve-up for years. The small fry, too, could anticipate some good pickings. It was a five-day sale; the catalogue was enough to make any dealer's mouth water. The first four days were devoted to the furniture, pictures, silver, and glass. On the fifth day the library was to be sold. It had been built up through several generations and was full of highly desirable collector's books. As one bookseller who went along put it somewhat luridly: "The castle was a carcass poised on the edge of a den, waiting for the auctioneer to throw it down to the jaws of the starved wolves. . . ."

In reality the waiting "wolves" were nowhere near starving; most were prosperous dealers from London and other major centers who, over the years, had found it well worthwhile to travel long distances to important country house auction sales. Local dealers would turn up as well, but few expected to be allowed to buy much, if anything. The best they could hope for was a nice little divvy at the knock-out that they knew would be held after the sale. While this was accepted as a fact of second-hand bookselling life by most, there were some not too happy to be hanging around all day to end up without one desirable book. It was, after all, their patch, and their regular customers would be looking in afterwards hoping for a Lowther book or two.

After the showdown over the activities of the ring in the antiquarian book trade in 1948, those members of the ABA who had been participants, or in some cases ringmasters, had bided their time, waited for the fuss to die down, and then for the most part returned to their bad old ways. They were fond of arguing that so long as auctioneers were too lazy or too ignorant to have their books properly catalogued or advise vendors on sensible reserves, rings would continue. After all, it was human nature to buy as cheaply as one could, wasn't it? And with a well run ring the big boys would see to it that the locals got something for their trouble — even if it was seldom books.

So ran the argument. By the early 1950s, as far as the small inner circle of the ringers was concerned, things were pretty well back to where they had been before the fuss in 1948.

The library at Lowther Castle was of a quality seldom seen outside the top auction houses. Apart from one or two novices in the trade, everyone knew that there would be a knock-out after the sale, which was the reason Percy and Laurie stayed away. Most of the thirty or more dealers who did go had little doubt as to who was going to end up with the cream. To them, it was worth going, all the same. The divvy from the knock-out would more than pay for the trip, and it was a chance to see and handle (during the viewing) many interesting rarities.

As usual the ringers had it largely their own way, the big boys having seen to it beforehand that there was little or no opposition. When the sale ended with some £2,200 worth of books sold, thirty-eight dealers gathered in a room in a nearby pub, hired for the occasion.

The first knock-out added £11,000 to the sum taken in the saleroom; a second, which excluded the smaller dealers, added another £5,000. Not everyone went away happy. There were grumbles about the sum deducted from the divvy for the hire of the room and what the ringmasters euphemistically called expenses, and some irritation among one or two local dealers at coming away with little in the way of books after spending the best part of two days viewing and attending the sale.

Whether it was the article in *Desiderata*, an antiquarian and second-hand book trade weekly, that first spilt the beans, or a letter to the press from a disgruntled Cumberland dealer (now long since dead) is debatable. A previous issue of *Desiderata* had carried an account of the adventures of a "Mr. Innocent," who had been introduced into the ring by a wimpish local colleague and had been less than happy in the company he found he was keeping. In a future issue there would be an all-out attack with no punches pulled.

"There is no question of the ring being a jolly brotherhood; a den of snarling wild beasts would be more appropriate," wrote Mr. Innocent, wisely wearing his cloak of anonymity. "The prevailing atmosphere is one of mutual mistrust . . . their conversation is boastful . . . how only they spotted a rarity and bought it for a song. . . ." There was a great deal more of this as well as some sensible advice to book collectors on how to buy at auction: "You will receive black looks and hear dark mutterings, but keep on bidding, and the book will be yours. In the end you will have bought it at a cheaper price than you would eventually see it listed in a catalogue. . . ." And there was further advice on how not to sell books of value. "If you allow a valuable library left to you by some bibliophile ancestor to be carted off by the local cattle auctioneer and catalogued like so many sheep, you are not the person to whom the library should have been left."

Mr. (now not so) Innocent, who was clearly speaking from bitter experience, regarded ringers as a thoroughly objectionable lot. The *Times*, spurred by letters from disgusted readers following the Lowther Castle sale, agreed with him and said as much in a Saturday leader headed "This Shabby Business." Why, the leader writer wanted to know, was the Antiquarian Booksellers' Association turning a blind eye to what were undoubtedly illegal practices going on under its nose?

Sir Basil Blackwell, of the old, established firm of B. H. Blackwell Limited of Oxford, booksellers and publishers, a past president of the ABA and still a member, had long been an opponent of the ring. As an important dealer who had always refused to "settle," he was heartily disliked by a section of the trade for that reason. When he turned up at auctions, they would groan, knowing that he would push up prices. The disclosures of the activities of the ring at Lowther Castle gave him the ammunition he needed for a renewed campaign against the participants. He fired off the first shot with a follow-up letter to the *Times* leader.

"The more publicity that is thrown upon `this shabby business,' the better," he wrote sternly, and after a side swipe at auctioneers who should be taking the lead in tackling the general problem both in their own interests and those of their clients, he went on to announce that he was prepared to compile and publish a list of bookdealers who would assure the public "by solemn and sincere declaration" that they were and would continue to be "innocent of participation in the Book Ring."

Publicity on this highly sensitive subject was the last thing the ABA committee wanted. Up to then the line taken by the majority had been the least said, the soonest mended. In any case, they could not see why the antiquarian book trade was being picked on when all or most of the other trades at the Lowther sale had held knock-outs. An aggrieved letter from H. R. T. Williams of Quaritch, the president of the association from 1955-56, had been sent to the *Times* in reply to the attack, protesting unfair allegations. But crying "not fair" was not going to make the problem go away.

"Our innocent editorials on the workings of the book-ring continue to attract much attention," wrote the editor of *Desiderata* gleefully in his comment column the following week, adding, "Let's hope that as a result a Kelmscott *Chaucer* will never again be knocked down for ten bob. . . ."

It could be thought that the editor was nursing a death wish for his little paper (it ran to only twelve pages and was intended as a link between libraries and booksellers) by running these revealing articles. Not surprisingly, advertisements began to be cancelled, and subscriptions from a number of dealers were not renewed. Within six months *Desiderata* had gone out of business. Meanwhile, the *Clique*, privately owned but for long the semi-official organ of the ABA (nonmembers were allowed to advertise, but their advertisements were segregated from those of members), kept mum and continued to thrive.

For *The Bookseller*, "The Organ of the Book Trade," the story was news, and it lost no time in reporting press criticism of the antiquarian book trade and Sir Basil's proposal of a list of non-ringers, soon to be dubbed his "Book of Saints."

While Percy was as worried as Sir Basil at the bad press the trade was suffering, not least because he felt it was bound to be harmful to the ABA's standing in the league, he was doubtful of the usefulness of a Book of Saints. He believed, rightly, as it turned out, that a number of ABA members who had never taken part in book rings would not wish to sign any document unauthorized by their trade association. In the event, only some sixty did so, including the directors of Elkin Mathews. By then all the customers on our mailing list had received a short statement, signed by Percy and Laurie, that made our position clear. "In view of the widespread publicity given recently to the prevalence of rings, settlements and knock-outs in the antiquarian book trade," it ran, "we wish to place on record our strong disapproval of these practices and state that since this firm came under its present directorship we have taken no part in them in any shape or form."

Laurie was already one of a group of younger members who had formed a self-styled "Ginger Group" to change what they considered fusty out-of-date attitudes prevailing in the ABA and to improve its public image. Anthony Rota, a future ABA president, was another. Their aim was to infiltrate the committee, and they were anti-ringers to a person.

That the ABA's image had become tarnished during 1955 and 1956, there was no doubt. In May 1956 there was more bad news for the ABA committee. The Sheppard Press, which annually published a directory of dealers in antiquarian and secondhand books, had sent out a circular inviting dealers to apply for a form of declaration that their firm had not contravened, nor would in future contravene the conditions of the Auctions (Bidding Agreements) Act of 1927. Booksellers who signed the declaration would then have an asterisk (not a halo) set against their names in the directory. This course was equally open to the several hundred dealers who were not members of the ABA either from choice or because they were in too small a way of business to be considered acceptable.

Peter Murray Hill had just been elected ABA president, and this was a hot potato to handle. Under his predecessor, H. R. T. Williams, the committee had been in favor of keeping their heads below the parapet and waiting for the dust to settle. Peter, who had privately discussed the whole problem with Percy, knew that this was not going to work. In any case something had to be done to prevent Sheppard Press from going ahead and awarding asterisks to virtuous dealers in the guide that they would be publishing in the late autumn, which had a large circulation both in the UK and overseas.

The Ginger Group reacted to the circular by sending a petition to the committee urging prompt action. In their view, if the committee had taken a stronger line from the first, the situation would never have arisen.

"We feel," ran their letter, "that publication of such a list by the Sheppard Press could do untold harm to any members who, for whatever reason, decline to sign Mr. [sic] Blackwell's declaration. Clearly those members whose names are not asterisked are by implication involved in the Ring. In fact many members prefer not to sign because they deplore the fact that a list should be compiled without the official support of the Association." The petition went on to urge the committee to take action against such an implied threat to members instead of leaving it to individuals to protest to the Sheppard Press. The matter was urgent, they insisted, and there ought to be an early statement.

Peter responded in a letter to Laurie Deval, one of the instigators of the petition, to say that he was doing what he could. He had had a constructive chat with two of the signatories and was going to see the association's solicitors: "Our main trouble in these matters is that nobody seems quite to know the legal position." All the same, armed with a brief from the solicitors, he intended "to pitch into them [the Sheppard Press] heartily."

No one doubted Peter Murray Hill's good will. He was no ringer and was as jealous as anyone of the good name of the trade. But there were those on his committee who still dragged their feet.

Shortly after this, armed with legal advice, Peter on behalf of his committee sent a stiff letter to the Sheppard Press, stating that the association had always set its face against book rings and that participation rendered a member liable to expulsion. Which on paper was true. The letter continued that the association believed the proposal would add nothing to the effectiveness of the existing sanctions and was open to considerable objection. After giving reasons for this, the letter finished with a veiled threat of possible legal action by dealers whose names were not asterisked, for implied defamation. In conclusion, if the Sheppard Press was determined to go ahead, the ABA would ask for a short statement to be included, setting out its views.

This did not satisfy the Ginger Group; it was something, but they were insistent that what was wanted was a special meeting to air the problem, revise the rules, and let the public know that the association had at last taken action against the ringers in its ranks. This also was Percy's view.

Worse was to follow. For a while, things seemed to have quieted down — as far as the press was concerned, the story had gone cold. It was, in any case, only a minority interest among readers. The Suez crisis was brewing up; there were plenty of matters of more moment to fill their columns. Then came the debate on the adjournment in the House of Commons before Parliament went into recess for the summer holidays.

The MP who chose to raise the matter of the persistence of "buyers' rings" in the antiquarian book trade was the member for Londonderry, Mr. R. Chichester-Clark, who rose to say he thought the Home Secretary should have a copy of Sir Basil Blackwell's list of booksellers who had pledged themselves not to take part in auction rings. "I hope with the aid of this list and with a more rigorous enforcement of the law my honourable friend will be able to do something towards bringing to an end this shabby business. . . ." He admitted that there were not the vast profits made from books as in some sections of the antiques trade, but abuses, nonetheless, did run into fairly high figures. He was equipped with figures of the amounts raised at various country house sale knock-outs, including the one at Wentworth Castle in 1948, when a marked catalogue of those who had taken part in the settlement was passed on to the *Times*. He recalled having asked questions about that particular sale in the House after an article had appeared about it in a 1949 issue of *The Bookseller*.

He could see the difficulties of a prosecution succeeding under the 1927 Lord Darling Act (there had in fact been only one prosecution since it came into force), but there was another method that might have a better chance of success — that being tried by "the famous Oxford bookseller, Sir Basil Blackwell." His speech included a sharp dig at the ABA when he pointed out that throughout the association's existence there had never been an expulsion for the infringement of their rule 16, which outlawed any dealings in auction rings and knock-outs.

He had plenty more to say before his time ran out and his seconder, Hugh Delargy from Thurrock, rose to ask the Home Secretary "to voice his strong disapproval of these brigands" and to say how the public could be protected from "their maraudings." While rather cagey about possible sanctions, the spokesman for the Home Office, Joint Under Secretary of State Mr. W. F. Deedes, was very willing to voice disapproval. The practices described had been called shabby, he said; they were also illegal. "They could only flourish," he continued pointedly, "with the connivance of many who know perfectly well what they are doing and ought to know better. But one enemy of any conspiracy is publicity."

He would be glad, he said, to receive Sir Basil's list, and there was another pat on the back for that gentleman "to whom the public should be grateful for putting them on their guard." After explaining the terms of the 1927 Act (which must have thinned out an already thin house), he concluded vigorously: "That means that those who indulge in the practice are not merely anti-social but crooks!"

The debate was, predictably, given a good deal of space in the *Times* and was fully reported in *The Bookseller* the following week. Through having done nothing other than write a couple of unconvincing rebuttals, the ABA committee was on a thoroughly sticky wicket. A reply had to be made to Chichester-Clark's charges, and a statement for the press was hurriedly put together and duly appeared in the *Times*. Unhappily, it was couched in such a way as to make the situation even worse. After affirming "wholehearted belief in the integrity of the Association's members," it protested that the "evil practices" imputed to the antiquarian book trade in the debate were "to put it mildly, greatly exaggerated." The statement went on, somewhat unwisely, to compare Sir Basil Blackwell's proposal for dealers to sign his declaration to an invitation to members of the medical profession to sign a declaration to say that "they had not, did not and would not perform illegal operations." In conclusion, it was stated that an extraordinary meeting would take place during the first week in October, when the whole matter would be reviewed.

The phrasing of this statement was a gift to the leader writer of the *Times*. Under the heading "Only a Little Crooked," he tore it to shreds. "For a body concerned with the written word the Antiquarian Booksellers' Association is singularly inept in its public statements," was the opening sentence. "To what grade of crookedness would the Association plead guilty?" the writer asked unkindly, taking up the plea that there were few if any organizations that could claim never to have members who stepped out of line. "The protest of `only a little one' leads to the speculation — how little?"

It was something, said the writer, that an extraordinary meeting had been arranged. Nothing would save the reputation of the association short of "an unequivocal undertaking by all members to observe the law and maintain respectable trading practices."

"Worse than useless!" cried Percy in despair after reading first the ABA statement and then the leader in the *Times*. "We have got to get a meeting called before the conference opens [on September 9th, 1956]. They must be made to realize that to take part in a debate in the general assembly on book auction rings when we still haven't put our own house in order is an impossible situation."

He had already made this point to Peter, who had pleaded on behalf of the committee that they were all so busy preparing for the conference that they simply couldn't spare the time.

After the publicity from the debate in the Commons, Percy, Laurie Deval, James Bain, and Boris Harding Edgar decided to wait no longer. They would call their own extraordinary meeting at the earliest possible time (they settled on August 16th) for the single purpose of demanding that the committee put forward the October meeting to a date prior to the opening of the conference.

A room was booked at the National Book League, our duplicator went into action, and a letter was sent out on August 10th to every ABA member in the name of Elkin Mathews, Charles Rare Books (Harding Edgar's firm), and James Bain. Inevitably, with such short notice there were many with prior engagements or absent on holiday. Despite this, the response was good. In the main, the large majority approved of this initiative taken by the three firms, all well known in the association, and wrote to say so.

As a past president of the ABA and President of Honor of the ILAB, Percy still had considerable status; he was trusted and his integrity was not in doubt. He had asked Basil Blackwell to put his Book of Saints on ice for the time being and had had a promise to that effect (as a member of the ABA Sir Basil was loath to explode this bomb unless he had to anyway). He also let Peter Murray Hill know his intention when the letters went out.

Some correspondents were pessimistic, although promising to come. "It's human nature to want to buy at the lowest price. I can't see how the

Association can stamp it out," wrote one. "I could write an essay on the Ring," wrote another, admitting to having taken part in the past. "We should have smashed it long ago. . . ." Yet another thought it ridiculous that dealers should "be compelled to bid against each other at auctions" and wanted the ABA to support "group buying" with self-selected groups of dealers sending up their names with their bids to the auctioneer. In general, the feeling was that the whole business had been badly mishandled.

Of the thirty-two members who turned up, including Sir Basil, only four formed an opposition. Many others who were unable to attend pledged their support. As chairman, Percy set the tone of the meeting, making it clear that he would allow no grudges to be aired. They would stick to the one purpose of the meeting, to ensure that the public should be given an unequivocal statement "rehabilitating our trade and our Association in particular in the face of the charges brought against us."

The result of the general discussion was never in doubt. The resolution put to the meeting, carried by twenty-eight votes to four, pulled no punches. There was trenchant criticism of the ABA committee, whose statements to the press were described as "totally inadequate," and a strongly worded request that rule 16 be changed and the forthcoming extraordinary meeting be called by the end of August, or at least prior to the league conference. A handful of the opposition, all well-known members of the ring, was there to fight a rear-guard action, but when they moved an amendment expressing confidence in the ABA committee, they could only muster four votes. When the meeting ended, with relief all round at the outcome, Percy and Laurie lost no time in personally delivering the resolution to Peter Murray Hill, who accepted it with good grace and promised a response as soon as he could gather a forum.

Confronted with a petition by nearly fifty members (some members joined the protest after the meeting), the committee caved in. A meeting to deal with last-minute arrangements for the conference had already been fixed for September 5th; this was now suggested as the date for the extraordinary general meeting. And this time, Percy was determined, the ABA was going to get it right.

With time running short and an agenda to be drawn up, Peter proposed getting together at the Murray Hill home in Hertfordshire. He would collect a few mates on the committee to discuss in peace and comfort what was to be done. If rule 16 was to be amended and a resolution passed, Percy was the obvious person to do it. "So you'd better come over . . . and help us sort it all out," said Peter.

Percy came home from the Murrey Hill's in great good humor. All had gone well. "It's going to be a tight thing, but we'll be able to get out a statement to the press before the opening of the conference," he told me. There had recently been an article on the ring in a Belgium magazine, strongly condemning the practice, and there had already been comments on the ABA's problems by foreign colleagues. Now they should be in a position to contribute to any discussion of the subject without embarrassment.

With the business at the Murray Hill meeting satisfactorily concluded, everyone had been relaxing over a pre-lunch drink, when Peter's young daughter, Auriol, had rushed excitedly into the room.

"Daddy, we're going to have a gymkhana in the village," she cried, "and they want *you* to be ringmaster!"

"The poor child couldn't understand why we all burst out laughing," Percy said.

"I am sending you herewith a copy of the three-line whip we have just sent out to all our people with a copy of the amendment [to rule 16]," Percy wrote to Peter a few days later. It had been settled that he should put the proposal, and he wanted ten to fifteen minutes in which to do so. Then there was the question of a seconder.

"I think it would be very effective," he wrote, "that a member of the committee . . . should speak on the amendment and second it. Kenneth Maggs would be an ideal person to do so. . . ."

By this time the number of members in support of the action taken by Percy and Laurie and their two fellow ABA members had risen to nearly seventy. "Most of them will be coming to the meeting," Percy told Peter, "and with your own supporters on the committee, we should form a very solid block. . . ."

His expressed hope for "a minimum of disturbance, personalities and slanging matches" at the meeting must have been met with a heartfelt response from Peter, a peaceable man, whose bad luck had been to be chairman when the long-term problem of the ring had come to the boil.

Percy had rather hoped that Basil Blackwell, who had put his pen to the resolution passed on August 16th, would be satisfied to wait for the outcome of the extraordinary general meeting three weeks later. But the old campaigner still had some doubts.

"I cannot see how the expulsion of a member (or indeed any number of members) from the ABA can help much to achieve our declared purpose to stamp out the activities of `The Ring' within the antiquarian book trade," he wrote to Percy on August 24th. "If it is so grievous a thing not to belong to the ABA why are there only some 300 antiquarian booksellers in our Association and some 1,475 outside it?"

Were the outsiders to be allowed to practice their 'Ringcraft' while the ABA members abstained, he wanted to know? And who would be making the allegations against the culprits? He thought it unlikely that it would be members of the public, for "The Ring is in effect a secret society and the public might not even know the names of booksellers who are operating it." For that reason, he wrote, his list was being compiled for all members of the trade. His method, he concluded, "required no policing and no allegations. The declaration bound the conscience of the individual and had the force of an oath." Few, he believed, were so corrupt that having made the declaration they would deliberately perjure themselves. What was more, he added somewhat complacently, he had the approval of the Home Office for his method.

Percy, however, was not to be converted to the Blackwell method. All the issues Sir Basil had raised in his letter hung, he maintained, on "making the ABA a worthwhile and responsible body that the public could trust." As to the declaration "binding the conscience of the individual" — his comment, scribbled in the margin of the letter, was the one word "nonsense!"

A diplomatic response was called for; the last thing needed just then was for Sir Basil to ride once again into the fray. So Percy asked once more for patience and forbearance.

This brought a brief reply: "I am pondering."

It was all a great rush and, as Percy had been saying, should not have been had the ABA committee been willing to face facts months earlier. He was well aware that he had come in for considerable criticism from some sections of the membership for pressuring the committee and forcing the issue. This did not much bother him. As he would say later, "They never forgave me for what had happened in 1948 and would have slung me out of the association had they been able."

The venue for the extraordinary meeting, five days before the opening of the second London ILAB conference, was the Monico Restaurant, once the scene of fashionable Edwardian revelry. Predictably, there was a large turnout and no revelry. Very much aware that the spotlight of the press was now on them, and with delegates to the conference already arriving in London, no one wanted a shouting match or dirty linen aired. As he surveyed the faces in the room, with many old friends among them, Percy knew that he had no need to worry when he rose to propose his resolution. The meeting was enthusiastically with him.

The proposed amendment to rule 16 had been drafted and re-drafted with much thought and care and was, he felt, as tough and comprehensive as it was possible to make it. In essence it declared that in future any member who contravened the 1927 Auctions Act should, whether legally convicted or not, be asked to resign from the association. Moreover, a standing subcommittee was to be appointed (two committee members and two others) to investigate any complaints of infringement. The sting in the tail was that all members were to be asked to sign an undertaking that they would observe the amended rule 16 and give full support to the committee in its "declared object to stamp out the illegal activities of `the ring' within the Association." All new applicants for membership would have to sign the document before being accepted.

This time the *Clique* felt free to publish a report of the meeting, but without editorial comment, although Mr. Murray, the editor, was present. "The Resolution was carried by an overwhelming majority," he reported.

A lengthy report in the *Times* the following day made welcome reading to all concerned. Not only was the result of the meeting headlined in bold type: "Stiffer Attitudes to Auction Rings," the second leader was devoted to the substance of the meeting, with congratulations to the ABA for setting an example to other trades "in which illegal and disreputable practices" were rampant.

It was, said the *Times*, "thanks to the determined pressure of men of good will, who form an overwhelming majority of the antiquarian bookselling profession, [that] the minority of cave dwellers has suffered defeat."

A comment was naturally sought from Sir Basil, who told the *Times* reporter that he was highly satisfied. The ABA had done the right thing, and he only wished they had done it a year ago. And what did he propose to do now? The reporter wanted to know if he would continue with his campaign.

It was a pertinent question because his signatories represented a fairly small proportion of dealers who were not members of the ABA. He replied that he would now "mark time" and give the association his support in putting its policy into effect. If it broke down, he asserted sturdily, his campaign would then go ahead.

Roundly defeated as they had been, the habitual ringers were unrepentant. They had been out maneuvered, but some still hoped to live to fight another day. There was no question of repentance. They did not feel guilty for ignoring what they considered an unenforceable law. Knock-outs at auctions, they argued, were the sensible way for dealers to buy. The auctioneers could stop them if they chose; the fact was that they were glad enough to leave it to the trade. And hadn't the dealers who ran the settlements always made sure that everyone got a share?

There were no resignations. Nor, as the months went by, were there any expulsions. Every member duly signed as required. Among the un-repentant a sour joke circulated:

Sam was shaking his head over the ABA's revised rule book for 1956, newly issued with the agreed amendments to rule 16.

"I don't know what the association's coming to," he grumbles to his friend Tom. "Now they want us all to sign this blankety-blank state-ment. Seems to me they're trying to ruin us. Look, old man, what d' *you* think? Do I really have to sign?"

"I know just how you feel," says Tom. "But I'm telling you, you've got to sign it. If you don't, I'll never ` settle' with you again."

Few if any were naive enough to believe that the new ABA rules sig-nalled the death knell of book auction rings. But while small local groups around the country would continue to agree not to bid against each other and "knock it out" after the sale, the days of the lords of the rings were over. The times were changing; the big country house libraries were more often than not removed to one of the London auction houses, or would be handled in situ by experienced auctioneers who understood current values. The ABA would no longer have the field to itself. The trade would increasingly attract a different type of dealer in rare books, well educated and independent minded, who would provide a healthy opposition to "group" buyers. In later years I would attend provincial auctions myself and have no problems.

One day, many years on, Percy and I looked in to see Sir Basil at his shop in Oxford. He had recently celebrated his ninetieth birthday and was sitting at his large uncluttered desk in an office above the shop in the High. He looked as spry and dapper as ever in his formal business suit and bow tie. He greeted us warmly. His sons, he said cheerfully, now did all the work, but he liked coming into the shop to see how things were going.

He never did feel the need to publish his Book of Saints, some of whom had by then gone ahead of him and no doubt been welcomed by Saint Peter — put to work, perhaps, on some biblical collating. As for the sinners no longer with us, I wouldn't put it past them to be still at it, flogging Satan and his minions defective copies of Goethe's *Faust*.

Index

346

348